CHURCH DO(

For further resources, including the forewords to the original 14-volume edition of the *Church Dogmatics*, log on to our website and sign up for the resources webpage:
http://www.continuumbooks.com/dogmatics/

KARL BARTH
CHURCH DOGMATICS

VOLUME IV

THE DOCTRINE
OF RECONCILIATION

§ 65–66

JESUS CHRIST, THE SERVANT AS LORD II

EDITED BY
G. W. BROMILEY
T. F. TORRANCE

t&t clark

Published by T&T Clark
A Continuum Imprint
The Tower Building, 11 York Road, London, SE1 7NX
80 Maiden Lane, Suite 704, New York, NY 10038

www.continuumbooks.com

Translated by G. W. Bromiley

Authorised translation of Karl Barth, *Die Kirchliche Dogmatik IV*
Copyright © Theologischer Verlag Zürich, 1953–1967
All revisions to the original English translation and all translations of Greek, Latin and French
© Princeton Theological Seminary, 2009

British Library Cataloguing-in-Publication Data
A catalogue record for this book is available from the British Library

ISBN13: 978-0-567-62721-6

Typeset by Interactive Sciences Ltd, Gloucester, and Newgen Imaging Systems Pvt Ltd, Chennai
Printed and bound in Great Britain by CPI Antony Rowe, Chippenham, Wiltshire

PUBLISHER'S PREFACE TO
THE STUDY EDITION

Since the publication of the first English translation of *Church Dogmatics I.1* by Professor Thomson in 1936, T&T Clark has been closely linked with Karl Barth. An authorised translation of the whole of the *Kirchliche Dogmatik* was begun in the 1950s under the editorship of G. W. Bromiley and T. F. Torrance, a work which eventually replaced Professor Thomson's initial translation of *CD I.1*.

T&T Clark is now happy to present to the academic community this new *Study Edition* of the *Church Dogmatics*. Its aim is mainly to make this major work available to a generation of students and scholars with less familiarity with Latin, Greek, and French. For the first time this edition therefore presents the classic text of the translation edited by G. W. Bromiley and T. F. Torrance incorporating translations of the foreign language passages in Editorial Notes on each page.

The main body of the text remains unchanged. Only minor corrections with regard to grammar or spelling have been introduced. The text is presented in a new reader friendly format. We hope that the breakdown of the *Church Dogmatics* into 31 shorter fascicles will make this edition easier to use than its predecessors.

Completely new indexes of names, subjects and scriptural indexes have been created for the individual volumes of the *Study Edition*.

The publishers would like to thank the Center for Barth Studies at Princeton Theological Seminary for supplying a digital edition of the text of the *Church Dogmatics* and translations of the Greek and Latin quotations in the original T&T Clark edition made by Simon Gathercole and Ian McFarland.

London, April 2010

HOW TO USE THIS
STUDY EDITION

The *Study Edition* follows Barth's original volume structure. Individual paragraphs and sections should be easy to locate. A synopsis of the old and new edition can be found on the back cover of each fascicle.

All secondary literature on the *Church Dogmatics* currently refers to the classic 14-volume set (e.g. II.2 p. 520). In order to avoid confusion, we recommend that this practice should be kept for references to this *Study Edition*. The page numbers of the old edition can be found in the margins of this edition.

CONTENTS

§ 65–66

THE SLOTH AND MISERY OF MAN

The direction of God, given in the resurrection of Jesus Christ who was crucified for us, discloses who is overcome in His death. It is the man who would not make use of his freedom, but was content with the low level of a self-enclosed being, thus being irremediably and radically and totally subject to his own stupidity, inhumanity, dissipation and anxiety, and delivered up to his own death.

1. THE MAN OF SIN IN THE LIGHT OF THE LORDSHIP OF THE SON OF MAN

So far we have been occupied with the existence of the Son of Man, who is none other than the humiliated Son of God. We have seen that as it is attested in the New Testament this existence is that of the true and exalted and royal man Jesus. And we have considered the problem of the connexion, the transition from Him to other men, the divine direction as it has been given, and is still given, by this man in the power and work of the Holy Spirit. But the alteration of the human situation as it is brought about by this man and His direction in the act of His lordship works itself out in the fact that there were and are and will be a Christian community and Christians in the world. It is of this alteration that we shall have to speak both in general and in detail in the sections which follow; of the sanctification and upbuilding of the Christian community and of Christian love.

To see it and understand it, however, we have first to consider the human situation in the form which precedes this alteration and is not yet affected by it. It is determined by human sin, or, more strictly, by the fact that the man with whom the royal man Jesus has to do in the act of His lordship is the man of sin: the man who wills and commits sin; the man who is determined and burdened by it. It is this man as such who is sanctified by the existence of the man Jesus, by the direction which is given by Him. In the Christian community and the individual Christian it is still a matter—with an incisive modification—of this man and the overcoming of this man. The Son of God abased Himself to be the Brother of this man, the Bearer of his responsibility, when He was made flesh and put to death in the flesh. And when He overcame him in Himself, [379] neither willing nor committing his sin, He set him aside, making him the old and superseded and outmoded man, becoming and being in his place the new

1

and true and exalted and royal man, heading a new and reconciled world and humanity, sending out in His resurrection His mighty direction, and bringing about in the work of the Holy Spirit the act of His lordship, the great alteration, within the human situation as determined by sin. In order that we may know what this means in all its concreteness and significance, we have first to see and understand as such this situation as it was determined by sin, and the old man who was overcome in Jesus and set aside by Him.

The light in which this man is to be seen and understood is none other than the light of his overcoming. It is in view of the lordship of the Son of Man, in the power of His direction, and therefore in the knowledge of Jesus Christ by the Holy Spirit that we may know sin and the man of sin.

The general basis of this proposition (*C.D.* IV, 1, § 60, 1) need not be developed again, but only sketched. As the opposition of man to God, his neighbour and himself, sin is more than a relative and limited conflict which works itself out only in himself and which can therefore be known in the self-consciousness and self-understanding which he can have of himself. As the one who commits sin man is himself totally and radically compromised. Where this is a true knowledge of sin, it can be only as an element in the knowledge of God, of revelation, and therefore of faith, for which he cannot in any way prepare himself. Man is corrupt even in his self-understanding, even in the knowledge of his corruption. He cannot see, therefore, beyond the inner conflict and its purely relative compass. He can never really see his sin, and himself as the man of sin. He cannot turn to a true knowledge of his corruption, but only evade it. God and His revelation and faith are all needed if He is to realise the accusation and judgment and condemnation under which he stands, and the transgression and ensuing need in which he exists. But faith in an idol and its revelation has no power to give him this realisation. It cannot be given by any further work of corrupt man; by any normative concept that he himself may freely construct of majesty, goodness, righteousness and holiness; by any law that he thinks he has discovered but has really invented and planned and built up of himself. A law of this kind can never have the power to bind and commit, and therefore really to accuse and judge and condemn, because in his encounter with it man is finally in encounter only with his own shadow, and in his discussion with it he is finally engaged only in discussion with himself. Any normative concept that he may construct is ultimately himself. By means of it he may well be conscious of that inward and relative and redemptive conflict with himself, but not of sin as his destructive opposition to God, his neighbour and himself.

[380]   He may perhaps achieve this so long and so far as the materials that he uses to construct this concept are taken from the statements of Holy Scripture and do actually give the necessary sharpness in virtue of their context. This was the case with the regulative concept of the Law as it was adopted and applied by the theology of the Reformation. But in this as in other respects it is a very doubtful and dangerous enterprise to take materials out of the Bible rather than allowing them to speak in their own context and substance and from their own

1. *The Man of Sin in the Light of the Lordship of the Son of Man*

centre. For the critical question then arises on the basis of what presupposition they will be read and according to what plan they will be—even in the most strictly biblicist manner—constructed. In other words, how is it to be decided what is meant by God and His majesty and will and Law? May it not be that in the answering of this question some other source of revelation and knowledge is secretly or even openly tapped as well as the Bible: the book of rational law; the consensus of all races as to what is generally and self-evidently right and fitting for man; the decision of the innate individual conscience; in short a *lex naturalis*[EN1] which is merely rediscovered in the Bible as the true *lex aeterna*[EN2] because it has found in what the Bible calls good and evil only its positive revelation, application and concretion? (On the questions of the origins of this pregnant concept, and its incursion into Christian theology, we cannot be too emphatic in our recommendation of the important book by Felix Flückiger, *Geschichte des Naturrechts*, Vol. 1, 1954.) May it not be that it has its effect, and is brought to light, that the builder of this Law which is presumed to be superior to man, and to confront him, is really man himself—the law being only an ideal by which he measures himself but which he himself has established? Is it not likely that the biblical elements used in its construction, having lost the distinctive power which they have in their own context and substance and from their own centre, will necessarily appear in the long run to be intrusive and dispensable? Is it not inevitable that a synthetic outlook and thinking will triumph, for which there is only the tension of a relative and redemptive antithesis between good and evil, between what man should be and what he is, and in the sphere of which there is no real place for genuine sin and a man of sin (in the serious meaning of the term)? Is it not possible that there is betrayed at this point the latent rationalism and immanentism of the biblicist enterprise? These questions are not merely hypothetical. They are a description (cf. *C.D.* IV, 1, 369 ff., 374 ff.) of the development which, in repetition of the mistakes of the early and mediaeval Church, actually took place, in respect of the concept of law and the corresponding concept of sin, in the history of Protestant theology from the closing stages of the Reformation to the apogee of Neo-Protestantism.

If man measures himself by a normative concept, a concept of God and His revelation, which is in some way—planned and constructed with or without biblical materials—his own work and therefore a reflection of himself, it is basically impossible that he should see his aberration as a destruction of his peace with God, his neighbour and himself, and therefore as his exposure to the threat of eternal perdition. Even in his aberration he will then see and think always of himself together with that norm. He will always be able to order and control his encounter with it, i.e., with himself. He will interpret his transgression as an incident, a point of transition, a stage in development. But he himself will not really be affected by even the sharpest judgment which he may find in it. He will never see himself so humiliated that he does not stand at some level and is not capable at least of climbing higher. *Quanti ponderis sit peccatum*[EN3], that as a sinner he is under sentence of death, and that he needs [381] redemption and total renewal will always be truths which are quite alien to his thinking.

[EN1] natural law
[EN2] eternal law
[EN3] How great a weight is sin

A genuine knowledge of sin is possible, and actual, as an element in the genuine knowledge of God, of revelation and of faith. But as an element in this knowledge it does not consist in the assertion of this or that general or specific accusation which man may make against himself but which he can always evade because it is he who makes it. Nor does it consist in the acknowledgment and acceptance of individual passages in the Bible which accuse and condemn man in the name of God but which are robbed of their true force because they are taken out of their context and given a purely arbitrary interpretation. It consists in the insight into the human situation which is given by the substance and centre of the biblical message; by the direction which is given us by the existence of Jesus Christ, in and with His resurrection, in and with the witness and work of the Holy Spirit. Where the Word of God became and is flesh, there it is disclosed that man is flesh, and what it means and involves that this is the case. Where the grace of God encounters him, there his sin is revealed, and the fact that he is a sinner. Where his salvation is achieved, there the perdition from which he is snatched cannot be overlooked or contradicted. The Gospel alone, which no man has invented or planned or constructed, but which encounters man, if at all, only as God's free revelation, is the Law in the knowledge of which man finds himself accused and judged and condemned. But the Word made flesh, the grace of God encountering man, his salvation, the Gospel, is Jesus Christ. He and His existence as the Son of God and Son of Man are the light in which man as the man of sin is made known to himself, in which he must see and confess himself as such. Where there is a genuine knowledge of sin, it is a matter of the Christian knowledge of God, of revelation and of faith, and therefore of the knowledge of Jesus Christ. We will now attempt a more specific formulation and establishment of this statement in our present context.

We must first bring out the truth and significance of what has to be said concerning the *humanitas Christi*[EN4], the existence of the man Jesus. He is the Son of God humbled to be a servant. And as such He is the Son of Man exalted to be the Lord. Both His humiliation as God and His exaltation as man as fulfilled in His death, both the true deity and the true humanity of His existence, are revealed in His resurrection from the dead. It is the second aspect which now concerns us: His true humanity as fulfilled in His death and revealed in His resurrection; His exaltation to be the royal man who in virtue of His identity with the Son of God lives and rules in full communion and conformity with God the Father. In this man God has elected humanity as such, and therefore all men, to the covenant with Himself. This man is the Representative and Head and Lord of all other men. But this being the case [382] they are all established in Him and directed to an eternal life in the service of God. Therefore the revelation of His exaltation as it has taken place in His resurrection is the revelation of theirs too. There thus went forth, and still goes

---

[EN4] humanity of Christ

4

forth, in the work of His Holy Spirit the direction of Eph. 5^{14} to them and all of us: "Awake, thou that sleepest, and arise from the dead, and Christ shall give thee light." It is not always and everywhere effective, or equally effective. It is not yet, or no longer, received and genuinely taken to heart by all. Yet in the present context it is not these and similar questions that are important, but the reality which is presupposed in all these questions and which precedes all acceptance or non-acceptance on our part—the objective fact of the existence of Jesus Christ among all the other men of every time and place.

"The rays of dawn were still concealed, That flood the world with light; But, look, the Light is now revealed, Which shines for ever bright. The sun itself its slumbers kept, But forth in all its power there leapt The uncreated sun" (P. Gerhardt). But the light which has arisen before any dawn is the reality of the exaltation and institution which have come to man in the death of Jesus; of his establishment in a vital fellowship with God. It is the reality of the revelation, in His resurrection, of this decisive alteration of the whole human situation. It has happened once for all and radically for all men in the man Jesus. What is said of the final and conclusive revelation of Jesus (Lk. 17^{24}) is virtually true of His first revelation which initiated the closing epoch of human history: "For as the lightning, that lighteneth out of the one part of heaven, shineth unto the other part under heaven; so shall also the Son of man be in his day." "The true Light, which lighteth every man, came into the world" (Jn. 1^9). It "shineth in darkness," although the darkness apprehended it not. The fire which Jesus came to kindle on earth (Lk. 12^{49}) burns and cannot be put out.

Since God humbled Himself and became man, thus exalting man to Himself, there is no more peace in the lowliness of human existence. In the power of the eternal divine election of grace and its execution in time, i.e., in the existence of the man Jesus, and by the fact of the direction which has been, and is, given by Him, all other men, whether they realise and accept it or not, are already estranged from the place which in itself would necessarily be, and continue to be, their place, if this man had not existed among them. They are already startled out of it. They are already alarmed. They are already summoned to make the movement within which they too are put in virtue of the exaltation of this One. Because and as this man lives, and God is lowly and man exalted in Him, man is no longer bound absolutely to his lowliness, nor is there now any absolute impossibility of his being in the height of a vital fellowship with God and in the service of God. He is no longer imprisoned, if secure, below. He is no longer unfree to let himself be exalted and to exalt himself. The existence of this One, and the fact of the direction of the Holy Spirit which He gives, is equivalent in practice to a *Sursum corda*[EN5]! *Sursum homines*[EN6]! which is called out, and applies and comes, radically and objectively to all men, even though they may be at the very lowest point and have never so much as heard of Him. Because this man exists, there is no man who does not exist under the sign of this *Sursum*[EN7]! For this man is not a private   [383]

[EN5] upward, hearts
[EN6] upward, men
[EN7] upward

person. As this One, this Individual, this First-born, this Lord and Head, He has taken the place of all others, to die for them and to live for them, to live for them as the One who dies for them. No one can alter the fact that he, too, is a brother of this One, and that this One lives for him.

It is the knowledge of the man Jesus which forces us to, or rather frees us for, a knowledge of sin; a knowledge of man as the man of sin. It does so, in short, because human existence as we taste and know it is set in the light of the exaltation of our humanity as it has taken place in Him. It is set under the sign of the great *Sursum*^{EN8}!, the Forward! and Onward! It is set under the command and the promise and the power of the "Follow me" that He addresses to every man. We shall speak of this positive aspect in our next section, which treats of the sanctification of man. But we cannot speak of it meaningfully unless we are aware of the negative aspect which on our side is also and primarily revealed in the same light of the exaltation of humanity as it has taken place in Jesus; of the depth from which it is (validly and effectively and for every man) lifted in Him.

The alteration of the human situation as it has taken place in Him is differentiated from a prior state in which it is not yet altered. The movement in which He has set it is preceded by an earlier immobility. To the above of man actualised in Him there corresponds a very definite below, and to the fellowship with God in which he is placed a separation from God. In order to overcome this prior state, this immobility, this below, this separation of man from God, and therefore to draw man to Himself, God took them to Himself in His Son. At this point of departure He accepted solidarity with us; He became our Brother. Willing to accept and suffer the conditions and consequences of this situation, He took our place and died on the cross. Hence He became and was and is, in this very act of His suffering and dying, the Conqueror, the Victor: exalted as man; entering into that above; passing from dereliction by God to perfect fellowship with Him; being set as man at the right hand of the Father; and therefore putting into effect in our place and for us that alteration of the human situation. The prior state, the immobility, the below, the separation from God which He made His own in order to overcome, is the sin of man. It is quite useless to try to see or state or know this except in relation to this gracious act of God toward man. This is the Law which reveals it where any other law imagined and invented by man, no matter how holy or pitiless he may think it to be, can only lead to illusions as to his own true nature. It is only where man has ground for thanksgiving that he has ground for the remorse which involves also repentance, conversion and sanctification.

[384] To put the same thing in another way, the life of a new man lived by Jesus is preceded by the dying of an old man suffered by Him, the rising of the true man in His existence and death by the destruction of a false and perverted, His being as the royal man by the accepted and conquered being of the

---

^{EN8} upward

enslaved, His life in the spirit by the vegetating and passing flesh in which He willed to be like us, to be one of us. God has had mercy on the man who even in the form of that old, perverted, man, even as that slave, even as flesh, is still the good creature which He elects and loves. He has received him so basically and radically that He was ready to make Himself his Brother in His own Son, to share his situation, to bear his shame, to be put to shame in his place and on his behalf, thus removing man from the situation which contradicts His election and love and creative will, divesting him of his shame and clothing him with His own glory: Himself being the new and true and royal and spiritual and worthy man in his place and on his behalf; the man in whose person the covenant was kept and fulfilled even on the part of man, and who in peace with God may also be at peace with himself and his neighbour. The first, perverted, fleshly man, whom God has so graciously pitied and accepted, is the man of sin. He is revealed in the light of the divine act of grace done to him in Jesus. In the light of this act, confronted with its law, this man is shown to be the man of sin. Where he has the most reason to praise God, no place whatever is left for any praise of self.

We will try to bring what we have to say concerning the knowledge of this man, and therefore the knowledge of sin and the man of sin as it is enclosed in the knowledge of God, of revelation and of faith, under a single common denominator, by saying that the existence of the man Jesus and the event of the direction of the Holy Spirit as issued by Him involve the shaming of all other men. Shaming is the disclosure of shame. Jesus is distinguished from all other men, and the knowledge of Jesus from that of all other men, from that of all other real or possible objects of knowledge, by the fact that they involve our incontestable shaming; the disclosure of our shame. When we say this we affirm in the first instance the purely factual element in the relationship between Him and us that He is the One who shames us and we are those who are shamed, quite irrespective of whether we are aware of the fact and are ashamed of ourselves, or still close our eyes or close them again to that which has happened and still does so. In this respect, too, the reality precedes the knowledge of it. But at any rate it is a decisive criterion of our knowledge of Jesus that, in accordance with the fact that He is the One who shames us and we are those who are shamed by Him, we should be ashamed of ourselves. If there is not this corresponding result, we are sadly mistaken if we imagine that we have even the remotest knowledge of Jesus.

The parable of the Pharisee and the Publican (Lk. 18[9f.]) speaks of two men who are both [385] equally shamed before God but who are completely different because of their knowledge or ignorance of the fact. On the one hand we have here in the temple, proudly displayed before the face of God, the man who is ignorant and therefore quite unashamed. He thanks God so beautifully that he is as he is and therefore not as other men, extortioners, unjust, adulterers, or even as this publican. He can claim that he is free from carnal appetites: "I fast twice in the week"; and he can also claim that he is free from the rule of Mammon: "I give tithes of all that I possess." On the other hand, also in the temple and before the face of God, we have the man who knows and is therefore ashamed. He can only stand afar off, and dare not lift up so much as his eyes unto heaven, but can only smite on his breast, his confession of faith being simply this: "God be merciful to me a sinner." The shame of both is already disclosed. But the one knows that this is the case and the other does not. The one can only humble himself whereas the other sees many things which encourage him to exalt himself. It is by this problem of shaming, whether it becomes acute or remains latent, that the decision is made and the ways divide.

But man is shamed (whether or not he is correspondingly ashamed) because he finds that he is compared with God. With God? Yes, if he is radically and totally shamed it is because he is compared with God, and measured by His holiness he necessarily sees his own unholiness revealed. When we compare man with man there can and will be occasional and partial and superficial shamings. And because, in view of the difference in the relationships in which men may be compared with one another, these shamings are always at bottom reciprocal, it is always possible either on the one side or the other, or both, to find good reasons for evading them. The basic and total shaming which we cannot avoid is either from God or it does not take place at all. But we must add that it is from the true God who meets us concretely in a living encounter. A supposed direct confrontation of man with a God who is only a God at some height or depth in and for Himself is not an encounter with the Holy One, measured by whose holiness man finds that he is revealed to be unholy. In these circumstances he is dealing only with an idea or concept of God which, however lofty or profound it may be, cannot give rise to any shaming, any disclosure of his shame, so that he can never really be ashamed before it because he is not really shamed by it. A God who is God only in and for Himself is not the true God. The concept of this God is that of an idol. Between Him and man there can be no comparison, with the result that there can be no serious shaming of man. And it is tempting to ask whether man does not usually invent and deck out for himself this idol just because he knows that he cannot be compared with it and therefore that there is no risk of his being put to shame by it.

But he is compared already, and in this comparison seriously and basically and totally shamed, in his encounter with the God who is distinguished from all idols as the true God by the fact that He is not merely God in and for [386] Himself but also Emmanuel: "God with us"; very man even as He is very God. Between us men it is not the case that the one encounters God in the other. It may well be that we mutually attest God, and therefore the fact that we are compared with Him and shamed by Him. It may well be that we can and must lead one another to shame before Him. But none of us is confronted with God Himself, or shamed by Him, in the existence of another man. This takes place only, but genuinely, in the existence of the true man in Jesus, the Son of God. It is in relation to Him—and we all stand in relation to Him—that there is the comparison with a man which is also our comparison with the holy God. And in this comparison with His of our actions and achievements, our possibilities

8

and actualisations, the true expression of that which is within us, and the inwardness of that which we express, our whole whence and whither, the root and crown of our existence, we are genuinely shamed. We are shamed because our own human essence meets us in Him in a form in which it completely surpasses and transcends the form which we give it. In Him we are not encountered by an angel, or a being which is superior and alien to our own nature, so that it is easy to excuse ourselves if we fail to measure up to it. We are confronted by a man like ourselves, with whom we are quite comparable. But we are confronted by a man in the clear exaltation of our nature to its truth, in the fulfilment of its determination, in the correspondence to the election and creation of man. We are confronted by the man who is with and for God as God is with Him, at peace with God and therefore with His fellows and Himself. But this means that we are all asked by Him who and what we ought to be as His brothers. What about human life as we live it? What about our thinking and willing and speaking and acting? What about our heart and actions? What about the use we make of our existence, of the time which is given us, of our own distinctive opportunity both as a whole and in detail? What about our coming and going? What about our motives and restraints, our plans and attainments? What about the ordering of our relationship to God and our neighbours and ourselves? And finally and comprehensively, what about our life-act as God's good creatures within the cosmos of God's good creation? If we had the freedom to orientate and measure ourselves by other men, or by an abstraction that we regard as God, or by a law invented and established by ourselves, it might well be possible to acquit ourselves creditably, or not too discreditably, in face of these questions. But we do not have this freedom. We can only imagine that we have it. The measure by which we are measured is the true man in whom the true God meets us concretely in a living encounter. Compared with Him we stand there in all our corruption. The failure of all that we have and do is revealed. The lost state of our humanity is exposed. Our holiness, however great or small, drops away. Our brilliance is extinguished, our boasting reduced to futility, our pride deprived of its object. The untruth [387] in which we are men is disclosed. The need in which God has accepted us in His Son, and which consists in the untruth of our humanity, is incontestable. This is our actual shaming, whether we see it or not, whether we are ashamed of ourselves or not. We stand there as those who are shamed in this way, in this shame, because and as the man Jesus is among us.

And if we are ashamed of ourselves, this means that we are aware of the way in which we are shamed by the man Jesus, of the shame in which we stand when we are measured by Him, and that we are grieved at it, but are quite unable, however ardently we may desire, to free ourselves from it. Even if the whole world takes our part, we cannot satisfy ourselves as those who are responsible for it. Even if no one else sees it, we see it. Even if no one else accuses us, we can only accuse ourselves. And if we try to conceal it from ourselves, it is always the more painfully present, for we cannot conceal ourselves from ourselves. We are forced to see and know ourselves in the loathsomeness in which we find ourselves exposed and known. We may perish and disappear, but we now know of no place in which we are no longer the terrible creature which we are known, and know ourselves, to be. We have to put up with ourselves as such. We need to be Christians, to know the man Jesus, if we are to be aware of the shaming which has come to all men in the existence of this One, and if we are to be affected by it, taking it to heart and accepting the fact of our shame. We can try to resist it, and to be without shame, only so long and so far as we have not yet seen Jesus, or still try, or again try, to ignore Him; only so long and so far as we have not realised that as men we all stand in relation to Him, and are compared with Him and measured by Him, and are therefore shamed, like all other men, by this true man and therefore by the true God. The Christian cannot and will not refuse this knowledge. He does not do anything strange when, in the eloquent expression of the Bible, he "smites upon his breast." He would not be a Christian if he did not do this. He does only that which it is for every man without exception to do, and that which in the day of judgment every man will do. We will all be ashamed before Him then as those who are compared with Jesus and measured and therefore shamed by Him.

It is striking, and worth considering, that in the Gospels the shaming of man is expressly revealed in a figure which is given great prominence—that of Peter. Peter is obviously shamed already (although the word itself is not used) in Mk. 8³³ and par. when, because he does not conceive of the death and passion announced by Jesus in divine but human terms, he is rebuked or "threatened" by Him, and has to be told quite plainly: ὕπαγε ὀπίσω μου, σατανᾶ EN9, i.e., that he must remove himself from the sight of Jesus. He is shamed already when according to Lk. 22³², in a saying which stands between a supreme promise given to all the disciples (that they will eat and drink and sit on thrones and exercise a judicial office in the coming Messianic kingdom) and a supreme assurance of loyalty from this first disciple, [388] Jesus tells him that He has prayed for him that his faith should not fail in the great trial which is at hand: "And when thou art converted strengthen thy brethren." He is ashamed already when in Mk. 14³⁰f. and par. his far too rash (ἐκπερισσῶς EN10) assertion of his own trustworthiness receives at once the answer: "Even in this night, before the cock crow twice, thou shalt deny me thrice"; when according to Mk. 14³⁷ he is asked: "Simon, sleepest thou? couldest not thou watch one hour?"; and when in Mt. 26⁵² and Jn. 18¹¹ he is commanded to put up his sword. Again, his particular distinction and commission as they are described in Jn. 21¹⁵f. are preceded by the shaming question whether he really loves Jesus; whether he loves Him more than the other disciples as he had previously boasted; whether he really loves Him at all. It is not only in Mt. 14³¹ that the one who is caught by the saving and uplifting hand of Jesus is the Peter who sinks before Jesus because of his little faith, his doubt. And we find a remarkable echo of the Gospel picture in the fact that it is he whom Paul has to "withstand to the face" in Antioch because of his hypocrisy (Gal. 2¹¹f.). But again, it is said expressly of Peter that he knows that he is shamed, and that he is ashamed of himself accordingly. "Depart from me; for I am a sinful man, O Lord" (Lk. 5⁸), is the first saying of this first disciple that has come down to us, and it is his first reaction in his encounter with the Lord. And then, more drastically, we have the description of the scene after his denial

---

EN 9 get thee behind me, Satan
EN10 more exceedingly

1. *The Man of Sin in the Light of the Lordship of the Son of Man*

(Lk. 22$^{61f.}$): "And the Lord turned, and looked upon Peter. And Peter remembered the word of the Lord, how he had said unto him, Before the cock crow, thou shalt deny me thrice. And Peter went out, and wept bitterly." And finally in Jn. 21^{17}: "Peter was grieved because he said unto him the third time, Lovest thou me?" It is obviously the intention of the New Testament tradition that everything else that it can say concerning him, or that is known concerning him in the primitive Church, should be seen and understood against this background. This was the appearance, in relation to Jesus, of the rock on which He willed to build His community, and did in fact do so. Again, it is obviously the intention of the tradition to characterise in the person of this first disciple *mutatis mutandis*^{EN11} the situation and shame of all others in their relation to their Lord; the Christian situation in its typical significance for the human situation as such. As it sees it, neither in the community nor the world is there anyone who is not shamed by Him as Peter is when measured by Jesus.

But the statement that man is shamed in the light of the lordship of the Son of Man needs to be filled out and explained before we can pass from the question of knowledge to that of fact. That there is a serious and radical and total shaming of man must not seem to be only a statement made and accepted at random. It is a matter of the truth of man in this shaming, and of the knowledge of this truth, when a man, the Christian, has to be ashamed of himself in accordance with the shaming of all men as it proceeds from the existence of Jesus. If he sees himself forced, or rather freed, to do this by the direction of Jesus Christ and therefore by the Holy Spirit, this is not a dead and formless and irresponsible awareness. He finds himself set in the light of the lordship of the Son of Man. He comes to participate in a knowledge of Him, and of himself. He is demanded and set in a position to give an account of his situation, to reflect on its origin and nature and significance and difficulty, to be clear about his sin and himself as the man of sin, and to make it clear to others and the world. He does not speak in the void. He does not merely assert. He does not merely appeal to an uncontrollable experience. He knows what he is saying when he confesses that he is one who is shamed by Jesus, and when he approaches other men with the presupposition that in them too, whether they know and accept it or not, he has to do with those who are in fact shamed by Jesus. What the Christian knows of himself and all other men must now be developed in more specific statements and deliberations. [389]

1. We must begin with the factual question whether it is really the case that all men do undoubtedly confront the one exalted man Jesus in the depths of abasement. Does the phenomenon of the shamed and sinking Peter really have a basic and general significance? Are there not those in whom humanity confronts us, at least in tendency, or in part, in a certain exaltation? Are there not those who can be compared with this One and do not emerge as men who are absolutely and unreservedly shamed in this comparison? Are there not those who are at least nobles or princes beside this one royal man? Is there not even something noble to be found in every man, even in those whose aspect is dominated by their abasement? May it not be that the statement that all men

---

^{EN11} allowing for differences

are shamed by Jesus is true only in a relative sense? Are we perhaps guilty of an exaggeration when we oppose to Him as the one true man the corruption of all the rest? How is it that as Christians we know concerning ourselves and all other men that, however lofty or lowly we may be in other spheres, in face of Him, measured by Him, we do not find ourselves half-exalted, but in the very depths of a perverted humanity?

The answer to this factual question is given by the simple fact that Jesus lives for the Christian, who alone knows what he is saying when he utters this name; that He lives as the man of the history handed down in the Gospels; and that the Christian himself has a personal share in this history, so that he cannot avoid recognising himself and all other men in the figures and manner and situation of those by whom Jesus is surrounded in this history. They may be distant and strange in other respects. But in the relation to Jesus he sees his own—and not only his own, but the characteristic relation of all men. In this respect he regards himself and all other men as one with them—no worse, but certainly no better, no different, when measured by this standard. What would he have to do with the Jesus who lives in the Gospel history if he had no share in it; if he were not in solidarity with those who surrounded Him: with the people of Galilee and Jerusalem; with the publicans and sinners; with the sick and possessed; with the scribes and Pharisees; with Caiaphas and Pilate and their men; with the disciples of Jesus from Peter the rock to Judas who betrayed Him; and if he were not forced to see and understand all other men in the same solidarity with them in relation to Jesus? It is on this ground that the Christian knows that he and all other men, however noble or princely they may be compared with men, are shamed by this One, and that no matter what

[390] may be attempted or done in other respects this shaming cannot be explained away or relativised or weakened either in his own case or that of others. He stands together with those who confront this One in the Gospel history. This does not mean that he finds himself in particularly bad company. This may be said of Barabbas and the two who were crucified with Jesus. But by and large there are no outstanding villains, no titans of iniquity, no palpably disturbed social relations, in face of this One. He is set in an environment in which He has no serious opponent. But it is also the case that He has no serious companion or helper or fellow-worker. In the positive sense, too, there is a dearth of figures who stand out in some way when they are measured by Him. The only possible candidate for this position is John the Baptist, but he belongs only to the beginning of the story, and the Gospels take good care to characterise him in such a way that there can be no place for any thought of an equality or even a similarity in the comparison between him and Jesus. For the rest, there are the sick who are healed, those whose sins are forgiven, those who seem to be, and are, affected and shaken by the preaching of Jesus, those to whom He turns in a way which completely surprises both themselves and others, and finally those who are called to follow Him, and do in some sense do so. There is not a single one among them who has any independent significance or weight

12

in face of Him. They see Him, and hear Him, and are helped by Him, and believe in Him, or think they do so. And in all these relationships He is always the One who gives, the One to whom none of them has anything to give. He goes through the midst of them in splendid isolation as the Lord. The men around Him, measured by Him, have no particular distinction either in good or evil; and if they have this in other respects, it pales in comparison with Him. They fall away beside Him. Measured by Him, they exist on a different level. What is revealed in the encounter with Him, in His light, is only the usual run, whether in good or evil, of mediocre and trivial humanity. And that the distinction and antithesis in relation to Him are not relative or temporary is proved by the fact that this humanity which is trivial in both good and evil is finally united in the fact that it doubts Him, that it does not understand Him, that it forsakes Him, that it rejects and denies and betrays, or at the very best impotently bewails, Him, that it judges Him either on spiritual or secular grounds, that it brings Him to the cross and that it finally abandons Him on the cross. It is the average man who does this. It is he who is the rebel that will not have this man to reign over us. It is he that is the perverted man who is so sharply distinguished, who so flagrantly distinguishes himself, from the true man. It is he who is the man of sin. And his sin consists in the very fact that he is the average man. The Christian knows that he belongs to this group, and he confesses that—whether he is a little above or a little below the average—he is in this group, together with all other men, man as such. He knows the Jesus who lives [391] in this history and therefore in this human environment. He thus knows who and what all other men are. He knows the lowliness and misery in which we confront Him, both as individuals and in the mass, both in our better impulses and desires and our worse. He knows the descent in which we are all implicated as compared with His ascent. He knows that the best possibility of man is only to be like sinking Peter, who without the hand of the Lord to save him and lift him up could only sink in his triviality. This is the first thing that has to be said concerning the factual question. It may not bring out the distinction and the antithesis between the one Son of Man and other men in all its clarity and strictness and danger. But its seriousness is already apparent. All our mediocrity is revealed, and it is revealed as the form in which we are unequivocally opposed to Him.

2. But the question arises, and demands an answer, whether and how far there is really any disqualification of others as sinners in and with this distinction between Him and them. Can the mediocrity, or triviality, with which they confront Him really be regarded as bad or evil? Is it really the case that in this confrontation with the man Jesus there is revealed a triviality of others in which they are not merely different from, but finally opposed to, Him? Is it really the shame of man which this discloses? Is he really shamed by Him because of it? Is triviality real corruption? Ought not mediocrity to be at least permitted as an optimum which is accessible to all? May it not even be commanded as that which is basically normal? Explanations and excuses might be

sought and found for all those men in the environment of Jesus who were not prepared to be wholly with Him or definitely against Him, and therefore for us to the extent that we are like them, and in solidarity with them. Indeed, it might even be asked whether they were not right. Was it not this One that was so different and strange and isolated among them—so one-sidedly orientated on God, so imprudently occupied with the cause of man, so singleminded and emphatic in the proclamation of Himself—who was really perverted? Was it not a sound instinct for that which is possible and to that extent right for men that caused the others to keep Him at a distance, not to commit themselves to Him absolutely or without the freedom to withdraw at the last minute, even perhaps to shake their heads and turn away from Him at once, or nonchalantly to pass by on the other side, and let Him go His own way, or, if He could not be resisted in any other way, and obviously willed to have it so, to make an end of Him altogether, driving Him out as One who was not wanted, as a disturber of the peace? As Goethe put it: "Let every fanatic be nailed to the cross in the thirtieth year." Was it not most likely that they were all in the right against the One rather than He against them? And may not we, if we belong to this company of those who are different from Him, regard ourselves, not as disqualified by Him, but as excused in face of Him, and basically and finally in the right against Him?

[392]

The question is a serious one to the extent that it undoubtedly brings before us an important aspect of the critical point where Christians and non-Christians necessarily divide. Decided non-Christians, however lofty their spiritual and moral principles, are always characterised by the fact that (more or less consciously and explicitly, but always resolutely) they usually defend those who are ordinary in relation to Jesus against the charge that in their ordinariness they are sinners. Many things may be conceded to the man Jesus, but not the fact that in their difference from Him all others are disqualified and shamed and ought therefore to be ashamed. Assuming that we ourselves are Christians, what is it that we know if in practice we regard this obvious question as just as self-evidently unimportant as it seems important to them? What was it that Peter began to know when, as the first and best of the many who then surrounded Jesus, he could not bear the look of Jesus after the denial, but "went out and wept bitterly"?

The first point is obviously that, if we know Jesus at all, we can never completely (but only temporarily) forget, nor can we absolutely (but only superficially) abstract from the fact, that this One is not a private person beside and among many others so that we can escape Him and keep ourselves to ourselves, but that in all the omnipotence of the merciful will of God He is the One who in all His isolation took our place, and the place of all men, so that what He is necessarily includes in itself our true being as it is ascribed and given us by God. If, then, He is very different from us, if there is this distinction between Him on the one side and all other men on the other, if we all confront Him in our ordinariness, we cannot excuse and vindicate and justify ourselves against Him in this ordinariness, or try to accuse Him because He is so different. In and with the existence of this One the ground is cut away from under our feet as those who are ordinary men. In and with this One who has taken our place there has come to us grace and liberation. This ordinariness is behind us and under us. We have become new men who are lifted out of this ordinariness and separated from it. This is the first thing that the Christian knows as he knows about Jesus Christ and himself and man. He belongs to Him, to His side; and not therefore to that of the trivial humanity in which he confronts Him.

From this first thing there follows necessarily the second, that it is not normal or excusable or justifiable, but evil and wicked, that he does not stand at His side. He contradicts himself as he contradicts Him. Even from his own standpoint, he does that which is impossible. He cannot be below, but has to be above with this One who is there for him. His mediocrity and triviality, the ordinariness of his manner and place, is actually sin, and as such it is intoler- [393] able and inexcusable. It is undeniable ingratitude to the grace which is shown him. In it he is like a prisoner who when the doors are opened will not leave his cell but wants to remain in it. It clearly disqualifies him. As the ordinary man he is like all others, he cannot be endured. His shaming is an event. This is the second thing that the Christian knows.

And from this there follows the third—he knows that every attempt to escape his shaming, to defend and justify and excuse himself, to regard the abnormal as normal and his wrong as right, to turn the tables, not only has no prospect of success and cannot alter his actual shame, but can only confirm his shame. Is it not enough that he stands where he does, in the impossible contradiction to himself where he does not really belong? When he is absolutely assailed in his being below, is he still going to espouse it? Is he going to pretend that that which is so harmful is really innocuous? Is he going to acquiesce in that which cannot be? Is he going to glorify that which is plainly infamous? Is he going to reject and contest that which is his own health and greatness and glory? Surely it is clear that every step in this direction, all the activity or inactivity in which he participates in the repudiation of the One by the many, even the impulse of superior indifference or rejection, merely recoils upon himself and threatens to make his shaming final and definitive. This is the basis of the Christian answer to the question. The Christian is no real Christian, i.e., he does not know Jesus and himself, if he cannot give this answer at once, shaking it off as no less self-evidently meaningless than the non-Christian regards it as meaningful and profound. He knows that man is quite defenceless in face of the accusation arising from his confrontation by the man Jesus. In their differentiation from this One all others are indeed disqualified as sinners. This statement, too, which is directed primarily against themselves, belongs to the witness which Christians cannot withhold from non-Christians—quite irrespective of whether or not they receive it.

3. It might also be asked, however, whether and how far it is directly the individual himself who is actually implicated in this disqualification as a sinner which arises in his relation with Jesus. How far is the sin disclosed in his confrontation with Jesus really to be understood as a determination of his being, of all that he does or refrains from doing? May it not be that the term "man of sin" is too strong? We have to agree that the evil act of a man is not something that takes place automatically from within himself, nor is it a function of his creaturely nature. It is a new and responsible work, and it is in contradiction to his nature, so that when he does it he is a stranger to himself. We have also to agree that even as the doer of this act he does not cease to be in the hand of God, and to be the man who was not created evil but good. From this it might

[394] be deduced that although it is right that he is disqualified in so far as he sins, i.e., as he frequently and seriously denies what he ought to be and might be as a man, yet the disqualification is not so far-reaching that it affects himself, his being, and all that he does or refrains from doing. The sinful act is a regrettable but external, incidental and isolated failure and defect; a misfortune, comparable to one of the passing sicknesses in which a healthy organism remains healthy and to which it shows itself to be more than equal. On this view, the individual—I myself—cannot really be affected by the evil action. I do not have any direct part in its loathsome and offensive character. In the last resort it has taken place in my absence. I myself am elsewhere and aloof from it. And from this neutral place which is my real home, I can survey and evaluate the evil that has happened in me in its involvement with other less evil and perhaps even good motives and elements; in its not absolutely harmful but to some extent positive effects; in its relationship to my other much less doubtful and perhaps even praiseworthy achievements; and especially in my relationship to what I see other men do or not do (a comparison in which I may not come out too badly); in short, in a relativity in which I am not really affected at bottom. I may acknowledge and regret that I have sinned, but I do not need to confess that I am a sinner. The alien nature of my act has not alienated me from myself. I am not really shamed, and therefore I do not have to be ashamed of myself. That there have often enough been, and will be again, mean and trivial and even unworthy things in our relationship to God and our neighbours and ourselves need not be concealed or unacknowledged, but this does not mean that we ourselves are mean in the totality of our achievements, and that we have to reckon with this fact. It is an illegitimate hyperbole to say that I am a man of sin, that I myself am ordinary and trivial and mediocre. How and why am I to see that I am prevented from regarding myself as secured against my sin, when all is said and done, by a kind of protective covering, by an alibi of this kind?

Our attitude to this question is a further test whether we are Christians or non-Christians. Do we realise that it is quite impossible to think and speak in this way, that it is not only difficult but out of the question to take even a first step in this direction? To be sure, we can follow this kind of argument. To be sure, it is all uncannily familiar, as though we ourselves do sometimes argue this way in our dreams. But in our waking thoughts we cannot possibly make it our own. It is self-evident that nothing less than the whole of it is basically false; that it is not at all the case that in virtue of the goodness of his creaturely nature as it is undoubtedly maintained by man even as the doer of sin he is protected from being the one who does it, and therefore a sinner who is alienated from himself in committing this alien act; that there is no neutral place from which he can relativise his evil and therefore be, and claim to be, a free [395] man in respect of it; that he has no alibi and cannot find one; that he himself is really mean as the doer of these mean actions; and that he has every reason to be genuinely ashamed of himself.

What reason? Simply that he knows that the place which he might occupy and maintain in face of his doing and non-doing in order to secure himself against its loathsome and offensive character, and the disqualification and shaming which are involved for himself, is a place which is already occupied, so that it gives rise to quite a different train of reasoning from that which he himself might pursue. For it is at this very place that there stands the man Jesus, the Other beside him and among all other men, but as this Other beside him and among all other men the Son of God in his and their stead, who is instituted and determined and empowered as man to conduct his and their case—really in their stead and on their behalf. His existence, therefore, is the decision who and what they are and are not with what they do and do not do; the decision as to their whence and whither. Thus the decision is taken wholly and once for all out of their hands. It is no longer a matter of what they themselves think. For all of them it can be only a matter of knowing the decision which has been made in His existence concerning them all, and of accepting and confessing it. For none of them can there be any retreat into the fantasies of stricter or milder self-judgments. The omnipotent mercy of God has introduced this man among them. It stands behind the decision which has been made in His existence and makes it incontestable and irrevocable. This is the first thing that the Christian knows in this matter. He can confess as his own only the being in which he finds himself known by the existence of the man who has taken and occupies the place of himself and all men.

But in this man Jesus who has taken his place he can and should also find himself known as a new man exalted into peace and fellowship with God, as God's dear child and welcome saint. In Him he can and should also find the reconciliation of the world, and his own reconciliation, with God. This is the goal of the divine decision which has been made concerning all men in Him. This is the goal of the movement in which the whole human situation is set by His existence. If the decision was made in the man Jesus in the place of all, in his place; if in his and their place, as his and their Brother and Fellow, He was and is the new man in whom all others, and he too, may discover that they are known and proclaimed as regenerate, it is also fixed what his and their place is which He has taken and whose Brother and Fellow He has become, to be for

17

them this new and different man, and as such their reconciliation with God. This is the second thing that the Christian knows in this matter. If his own whence is revealed in the existence of this man, information is also given in this existence concerning his whither. He could not find comfort and joy in the reconciliation with God which has taken place in this man, in the divine sonship and sanctification which have been won in Him, if he were not prepared to be told, as this man has taken his place, who and what he himself is as the one for whom this Other has intervened, and whose hope and confidence are grounded wholly and utterly in Him.

[396]

And this Other, to be the new man and the hope and confidence of all men, is the Son of God who has become unequivocally lowly, the Bearer of human mediocrity and triviality, the Friend of publicans and sinners, the Brother of the ordinary man, in order to reconcile the world as it is to God, in order to take up man to himself as the elect and beloved creature of God in the state in which he actually finds himself. It is not at a height far above us, but in our depths, as one of us, that He was and is the new man. If we do not see Him in these depths we do not see Him at all, and therefore we do not see the exaltation that took place in Him. These depths are the place which He has taken for us. This is the third thing that the Christian knows. In the Son of God come down from heaven he recognises the exalted Son of Man who as such is the Reconciler of all other men with God, their hope and confidence.

And this brings him to the fourth and decisive point. He finds himself in these depths, and therefore he himself is mean and lowly in what he does and does not do. It is with him as such that the Son of God has associated Himself in becoming man. It is he as such, the publican and sinner, estranged from himself and therefore disqualified, who in Him as the new man is reconciled with God, the child and saint of God. If he is not prepared to be such, to be a man of sin, this can only mean that he does not want to be one of those whom God has taken to Himself in this one man, with whom He has made Himself equal, whose place this One has taken to their salvation. In the measure that he tries to contest his disqualification, or to hedge it around with reservations, or not to be one of those to whom it refers, he only compromises his real qualification as a child and saint of God. The only alibi that he can find is hell. If we are not ready to be in the far country, we are not ready to allow that the Son of God has come among us. We want to be in hell. In the very One in whom the Christian sees himself qualified and exalted, he has also to see that he is disqualified and abased. The joy in which he can boast in relation to Him is absolutely bound up with the humility in which he is necessarily ashamed in relation to Him—necessarily because otherwise he would dash away fellowship with Him and therefore his own exaltation as it has taken place in Him, thus condemning himself. This One confesses *in toto*EN12 those who are shamed by Him, but only those. Hence no one can confess Him, and therefore be a Chris-

---

EN12 as a whole

tian, unless he confesses that he is totally shamed by Him. It is for this reason that there can be no escaping the recognition that we are sinners. Only the [397] Christian can see the force of this reason. But it is valid and momentous for all men. For it is for all men that the Son of God has become lowly, and takes place in lowliness as the new man, and is their hope and confidence. What distinguishes Christians is that they know this reason, and therefore cannot conceal either from themselves or others that we cannot withdraw or protect ourselves from our sin, that in this matter there can be no question of an alibi.

4. We will assume that the first three questions have all been answered along the lines suggested, i.e., that they have been rejected as impossible questions. In comparison with the man Jesus (1) we are all shown to be opposed to Him; this opposition (2) involves our disqualification; and this disqualification (3) actually and inescapably applies to ourselves. Yet even if this is conceded, the three statements might still be over-arched or bracketed by the final question whether there is not a higher or deeper synthetic view on which the situation of man as one who is shamed is indeed necessary, but as a kind of metaphysical *datum*, so that in spite of its seriousness it does not prove to be finally or genuinely disturbing. Is it not perhaps the case that it is simply laid on man as an unavoidable destiny to be a man of sin, and to be revealed as such, and objectively shamed, and therefore necessarily to be ashamed of himself? Might it not be conditioned, for example, by his different nature and essence as a creature; by the limit which is set for him as such; by the fact that he does not confront that which is not with the same sovereignty as God but is exposed to its temptations and threats; by the fact that he cannot avoid the proximity and co-existence of darkness and its power but has to participate in them, and cannot ignore or deny this participation? Might it not be that his shaming is the characteristic feature of his existence as a man in the rest of creation (which might have the same experiences without being either shamed or ashamed)? Might it not be that simply to be a man is also to be disqualified by this opposition and to be directly and most intimately affected? Or, finally and decisively, might it not belong to the perfection of God, to His inaccessible and incomparable majesty encompassing both man as His good creature and the nothingness which menaces him, to have in the man who sins against Him and is therefore shamed by Him a kind of shadow, and therefore a counterpart with its negative attestation? Might it not be that man in his abasement, his sin, he himself as the man of sin, and his shame as such, are all integrated in the all-embracing nexus or system of a harmony of being in which he is affirmed as well as negated, and in this twofold determination is concealed, and knows that he is concealed, in a final and supreme and assured and reassuring compulsion: not lost but sustained and upheld even as the one he was and is, in all his shame; a free man ultimately even in that which speaks against him, and in their resultant misery, and in the knowledge of this situation? Might it not be [398] that in the existence of the man Jesus, and the majesty and lowliness of the

surrounding humanity which He receives and adopts, we have a supreme attestation and confirmation of this harmony which spans even the discord of human sin and is therefore all the more glorious in its universality, so that a basic calm is legitimate in spite of all the unsettlement to which our situation may give rise?

Is there a penetrating Christian answer to these questions too? Can it be shown that even this attempt to throw light on the human situation, inviting though it may be by reason of its largeness, only obscures it—and perhaps more deeply than ever? We must not be too ready with our answer. It will not do merely to protest, attaching perhaps the derogatory label "monism." The question is the more seductive and dangerous because it seems to have overcome the first three questions by exposing their superficiality, and to have approximated in some sense to Christian truth. Even in a Christian doctrine of sin, although there can be no question of an innate potentiality for evil in accordance with creation, we have to reckon with the fact that, unlike God, man is indeed exposed to the assault of chaos by reason of his creatureliness, that he confronts the nothingness which is intrinsically alien to him, not with the superiority of God, but—although no possibility in this direction can be ascribed to him—with a certain reversionary tendency. Nor can it be contested, but only asserted, that within the created order it is the place of man to be not only the field and prize of battle, but himself the contestant in the divine conflict with nothingness which began with creation. Finally, there has to be confessed as in no other teaching the absolute superiority with which God controls and conquers nothingness even in the form of human sin, not in any sense being arrested by it, but setting it to serve His own glory and the work of His free love. All these are assertions which we cannot avoid if we are determined to derive our thinking on God, the world, man and even evil from Jesus Christ. And the fourth question which now engages us seems to be co-extensive with these assertions, aiming at the same bracketing of sin as we necessarily find in Christian doctrine. We have to be all the more careful, therefore, in our consideration whether we can decide for the view represented in this question, or whether as Christians, and therefore from the centre of Christian knowledge, we must return a negative answer, i.e., reject it, because even if we put only one foot on the ground indicated by this last question, it means that at the last moment we again obscure and even destroy the knowledge of sin and the man of sin.

What is it that the Christian knows if he finds that he is in fact absolutely prevented from having any part or lot at all in this higher or deeper view of his own and human sin? from understanding it, in the light of the relationship between the Creator and the creature, or in relation either to man or to God Himself, as a necessary *datum* co-ordinated into an embracing nexus of being, as an unavoidable but not finally or genuinely disruptive discord in a superior harmony? from finally explaining the fact that man is shamed and has therefore to be ashamed? from a calm acceptance of the fact because there can be

[399]

no question of any real damage to God or fear of perishing, or of anything monstrous and terrible, any incurable wound, any absolutely fatal contradiction, in the being of man in the abasement of sin? What is it that the Christian knows which forbids him to regard himself as finally secure even as the doer of sin, the man of sin, within the framework of a universal systematisation of this kind? What is it that he knows when he knows that there can be no question of any universal systematisation; that he cannot find any framework within which he may be finally secure as a sinner; that he cannot avoid the fact that as the man of sin he has every reason seriously to fear; and that he can find himself secure, and therefore free not to fear, only at the place where he has no option but seriously to fear?

In answer to this question the decisive content of Christian knowledge is again the man Jesus, and therefore the actuality in which the Christian finds that his sin, and that of the world, is contained, that in all its frightfulness, it is cancelled and overcome, and that it already dispersed like a fleeting shadow. It is the actuality by which all respect for sin, or anxiety before it, is in fact forbidden because sin has lost its power, because it has been made contemptible, because he has been freed and set on his feet in face of it, because he had already been lifted up out of its abasement. It is true enough that it is only subsequently that the light of the lordship of the Son of Man, His direction as it is issued in the might of His resurrection and the power of the Holy Spirit, discloses who and what is already overcome in His death, and from what situation this one is already snatched. But this radical limitation of sin and man as its doer, as it is known by the Christian to have taken place already in the one man Jesus (for how could he be a Christian if he did not know this?), has nothing whatever to do with a harmony of being in which sin and its shame are systematically co-ordinated, and God and man and sin peacefully united. Indeed, if any idea is excluded, like sin itself, in this limitation, it is that of this peaceful co-existence of God, man and sin, and of the comfort which can be derived from it.

For who and what is overcome in the death of the Son of Man is revealed in His resurrection. The Son of God died in our place the death of the old man, the man of sin. And the One who undertook to suffer the death of this old man in our place was the new man who lives in our place again as the Holy One of God in whom we are all exalted to be saints of God. There is no continuity or harmony or peace between the death of that old man and the life of this new. The containment of sin as it has taken place on the cross of the Son of [400] Man, the complete replacement there of the man of sin, took place in the conflict of an irreconcilable and unbridgeable opposition in which only the one or the other could remain and one or the other had necessarily to give place. The old man could not be co-ordinated with the new, nor the new with the old. The new could only live, and the old yield and die. The divisive No of the wrath of God, which is the consuming fire of His love, lay on the old man, destroying and extinguishing him. This is the first thing that the Christian

21

knows in relation to this question as he knows what took place for him and all men in the man Jesus. No compromise was made, no armistice arranged, no pact of non-aggression concluded at the place where he and all men were helped, but an unequivocal and intolerable and definitive enemy of God was treated as he deserved and utterly destroyed. This enemy is the sin of man; it is he himself as the man who wills this sin. He was not tolerated at that place. No pardon was given him. An end was made of him. This is how he stands as a sinner in the light of the resurrection of the Son of Man. This is what his sin looks like in that light. It is unambiguously defined as that which God did not and does not will, and will never do so; as that in which He has no part; as that which He did not create; as that which has no possibility in Him and therefore in itself. It is that which is absurd before Him, and therefore that which He has rejected and forbidden. God can be thought together with it only in the act of opposition in which He masters and contests and overcomes it. This is what He did at Calvary. Any systematic co-ordination of God and sin is made quite impossible for the Christian by his knowledge of what took place there. But so, too, is any co-ordination of himself with sin; any attempt to make himself comprehensible, to explain and understand himself, as the doer of sin; any desire to find security in the peace of a higher view or synthesis. To be sure, he may know, as the creature of God, that he is preserved and blessed by Him, and in the man Jesus that he lives in and with Him. But this knowledge stands or falls with the recognition that as the man of sin he is cursed and slain by God, thrust out into the void, dark in the darkness, a lost soul. There cannot, then, be any talk of harmony. In sin man strikes a chord which cannot be taken up into any melody. The Christian can understand it only as something which is overlooked, covered and forgiven—not as a reality which is adapted to his human nature or co-ordinate with his human destiny, but only as that which cannot be co-ordinated. And he can understand himself only as one who is delivered from its kingdom as a brand is plucked from the burning, as one who can only avoid and withstand it. If he knows the radical decision that has been made in Jesus Christ for the world and himself and against evil, how can he still try to create a synthesis of God and evil, the world and evil and himself and evil?

[401]   The first point gives rise to a second. The One who in this decision acted against sin, i.e., who suffered in our place the death of the old man, the man of sin, is none other than God Himself in the person of the Son of Man. It is not only from a distance that God has reacted against this enemy as against one who has disturbed the peace of the created reality distinct from Himself, but whose evil work did not in any way affect His own life and being. As He sees it, this evil work is obviously not merely an imperfection, but something quite intolerable. It is not merely a final and relative, but an infinite and absolute evil. It is not an evil that can be countered by a mere arrangement within the world, or averted through the instrumentality and mediation of a creature. It is not an evil which any creature is good enough, or competent, or adapted to contest and remove. God Himself had to come down, to give Himself, to sacri-

fice Himself, in order that a place should be found for a man freed from this evil, and a reconciled world introduced in this man. On the cross of Golgotha God Himself intervened to accomplish this liberation, paying the price Himself, giving Himself up to death. If this was not too much for Him, if this intervention was not too big a thing or this price too high, if this decision against sin and man as the doer of sin could be taken only in this way, this brings home to us how great is the absurdity of sin, and how serious it is. God Himself is affected and disturbed and harmed by it. His own cause, His purpose for man and the world, is disrupted and arrested; His own glory is called in question. He Himself finds Himself assaulted by it in His being as God, and He hazards no less than His being as God to encounter it. This being the case, we have every reason to repudiate resolutely and once and for all any idea of a limitation, counter-balancing or relativisation of sin apart from that which is accomplished in this way. The seriousness of this disturbance can be measured only by the fact that it is met and overcome by God Himself. As He is for us and against it, it is in fact limited and counter-balanced and relativised, but only in this way, only by the occurrence of this history in which God is the active, militant and suffering Subject, and not in a co-ordination in which sin, and we ourselves as the doers of it, are tolerated alongside Him. What has taken place for us and against sin in this history proves that it is not in any sense tolerated, and that we ourselves are not tolerated as the doers of it. The Christian knows this, and does not cherish any illusions, even the most kindly and beautiful, in this respect.

But this leads us to a third point. The dying of the old man of sin, and the rising of the new man in whom we are liberated from sin for God, did not take place as our own act, but as the act of the true Son of God and Son of Man in our place. Neither the destruction nor the emergence, neither the death of the old nor the life of the new, is our own achievement. We can participate in it only in such a way, and our sanctification, our exit as sinners and our entry as disciples of God and Jesus Christ, can consist only in the fact, that we love in return the One who has first loved us in this act. It is God's free grace that the battle which He Himself and alone has fought for His own glory is also a battle for our salvation, and that the victory includes also our deliverance and liberation. It is again His free grace that we have a part in this battle, being called and empowered to fight and suffer and triumph with Him in this cause. We cannot presume to do this of ourselves. It can only be given to us. No Christian can stand before the decision made at Calvary in the person of the true Son of God and Son of Man except in the pure gratitude of the knowledge that it took place for him but quite apart from him and against all his merits and deservings. And no Christian will obey the divine direction of the Holy Spirit as it was and is issued in the power of the resurrection of Jesus Christ except in the pure gratitude of this knowledge; not, therefore, in the sense of an original achievement, but in that of a secondary correspondence, which he cannot evade because he knows that, apart from and even against him, disposition was

[402]

23

made concerning him in that decision. It is free grace, an unmerited gift, that what took place on Golgotha as the death of the old man and the life of the new is valid for him too, and takes shape in his existence, when he must not and may not fear, when he may become and be a man who is liberated from sin for God. But the one who may become and be a man liberated in this way, by the free grace addressed to him in the person of another, is obviously completely enslaved when regarded in and for himself and his own person. He is not in a position to see his own imprisonment as limited in a higher synthesis, and therefore to understand his situation as finally harmful. Free grace is not one element in the totality of a nexus in which even that which man is without and against it also has its secure meaning and place and if possible a positive significance. Free grace is the event of the shattering and destroying of what he is without it and against it. It means his total disqualification from which he cannot find refuge in any system in which it has a relative significance and range—but also a limit. His only way of escape is forward. He can escape only to the place from which this disqualification comes; to the free grace which also judges him, which disqualifies him as it qualifies him, which humbles him as it exalts him. Except in the light of this grace, and therefore in the knowledge of the Son of Man in whom it comes to us in this twofold form, there can never be this mercilessly critical self-judgment of man. It is the self-judgment of the Christian man, and the Christian man alone. It is impossible, however, that love for the Son of Man, who is the Lord over all, should allow the Christian man any other judgment of the human situation; that it should not exclude absolutely the worthless consolation of a harmonising view. The light of the liberating lordship of the Son of Man, in which he views himself and all men, is what impels him towards, or rather liberates him for, this uncompromisingly sober assessment of the human situation; the knowledge that in its determination by the meanness and lowliness of man it is an untenable situation. "There is no peace, saith the Lord, unto the wicked" (Is. 48^{22}).

[403]

2. THE SLOTH OF MAN

We now turn to the material question: What is sin as seen from the standpoint of the new man introduced in Jesus Christ? What is the action of the old man overcome in the death of Jesus Christ? What is the character of this man as he is subsequently revealed in Christ's resurrection, in the light of the divine direction which falls on him from this source? Our present answer is that the sin of man is the sloth of man. The christological aspect which now occupies us calls for this or a similar term. We might also describe it as sluggishness, indolence, slowness or inertia. What is meant is the evil inaction which is absolutely forbidden and reprehensible but which characterises human sin from the standpoint presupposed in the deliberations of our first sub-section.

There is a heroic, Promethean form of sin. This is brought to light—as the pride of man which not only derives from but is itself his fall—when we consider man in his confrontation with the Lord who humbled Himself and became a servant for him, with the Son of God made flesh. Sin was unmasked as this counter-movement to the divine condescension practised and revealed in Jesus Christ when we reached the corresponding point in the first part of the doctrine of reconciliation. In its unity and totality human sin always has this heroic form, just as, in its unity and totality, the free grace of God addressed to man always has the form of the justification which positively encounters this pride. But as reconciling grace is not merely justifying, but also wholly and utterly sanctifying and awakening and establishing grace, so sin has not merely the heroic form of pride but also, in complete antithesis yet profound correspondence, the quite unheroic and trivial form of sloth. In other words, it has the form, not only of evil action, but also of evil inaction; not only of the rash arrogance which is forbidden and reprehensible, but also of the tardiness and failure which are equally forbidden and reprehensible. It is also the counter-movement to the elevation which has come to man from God Himself in Jesus Christ.

In Protestantism, and perhaps in Western Christianity generally, there is a temptation to overlook this aspect of the matter and to underestimate its importance. The figure who claims our attention is Prometheus who tries to steal the lightning from Zeus and turn it to his own use: the man who wants to be as God, not a servant but the Lord, his own judge and helper; man in his hybris as a defiant insurrectionary. We do well to consider this figure, and constantly to realise how powerfully he is contradicted by the grace of God which justifies the sinner and exalts the abased and only the abased; how decisively he is routed by Jesus [404] Christ, the Son of God, the Lord who became for us a servant. But the man of sin is not simply this insurrectionary, and his sin has more than the heroic form in which (however terrible it may seem to be) we can hardly avoid finding traces of a sombre beauty—the beauty of the Luciferian man. We are missing the real man, not only in the mass but individually, not only in the common herd but in the finest and most outstanding of all times and places, and especially in ourselves, if we try to see and understand his sin consistently and one-sidedly as hybris, as this brilliant perversion of human pride. At a hidden depth it certainly is this brilliant perversion in all of us. But sober observation compels us to state that, as it may be seen and grasped in the overwhelming majority, it has little or nothing of this Luciferian or Promethean brilliance, this sombre beauty; and that even among those who may be regarded as exceptions there is a hidden depth at which, although they are still sinners, they are not at all insurrectionaries, but something very different and much more primitive, in which sin is merely banal and ugly and loathsome. It gives evidence of a very deficient or, from the Christian standpoint, very unenlightened self-knowledge if we try to deny that, beyond all that we may see and bewail in ourselves as pride, we have also to confess this very different and much more primitive thing in which there is nothing at all even of that doubtful beauty. And is it really "beyond" what we call pride? Sin may have different dimensions and aspects, but it is a single entity. Ought we not to say, therefore, that this different form is there at the very heart of our pride and forms its final basis? And yet the connexion between the two forms cannot easily be reduced to a common denominator. We might equally well say that this other, more primitive form has its final basis in human pride. The important thing is that we have every reason closely to scrutinise this second form. If we consider sin only in its first and more impressive form it might easily acquire an unreal and fantastic quality in which we do not recognise the real man whose heart, according to Luther's rendering of Jer. 17[9], is not merely desperate but also despairing. And the result would be to obscure the concrete point at issue in the sanctification or exaltation of sinful man. The sin of man is not merely heroic in its perversion. It is also—to use again the terms already introduced in the first sub-section—ordinary, trivial and mediocre. The sinner is not merely Prometheus or Lucifer. He is also—and for the sake of clarity, and to match the grossness of the matter, we will use rather popular expressions—a lazy-bones, a sluggard, a good-for-nothing, a slow-coach and a loafer. He does not exist only in an exalted world of evil; he exists also in a very mean and petty world of evil (and there is a remarkable unity and reciprocity between the two in spite of their apparent antithesis) In the one case, he stands bitterly in need of humiliation; in the other he stands no less bitterly in need of exaltation. And in both cases the need is in relation to the totality of his life and action. We will gather together what we have to say on this second aspect under the term or concept "sloth."

The forbidden or reprehensible tardiness and failure of man obviously fall under the general definition of sin as disobedience. In face of the divine direction calling him to perform a definite action, man refuses to follow the indication which he is given. Even in this refusal to act, however, and therefore in this inaction, he is involved in a certain action. The idler or loafer does something. For the most part, indeed, what he does is quite considerable and intensive. The only thing is that it does not correspond to the divine direction but is alien and opposed to it. He does not do what God wills, and so he does what God [405] does not will. He is disobedient and he does that which is evil. In all that follows we must keep before us the fact that because sin in its form as sloth seems to have the nature of a vacuum, a mere failure to act, this does not mean that it is a milder or weaker or less potent type of sin than it is in its active form as pride. Even as sloth, sin is plainly disobedience.

Again, this form obviously falls under the even more penetrating definition of sin as unbelief. For the disobedience in which man refuses the divine direction and does positively that which God does not will has its basis in the fact that he does not grasp the promise given him with this direction, but refuses to trust in the One who demonstrates and maintains His faithfulness in this overwhelming way, not claiming his obedience with the severity and coldness of an alien tyrant but as the source of his life, in the majesty and freedom of the love with which He has loved him from all eternity. He hardens himself against the divine benevolence addressed to him in the divine demand. The sloth of man, too, is a form of unbelief.

But we must define the term rather more closely as we use it of human sloth. In its form as man's tardiness and failure, sloth expresses much more clearly than pride the positive and aggressive ingratitude which repays good with evil. It consists in the fact, not only that man does not trust God, but beyond this that he does not love Him, i.e., that he will not know and have Him, that he will not have dealings with Him, as the One who first loved him, from all eternity. In relation to God there is no middle term between love and hate. The man who does not love God resists and avoids the fact that God is the One He is, and that He is this for him. He turns his back on God, rolling himself into a ball like a hedgehog with prickly spikes. At every point, as we shall see, this is the strange inactive action of the slothful man. It may be that this action often assumes the disguise of a tolerant indifference in relation to God. But in fact it is the action of the hate which wants to be free of God, which would prefer that there were no God, or that God were not the One He is—at least for him, the slothful man. This hatred of God is the culminating point of human pride too. The overweening pride of man, which consists in the fact that he wants to be and act as God, may at a pinch be understood—and this is perhaps the reason for its sinister beauty—as a perverse love of God, whose frivolous encroachment and usurpation, whose illegitimate attempt to control its object, do of course culminate in a desire that the object should disappear as such, that there should be no God or that God should not be God, that man should be able to sit unhindered on his throne. But sin as man's subservient and obsequious sloth is from the very outset his desire not to be illuminated by the existence and nature of God, not to have to accept Him, to be without God in the world. The slothful man, who is of course identical with the proud, begins where the other leaves off, i.e., by saying in his heart: "There is no God." This is the characteristic feature of sin, of disobedience, of unbelief, in this second [406] form. It is from this root that all the constitutive elements of human sloth grow.

Sin in the form of sloth crystallises in the rejection of the man Jesus. In relation to Him the rejection of God from which it derives finds virulent and concrete and forceful expression. For it is in Him that the divine direction and summons and claim come to man. It is in Him that the divine decision is made which he will not accept, which he tries to resist and escape. It is to be noted that in the main there is no radical opposition to the idea of God as a higher or supreme being to whom man regards himself as committed, nor to the thought of a beyond, of something which transcends his existence, nor to the demand that he should enter into a more or less conscious or unconscious, binding or non-binding connexion with it. He will never seriously or basically reject altogether religion or piety in one form or another, nor will he finally or totally cease to exercise or practise them in an open or disguised form. On the contrary, an escape to religion, to adoring faith in a congenial higher being, is the purest and ripest and most appropriate possibility at which he grasps in his sloth, and cannot finally cease from grasping as a slothful man. His rejection of God acquires weight and seriousness only when it is made with a final and concentrated piety. But that in this piety it is really a matter of rejecting God, of rendering Him innocuous, emerges clearly in the fact that man definitely will not accept in relation to himself the reality and presence and action of God in the existence of the man Jesus, and the claim of God which they involve. He definitely will not accept them as the reality and presence and action of God which refer absolutely and exclusively and totally and directly to him, and make on him an absolute, exclusive, total and direct demand. As one who worships a higher being, as a religious or pious man, he is able to resist this. It does not matter what name or form he gives to the higher being which he worships; he finds that he is tolerated by it, that far from being questioned and disturbed and seized he is strengthened and confirmed and maintained in equilibrium by it. And he for his part can always show equal toleration to this being—and in this form to "God." It does not cause him any offence, and so he has no need to be offended at it. But he is not tolerated, let alone confirmed, by the reality and presence and action of God in the existence of the man Jesus. He is basically illuminated and radically questioned and disturbed and therefore offended by the deity of God in the concrete phenomenon of the existence of this man. His own tolerance is thus strained to the limit when he has to do with God in this man. His rejection of God finds expression in his relation to this man. Tested in this way, he will unhesitatingly avoid God even as the religious or pious man. But this means that he will unhesitatingly resist God. In his relation to God he will show himself to be the slothful man, turned in upon himself and finding his satisfaction and comfort in his own ego.

[407]

Why is it that this is expressed in the rejection of the man Jesus? The reason is that in this man, as opposed to all the higher beings and transcendencies which he knows to be congenial and to which he may therefore commit himself, he has to do with the true and living God who loved this man, and was His God, from all eternity, and who will love this man, and be His God, to all eternity; the God whose outstretched hand of promise and preservation, of deliverance and command, has always been, and always will be, the existence of this man. The reason is that what God always gave to all men, what He was and is and will be for them, is simply a demonstration of the free grace which became a historical event in the appearance and work, the dying and rising again, of this man. The God of this man, and therefore concretely this man, offends us. Our sloth rejects Him. In relation to Him it is our great inaction, our hesitation, our withdrawal into ourselves. Man rejects Him because he wants to elect and will himself, and he does not want to be disturbed in this choice. For he is disturbed, and he finds that he is disturbed, by Him; by the will of God which always has and will have the name of Jesus, which has in this name its unalterable goal and ineffaceable contour. When he comes face to face with the will of God in Him he comes to the frontier which he can cross only if he will give up himself and his congenial deities and find God and himself in this Other: At this point he can only protest, for he is not tolerated and therefore he cannot tolerate. He regards it as vitally necessary to be free of this man, i.e., of the God of this man. This is a pious act which he must execute in his reverence for the higher being which does tolerate him. "There is no God" means concretely that there is no God of this kind; that a God of this kind cannot and may not be.

Why not? Why is it that human disobedience, unbelief and ingratitude in sloth have this culmination? Why is the sin of man revealed in this opposition? Our first and general answer is that it is because in himself and as such man will not live in the distinctive freedom of the man Jesus and is therefore forced to regard this Fellow and Brother as a stranger and interloper, and his existence as an intolerable demand.

He wants to be left alone by the God who has made this man a neighbour with His distinctive freedom, and therefore by this neighbour with His summons to freedom. He regards the renewal of human nature declared in His existence as quite unnecessary. He sees and feels, perhaps, the limitation and imperfection of his present nature, but they do not touch him so deeply that he is not finally satisfied with this nature and the way in which he fulfils it. A serious need, a hunger or thirst for its renewal, is quite foreign to him. He therefore sees no relevance in the man Jesus with His freedom to be a new man.

Again, he thinks he has a sober idea of what is attainable, of what is possible [408] and impossible, within the limits of his humanity. This leads him to question the real significance of this renewal, of man's exaltation. The limited sphere with which he is content seems to him to be his necessary sphere, so that its transcendence in the freedom of the man Jesus is an imaginary work in which he himself can have no part.

Behind the indifference and doubt there is a definite mistrust. In the freedom of the man Jesus it seems that we have a renewal and exaltation from servitude to lordship. But this is an exacting and dangerous business if it necessarily means that we acquire and have in Jesus a Lord, and if His lordship involves that we are demanded to leave our burdensome but comfortable and secure life as slaves and assume responsibility as lords.

Again, if the freedom of the man Jesus as the new and exalted and lordly man has its basis and meaning in the fact that he is the man who lives in fellowship with God, the indifference and doubt and mistrust in which we confront Him have their basis and meaning, or lack of meaning; in the fact that we regard it as unpractical, difficult and undesirable to live in fellowship with God. A life which moves and circles around itself, which is self-orientated but also self-directed, seems to hold out far greater promise than one which is lived in this fellowship.

It is for this reason that our brother Jesus is a stranger, and His existence among us is an intolerable demand, and the God who is His God is unacceptable. This is, in very general terms, the deployment, or rather the rigid front which human sin presents to Him, and in which it is actual and visible in face of Him, in the form of human sloth.

Why and to what extent is it sin? The reason is that, as the rejection of the outstretched hand of God, the refusal of His grace, all this means that man neglects his own calling, that he is untrue to his own cause, that with his true reality he goes out into the unreal, into the void, where he cannot stand and be what he wants to be, where he cannot be a man, himself, but only his own shadow. The One who confronts him in the freedom of the man Jesus is not merely this Fellow and Brother as such, nor is it merely the God of this man. It is the God of every man, without whom none either is or can be who he is. And in the person of this Fellow and Brother given him by his own God it is he himself, his own true reality, his own humanity as it is loved and elected and created and preserved by his God in the person of this One. The terrible paradox of his sin in this form is that if he refuses the man Jesus, he does not refuse only this man and His (and therefore his own God) but he also refuses to be himself, breaking free from his own reality, losing himself in his attempt to assert himself, and thus becoming his own pitiful shadow. It is no light thing [409] that man can unthinkingly accomplish when he takes his stand as a denier on this front of human sloth. He becomes and is "man in contradiction": the man who contradicts God and therefore contradicts and hopelessly jeopardises himself; the man who would be lost if in this self-contradiction which he achieves he were not confronted, in the man Jesus on whom he stumbles and falls, by the superior contradiction of God, whose will it never was or is or will be that slothful man should perish. We must now develop four main aspects of his mortal refusal of the freedom which he is promised in the man Jesus.

We are confronted by man's refusal (1) in his relationship with God; (2) in his relationship with his fellow-men; (3) in his relationship with the created order; and (4) in his relationship with his historical limitation in time. These are the same four groups in which, in the light of the true humanity of Jesus Christ, we developed the doctrine of man as the creature of God (*C.D.* III, 2) and, in the first part of theological ethics, the doctrine of the command of God the Creator (*C.D.* III, 4). Again in the light of the *humanitas Jesu Christi*[EN13], we are now considering the sin of man in the form of his sloth, and therefore his refusal of his own reality as it confronts him in Jesus Christ. For all its varied character, this refusal constitutes a single inter-related and connected whole. We will thus turn our attention specifically to each of the relationships in turn, but we shall always look either forwards or backwards, as the case may be, to see how far his refusal in one of these relationships necessarily includes, presupposes and involves it in the other three.

1. The Word—God's eternal Word—became flesh. In the existence of the man Jesus it was and is spoken in human form to us men. It is with this Word, which was and is this man Himself, that we have to do in Him: proclaimed in and with what He was and spoke and did and suffered in His history; proclaimed as He died on the cross; proclaimed as He lives and reigns as the Crucified. It was and is His royal freedom to be as man the perfect hearer of God; the One who knows God perfectly, and therefore the perfect servant and witness and teacher of God; the light of God shining in the world for us; the revelation in which He disclosed and discloses Himself to us and us to Himself; both ear and mouth for the wisdom and purpose and plan and meaning of His omnipotent mercy; sagacious and therefore able and equipped to make us wise and sagacious. Among all other men, as one of us, but exalted above us, and therefore the divine direction to us, He was and is the One who fulfils and brings and establishes the knowledge of God and His existence and nature and work, His presence and action. Nor is this knowledge which He fulfils and

---

[EN13] humanity of Jesus Christ

brings and establishes a superfluous or idle or partial or uncertain knowledge. On the contrary, it is universally relevant and indispensable, vital and active, total and firm and sure. It is to be grateful participants in this knowledge of God which He has fulfilled and disclosed and established on our behalf among us, so that we ourselves should be wise in virtue of His wisdom, that we are elected and created and determined in Him.

But we on whose behalf, for whose enlightenment and information and [410] instruction, He has this freedom, refrain from making use of this freedom which is also, and precisely, our own freedom. The clear light of day has come, but we close our eyes and persist in the darkness which has been penetrated and dispersed in Him. We harden ourselves in our unreason, our ignorance of God, our lack of wisdom, our folly and stupidity. And this refusal to move where we can and should bestir ourselves and follow Him is the unreason and ignorance which makes us the stupid fools we are. This is the folly in which we want to remain as we are instead of being those we are in Him and by Him.

It belongs to the vanity of this human refusal and failure to budge that it is finally and objectively futile. That is to say, it cannot alter in the least what the man Jesus is for us and for all men in the freedom of His knowledge of God. Our refusal cannot make the Word of God spoken in Him an unspoken Word, nor can it kill His life nor silence His proclamation. It cannot conceal, let alone quench, His light, nor arrest His revelation, nor destroy His direction, nor dam up the stream of the knowledge of God of which He is the source. It is paradoxical and absurd, but it cannot cancel the fact of the new man Jesus who has a vital and active and total and sure and certain knowledge of God. It cannot control the fire which He came to kindle on earth. In face of Him it can be only the sloth of man—his puerility, his senility, his mediocrity. It cannot alter the fact, therefore, that in this one man all other men—even the most untaught and unteachable amongst countless thousands who are yet untaught—are elected and determined to be taught about God. I may close my eyes, I may shut them as tight as I can, or I may turn away from the sun, but this does not alter the fact that the sun shines on me too, and that I have eyes to see it. I may try to cease or refuse to be the man I am in that one new man, but I cannot in fact cease to be this man. Evading the knowledge of God, I may contradict myself. It is my folly that I do this. But in my folly I can only contradict myself. I can no more destroy myself than I can the light of the man Jesus in which I exist. My self-contradiction cannot touch the fact that in Him I am known by God even in my evil ignorance of God. It cannot set aside the reality in which I live by this divine knowing. As my proud attempt to be like God is futile, because this is quite impossible, so too is the slothful refusal in which I am content to be without God in the world, because He who has revealed Himself and acted in Jesus as the God of man, of every man, and therefore as my God, will not be God without me, so that even in the most secret recesses of this world I for my part can never be without Him, outside His light, without the eyes with which I may and should see Him, with which I am elected and determined to see Him as the fellow and brother of this One. The outcome of my refusal can be only another refusal, or the revelation of a refusal—the demonstration of the futility of my remaining at a place which does not exist. I cannot in fact remain alone. I can try to do so. And in so doing I can, and do, create a reality. But this reality is from the very outset a limited reality. It is a reality of the second—and inwardly and materially an inferior—degree. It is a reality which is condemned as such to failure. My folly can only reveal and express my sin and shame.

[411]

We do have to do, however, with this reality of the second degree, with the sin and shame (however limited) of the folly in which we make no use of the freedom which we are given in Jesus. The inner futility of human sloth, like the impotence of human pride, does not alter the fact that it does actually take place as a form of human corruption. It is a fact. Its character is purely negative. It is not necessary or genuine or, in the strict sense, possible. It is only impossible. It has no true basis. It cannot be deduced or explained or excused or justified. But it is still a fact. It is a fact in the whole futility in which it is created and posited. It is not, therefore, nothing. It is something. It is the something of our persistence in turning to that which is not, to that which God has not willed but denied and rejected. It is the something of our ignorance of God and therefore our self-contradiction. Man does actually will the impossible. He does actually will not to know God as he might and should know Him thanks to the freedom in which the man Jesus does so for him, in the bright light of the existence of this Fellow and Brother. And his thoughts and attitudes and actions express this non-willing, this refusal. He sets himself in mortal self-contradiction. This does not mean that he can set aside his Fellow and Brother Jesus, and his own reality as established in Him. All that he can do is to make himself impossible. And even this "ability" is as baseless as the nothingness to which he wills to turn in this non-willing. Yet he does will it, and in this will which is opposed to the good will of God he creates a fact and lives in it. He does not live as a wise man, but as a stupid fool.

We are thus forced to the rather unusual and hazardous statement that sin is also stupidity, and stupidity is also sin. By stupidity we mean, of course, that which the Bible describes and condemns as human folly. Of this it cannot be said that man would at once leave it if he were better informed. It cannot be advanced as an excuse or mitigation of man's corresponding thoughts and words and attitudes and actions. It is not just an unfortunate weakness, a vexatious drawback, which can be partially or totally removed by education and enlightenment, and which has perhaps to be suffered with tolerance and equanimity, and compensated by other and better qualities. It is the evil act of man; of the whole man. Or better—for we have here the basic dimension of his sloth—it is his inaction, his responsible and culpable refusal to act.

When the Bible speaks of the *nabal* or *kesil*[EN14], as, for example, of those who say in their

---

[EN14] dolt or fool

hearts that there is no God (Ps. 14¹), there can be no question of any lack of intellectual   [412]
endowment, or of powers of thought and comprehension, or of the erudition which we both
need and desire. The biblical dolt or fool may be just as carefully taught and instructed as
the average man at any particular cultural level. He may be below the average, but he may
also be above it, and even high above it. What makes him a fool has nothing whatever to do
with a feebler mind or a less perfectly attained culture or scholarship. It is not in any sense a
fate. Those who have only weak intellectual gifts and a rudimentary scholastic equipment—
the "uneducated"—are not necessarily fools as the Bible uses the word. We have only to
think of the νήπιοι[EN15] of Mt. 11²⁵ to realise that they may very well be wise. In the biblical
sense a man is a fool or simpleton when (whatever may be his talents or attainments) he
thinks that he has no need of enlightenment by the revelation and Word of God; that he
ought, indeed, to oppose it; and that he can live his life on the basis of the resultant vacuum,
and therefore by the norm of maxims and motives which are perverted from the very outset—on a false presupposition and therefore by a false method.

Anselm of Canterbury was quite right when, introducing the denier of God's existence of
Ps. 14¹ at the beginning of his proof of the existence of God (*Prosl.* 2), he did not describe
him as *ignorans* but as *insipiens* (= *insapiens*) [EN16]. His objection, which Anselm discusses, is
that God is not a real object, but only one which we think or can think; that He is not a
res[EN17], and therefore does not exist: *non est Deus*[EN18]. He does not think and speak in this
way because he is limited or uneducated. He does so because of a fundamental lack which
consists in the fact that he is not an *intelligens id quod Deus est*[EN19] (*Prosl.* 4). He does so
because of his lack of understanding, grounded in his unbelief, of the revealed name of
God, in virtue of which God is *quo maius cogitari nequit*[EN20]. Anselm opened his own argument with a confession of his faith in God as the One who bears this name (the name of the
Creator above which no legitimate thinking can exalt itself, but from which it can only
derive). His enquiry and demonstration have reference to the knowledge of this faith, which
necessarily includes the knowledge of the existence of God. They are evoked and stimulated
by the objection of the denier, but it is obvious that the latter can have no part in the ensuing
discussion. For he thinks and speaks as *insipiens*, and therefore from the point where he does
not know, and as an unbeliever cannot know, the One whose existence he questions. This is
his folly in which he excludes himself from the outset from the knowledge of God's existence. And it is in answer to his folly that Anselm deliberately proves that, presupposing the
understanding of His revealed name, God's existence *cannot* be questioned. What a mis-
apprehension it was that the good Gaunilo found it necessary to rush to the help of the
atheist with the defence, *Pro insipiente:* as though his denial, deriving as it does from his folly,
and denying what he does not know and understand, could still be championed and discussed; as though, proceeding from stupidity, it could be anything else but stupid.

We have to realise that as the basic dimension of human sloth stupidity is sin.
It is disobedience, unbelief and ingratitude to God, who gives Himself to be
known by man in order that he may be wise and live. It is thus a culpable
relapse into self-contradiction; into incoherent, confused and corrupt
thought and speech and action. We have to realise this if we are to estimate its

---

[EN15] babes
[EN16] ignorant but as foolish
[EN17] thing
[EN18] God is not
[EN19] one who understands what God is
[EN20] that than which nothing greater can be conceived

power; the strange but mighty and tumultuous and dreadful force of the role—the leading role—which it plays in world-history, in every sphere of human life, and either secretly or flagrantly in each individual life. Whether great or small, every confidence or trust or self-reliance on what we can, and think we should, say to ourselves when we reason apart from the Word of God is stupid. Every attitude in which we think we can authoritatively tell ourselves what is true and good and beautiful, what is right and necessary and salutary, is stupid. All thought and speech and action which we think we can and should base on this information is stupid. And this whole frame of mind is self-evidently, and even more acutely, stupid in the form in which we think we have so heard the Word of God, and so appropriated its direction and wisdom in the guise of a principle or system, that we have no need to hear or practise it afresh; in the form, therefore, in which we regard ourselves as so enlightened by the Word of God that we think we can throw off our openness to further and continuous instruction. Where an uncontrolled truth or rule, however clear, possesses man or men in the way in which they ought to be governed only in the knowledge of God Himself and by His living Word, we certainly have to do with a revelation, and in principle with the whole economy; of stupidity. And where men think they have a goodness which is assured, not in the active fulfilment of their knowledge of God but in itself, and try to live and act and assert themselves as good in this sense, this is not merely the self-righteousness in which faith is denied but also the stupidity which is forbidden by the Word of God and which wastes and destroys all the goodness that is really given. When Adam and Eve were not content with the Word and commandment of God, but wanted to know for themselves what is good and evil, this was disobedience, but it was also a step into the stupidity which cannot and never will know what is good and evil, but will always exchange and confuse them. And there is a deeper meaning in the common expression that for all his devilish cleverness and cunning the devil is finally stupid. This is inevitable when he is obviously the *insipiens*[EN21] in principle, the personification of ignorance of God and the corresponding independence and autonomy in face of Him.

The stupidity of man consists and expresses itself in the fact that when he is of the opinion that he achieves his true nature and essence apart from the knowledge of God, without hearing and obeying His Word, in this independence and autonomy, he always misses his true nature and essence. He is always either too soon or too late. He is asleep when he should be awake, and awake when he should be asleep. He is silent when he should speak, and he speaks when it is better to be silent. He laughs when he should weep, and he weeps when he should be comforted and laugh. He always makes an exception where the rule should be kept, and subjects himself to a law when he should choose in freedom. He always toils when he should pray, and prays when only work is of any avail. He always devotes himself to historical and psychological investigation when decisions are demanded, and rushes into decision when historical and psychological investigation is really required. He is always con-

[EN21] a fool

34

tentious where it is unnecessary and harmful, and he speaks of love and peace where he may confidently attack. He is always speaking of faith and the Gospel where what is needed is a little sound commonsense, and he reasons where he can and should commit himself and others quietly into the hands of God. In Eccl. 3 we are given a list of different things for which there is a proper time—in accordance with the fact that God Himself does everything in its own time. The genius of stupidity is to think everything at the wrong time, to say   [414] everything to the wrong people, to do everything in the wrong direction, to lose no opportunity of misunderstanding and being misunderstood, always to omit the one simple and necessary thing which is demanded, and to have a sure instinct for choosing and willing and doing the complicated and superfluous thing which can only disrupt and obstruct.

Again we have to realise that stupidity is sin if we are to estimate the dangerous nature of its power. Its very character betrays how dangerous it is to life and society, to state and Church. Like the demons, and as one of the most remarkable forms of the demonic, stupidity has an astonishingly autonomous life against whose expansions and evolutions there is no adequate safeguard. It has rightly been said that even the gods are powerless in face of it. And it is in vain that we appeal to many gods to counter it. We may meet it in righteous anger, or with ironical contempt. We may play the school-master. We may try to overcome it by approximation or advances. We may try to use it, to harness it for better ends. But even when we are trying to overcome it in ourselves, to liberate ourselves from it, we must always be on the watch lest we merely augment stupidity with stupidity, either secretly or openly giving it place and nourishment, and being only the more completely overrun by it as we seek to encounter it.

It is particularly and supremely dangerous because it has an uncanny quality of being able to attract, to magnetise and thus to increase. The folly of one seems irresistibly to awaken that of another or others: whether in the form of mutual boasting or sinister collusion, of cold or hot warfare or the formation of massive collectives and majorities which trample down all opposition like a herd of elephants; or even more dangerously by an inward process, in the form of winning others, of begetting children, and of acquiring fresh vitality in them. It is also dangerous in the fact that we do not usually recognise it (or only when it is too late) as the beam in our own eye, our own stupidity, so that in our unconcerned and self-conscious pandering to it we only help it to gain a greater hold on others. It is also dangerous because it is only very seldom, and probably never, that we see it unmasked and undisguised and unadorned. It normally takes, as we shall see later, the form of its opposite, of a superior cleverness and correctness, or even of an excess of noble feeling. For how sure and quick and persistent it is in finding and building up reasons for what it thinks and maintains and does and impels to do! With what assurance it always presupposes that it is right, and has always known better ("What did I tell you?")! How it loves to make itself out to be either the pillar of society or the sacred force of revolutionary renewal! How powerfully (in contradiction or agreement with the form in which it encounters one in others) it can strengthen and deepen and advance itself by itself, continually preparing for, and embarking upon, fresh adventures of basic inactivity! It is also dangerous because at a first glance it is so innocuous, so kindly disposed, so familiar, knowing how to awaken tolerance or a pardoning sympathy or even a certain recognition, but concealing somewhere, and probably behind its probity and gentleness (like the claws of the feline species behind their soft pads), the supreme malice and aggressiveness and violence which will pounce on a victim and tear it to pieces before it is even aware of them.

[415]   But what is the value of marking its symptoms and warning against their particular dangers? It is not merely in its symptoms and fruits but in its root that stupidity is sin; nor is it merely because the symptoms and fruits are dangerous, but by reason of its root that stupidity as sin means destruction. It is from its root that the stupid action of man is sin, and that it is dangerous as such. But it is only from its root. There is thus no point in seeing it in its stupidity, and being on our guard against it, if we do not know the root which makes it sin and therefore dangerous. At its root it is the perverted action of that great omission which Paul described in 1 Cor. 15^{34} as the ἀγνωσία θεοῦ^{EN22}, man's evil and culpable and irresponsible failure to know God. Anselm was right when he regarded even the stupid confession in his heart of the fool of Ps. 14^1 ("There is no God") as only one of the symptoms and fruits of his folly, and pointed beyond this confession to its root in his true atheism, which consists in this wicked ignorance of God. The really stupid element in his stupidity, the true atheism of the fool which comes to light in that stupid confession and all the other symptoms and fruits, is not his theoretical but his practical atheism. It is only seldom, and seldom explicitly or definitively, that he comes to the point of theoretical rejection. He may regard it as unnecessary and even be opposed to it without being any the less an atheist in practice. There is a whole ocean of religious and even Christian stupidity, and those who swim in it always do so as those who are religious and even Christians. But practical atheism, of which the wise man will know and confess that he is no less guilty than the fool, and therefore human stupidity at its root consists in the fact that God is revealed to man but that man will not accept the fact in practice; that in the knowledge of God, in the clear light of His reality, presence and action, he is radically known by God but refuses and fails to know God in return and to exist in this knowledge; that he lets himself fall as one who is already lifted up by God and to God. It is this letting oneself fall—a process in which we are all implicated—that is the really stupid element in our stupidity, whether or not it is accompanied by theoretical atheism on the one hand or religion or even Christianity on the other.

But it would not be what it is—the primal phenomenon of sin in one of its most remarkable aspects—if there were any reason and explanation for this process. The stupid and inopportune movements of the fool in which stupidity reveals itself are always relatively explicable. They always have their more or less demonstrable grounds and causes, their active and passive impulses both internal and external, by which they can in large measure be understood. But their root, the stupid element in a fool's stupidity, the sin revealed in what he does and seeks to do, baffles understanding or explanation. There is no reason for it. It derives directly from that which is not, and it consists in a move-

---

^{EN22} ignorance of God

ment towards it. It is simply a fact, *factum brutum*[EN23]. We can only say [416] concerning it that he does it. He is free, but makes no use of the fact. He is lifted up, but he lets himself fall. He is in the light and has eyes to see, but he does not see and therefore remains in darkness. He hears, but he does not hear or obey. Why? For what reason? There is neither rhyme nor reason. It is simply a fact. To try to find a reason for it is simply to show that we do not realise that we are talking of the evil which is simply evil.

Of all the symptoms there is only one—a very striking one—which points with any clarity to the depths of primitive stupidity from which stupidity derives. This is the fact that it always appears and acts in disguise. Who has ever seen it gape, even in his own heart, as it would necessarily gape if it were seen and known openly and directly for what it is? What fool will ever confess his own folly, his ἀγνωσία θεοῦ[EN24], his practical atheism, the fact that he lets himself fall? The moment we admit our folly, have we not become truly wise? Even the theoretical atheist, who is only one species of the practical, will not and cannot openly declare his folly, because he does not and will not know whom and what he denies. How, then, can he ever confess his folly? What is the reason for this shyness? Why is it that no one will allow that he is stupid? Why is this impossible? Why does stupidity always appear in disguise, in an incognito, anonymously or pseudonymously? The obvious explanation is that in the depth where he is a fool man knows that his folly derives from that which is not and consists in his movement towards it. He cannot see what is wrong, but he has instinctive awareness like a blind man who is groping towards an abyss. He is frightened to confess, or to be told or accused, that he himself belongs to that which is not. He is on the point of realising it, but he will not accept it. Nor is it really true. He does not belong to nothingness. Even in and in spite of his folly he belongs to God and is the good creature of God. How, then, can he accept and confess that this is not the case? May it not even be that the God whom he does not know, but who knows and does not cease to know him, keeps him back from this and makes it impossible, that the fact that he has this awareness and is frightened is the work of His gracious hand? This will, of course, only turn to his judgment, to which, in his attempts at concealment, he will react in the most perverse and perverted way.

However that may be, the folly of the fool shuns the light. It does not want to be known as such. And it hides itself with a sure instinct and touch in its opposite. It pretends to be wisdom. Not, of course, the wisdom whose beginning is the fear of the Lord. Only the fool who is converted from his folly, from his ignorance of God, will be prepared in a profound horror at himself to accept this wisdom, to humble himself before it, to be clothed by it and to take refuge in it. When this happens, he will not pretend to be a wise man, but exercise

---

EN23 brute fact
EN24 ignorance of God

[417] and reveal his true wisdom by the fact that—in the fear of the Lord—he confesses his folly and in his folly cleaves wholly to the wisdom of God. We are now speaking of the unconverted fool who does not know the Lord and the fear of the Lord and necessarily lacks the wisdom which begins with this fear. How can he confess his folly? Is it not inevitable that he should deny and conceal it? And how else conceal it but with what he regards as wisdom—his own wisdom, what Paul in 1 Cor. 1[20] calls the "wisdom of the world" or in 1 Cor. 2[5] the "wisdom of men"? We might define this theoretically and generally as the fulness of all the knowledge of truth and reality and experience accessible to man minus the knowledge of God in His revealed Word. Practically and in detail it will never appear in its fulness, but only in an excerpt, in a particular form, in the realisation of one of many possibilities. Within the framework or brackets of this minus, it may be either a rather limited or a very imposing matter. It may take either the modest form of the self-assertion of sound commonsense or the prouder guise of an inspired profundity of thought. It may affect a childlike merriness or a deeper melancholy. It may have the appearance either of scepticism or of the ripe wisdom of old age. It may be academic, or aesthetic, or definitely moral, or non-moral, or even political. And because even in his folly man is always the good creature of God it is inevitable that in all its forms, even the most primitive and suspect, his own wisdom, or what he regards as such, should exhibit positively significant and impressive elements and aspects which enable it to commend itself both to him and to others. The wisdom of the world or of men is not, therefore, something which we must rate too low. In many cases it may have a very high value. It is never simply and unequivocally devilish. Within its limits, it is often worthy of the most serious respect.

In its own way it may even have exemplary significance for those who are truly wise—for Christians. When he described it as he did, Paul clearly indicated its limits. It was the wisdom of the (passing) aeon (1 Cor. 2[6] and 3[18]). But the same Paul had no hesitation (in Phil. 4[8]) in giving to his exhortation to Christians a form which in terminology might well have been the worldly wisdom of a Stoic teacher of his day. They were to consider and ponder ($\lambda o\gamma i\zeta\epsilon\sigma\theta\alpha\iota$) "whatsoever things are true, whatsoever things are honest, whatsoever things are just, whatsoever things are pure, whatsoever things are lovely, whatsoever things are of good report." And this comes immediately after the saying about the peace of God which commands and encloses their understanding like a wall, keeping their hearts and minds through Christ Jesus. Again, in Lk. 16[8] we read that the Lord Himself praised the "unjust" steward, or his worldly skill, concluding that the children of this aeon are in their generation (on their own level or in their own sphere) wiser than the children of light are in theirs.

The worldly wisdom which conceals human stupidity can hardly ever be effectively attacked and unmasked and overcome in a direct encounter. In virtue of the qualities or excellencies which cannot be denied to it in its own sphere, it is in a real position to serve as a covering, to provide an alibi, for

[418] stupidity. The fact is that (in this as in all its forms) sin profits by the goodness of the divine creation in which even the godless and foolish man does not cease to participate. In this pseudo-wisdom it is not, therefore, necessarily or

certainly or exclusively a case of pure pretence. Bracketed by that minus, there are probably in most cases many things that are in a higher or lower degree beautiful and true and good, or at any rate incontestable, behind which the fool can find solid cover, and in the development of which he can have the satisfaction of a good conscience and even make an impression on his fellow-creatures. If he is not unsettled by the knowledge of God, how can he even be aware of the fact that his witness is actually deployed within this bracket? How can he fail to find comfort and even joy in the fact that within this bracket he is doing his relative best with more or less zeal and success?—especially when in so doing he finds himself in the helpful company not merely of the over-whelming majority but at bottom of all his fellow-men, in whom we find other forms of exactly the same process of concealment as that in which he himself lives. It may well be that within this company it is inevitable that there should be constant friction and collision between the different forms of worldly wisdom; that mutual animosity and depreciation and even conflict should be the order of the day in the most violent of subterranean and global hostilities. This does not alter the fact that as a fool man finds that he has the inestimable advantage of being able to march in rank and step with countless thousands of his fellows. For at bottom all fools understand each other very well, because the norm or standard of the different wisdoms of the world behind which they conceal their stupidity is always the same within this bracket for all the differences in detail. Thus, although they may and necessarily do fight amongst themselves in the most devastating way, yet in some way and at some point they can always come to terms, and they often do so with astonishing suddenness if seldom with any permanence, as in the case of Pilate and Herod in Lk. 23^{12}. In the fact that they all try to take into their own hands control of the good creation of God and the affairs of men as if they belonged to them, and negatively in the fact that the wisdom deployed and exercised by them never begins with the knowledge and fear of the Lord, they are all united in spite of their differences in other respects, and at bottom there can and will be mutual understanding and mutual confirmation. This is infallibly revealed and operative when they suddenly come up against the question whether, for all its advantages and excellencies, the wisdom which they deploy in some form within this framework is or can be genuine wisdom; or against the protest that they are abusing the good creation of God; or against the demand that prior to anything else this framework should be broken, this bracket with the presupposed minus dissolved, the whole purpose and character which is the mark of the evolution of worldly wisdom abandoned, and the knowledge and fear of God [419] given their contested right as the true basis and beginning of wisdom. The trouble is that this question, protest and demand are perhaps encountered only in the unauthentic form of the pride of an ill-advised and at bottom worldly-wise Christianity in face of which they find themselves justified in the human sense and therefore grow all the more obdurate.

Who can say whether it was not due to his encounter with an ill-advised Christianity that the great Goethe took such offence at the saying in 1 Cor. 3$^{18f.}$ ("Let no man deceive himself. If any man among you seemeth to be wise in this world, let him become a fool, that he may be wise. For the wisdom of this world is foolishness with God")—even arguing that life would not be worth living if this were true. It may well be, of course, that he would not have accepted the saying from a better advised Christianity. We can only say that as far as he himself is concerned he now knows better.

There can be no doubt that in spite of their divergence all the unfolding wisdoms of the world—even those within an ill-informed or better informed Christianity—attain mutual recognition and practical unity in the fact that they cannot admit that question, protest and demand, preferring every kind of compromise or settlement amongst themselves to surrender on this point. And this agreement always involves a further enhancing and intensifying of their activity as concealments—the one great concealment—of what man wills to be and do, or rather not to be and do, not to admit and confess that he is and does, a fool who commits folly. Nothing is more tempting at this point than to turn the tables, to represent that ignored and rejected wisdom of God as folly, as stupid, ridiculous, contemptible and even dangerous from the point of view of what he regards as wisdom, so that it can only be hated and contested. Without realising what is really taking place, he will again find that he is not tolerated, and therefore cannot tolerate. He will see and feel the point of the sword which according to Mt. 10^{34} Jesus came to bring on earth, and he will try to protect himself against this threat with an energy which far surpasses the violence of all the internecine conflicts of different human wisdoms. What he does not really like and would rather ignore, what can only be the object of his unconcern and passive resistance—the knowledge of God—will always appear to be irrational and nonsensical when in some form it comes, as it may suddenly do to anyone, with its insistent summons. In face of it he can only defend to the death his own stupidity, the great minus within whose sign he thinks he can and should be wise, as that which is truly rational. The wisdom of God, the cross of Christ (1 Cor. 1^{18}), is foolishness as he sees it. So much the better if he can feel justified in this view by reason of the pride of an ill-advised Christianity which in face of him regards itself *per nefas*[EN25] as the wisdom of God. But even if it were set before him in the greatest humility by an angel of God, he would be adept at finding it quite incredible, regarding and expounding and defaming it as irrational nonsense, and belligerently maintaining his own wisdom in face of it. He can only evade it in some way, and therefore he will never find himself at a loss for ways and means to do this, maintaining that he himself is wise. And because in so doing he makes use of the good gifts of God Himself, he will always be relatively successful in escaping the knowledge of God, in maintaining and securing the incognito of his stupidity, in causing it to illuminate himself and others as true wisdom. His success can be only rela-

[420]

[EN25] mistakenly

tive because the good gifts of God are neither ordained nor adapted to author-
ise or empower man in an absolute opposition to their Giver, and therefore to
be used as the means of this concealment. But there is undoubtedly a relative
success, and it is strong enough to create a fact which can be removed only by
God's own Word and Holy Spirit.

Yet even the most effective concealment cannot alter the fact that the fundamental stupidity of man, hidden behind his supposed wisdom, is revealed as
such on every hand. He may pretend that he knows God well, and try to be
wise under the sign of this minus. But he cannot do so without serious consequences.

In and with the knowledge of God he necessarily loses (1) the relationship
which gives to his existence the character of humanity—his relationship to his
fellow-men. It is God who guarantees this relationship. Its order has its basis in
that of his relationship to God. Without this it cannot be maintained. The
knowledge of the divine Other by whom he is confronted, and therefore the
knowledge that this Other is the triune and not a lonely God, is the indispensable presupposition of the necessity, dignity, promise and claim of the other
who also confronts him in the form of man. But the fool lacks this knowledge.
He tries to evade it. It is foolishness to him. He thinks that he can replace it by
his own better wisdom. How, then, can he have the further knowledge to
which it gives rise? If God is dispensable, so is his neighbour. If he prefers his
own society to fellowship with God, he will also prefer it to the company of his
fellows. If he tries to keep God at a distance, he will do so all the more emphatically in the case of his equals. Who is to prevent him? And conversely, how can
the problematic being of his equals, his fellow-men, cause him to seek himself
only in the encounter, fellowship and partnership of I and Thou, if God does
not do so? How can man seek and find his brother in man if he will not allow
God to be his Father? The necessary consequence of vertical self-withdrawal is
horizontal self-withdrawal and isolation. It is possible, and it will indeed take
place, that he may need another man, and claim him, and try to exercise a far-
reaching control over him. But this does not involve a genuine fellow-
humanity. It does not mean that the one sees and understands the other as a
man, or that he accepts him as his ordained companion and helper, and himself as his. On the contrary, it means a radical superiority over him, an emancipation from him which because it has the character of a needing, claiming and   [421]
controlling in which the other may not readily acquiesce, necessarily has, and
will sooner or later reveal, the character of opposition to and conflict with him.
The solitary man is the potential, and in a more refined or blatant form the
actual, enemy of all others. The outbreak of war between him and them is only
a matter of time and occasion, and often enough it will be caused by a ludicrous accident. The stupidity of man, the false estimation of his own (in other
respects very worthy and excellent) wisdom, wills that this should be the case,
and inevitably calls for it. Without the knowledge of God, which the stupid
man despises, there is no meaningful companionship between man and man,

no genuine co-operation, no genuine sharing either of joy or sorrow, no true society. But work which is not co-operation is busy indolence. Joy which is not shared is empty amusement. Sorrow which is not shared is oppressive pain. The man who is not the fellow of others is no real man at all. And a society composed of men like this breaks up as soon as it is formed and even as the most zealous attempts are made to build and maintain it. But the stupidity of man calls for this. Even in its noblest forms humanity without the knowledge of God has in it always the seed of discord and inhumanity, and sooner or later this will emerge. From the vacuum where there is no "Glory to God in the highest" even the sincerest longing and loudest shouting for peace on earth will never lead to anything but new divisions. This is the first thing which all the concealment of human folly can never alter.

This vacuum also involves inevitably (2) a dualism between the psychical and physical elements in his being. It is God who guarantees his unity, the whole man as such, who is not just soul and not just body, who does not consist of body and soul as two separate parts, but who is the soul of his body. God has created man in this ordered unity. He pledges its maintenance, so that man's responsibility in relation to this unity and its order has its basis in his responsibility to God. Thus his knowledge of himself in this unity is an expression of his knowledge of the one God, the Lord of heaven and earth, of all invisible and visible reality. If he renounces his responsibility to God and lacks this knowledge, he will also lack that which he can know only as its expression. This does not mean that he will destroy the work of God or himself in this unity. Only God, who has created him in this unity, could do that. But everything that he does of himself (in his folly as it is concealed by his supposed wisdom) will result in a disturbance of this unity, a dualism of the two elements, and a confusion of their relationship. In one of the countless fatal variations which are possible he will then lead a life which is either more abstractly psychical or more abstractly physical. He will live alternately to the spirit and to matter. He will let himself be ruled alternately by his head and by his nerves and appetites.

[422] He can never wholly do either. On both sides he will always find himself hampered and contained. On neither side will he be able to escape tension. He will never know peace or satisfaction. He will never have a good conscience. He will always be pressing and pressed from the one to the other. He will never be able to destroy, and never wholly to forget, the order, the super- and subordination, in the unity of his nature. Nor will he ever be able to maintain it. He will never rid himself of the unrest caused by the twofold character of his existence. Or he will do so only by means of strange compromises and hypocrisies between an abstracted higher part of his nature and an abstracted lower, and therefore only in appearance. He will take refuge in an inner world, trying to build up a world of the spirit, in which, to be happy, he must close his eyes to the forces of his physical nature. In face of these forces he will find himself forced to make concessions of which he is basically ashamed—in view of the fact that he is primarily a soul and only then and as such a body. When he seeks

this higher level he will always have a desire for the lower, and when he is on the lower he will always be homesick for the higher. He will never be healthy on either. In the depths or on what seem to others remarkable heights he will always be a man of disorder. For he does not know the All-Highest, and therefore he has no true knowledge of the higher and lower levels of his own structure as a human being. He does not understand the norm of their relationship, and therefore he cannot direct himself by it and live as a whole man. His primary folly inexorably entails this secondary folly which cannot be radically amended by even the cleverest of psychical or physical diagnosis and therapy. The injuries which are continually caused can certainly be stated and described, and hints and advice can be given to mitigate them. But the problem of changing the man of disorder into a man of order is the problem of overcoming this vacuum, the primary folly, in which man will not and cannot understand God, and therefore, in spite of every concealment, cannot understand himself and be fit and healthy. This is the second point that has to be made.

Again as a result of the basic failure, and in spite of every concealment, man is inevitably involved (3) in a perverted relationship to the limited temporality of his being. God is the Lord who guarantees the time and times of all individual men. The Yes of God makes both the limited individual time and all time with its beginning and end a time which is filled—filled by His dealings with man, by His call and claim and promise and patience and blessing. This relationship of man to God is the meaning of all his coming and going both individually and *en masse*[EN26]. It is the meaning of history, of every human past and present and future. Thus the knowledge of God is the presupposition of all man's knowledge of his historicity, i.e., of his being as a being in time and in the limits of time. The loss of the one necessarily carries with it the loss of the other, and therefore of any clarity or certainty in the practice of life in its temporality, in the acceptance of historical responsibility. Whence do we come, and whither do we go, if not from God and to God? What are we, and what is it that we think and will and do, if this beginning and end of our existence have no interest or relevance for us, and are even quite unknown to us? What, then, is the meaning of our present? In what sense is it to be taken seriously by us— yet with a seriousness which is not incompatible with a happy freedom? In what sense are we continually committed by it, passing courageously through it from yesterday to to-morrow? What is the meaning of the unique opportunity of the long or short life that we are given? God is the only answer. He Himself gives and reveals Himself to us as this answer. The folly of the fool may be seen in the fact that this answer has no significance for him because he does not know God. We may each know what great fools we all are by considering how often we are tempted, and how vulnerable we are to the temptation, to regard

[423]

[EN26] collectively

this answer as without significance. And yesterday becomes to-day, the morning evening, youth old age, and time and its unique opportunity pass, and all that man does is to dream: perhaps of a finer or even more wretched past; perhaps of a finer or even more wretched future; perhaps of the possibilities of general or individual progress which he thinks he can advance and experience; perhaps of its impossibility; perhaps of a lasting fame that he can secure for his own name, at any rate in the immediate circle of his acquaintances, by his virtues and achievements; perhaps of supernatural developments beyond this life either of a personal or a cosmic nature. He may even dream as a child does of its games and its little anxieties at school and its dislike of instruction. He may not even dream at all, but sleep a wakeful sleep in which there are neither dreams nor thoughts nor ends, forgetting himself in more or less ceaseless activity and the satisfactions which he can attain. The wisdom with which he hides the full wretchedness of his plight may consist in the opinion that this is what life is, and in the resigned determination to see it through as bravely as possible, to make the best of it, perhaps with a higher or baser frivolity or the corresponding depression, perhaps with an anxious concern at approaching death or an unthinking forgetfulness. But what is all this if there is nothing more? Yet if we are fools there is nothing more than this—with accidental or necessary variations. This is the whole fulness of our being in the limits of our temporality. This is the fulness of our history. In the light of our basic folly we will always have too much and too little time. There will never be any content for our time. And for the foolish man world-history with its greatness and misery, its marvels and horrors, will be much the same in its own appointed limits, except that everything is now on a greater scale and has therefore an even darker aspect. It is simply a riddle which he may more or less

[424] boldly attempt to solve, or more or less boldly despair of solving; regarding himself either as responsible on the one hand or not responsible on the other. There is no lack of ways—optimistic and pessimistic, sceptical, idealistic and historical, moral and non-moral, highly aesthetic and starkly brutal—in which we may try to conceal this situation, the being in time of the man who cannot understand because he will not know the Lord of time, of his own and all history. But there can be no alteration of this situation by any such concealment. This is the third consequence of this vacuum, of the basic stupidity of man.

This, then, in a first form and aspect, was the man whom God reconciled and seized and exalted to Himself in the man Jesus. Seen and measured by that One, he is this slothful man; the man who from the standpoint of his own action, or inaction, lets himself fall in this way, and is so stupid, such a fool. God has taken this man to Himself—not in ignorance but with a full awareness of this sin. What God willed and accomplished in the existence of that One was the healing of the sickness from which we all realise that we suffer in the light of that One; the instruction of the fools that we must all confess ourselves to be. His light shines in the darkness. And if it is true that the darkness has not comprehended it, it is even more true, and a better translation of Jn. 1^5, that the darkness has not overcome it.

The fool or simpleton in his godlessness and the resultant imprudence and insecurity gives us a very concrete picture, as he is portrayed especially in Proverbs and Ecclesiastes, of the folly which stands in such marked contrast to the divine and practical wisdom of which these two books speak and which is personified in the wise man, the man of prudence and understanding, the man who fears God. We may recall at this point some of the basic traits in the character of the fool. He is the man who trusts in his own understanding (Prov. 28^{26}). He does not think it necessary to take advice but thinks that his own way is right (12^{15}). He thus gives himself heedlessly to that which is wrong (14^{16}). Folly is joy to him (15^{21}). He wears it like a crown (14^{24}). He proclaims it (12^{23}). The awful thing about him is that the speech in which he shows himself to be a fool continually emphasises the fact. His own lips "will swallow up himself. The beginning of the words of his mouth is foolishness: and the end of his talk is mischievous madness" (Eccl. $10^{12f.}$). He might pass for a wise man if only he would be silent, and for a man of understanding if only he would keep his lips shut (Prov. 17^{28}). But he does not do so, and this means that he has a mouth which is "near destruction" (10^{14}), for it covers violence (10^{11}). Foolishness pours out from it (15^2). We need to beware of a fool, because he is always meddling (20^3). His lips bring contention and his mouth provokes blows (18^6). "If a wise man contendeth with a foolish man, whether he rage or laugh, there is no rest" (29^9). "A companion of fools shall be broken" (13^{20}). "Let a bear robbed of her whelps meet a man, rather than a fool in his folly" (17^{12}). There is also an infectious quality in folly. The fool passes on folly as the wise man bequeaths wisdom (14^{18}). "A stone is heavy, and the sand weighty; but a fool's wrath is heavier than them both" (27^3). It is even worse when he is clever. As "the legs of the lame are not equal"—or "as a thorn goeth up into the hand of a drunkard, so is a parable in the mouth of fools" ($26^{7\ 9}$). Even his prayer is an abomination (28^9). Can we do nothing for him? Can he not improve himself? No, "as a dog returneth to his vomit, so a fool iterateth his folly" (26^{11}). "Though thou shouldest bray a fool in a mortar among wheat with a pestle, yet will not his foolishness depart from him" [425] (27^{22}). For his heart is corrupt (15^7). He will die in his lack of understanding (10^{21}). He will always be a fool, for he cannot and will not receive admonition (12^1).

Who is this fool of the wisdom literature? There can be no doubt that its authors have in mind specific individuals or groups. They are thinking of certain signs of decadence in the society of later Judaism. The reference is to concrete situations. Not all those whom they addressed were guilty of all the individual follies indicated—disobedience to parents, sexual and economic dissipation, drunkenness, blatant hardness of heart, bloodthirstiness, raillery, etc. We also misunderstand these proverbs if we expound them with reference to a recognisable group, an unpleasant stratum or party, that of "fools," which can be differentiated from the opposing group or stratum or party of the wise, and accused and condemned. The sign of decadence to which the term "fool" has reference is basically a characteristic of the whole life of Israel in its later stages. It applies virtually and even actually to all its members. And in the last resort it is a characteristic of the life of all men. "Therefore the Lord will cut off from Israel head and tail, branch and rush, in one day ... for everyone is an hypocrite and an evildoer, and every mouth speaketh folly," is what we are told concerning Northern Israel in Is. $9^{14\ 17}$; and in a condemnation of idolatry in Jer. $10^{8\ 14}$ the same is said concerning the Gentiles: "But they are altogether brutish and foolish: the stock is a doctrine of vanities .... Every man is brutish in his knowledge." It is also to be noted how in Rom. $3^{10f.}$ Paul quotes from the context of the saying in Ps. 14^1 about the man who denies God: "They are corrupt, they have done abominable works, there is none that doeth good. The Lord looked down from heaven upon the children of men, to see if there were any that did understand, and seek God. They are all gone aside, they are all together become filthy: there is none that doeth good, no, not one" (Ps. 14$^{1-3}$, cf. Ps. 53$^{2f.}$). This is why even the righteous man (not the godless) has to confess (Ps. 69^5): "O God, thou knowest my foolishness," and (Ps. 73^{22}): "So foolish was I, and ignorant: I was as a beast before thee"—although he can then continue: "Nevertheless I am continually with thee: thou hast holden me by the right hand." Folly even extends to the heart of the child (Prov. 22^{15}), and the rod of affliction which is to drive it from him has much wider and deeper reference than to corporal punishment and other pedagogic measures. In Eccl. 9^3 we read that "the heart of the sons of men is full of evil, and madness is in their heart while they live, and after that they go to the dead." If this is the case, the folly envisaged in these writings does not refer—for all the concreteness of its manifestations—only to specific individuals as opposed to others who are superior and unaffected. It is not just the affair of a group. It is a determination under which the wise and clever who understand and seek after God, while they are certainly distinguished from the fools and simpletons who do not understand and do not seek after God, are also united with them, because the latter are at the very place from which they themselves have come and continually come, from which they have constantly to break away, at which they would spend their whole lives were it not given to them—and this is what makes them wise—by the omnipotent Word of God, which liberates them for knowledge, to break away from it, to turn their back on their folly; so that they too have need always to be recalled, and to recall themselves, by these proverbs. Folly is something which concerns Israel—for when was Israel not addressed by the prophets as a foolish people in its relationship to God? It is also something which concerns the nations who come under the light of the history of Israel, i.e., of the God who rules Israel. It is the concern of every man as he is revealed in the divine judgment. This picture of the fool is the mirror of the merited rejection held out to all men—a rejection from which there is no escape except by the gracious election of God, by the mighty Word of God which calls and chides. Thus the unfolding of this picture involves [426] the call to decision as it has been heard, and must be continually heard, by the wise man, and as he loves to hear it. Who is the wise man but the fool of yesterday who will also be the fool of to-day and to-morrow without a fresh issue of this summons and fresh obedience? And who is the fool but the man who is summoned by the Word of God to be the wise man of to-day and to-morrow? Even the fool who is incorrigible as such is man before God—or, rather, man in the history in which God is about to fulfil and realise His covenant with him, the covenant which he himself has broken but God has kept. The picture of the fool shows with pitiless clarity where it is that man comes from, who and what he is there where he does not seek but is found by God, and who and what he would remain if he were not found by God. No wise man will obviously see fools except as they are seen in the wisdom literature. None will fail to take with absolute seriousness their godlessness and their consequent imprudence and insecurity. On the other hand, it is not a wise man, but only a fool, who will not remember that God is also the God of the fool, and only as such the God of the wise; who will therefore only contrast himself with the fool, and not admit his solidarity with him, and speak about him and to him in this solidarity. The picture of the fool in the Book of Proverbs is not an invitation to this unwise wisdom. The Book of Ecclesiastes can and must also be regarded as a warning against this misunderstanding of Proverbs. Particular attention must be paid in this respect to the remarkable passage in Eccl. 7$^{16-18}$: "Be not righteous over much; neither make thyself over wise: why shouldest thou destroy thyself? Be not over much wicked, neither be thou foolish: why shouldest thou die before thy time? It is good that thou shouldest take hold of this; yea, also from this withdraw not thine hand: for he that feareth God shall come forth of them all." But even in the Book of Proverbs itself we have to take note of the surprising words of Agur the son of Jakeh (30$^{2f.}$): "Surely I am more brutish than any man, and have not the understanding of a man. I neither learned wisdom, nor have the knowledge of the holy. Who hath ascended up into heaven, or descended? who hath gathered the wind in his fists? who hath bound the waters in his garment? who hath established all the ends of the earth? what is his name, and what is his son's name, if thou canst tell?" There can be no doubt that it is a wise man who puts these questions. But there can also be no doubt that it is one who is wise in the fact that in and with these questions concerning God he ranges himself with the fool, acknowledging himself to be a fool. Is he wise all the same, and able and called to teach the fool wisdom? This is undoubtedly the case, for in vv. 5f. he is given and gives himself the answer: "Every word of God is pure: he is a shield unto them that put their trust in him. Add thou not unto his words, lest he reprove thee, and thou be found a liar."

It is of a piece with this—with the required modesty with which alone the wise man, if he is to be truly wise, can look upon (and not therefore look down upon) the fool—that in Mt. 5^{22} the address $\mu\omega\rho\acute{e}$, thou fool, is forbidden on the severest penalties as a term of reproach directly and personally flung by one man at another. It is, indeed, the most terrible form of what Jesus describes as "murder" in exposition of the Old Testament commandment. It does, of course, occur several times in the New Testament in the context of teaching or prophecy. For example, we find it in Lk. 11^{40} in the condemnation of the Pharisaic view of cleansing: $\check{\alpha}\phi\rho o\nu\epsilon\varsigma$[EN27], "did not he that made that which is without make that which is within also?"; in Mt. 23^{17} in the attack on the pharisaic practice as regards oaths: $\mu\omega\rho o\grave{\iota}$ $\kappa\alpha\grave{\iota}$ $\tau\upsilon\phi\lambda o\acute{\iota}$[EN28]: "for whether is greater, the gift, or the altar that sanctifieth the gift"; in Mt. $25^{2f.}$, where in the parable five of the virgins are called $\mu\omega\rho\alpha\acute{\iota}$[EN29]; in 1 Cor. 15^{36}: $\check{\alpha}\phi\rho\omega\nu$[EN30], "that which thou sowest is not quickened, except it die"; and in Lk. 12^{20}, to the rich man who planned to build greater barns: $\check{\alpha}\phi\rho\omega\nu$[EN31], "this night thy soul shall be required of thee: then whose shall those things be, which thou hast provided?" It is to be noted that this is not said to him by a man, but by God. It is also to be noted that in all these passages the primary condemnation is not of the individual but of specific ways of thinking and acting. It is the former which is forbidden in Mt. 5^{22} as a qualified form of murder, as an absolute breach of communication with one's brother. In this respect there is again brought out the whole basic seriousness of the concept "fool." For all its lavish and drastic appearance in the Old Testament it is always used in the third person, never in the second. It is impossible not to speak of the fool. There are innumerable representatives of folly—its poor slaves, but also its priests and bold prophets and protagonists. And therefore there are innumerable fools. Yet no one has either place or right to see and treat another as such. It may well be that he confronts me as such in a terribly concrete way, so that I seem almost to get the touch and smell of the fool. But he does not confront me in such a way that I can really recognise him concretely as such. To say "fool" of another man is to curse him, and as such to murder him, to invade the divine prerogative as a qualified murderer, to act in ignorance of God, and therefore to show oneself a fool. The curse is one which recoils on the man who utters it. For it is only those who are themselves godless and stupid that will feel free to apply this murderous term of opprobrium and condemnation to their companions in stupidity.

There is, however, one notable example in the Old Testament (1 Sam. 25) of a man who is as his name is (v. 25)—Nabal, a fool. This man, sharply contrasted with his wife Abigail as the representative of wisdom and David as the exponent of the divine action and promise in and with Israel, plays in the form of folly a very important—if, as is only fitting, subsidiary—role.

[427]

[EN27] fool
[EN28] blind fools
[EN29] foolish
[EN30] fool
[EN31] fool

It will be worth our while briefly to consider the story. It certainly provides us with a "study in desert customs" (R. Kittel), but it is hardly for this reason that it has found a place in the collection of dynastic records of which the two Books of Samuel form the starting-point. Even the contracting of David's second or third marriage (with Abigail), which is the culmination of the story, is hardly a sufficient justification for so detailed an account of what precedes. It is evident that in the depiction of the strange happenings which took place between these three characters our attention is drawn to something of material significance. And the emphasis given to them, especially to Nabal and Abigail, shows unmistakeably that what we have here is an encounter of David, the bearer of the promise κατ ἐξοχήν EN32, with two contrasting types, the expressly foolish and the expressly wise, and his rejection by the former who is called Nabal, and acknowledgment and humble acceptance by the latter, Abigail.

The event takes place in Carmel, south-east of Hebron, which is the abode of the prosperous Nabal, the owner of 3,000 sheep and 1,000 goats, who is just about to keep the feast of shearing (v. 2). The story belongs to the records of David's experiences and activities when, although he is already elected and called and anointed to be the future king, he is forced into exile by the attacks of Saul. David and his 600 men are in the western part of the wilderness of Judah on the borders of Carmel, where the shepherds of Nabal have taken his sheep to pasture. David hears of the sheep-shearing, and sends ten of his men to Nabal. They are to greet him as a brother, saying: "Peace be both to thee, and peace be to thine house, and peace be unto all that thou hast" (v. 6). The message which they are to give is that no injury has been done to the shepherds (as they themselves can and do testify, v. 15) by the roving band into whose sphere of influence they have come, nor have the flocks themselves suffered the loss that might have been expected (v. 7). On the contrary, David and his men have protected the flocks and shepherds against alien robbers. Far from constituting a threat, they have been "a wall unto them both by night and day" (v. 16). David is not reminding Nabal of the positive achievement, but of the integrity and loyalty which he and his men have proved. And he requests only the customary hospitality at festivals of this kind when he [428] asks Nabal to be generous to his emissaries and to give them "whatsoever cometh to thine hand" for David and his servants. He even describes himself as "thy son David" (v. 8).

It is at this juncture, however, that Nabal lives up to his name and shows himself to be "churlish and evil," a true son of Caleb (v. 3), "this man of Belial," as he is later called by his own wife (v. 25)—and so much so "that a man cannot speak to him" (v. 17). "Who is David? and who is the son of Jesse? there be many servants now a days that break away every man from his master. Shall I then take my bread, and my water, and my flesh that I have killed for my shearers, and give it unto men, whom I know not whence they be?" What is the folly of this foolish speech? Is it that it is the speech of an unusually self-opinionated and standoffish and intolerably priggish bourgeois? This is one aspect of it. He seems to be completely lacking in any feeling for a neighbour in need, or even in ordinary civility in his dealings with his fellows. He is a quite impossible neighbour. But there is more to it than this if we are not simply to read the story in moralistic terms. Nabal was addressed "in the name of David" (v. 9). The different reaction of Abigail as soon as she heard the name of David shows where the decisive folly of the speech is to be found. Note the beginning and end of his words. It is not just a bedouin sheikh but the elect of *Yahweh* that he refuses to recognise, and thinks that he can scorn and despise, accusing him of being a runaway servant and so inhospitably refusing him food and drink. How could he possibly miss the threefold *shalom* EN33 with which David greeted him? But he did miss it. It was really an encounter with his own and Israel's salvation

---

EN32 above all others
EN33 peace

that he neglected and so rudely rejected. It was *Yahweh's* own presence and action in the person of this man that he despised, refusing his services, and insisting so snobbishly upon his own right of possession and therefore control. He had to do with *Yahweh* Himself, and he acted as one who was completely ignorant of Him. That is why he was so impossible.

David, of course, was a man like others, who normally give a rough answer to churlishness, replying with anger and vengeance to foolish words and actions, and in this way, i.e., in the name of avenging righteousness, with folly to folly. When he received news of Nabal's reception he took 400 of his 600 men, and when they had girded on their swords they set out westward towards Carmel—a thunder-cloud which according to the practice of the times threatened complete extermination to Nabal and all his house (v. 12). We can see later (v. 21 f., 34) how David looked at the matter: "Surely in vain have I kept all this fellow hath in the wilderness, so that nothing was missed of all that pertained unto him: and he hath requited me evil for good. So and more also do God unto David, if I leave any men of all that pertain to him by the morning light."

It is at this point that Abigail takes a hand. According to v. 3 she is a woman "of good understanding, and of a beautiful countenance." One of Nabal's servants has come (v. 14) and told her what has taken place (according to v. 25 in her absence): "Now therefore know and consider what thou wilt do; for evil is determined against our master, and against all his household" (v. 17). But her wisdom has as little need of lengthy deliberation as the folly of her husband. What is it that she knows and he does not know? That this is not the way to treat people? Yes, she knows this too. But this is not the decisive point. She hears the name of David and knows with whom they have to do (with the same immediacy as her husband does not know). She takes in the situation at a glance and acts accordingly (v. 18 f.). "Whatsoever cometh to thine hand" is what David had asked of Nabal. But she now takes two hundred loaves, and two bottles of wine, and five sheep ready dressed, and five measures of parched corn, and an hundred clusters of raisins, and two hundred cakes of figs, and loads them on asses. Some of the servants are to go on before, and she herself follows—eastward towards David. And she does all this without even consulting her husband. When the elect of God draws near, and with him the judgment, wisdom does not dispute with folly, but ignores it and does that which is commanded. [429]

There then follows her encounter with David and his band. According to v. 20 it takes place in the fold of a valley, and is a surprise meeting for both parties, Abigail coming down from the one side and David from the other. "And when Abigail saw David, she hasted, and lighted off the ass, and fell before David on her face, and bowed herself to the ground" (v. 23)—the full prostration of worship like that of Abraham before God (Gen. 17³) and Joshua before the angel (Josh. 5¹⁴) and before the ark (7⁶). A sign of anxiety? No, but of something very different—an unconditional respect. Abigail has no anxiety. She knows very well what she wants and what she has to represent with a very definite superiority. What she now does is the demonstration of the fact that in this situation she knows with whom she has to do in the rather threatening person of this man. This is the core and guiding light of the long speech which is now put on her lips (vv. 24–31). This is the reason for her attitude and for the gifts that she has brought to David. It is also the basis of the requests that she makes. It is on this account that she must and will make good the evil of Nabal, and prevent the evil that David himself is on the point of committing. It is in this respect that she shows herself to be of a good understanding. The point is that the name David means something to her. She knows and solemnly declares who he is and will be. Since the wordless anointing of David by Samuel in 1 Sam. 16¹⁻¹³—and it is not for nothing that the death of Samuel is reported at the beginning of this chapter—it has not been reported that anyone has said anything to this effect either of or to David: "*Yahweh* shall do to my lord all the good that he hath spoken concerning thee, and appoint thee ruler over Israel" (v. 30); and even more emphatically:

49

"For the Lord will certainly make my lord a sure house, because my lord fighteth the battles of the Lord, and evil hath not been found in thee all thy days. Yet a man is risen to pursue thee, and to seek thy soul: but the soul of my lord shall be bound in the bundle of life with the Lord thy God; and the souls of thine enemies, them shall he sling out, as out of the middle of a sling" (vv. 28b–29). Everything else depends upon, and has its meaning and power in, the fact that Abigail knows and has to say this of David, and therefore of the will and promise, the secret of the covenant, of the God of Israel.

It is this knowledge which commits and constrains her fearlessly and whole-heartedly to take up the cause of Nabal with David. As the one who does not know in this decisive respect, Nabal and all that he says and does in consequence can only be found wanting in this situation. This will be proved later in what is for him a terrible sense. In the first instance, it means that he does not even come into consideration in the discussion and bargaining with David: "Let not my lord, I pray thee, regard this man of Belial, even Nabal: for as his name is, so is he; Nabal is his name, and folly is with him" (v. 25a). Abigail can only ask David to listen to her and not to him: "Let thine handmaid, I pray thee, speak in thine audience, and hear the words of thine handmaid" (v. 24). But this means that she accepts responsibility for what Nabal has said and done; that she takes his place in relation to David. She knows and says that she had no part in the event: "But I thine handmaid saw not the young men of my lord, whom thou didst send" (v. 25b). And yet: "Upon me, my lord, upon me let this iniquity be" (v. 24a). The first practical meaning of her prostration is that she gives herself into David's hands for good or evil if only he will hear her, and hear her in the place of Nabal.

What is it that she has to say to him? In the first instance, she has to act: to make good the mistake that Nabal has made; to fulfil the request that he had rejected; to unload the asses and present the bread and wine and sheep and corn and raisins and figs to David. "And now this present which thine handmaid hath brought unto my lord, let it be even given unto the young men that follow my lord" (v. 27). And then: "Forgive the trespass of thine handmaid " (v. 28a). Why should David forgive? Because she has made good the mistake and given the present? No, but because David—there now follow the words of promise in vv. 28b–29—is already the anointed and future king of Israel. It is as the one who knows him as such that Abigail has interposed herself between him and Nabal. And it is as the one who knows this, and in view of what she knows, that she asks for forgiveness. And the granting of this request carries with it the sparing of Nabal and his house from impending destruction. Even to her personally there will not now occur (as we learn from v. 34) the worst evil that could come on any woman in Israel, the loss of her sons. But she is not concerned about this danger, as had been the servant who first told her what had happened and what it would necessarily entail. What moves Abigail is not that vengeance should be averted from Nabal and his house and indirectly herself, but that it should not be committed by David. In her intervention she is particularly unconcerned as to the fate of Nabal. Indeed, she counts on it as something which is as good as done that he will come to a bad end: "Let thine enemies, and they that seek evil to my lord, be as Nabal" (v. 26b). What she wills to prevent when she throws herself down before David, and accepts the guilt of Nabal, and asks that it should be forgiven, is that David should be the instrument of Nabal's destruction, and therefore incur guilt himself.

Does she only will to prevent this? The remarkable thing in her speech to David is that she regards it as something which objectively is prevented already. With such superiority does she confront the wrathful David (before whom she prostrates herself), so little does she fear him or doubt the success of her intervention, that from the very first she speaks in terms of an accomplished fact: "Now therefore, my lord, as the Lord liveth, and as thy soul liveth, seeing the Lord hath withholden thee from coming to shed blood, and from avenging thyself with thine own hand ... " (v. 26a). We find the same daring anticipation in the words of promise in relation to David's future as the one whom *Yahweh* has raised up and protected to

[430]

be a prince over Israel. When God has done this (and it is assumed that He will), "this shall be no grief unto thee, nor offence of heart unto my lord, either that thou hast shed blood causeless, or that my lord hath avenged himself" (v. 31). This is the wisdom of Abigail in her relationship with David, who in the act of vengeance which he purposes stands in the only too human danger of making himself a fool. She knows that as the one he is and will be he may not and cannot and therefore will not actually do what he plans to do. The elect of *Yahweh* may not and cannot and will not avenge himself, making himself guilty of the blood of Nabal and many others who were innocent, and thus violating the prerogative of *Yahweh*, which none can ever escape. She towers above David with this knowledge as she makes this pronouncement.

And what of David? The practical consequence is as follows: "So David received of her hand that which she had brought him, and said unto her, Go up in peace to thine house; see, I have hearkened to thy voice, and have accepted thy person" (and intervention, v. 35). But the reason why he forgives, and therefore forgoes his intended revenge, is not because he has received the present or changed his mind as to what Nabal deserves. He still fully acknowledges his purpose: "For in very deed, as the Lord God of Israel liveth, which hath kept me back from hurting thee, except thou hadst hasted and come to meet me, surely there had not been left a man unto Nabal by the morning light" (v. 34). The ground of his forgiveness is exactly the same as that of Abigail's request for forgiveness. And in his words as in hers it is one which has to be taken into consideration and therefore discussed, but one which is already realised and operative, excluding from the very outset the execution of his purpose. The beginning of his answer is decisive: "Blessed be the Lord God of Israel, which sent thee this day to meet me: and blessed be thy advice, and blessed be thou, which hast [431] kept me this day from coming to shed blood, and from avenging myself with mine own hand" (v. 32 f.). The request of Abigail did not need to be fulfilled. It had been fulfilled already—even before it was made. It simply reminded David of the accomplished fact that he could not and would not do what he intended to do. For, indicated by the voice of Abigail, it is *Yahweh* the God of Israel who withstands him as an absolutely effective obstacle on the way which he has planned to follow, arresting and turning him back again. And in face of this obstacle David can only break out into praise of God and of the understanding Abigail. As the one he is on the basis of the election of *Yahweh*, and as the one he will be in the power of the calling of *Yahweh*, he is not in a position to execute his purpose. As the Lord liveth— *Yahweh* and he himself would have to be other than they are if he were to be in a position to execute it. The wisdom of Abigail consists in the fact that she knows *Yahweh* and therefore knows David. When David hears the voice of this wisdom, no particular decision is needed. The matter is decided already. He is restrained from doing what he had intended to do.

The story has two endings. The first is a sombre one. Nabal has escaped the wrath of David. But he runs none the less to his destruction. The death overtakes him to which he has fallen a victim in his own corruption. The second is brighter. It speaks of the marriage of David and Abigail as the result of their encounter and remarkable agreement.

Nabal is removed. When Abigail returns from her enterprise to Carmel she finds this rash and foolish fellow engaged in a fresh act of madness: "He held a feast in his house like the feast of a king; and Nabal's heart was merry within him, for he was very drunken: wherefore she told him nothing, less or more, until the morning light" (v. 36). But he has to learn what danger he has incurred, under what threat he has actually stood, and above all how—while he himself feasted and amused himself so regally, and therefore so little deserved it—he was saved from destruction in the power of the redemptive will of *Yahweh* as it is focused on David and known and proclaimed by Abigail. Therefore "in the morning, when the wine was gone out of Nabal ... his wife told him these things" (v. 37a). But it is not the fact that he has been saved that makes an impression on this fool and causes him to think, although this might have been an excellent opportunity to learn to know the one whom hitherto he had not known. Even now that he is sober he is still the fool he was in and before his carousal. And it is the account of that from which he has been saved, and therefore of that by which (like the rider on Lake Constance) he was threatened, that suddenly comes home to him and obviously affects him like a stroke—his subsequent fear being all the greater than his previous sense of security. "His heart died within him, and he became as a stone. And it came to pass about ten days after, that the Lord smote Nabal, that he died" (vv. 37b–38). The message of salvation itself, not being recognised by him, turns to his own judgment and death. He can and does only disappear from the scene. And on learning of Nabal's end, and in the light of it, David can only praise *Yahweh*, that He has acted as his avenger, and that He has kept David himself from evil (v. 39a).

But the death of Nabal means that Abigail is now a widow. She does not remain so long. She becomes the wife of David. At first sight this is rather surprising, for there are no hints of any romantic developments in the earlier part of the story. The dealings between herself and David had been strictly matter of fact, and it would be wrong to allow artistic imagination to impart to them a different and preparatory character in the light of the outcome. There is, in fact, no trace of sentimentality even in the portrayal of the conclusion itself. It must be understood in the sober context of the main part of the narrative. "And David sent, and communed with Abigail, to take her to him to wife" (v. 39b). The proposal was made by the [432] servants of David (v. 40) and it was accepted by Abigail with the same unquestioning resolution as had marked all her previous speech and action, and the same unconditional subjection as that which she had known when she had fearlessly and critically instructed this great and fearsome leader, and told him the truth concerning *Yahweh* and himself. She does not compromise herself, but simply carries through to the end the role allotted to her in her wisdom, when we read that "she arose, and bowed herself on her face to the earth, and said (as though addressing David himself and not merely his servants), Behold, let thine handmaid be a servant to wash the feet of the servants of my lord. And Abigail hasted, and arose, and rose upon an ass, with five damsels of hers that went after her; and she went after the messengers of David, and became his wife" (vv. 41–42). We really ought not to be surprised by this development, for as by an inner necessity the main narrative hastens towards the death of Nabal and the new life of Abigail in union with David. The meaning is not to be sought in any special importance of Abigail in the future history of David. There is only one other mention of her, together with David's other wives, in 2 Sam. 3³, where we read that she was the mother of Chileab, who in the parallel in 1 Chron. 3¹ is called Daniel. Michal and later Bathsheba play a much more imposing role in the tradition. But we are forced to say of Abigail that of all the wives of David, or even of the Old Testament as a whole, she is outstanding as the only one to whom there is ascribed the function described in 1 Sam. 25: that of the woman of good understanding who recognises and honours the Lord's anointed, and therefore the Lord's will for Israel, at a time when he is so severely assailed and so deeply concealed, and when her foolish husband is so blind and deaf and stupid in face of him; but who also represents and declares to the elect himself the will and purpose of *Yahweh* and the logic of his election and calling, keeping him from putting his trust in his own arm and sword and therefore himself becoming a fool. In this function she belongs to David even before she does so in fact. She belongs to him as the wisdom which takes the place of folly and speaks for it, and without which he could not be the one he is as the elect of *Yahweh*, or be the king of Israel, as he will be in virtue of his calling. Ordained to be his help-meet (Gen. 2¹⁸ᶠ·) in this function, she belongs indispensably to him. This is what David actualises and confirms with his swift proposal—once the existence of the fool and the work of his folly have been removed—and which she herself also actualises and confirms with her swift and unquestioning acceptance. David would not be David without Abigail and without recognising Abigail; just as Abigail would not be the wise Abigail without David and without recognising David. Therefore He has to take her to wife and she has to become his wife, so that they are one flesh. To no other marriage of David, or indeed of the Old Testament, does the biblical account give the distinctive mark of this inner necessity in the context of the history of salvation.

2. We again begin with a christological statement. The Word of God became and is flesh. It was and is spoken to us, and present in power, in the existence of the man Jesus. The royal freedom of this one man consisted and consists in the fact that He is wholly the Fellow-man of us His fellows; wholly the Neighbour of us His neighbours; wholly the Brother of us His brothers; the Witness, Teacher, Doctor, Helper and Advocate given as a man to us men. In the actualisation which it has found in Him humanity means to be bound and committed to other men. In Him, therefore, man is turned not merely to God but to other men. In Him he is quite open and willing and ready and active for them. In Him he gives glory to God alone, but in so doing sees and affirms and exalts the dignity and right and claim of the other man. In Him he does not live only [433] in fellowship with God, but in so doing he also lives in fellowship with other men. In Him, in this man, God Himself is for all other men. This cannot be said of any other. In the fact that as He is with us He is also for us He remains exalted above all. In this exaltation above all He is also a direction for all; a summons to participate, as thankful recipients of His grace, in the humanity actualised in Him, to share this humanity with a concrete orientation on the fellow-man, the neighbour, the brother. To receive His Holy Spirit is to receive this direction and accept this summons. It is to see oneself in Him as one who is elected and created and determined for existence in this humanity.

But we, on whose behalf and for whose orientation He was and is man in this freedom, fail to obey the call to this freedom. Among all the others for whom He is a Fellow and Neighbour and Brother as we are, and who are therefore our fellows and neighbours and brothers, we remain in our isolation and seclusion and self-will and unwillingness, and therefore in our latent or patent hostility, in relation to them; in a word, in our inhumanity. We are again inactive where we can and should and must let ourselves be moved in the direction of these others. This is the second form of our sloth, in which we want to be alone instead of being those we already are in and by this One.

This human reluctance has again to be considered primarily in its futility. Nothing can alter the fact that the man Jesus is for all, not only the light of the knowledge of God, but also the power of humanity. He cannot be dismissed from the world, this One who is the Fellow and Neighbour and Brother of all men. The fire which He has kindled on earth in this sense too cannot be put out. His direction cannot be reversed. No absolute fact can be opposed to Him. Nor can anything alter the fact that in Him all men, even the most deformed and unnatural, are elected and created and determined for fellow-humanity, for neighbourly love, for brotherhood. It is as well not to keep this from even the worst of our fellows, but to tell it to him plainly, and above all to

53

accept it ourselves. In this respect, too, I can refuse to be the new and neighbourly man that I am already in this One. In this respect, too, we can involve ourselves in self-contradiction. But in this respect, too, we cannot destroy ourselves. We cannot, therefore, destroy the fact that others are there as our fellows and neighbours and brothers. We may cause them to wait, and wait in vain, for our corresponding action and attitude. But they are there as such, and we cannot alter the fact that they do wait for our corresponding action and attitude. They are always there and they always wait for us even though our indifference, our aversion and even our more refined or blatant wickedness in face of them is uppermost—especially so when this is the case! It is not for nothing that the Son of God has made Himself theirs and ours. It is our sloth rather than His direction which is futile—the sloth in which we cause others to wait for us in vain. In it we remain at a place where there is no solid ground under our feet, so that we cannot maintain ourselves. In face of the fellowship already established between all men in the one man Jesus, no man can withdraw into a final isolation. I can, and do, sabotage this fellowship. But I cannot make it a reality of inferior quality which is destined to perish. Even in my inhumanity I can only practise my sin and reveal my shame.

[434]

But this is bad enough, and we must now speak of it. For all its relativity and ultimate futility, our sloth even in this form is a fact. It is not nothing, but, in a way which is very painful for others and even more distressing for ourselves, it is the something of our persistence in the direction to that which is not. Man wills that which according to His incarnation God does not will. He wills the impossible. He wills to be man without and even in opposition to his fellow-man. His action and attitude in relation to others have nothing of the freedom in which the man Jesus causes him to participate in the power of His direction. For no real reason he dissociates himself from the movement to his fellows which proceeds from Jesus. Or perhaps he never really has any part in it at all, although he is in the sphere of it. He does not live a genuinely human, but an inhuman, life, because he does not live as a fellow-man.

Between humanity and inhumanity, divided by the criterion of fellow-humanity, there is no middle term; just as there is no middle term between wisdom and folly, between the knowledge of God and ignorance of God. "Inhuman" means to be without one's fellow-men. We can either be with them, i.e., orientated on them, and therefore human, thinking and willing and speaking and acting as men; or we can be without them, and therefore not human, but inhuman, in all our acts and attitudes. If we are without them we are against them. And as the stupidity of man does not have its origin in the theoretical denial of God, but is merely practised in a particular and not indispensable way in this denial, so inhumanity does not have its basis in individual actions and attitudes towards our neighbours, but either in these or without them in the fact that we think we can and should be without our neighbours and therefore alone—a distorted attitude which will necessarily find powerful expression in corresponding actions or omissions. It is from this basic attitude that our repressions and actions in relation to others acquire the character of sin, of a culpable lapse into self-contradiction in the fulfilment of which we deny and oppose and shame both God our Creator and ourselves as His good creatures, and therefore, while we do not cease to be men, become and are inhuman men. We are always inhuman from the very outset, even before we perform the corresponding action and either trespass against our neighbours and therefore ourselves or in some way leave ourselves and our neighbours in the lurch. The great rejection has already taken place even when and as it finds specific expression. It is not, therefore, determined by our more or less lofty, sociable, altruistic or egotistic impulses or qualities or inclinations, by our environment, or by the opportunities which we have or do not have. On the contrary, it is itself that which determines what takes place in the sphere of all these presuppositions as the activity, or inactivity, of our more or less lofty, sociable, altruistic or egotistic nature as such. What takes place reflects man's inhumanity as the second basic dimension of his folly. The form and texture may vary, but it is always his sin of disobedience, unbelief and ingratitude which is manifested in this sphere. It is his sin, because in it he turns aside from the grace which is given him by God to order his relationship not only to God but also to his fellows, violating the law of this grace, and therefore letting himself fall where he is in fact exalted and may and can and should stand.

[435]

We have to realise this if we are to see from what source the notorious inhumanity of human life and society draws its perennial strength and irresistible efficacy. It is so easy to say how simple and pleasant everything would be if only we were a little more human in our dealings, a little more attentive to one another, a little more understanding and ready to help one another. We may even suspect that all the essential evil of human existence could be avoided, and all the incidental evil mitigated and made supportable, if only it were not for this great and constant lacuna of our inhuman dealings. And the corresponding admonitions, to ourselves and others, are easily made and spring self-evidently to hand; just as great or small measares have been devised and executed, and will continually be devised and executed, to fill or bridge the gap. The only trouble is that in great and little things alike the gap always reappears. What the one thinks about another, and says to him, and does in relation to him, is decisively determined by the fact that he maintains a continual reserve, that he constantly withdraws into himself, that he has to do with him only from this standpoint and in the form of his own interests, that he is not really for him and therefore his fellow. This reserve common to us all is not affected by any admonitions or counter-measures, by any psychology or individual or social pedagogics, by any social revolution or individual conversion, however radical. On the contrary, it is appalling to see how all the great and little things which can and continually do and will take place around this centre can only reveal afresh at some point that in his relation to his fellows too man is this slothful and sinful being who falls back upon himself and acts and reacts in this inhuman fashion. If we do not realise this, if we will not accept it primarily of ourselves, we shall never understand the intrinsically incomprehensible fact of the continual complication of that which is so simple; of the human life which can be lived only as a life in fellowship, but which is not lived as a life in fellowship and is therefore lived in inhumanity—an inhumanity necessarily and indissolubly connected with its godlessness.

[436]

We have also to realise this if we are to see how dangerous is the effect of man's inhumanity. We will consider again its outward aspect. As it takes place first in the distorted attitude and then in the corresponding acts it has the character of power; of a force which once unleashed, as in the activity or inactivity of our refusal, escapes our control, follows its own law and has its own dynamic, whose effects we can experience only as spectators, thus adding to our own guilt. By renouncing our true humanity we do, of course, achieve a kind of liberation, an independence, a superior capacity to act, in the exercise of which we gain a peculiar advantage over others and seem to be the stronger. But even as we enjoy and assert it this power is strange and alien in relation to ourselves. It is stronger than we are. Our inhumanity sets us under a rule according to which every man's hand is necessarily against his brother's, and we are all subjects. Again, there is a certain finality about this power. Its development is along a line which moves from its origin to a definite end, and on which the first step is virtually the last, even if it is not taken in fact. It begins with the omissions and actions of an indifferent association with one's neighbour to which there can be no juridical and hardly any moral objection. It then becomes the secret or blatant oppression and exploitation of one's fellow. His dignity, honour and right are actively or passively violated. The final upshot is what we call actual transgression: stealing and robbery; murder in the legal sense; and finally war, which allows and commands almost everything that God has forbidden. It is obviously one and the same thing at every point on this way; just as everything that is done by one man to another is at every step the same in essence. Society may not see it in this light. Nor may a less well-instructed Church. But in the judgment of a conscience enlightened and sharpened by God, the hard and relentless citizen (perhaps a public prosecutor or judge) who keeps within the bounds of what is customary and decorous is in exactly the same boat as the flagrant criminal judged and condemned by him. He carries the latter within himself, just as the latter was perhaps for many years like him. The man has yet to be found who does not bear murder in himself, who might not become a murderer even though he never does so. How dangerous is this inhuman life, which is the life of us all, is seen at the end of the line in the outbreak of strife and global warfare. But this only gives it palpable expression. It consists decisively in the fact that it is life on the steep slope which leads in different ways to this end. And its real menace, like that of stupidity, lies particularly in the fact that it is so supremely infectious. It has such great powers of reproduction. Lived by one, it is a challenge to others to live it. One man imposes on another by the power won and exercised through great or little inhumanities because by its exercise he raises the question why [437] the other is so simple as not to exercise it himself. Is he not just as capable of doing so as anyone else? Indeed, when he is the accidental or intentional victim of someone else, he is given a legitimate reason to exercise it. Why should he be the fool? Why not repay like for like: indifference for indifference; threat for threat; pressure for pressure? Why not find a place for inhumanity in answer to inhumanity? Even the most pious man cannot live at peace if a bad neighbour will not let him. Why, then, should he remain a pious man, or the most pious? And in this way an endless series of aggressions and reprisals is initiated, as happens no less in the small sphere of personal relationships than in the greater of world-politics. Yet we cannot understand how irremediable is what we all do to one another and ourselves, but can know only a superficial and ineffective horror at it, unless we are aware of the root in which we are inhuman, and necessarily do sacrifice to inhumanity, and ourselves become its victim. It is there in the root—in the fruits too, but not primarily—that as sin it is the wasting and destruction which impends and falls. It is there where it consists so insignificantly in the fact that man does not follow the movement initiated for him by God, but evades it and lets himself sink and fall into the isolation in which he deludes himself that it is grander to live without his neighbour (as well as without God) than in the fellowship with him in which he is bound and committed to live if he is himself to be a man.

But here, too, we must remember the concealment in which man is inhuman. In this form of sloth, too, it is not the case that anyone will openly admit. We are prepared to admit that in some respects we are superhuman, and in others (rather ashamedly) subhuman. But surely not that we are inhuman? Our reluctance to admit this has a sound positive reason in the fact that a man cannot cease to be a man. He cannot change himself into another creature altogether. He cannot become an animal or a devil. For all the movement toward that which is not, of which he is guilty in his relationship to his fellows, he cannot reverse the good creation of God and therefore destroy himself as a man. This may well be the objective basis of his reluctance to confess his inhumanity. But the terrible nature of inhumanity is this. Without ceasing to be man, and as such the good creature of God, man acts as though he were an animal or devil and not man. Inhumanity is the denial of our humanity. But we deny our humanity when we think that we can and should exercise it apart from our fellow-men. And when we try to conceal this, to deny this denial of our humanity, we are not justified, but accused and condemned, by this sound positive reason for our reluctance. In our denial and concealment of that which we are and do we can and will only make it worse and really be and do it. Hypocrisy is the supreme repetition of what we seek to deny with its help.

The aim of hypocrisy is to conceal the inhumanity which we will not confess. [438] But the result is only to make it worse rather than better. The veil chosen is selected with the attention of giving the appearance of the very opposite of what is concealed. We take up a position and attitude in which we think we can persuade ourselves and others and even God that they are supremely human, not least in relation to our fellows. It can all be summed up in the quite respectable word philanthropy. Philanthropy carries with it the thought of a *causa*[EN34] in its exalted sense, a specific form of the great or little ideas, systems, programmes, institutions, movements and enterprises in which, under one name or another and in one direction or another, it is a matter of satisfying a more or less necessary and profound and general human interest or need, and therefore a matter of man himself, of his physical and psychical preservation, of the order of his collective life, of his education and culture, of the increase and safeguarding and exploitation of his material and spiritual resources, of his individual, social, scientific and cultural progress. Of course, in all this man is always understood in general. He is humanity, or simply man, anonymous man. Philanthropy, then, is the focusing and concentrating of human will and action on the prosecution of one such anonymously human cause to a victorious and successful outcome. And there can be no doubt that the genuine humanity which is fellow-humanity does include philanthropy of this kind. The fact that there are always in human society questions and causes which claim the attention and loyalty of individuals and groups is in itself, because the ultimate concern is always man, a sign of the great interrelatedness in which alone we men can be men. This brings us back to the good creation of God. To be concretely with the other means always to be occupied with some such cause in relation to him. In relation to him? This is the critical point. For it is not at all self-evident that when I am actually occupied with a cause of this kind I have concretely in mind the other, the fellowman, the neighbour and brother; that I am committed to him rather than free in relation to a purely abstract and anonymous man. I can so easily escape this being with him in the prosecution of a mere cause, and the more effectively the better and more important the cause by which I find myself claimed, and the greater the urgency with which it claims me. Even in the good creation of God, and as myself a good creature, I can still evade the knowledge of God and therefore be stupid. In just the same way, again in the good creation of God and as myself a good creature, I can apply myself to a human cause, and give myself wholeheartedly to the prosecution and success of the relevant programme and enterprise, yet always have my own activity and therefore myself in mind rather than the other man, thus thinking and speaking and acting with a complete disregard for his questions and needs and expectations, for his existence generally, and proving myself to be quite inhuman. The [439] inhuman element in us all is skilled to see and use this possibility. It plunges itself into philanthropy of this kind as though it were genuinely human. In this way it conceals its true intentions and projects. And because it is not human in fellowship, it is really inhuman. But the concealment cannot be stripped off

---

[EN34] basis

from inhumanity by frontal attack any more than it can from the stupidity which decks itself out as wisdom. In fact, we seldom encounter it in its naked form either in ourselves or in others. In the majority of cases we are most sure to find it where it is concealed in the service of a great or little cause, artfully clothing itself, in its application to this cause, as the friend and servant of anonymous man, and therefore the more energetically turning away from concrete, individual man, trampling over him as though he were a corpse, which indeed he is, since the living fellow-man is regarded as non-existent, and is treated accordingly.

The field which opens up before us at this point is so vast that we can only give the briefest sketch with the help of one or two examples. The inhumanity of man may sometimes clothe itself in the necessary establishment and defence of institutions, of law and order. On the other hand, it may equally well take the form of their no less necessary criticism and over-throw. It may work itself out in the conservation of old, or the introduction of new, political and social forms. It may be active in the functions of the sacrosanct compulsory organisation of the totalitarian, or the no less sacrosanct free play of the forces of the democratic state, thus pretending to espouse either the claim of society on the individual or the freedom of the individual in relation to society. It can sometimes, as in Europe and America, disguise itself as ceaseless activity. It can cloak itself behind pure scholarship or pure art, or behind the promotion of the common interests of a national or economic or intellectual group, or behind officialdom with its concern for the regular functioning of an official apparatus, or simply behind the refinement of a technique with its different applications. It can find an instrument in marriage to the extent that this has the character of an institution and there-fore a cause. The family and its stability and possessions and honour are a cause in the emotional respectability of which it can find particularly effective concealment. Again, it may give itself with particular zeal to the stern task of the schooling and education of the younger generation, which provides the necessary "educable material" for this purpose. Not least, the Church itself, the proclamation and hearing of the Word of God, the confession and doctrine and liturgy and order of the Church, and even its theology, offer a vast oppor-tunity for philanthropic activity which is devoid of true humanity. All these things are "causes" which in their context do not lack the appearance of human justification, necessity and value, which from some standpoint can and must also be the concern of the man who is directed to his fellow-man, which have therefore a real claim to attention and service, which therefore call for the appropriate devotion which we call philanthropy. But there is not one of them which does not leave open the question how their promotion is going to affect the concrete man envisaged and embraced by them. Is he really considered at all, and if so to what extent? How far is he only an end or goal, or even a more or less useful means, so much material for the purpose, perhaps a disruptive obstacle? There is not one of them which cannot be appropriated by the inhuman element in us, which is not in fact appropriated by it both in little things and great, so that, screened by their humanity, it can dismiss the concrete man, attaining sovereignty without him or over him, and therefore secretly or openly turning against him. It cannot easily be denied that somewhere at the back or in the depths of the promotion of even the best cause—simply because and as it is promoted by [440] men—there may usually be seen the hard and evil face of the man who at bottom has no more time for his fellow than he has for God, who refuses to consider him, but who, in order not to have to confess this either to him, to himself or to God, takes refuge in an activity in which his true purpose, or lack of purpose, will necessarily be all the more active and power-ful. The cause is carried through to success—and man is really brought under the wheel.

Sometimes, rather perversely, one could almost wish that there were not all these human causes the ceaseless promotion of which only seems to make everything worse, postponing the peace on earth which they all seem to desire, and merely intensifying an internecine warfare. In their service the inhuman element in all of us not only finds particularly effective concealment, but finds itself particularly well supplied with offensive and defensive weapons. Yet of what avail would it be to abandon the causes? It is not the different causes themselves that are evil, nor the philanthropic zeal dedicated to them, but the inhuman element in us which has such an uncanny power of mastering and using them on the pretext of serving humanity.

One such cause deserves particular mention. Could it be that the clearest antithesis to inhumanity—love itself, humanitarian and brotherly love—is calculated in its own way to create a cause, to give rise to philanthropic endeavour in the narrower sense, and therefore to offer particular concealment to inhumanity? It is a frightful thing to say, but this is actually the case. There is indeed a love which is mere philanthropy, a sympathetic and benevolent concern and assistance which we can exercise with zeal and devotion without taking even a single step away from the safe stronghold of being without our fellow-man, but in a deeper withdrawal into our shell. There is a form of love—mere charity—in which we do not love at all; in which we do not see or have in mind the other man to whom it is directed; in which we do not and will not notice his weal or woe; in which we merely imagine him as the object of the love which we have to exercise, and in this way master and use him. Our only desire is to practise and unfold our own love, to demonstrate it to him and to others and to God and above all to ourselves, to find for ourselves self-expression in this sublime form. There is thus a form of love in which, however sacrificially it is practised, the other is not seized by a human hand but by a cold instrument, or even by a paw with sheathed talons, and therefore genuinely isolated and frozen and estranged and oppressed and humiliated, so that he feels that he is trampled under the feet of the one who is supposed to love him, and cannot react with gratitude. The great tragedy is that it is perhaps in the sphere of the neighbourly love established and shaped by Christianity, in Christian families and houses and societies and institutions, that we seem to have more frequent and shattering examples of this than in that of the worldly love, courtesy, affability and fellowship which are so much more shallow and undiscriminating, and therefore so much the less exacting. Certainly we have no reason to think that as Christians we have easily escaped from this whole field of inhumanity and its concealment.

The effectiveness of the concealment of this inherent inhumanity by various forms of philanthropy is beyond question. As a rule it is broken only in relatively few individuals, and in the lives of the rest of us only occasionally in comparatively harmless and excusable forms. More widespread penetration can be expected at certain times of crisis. Then inhumanity may and can burst every barrier and emerge in all kinds of wild and savage forms—to the horror of those who are not directly implicated. The bottom of the steep incline may then be revealed in many people, even in individuals or circles where we would [441] least expect to see it. Man collectively may take on a terrifying and monstrous appearance. But these critical periods usually pass, and they are followed by periods of relative calm in which civilised life is resumed and these dangerous manifestations are again regarded as exceptional. The inhuman element withdraws for the most part into the wings. We are again ashamed of it. We would rather not mention the names which it has assumed and the events which betray its savagery. The face of society is again dominated by more or less sacred causes and the more or less sacred devotion they inspire. And in the light or half-light which they shed the situation again becomes fairly normal and tolerable. It again appears to be an excited and pessimistic and unjustifiable and disruptive exaggeration to point to certain unsettling but isolated phenomena as a reason for maintaining that this inhuman element is always present; that it is at work even in these various forms of philanthropy; that every man is at bottom inhuman; that according to the well-known and much contested formula of the *Heidelberg Catechism* he is inclined by nature to hate God and his neighbour. Those who say this are themselves open to accusation as troublers of Israel, enemies of the human race, and guilty of a genuine inhumanity. The inhuman nature within us laughs at prophets of this kind, lurking, until the next outbreak, where it best loves to lurk, in the concealment of a good and necessary and solemnly exercised activity. In the same way its outbreaks in the life of the individual are only the relatively few interruptions of its normal existence in the concealment in which its words and acts and attitudes are remembered as though it had never been, its whole activity now taking the very human rather than inhuman form of devotion to a cause. Everything now seems to be intact and in order again, so that the charge that everything is really in disorder, and profoundly inhuman, may easily be dismissed as irrelevant. The power and effectiveness of this concealment cannot be too highly assessed.

Yet the concealment cannot alter the fact that the inhumanity which disguises itself as philanthropy does actually emerge, not only in its occasional individual or collective outbursts, but also in all the other spheres of that which makes a man a man.

If the bond which joins us to our fellow-men is hazarded and mortally endangered, so too is (1) that which unites us with God. We have described the dissolution of our relationship with our fellows as the necessary consequence of the dissolution of our relationship with God. But the folly of man is caught in a vicious circle, and the converse is also true that stupidity is always a necessary consequence of inhumanity. The clear-cut statements of 1 Jn. 4^{20} are apposite in this connexion: "If a man say, I love God, and hateth his brother, he is a liar: for he that loveth not his brother whom he hath seen, how can he love God whom he hath not seen?" He cannot do so. The relationship of man with his visible fellow-man is not in itself and as such a relationship with God. But since God is the God of his fellow as well as his God, the latter inexorably [442] includes the former. The former is the horizontal line to which the vertical is related and without which it would not be a vertical. In non-mathematical terms, I cannot know and honour and love God as my God if in the words of the Lord's Prayer I do not do so as *our* God, as the God of the race which He has created, and therefore if I do not also know and honour and love in the appropriate way those who are members of this race as I am. If I choose myself in my isolation from other men, *eo ipso*[EN35] I enter the sphere of the even more terrible isolation in which God can no longer be my God. If they are indifferent to me, I am involved wittingly or unwittingly in indifference to Him. If I can despise men, the praise which I may bring ever so willingly and joyfully to God will stick in my throat. If I merely exploit my neighbour according to my own needs, I will certainly think that I can do the same with God, and it will be my painful experience to find that He will not permit this. I have in fact hated and despised and wounded and attacked God if I have done this—not perhaps in actions, but "merely" with my words or in my heart—in relation to my brother. And if I have not done to him what I ought to have done, *eo ipso*[EN36] I have not done it in relation to God. In short, if I am inhuman, I am also stupid and foolish and godless. The great crisis in which all worship and piety and adoration and prayer and theology constantly finds itself derives of course from the question whether and how far in these things we really have to do with the true and living God who reveals Himself in His Word, and not with an idol. But this question is decided concretely in practice by another one which is inseparable from it—whether and how far in these things we come before God together and not apart from and against one another. True Christianity cannot be a private Christianity, i.e., a rapacious Christianity. Inhumanity at once makes it a counterfeit Christianity. It is not merely a superficial blemish. It cuts at the very root of the confidence and comfort and joy, of the whole *parresia*[EN37], in which we should live as Christians, and of the witness which Christianity owes to the world.

For all that the lack of faith, or plight of doubt, is so profound and tragic, it has also to be asked whether the doubter has not also to consider how many men he has evaded and rejected, how many he has wounded and tormented, how many he may even have murdered in the sense of the Gospel, and whether he seriously thinks that he can find joy or even solid confidence in his faith in the light of this fact. And if—not without justice—we usually complain from the Christian angle that the increasing disintegration of human society is connected with the great modern apostasy from faith, the counter-question has also to be put whether it may not be the great secularisation and de-humanisation of human life in society which, having been so successfully accomplished without any serious or timely protest on the part of the Church or Christianity, have necessarily involved the great apostasy from faith.

[443] If man wills and chooses inhumanity, he can only imagine that he can believe and attain to a knowledge of God. After a time he is forced to admit that, however earnestly he may desire or seriously he may attempt it, he cannot actually do so. At the point where it is a matter of God and His words and acts, where there can and should and must be the *intellectus fidei*[EN38], he is dealing with pure illusions and myths. Without one's fellow-man, God is an illusion, a myth. He may be the God of Holy Scripture, and we may call upon Him as the

---

[EN35] by that very fact
[EN36] by the same token
[EN37] freedom
[EN38] understanding of faith

Yahweh of Israel and the Father of Jesus Christ, but He is an idol in whom we certainly cannot believe. This is the first thing which no concealment of our inhumanity can alter.

Again, the way leads directly from man's inhumanity (2) to a collapse of the structure and order of his human nature as the soul of his body, of the order in which he is he himself. Without his fellow-man he cannot be that which he would obviously like to be when he withdraws into himself—he himself in this totality, as the soul of his body. And I cannot and will not be an I without a Thou. If he does not see and hear the Thou, the other I which lives in this Thou (in distinction from all other objects), the automatic result is that he for his part is not seriously accepted and posited as a Thou (and therefore as the living I that he would like to be). How can he accept and posit himself when by his very nature he can be accepted and posited as himself, as this man, only in his co-existence with the other, only in his confrontation with him? If he will not give himself to this other, he himself withers and perishes. Nor can a preoccupation with causes afford any substitute for that which only his fellow-man can offer him—the acceptance and positing of himself. It can do this only when in it he has a concern for man, and not to be free from man. If it is merely an instrument of this concealment he will not find himself in it; he will lose himself. He will lose both soul and finally body and become a mere vehicle of the cause, a wheel which drives and is itself driven. He is then submerged in it. It consumes him. But this need not happen. The fellow-man in whose company he might come to himself is always there. Indeed, he is waiting for him. For he, too, might come to himself with him. But the help must be reciprocal. It is no use if he is indifferent or hostile to him. In the measure that he is this, he brings about his own undoing. He can only achieve his own destruction. He can only live to his death. He can only be sick: sick of the relationship in which he stands but which he also lacks because he refuses to fulfil it; sick of his fellow-man who is always there but to whom he will not be a fellow. The real truth is that we are all openly or secretly sick of one another, of our mutual refusals, of the isolation in which we each think that we can help ourselves better without the other, of the pricks or blows with which we all try to assert ourselves and only do ourselves more harm than others. In the process it is we primarily who are abused and abased. Who among us does not in some way get on the nerves of all others? We should have to take one another to heart if it were to be otherwise. But that is the very thing which our inhuman nature will [444] not have. And its lordship triumphs always in the fact that most of all we get on our own nerves. The order of our psychical and physical nature, to which the nerves also belong, is not attuned to the lordship of our inhuman nature. It can only break under it. The price of the self-contradiction in which we involve ourselves with our contradiction of others can only be suffering; the suffering which we heap up to ourselves. And it is a mortal sickness which we give ourselves and from which we necessarily suffer. This is the second thing which the concealment of our inhumanity may conceal but cannot remove.

Our inhumanity extends (3) to human life as characterised by its limited temporal duration. "It moves quickly away, as if we fled from it" (Ps. 90¹⁰). But how does it move away? The fulness, if there is such, of the time allotted to each of us (our life-time), that which when we have lived our lives will be before God and in His judgment, is our history. *Our* history? It is ours only as we have lived and experienced and actualised and suffered it together with others, in a stretch of time which is theirs too. It is our history as the history of our relations with our contemporaries in the narrower and wider and widest sense of the term, including the older generation which accompanied us yesterday and the younger which already accompanies us to-day. It is the consecutive series, constituted in our striding from the past, through the present and into the future, of our encounters and fellowship with concrete men, which may directly or indirectly include men of the preceding generation, and often does so, together with those who belong to the age which follows. It is our part, our responsible co-operation, in world-history. But if we are guilty of withdrawal, i.e., from our fellow-men, in this history, what are we in our time? What is the meaning of our life? Why have we been given time to live and work? How shall we stand before God and in His judgment? Will this not be brought against us? Will we not be accused? You were no help to me in my history which was interwoven with yours. You ignored me. I was of no interest to you. You disappointed me when I waited for you. You had no time for me. You merely played with me. Or again, you only appeared to help, but in reality harmed me. You led me astray, so that it was only with the greatest difficulty, if at all, that I was able to get back to the right path. You confirmed me in that from which you ought to have kept me. And you kept me from that in which I needed confirmation. Or again, you would not yield to me. In your great righteousness, or simply because you were the stronger, you pushed me to the wall. You humiliated and wounded me. You trampled over me contemptuously and perhaps even derisively, pursuing your own ends. For some reason which I cannot understand you blocked my path. You surrendered and betrayed me.

[445] You took from me the dearest that I had. The encounter with you cost me my life. Yes, we shall certainly have to render our accounts in relation to others, and we must see to it that they are in good order. But who of us will have any real advantage over the rest? Will we not all have our own burden of accusation? And what will be the net result for us all if the only upshot is an awful conflict of mutual recriminations? Will it have been worth while to have lived for this fulness, this harvest, of our time? We have to consider that the inhuman element in us all wills that we should pass our time in this way. It aims at this fulness, this harvest, of our time. It makes this history. Of course, it conceals this. It hides from us the fact that we give to our time this content. It consoles both itself and us with the reference to all kinds of causes which we finely and usefully espouse in the course of our time. It covers over the fact that we espouse them apart from and even against the other man who waits for us. Openly and under this cover it makes our life a history of these lost and wasted

opportunities. Nor will it save this history that it has also been a history in which we have actually been busy with various causes. This is the third consequence that we have to consider in this connexion.

Here, then, we have the second aspect of the man who is affirmed before God in the one Jesus and exalted with Him to fellowship with God. As seen in the light of this One, he is this slothful and wicked shirker, not only in relation to God, but also in relation to his fellow. God knows him as this sinner. In spite of his sin, He has had pity on him, and continues to do so. In his reconciliation it is a matter of raising him up out of his inhumanity. On the one hand, he will not know his fellow-man; he will not be his keeper (Gen. 4^9); he is his murderer. But on the other—and this is the greater and final truth—he is told, as the disciples were, by the One who was judged in the place of Barabbas (Lk. 23^{25}): "All ye are brethren" (Mt. 23^8).

We will again illustrate the situation from the Bible, and we will choose for this purpose the sin of Israel as it is exposed by the prophet Amos in his message of impending judgment. We call him the prophet, although he is not only the oldest of the so-called writing prophets of the Old Testament but also the one who in 7^{14} expressly refused to be called a prophet or a prophet's son. In Northern Israel, where he ministered, this could only mean concretely that he did not wish to be regarded or accepted as a successor in the tradition which had had its acknowledged representatives for good or evil in Elijah and Elisha. His own distinctive description of himself is as follows: "I was an herdman, and a gatherer of sycomore fruit," and in the title he is introduced as "the herdman of Tekoa" in the Southern state of Judah (1^1). He does not come from the peasant class, the agricultural proletariat, but, as his style seems to suggest, he is himself a proprietor. Yet his message cannot be explained by his social origin and situation. "*Yahweh* took me as I followed the flock" (7^{15}). Although he did not belong to the prophetic class but was engaged in farming, God gave him a function which seemed to be interchangeable with the speech and action of the prophets (as was recognised by Amaziah the priest of Bethel in $7^{10f.}$), but which he himself regarded as separate and distinct. He, too, speaks in the name of *Yahweh* and in proclamation of His will and purpose as the Lord of the history of Israel. He, too, comes forward with a public denunciation. He, too, appeals directly to visions which he has been granted. Even the fact that his addresses contain warnings is not regarded as anything intrinsically new, as we learn from the account of that interview with Amaziah. [446]

What is it then that gives him this consciousness of being out of the ordinary? It is the absolutely direct compulsion by which he is constrained to speak. He does not do so because it was foreseen and prepared in his earlier life. He does so because he is overtaken, as it were, by an impelling force which he cannot escape. "The lion hath roared, who will not fear? the Lord God hath spoken, who can but prophesy," he says himself in 3^8 at the end of a whole series of metaphors which all describe the same thing—that he is aware of himself only as the effect of an all-powerful cause which objectively is described in the first saying ascribed to him in 1^2: "The Lord will roar from Zion, and utter his voice from Jerusalem." Because and as he must lend his human mouth to this voice, he has to go to Northern Israel and cause trouble in the national sanctuary of Bethel, being advised to leave the country as an undesirable alien ($7^{10f.}$). His appearance is not just a continuation of the previous history of the country, but marks a critical turning-point which is no less surprising to himself than others.

But there is a second peculiarity closely bound up with the first. This is that his message is so unequivocally a message of judgment. The evil which he proclaims is definitive and total.

It is the destruction of the whole kingdom and nation and people of Northern Israel. As we read in $2^{13f.}$ at the beginning of the book: "Behold, I will press the ground under you, as a cart is pressed that is full of sheaves. Therefore the flight shall perish from the swift, and the strong shall not strengthen his force, neither shall the mighty deliver himself: neither shall he stand that handleth the bow; and he that is swift of foot shall not deliver himself: neither shall he that rideth the horse deliver himself. And he that is courageous among the mighty shall flee away naked in that day, saith the Lord." And then again at the end in 9^{8a} and 10: "Behold, the eyes of the Lord God are upon the sinful kingdom, and I will destroy it from off the face of the earth …. All the sinners of the people shall die by the sword, which say, The evil shall not overtake nor prevent us." The evil has not yet come. Amos speaks two years before the earthquake, as we learn from words in the introduction which are surely not without significance (1^1). But it is ineluctably determined and it draws inexorably near. The warnings given by the previous judgments of *Yahweh* had all been in vain: "Yet hath ye not returned unto me, saith the Lord" (five times in $4^{6f.}$). Amos had even entreated God for the "small" people Jacob. And "the Lord repented for this: It shall not be, saith the Lord." This was the result of the first two visions in $7^{1f.}$ and $7^{4f.}$. But then the result of the third is: "I will not again pass by them any more: and the high places of Isaac shall be desolate, and the sanctuaries of Israel shall be laid waste; and I will rise against the house of Jeroboam with the sword" ($7^{7f.}$). The result of the fourth is similar: "The end is come upon my people of Israel: I will not again pass by them any more. And the songs of the temple shall be howlings in that day, saith the Lord God: there shall be many dead bodies in every place; they shall cast them forth with silence" ($8^{1f.}$). So, too, is that of the fifth: "I saw the Lord standing upon the altar: and he said, Smite the lintel of the door, that the posts may shake: and cut them in the head, all of them; and I will slay the last of them with the sword; he that fleeth of them shall not flee away, and he that escapeth of them shall not be delivered. Though they dig into hell, thence shall mine hand take them; though they climb up to heaven, thence will I bring them down. And though they hide themselves in the top of Carmel, I will search and take them out thence; and though they be hid from my sight in the bottom of the sea, thence will I command the serpent, and he shall bite them … and I will set mine eyes upon them for evil, and

[447]

not for good" ($9^{1f.}$). It is all summed up in anticipation in the lament of $5^{2f.}$: "The virgin of Israel is fallen; she shall no more rise: she is forsaken upon her land; there is none to raise her up." The roaring of *Yahweh* from Zion, and the voice of the herdman of Tekoa, is that this is irrevocably resolved. And none of the recognised prophets prior to Amos had ever said this, not even Elijah.

But the third and decisive peculiarity of his message consists in the fact—and this is what makes it particularly interesting and relevant in our present context—that the accusation which he has to make against Northern Israel, and which is the reason for his proclamation of judgment, is so one-sidedly concrete and specific. Only a century has passed since the bitter conflict between Elijah and Ahab and Jezebel, but there is hardly a mention of the Baal-cult which then triumphed on so wide a front. Had this problem ceased to have any relevance? At any rate, Amos is not in any way concerned with it. Nor is he concerned, like his younger contemporary Isaiah, with actions in the field of high politics which are contrary to the covenant. Was Jeroboam II not guilty of similar actions? It is not on this account, however, that Amos proclaims the certain and imminent and total destruction of Israel. Nor is his accusation directed (except perhaps tacitly) against the person or internal policy of this monarch. It is simply and solely the inhumanity of the social relationships obtaining in this kingdom which so seriously and radically and blatantly challenges Amos—and in the first instance *Yahweh* himself—that there can be proclaimed to it only His wrath, and the outpouring of His wrath as it is irrevocably determined and menacingly impends, and the end of the nation as its final consequence. His accusation—the reason for this threat as it is

2. The Sloth of Man

laid on his lips with that direct urgency and that by-passing of the prophetic tradition—is focused with astonishing exclusiveness upon the one point that in this state one man does not live and deal with others as he ought to do according to the will of *Yahweh*; that wrong is done on the horizontal level of human relationships, and therefore on the vertical level of the relationship of the people of *Yahweh* to *Yahweh* Himself as the Creator and Lord of its history. The earlier prophets and their disciples had never spoken in this way. The prophecy of Amos acquires a new character even for himself from the fact that he refuses the role of a prophet and—apart from the commission of *Yahweh*—wants to appear and to be heard only as a herdman and a gatherer of sycomore fruits. In other words, he proclaims *Yahweh* as the God of the fellow-man who has been wronged and humiliated and oppressed by man, and as the Avenger who has been challenged to direct and implacable action by what has been done to him. It is to be noted that this is shown to be the decisive matter in the complaints made in the first two chapters against the neighbouring states—Damascus ($1^{3f.}$), the Philistines ($1^{6f.}$), the Edomites ($1^{11f.}$), the Ammonites ($1^{13f.}$) and the Moabites ($2^{1f.}$). The three, yes four transgressions of these other nations all consist in offences against humanity. They are not in covenant with *Yahweh*, but they are judged no less by the standard of His righteous will, and like Israel they fall victims to His judgment because of their transgression in this respect. But the charge acquires sharp and concentrated form only when it is made against Israel, and it is in this form that it dominates the whole collection of pronouncements made by Amos. As it is uttered with this one-sidedness and emphasis, the protest of Amos is something entirely new. The presentation given in the Books of Kings does not prepare us for the advancement of this as a reason for the wrath of *Yahweh* as it has obviously accumulated over a long period but has now suddenly become an imminent threat which cannot be averted. Certainly we find the same strand in Isaiah, but in his case it is only one among many. It is not omitted by the younger prophet of Northern Israel, Hosea, but the main attention of Hosea is directed elsewhere. The note sounded by Amos occurs again and again in later prophecy—and sometimes very loudly. But the remarkable feature of the message of Amos as the [448] first to sound it is that his accusation is confined to this strand. That is why we cannot fail to hear him. That is why his particular contribution to the biblical message is that the affair of God is the affair of man; the affair of the fellow-man who is so severely and constantly hurt by man, and so inflexibly and relentlessly championed and defended by God. In the history of the active exposition of the Bible it is not for nothing that on the one hand Amos has been so frequently neglected and that on the other he has been the classical biblical witness for all the movements in which the conscience of the Church has been reawakened in this direction, and therefore to a repudiation of the base and dangerous overlooking of this basic element in Christian truth and the revealed Word of God Himself.

The middle of the 8th century, in which the accusation of Amos was made, was not a time of war or crisis. On the contrary, it was for both the Northern and Southern kingdoms (cf. M. Noth, *Geschichte Israels*, 1950, 216 f.) a kind of golden age—the period of restoration after their long oppression by the Aramaeans, who had succumbed to the Assyrians about 800 B.C. It is true that according to 2 K. $14^{23f.}$ Jeroboam II fell under the stereotyped judgment passed on all the Northern rulers. He had done that which was not pleasing to *Yahweh*, and had not separated himself from the sin of the first Jeroboam, which according to 1 K. $12^{25f.}$ had consisted in the institution of a separate cult of *Yahweh* before images of bulls erected in Bethel and Dan. Yet the same passage acknowledges his services in the recovery of Israel's former territory (from Hamath to the sea of the plain) and the military skill and valour which he had demonstrated in this achievement. Indeed, it is expressly said that *Yahweh* did not will to "blot out the name of Israel from under heaven: but he saved them by the hand of Jeroboam the son of Joash." This relatively happy state of political affairs must be considered together (M. Noth, p. 189) with a certain high-water-mark in a development which had begun already in the time of David and Solomon—that of a civic life modelled on the customs of the Canaanites, and the corresponding civilisation, the emergence of trade and commerce, the beginning of a monetary economy, and the consequent creation of distinctions between those who were economically, and then socially and politically, strong and those who were weak. This is the situation in which the Lord roars from Zion and the herdman of Tekoa speaks.

Is he merely voicing the resentment of the older farming community against this modern development as such? As an educated countryman he might well have seen how mistaken it was far more clearly than those who had a direct part in it. But his accusation is far too basic and radical to be understood merely in terms of this kind of opposition. The prophet is not a statesman or sociologist. We must remember this if we are to understand his denunciation. For it means that, apart from a few flagrant instances, the evils of the situation as Amos censured them were not perhaps quite so palpable and blatant as his actual words might seem to suggest. To their own and our advantage and disadvantage, politicians and sociologists do not usually see visions. But a prophet does. And this means that in the historical reality around him he not only sees what is obvious and characterises it as any other critical and far-seeing observer might do. He is also given to see with the eyes of God, and he therefore sees to the bottom of things, and therefore gives them the name which they might not have, or generally have, in their external appearance, but which they have at root, in the light of the dominating factor in them, so that if they do not deserve the name according to human righteousness, they certainly do so according to the righteousness of God. It is for this reason that Amos stands under the compulsion, which is also as such his prophetic freedom, to foresee and proclaim their inevitable consequence—the judgment to which they irresistibly move. How could Amos have been a prophet (the prophet who did not wish to be a prophet) if his picture of the present and future had not stood in opposition to the more harmless or equivocal pictures which any acute contemporary might have painted of the same situation, or any pragmatic historian might still form of it. On the level of ordinary human perception and thought and speech (apart from the fact that he spoke the true Word of God), the truth of his vision was and is guaranteed only by the fulfilment of all that he had seen and said in the year 722. It is in this sense, therefore, that we have to ask what it was that he saw.

[449]

He saw first the prosperity and even luxury enjoyed by the circles which exploited that development and acquired power and authority and influence by means of it. He saw their accumulated possessions (3^{10}), their houses of hewn stone and pleasant vineyards (5^{11}), the convenience of separate residences for winter and summer (3^{15}), and the lavishness of their furnishings, especially the comfortable divans (3^{12} and 6^4) and the ivory-work (3^{15} and 6^4) that king Ahab had already so extravagantly affected (1 K. 22^{39}). He saw them luxuriously reclining at their meals. He saw and heard those "that chant to the sound of the viol, and invent to themselves songs, like David; that drink wine in bowls, and anoint themselves with the chief ointments" ($6^{4f.}$). He saw the "kine of Basan" on the mountain of Samaria (4^1), namely, the ladies of this society, the fat and greasy wives of these pashas (to use the words of B. Duhm, *Israels Propheten*, 1916, 129), who say to their husbands: "Bring, and let us drink." Do we really hear in these descriptions "the champion of the old and simple customs ... his opposition to new ways and foreign extravagance" (Duhm, p. 130)? Is Amos to be hailed as a precursor of J. J. Rousseau? Or when all these things are severely denounced and threatened with divine judgment, are they contested in the sense of modern reforming movements directed against luxury, gluttony and drunkenness (as interpreted by L. Ragaz in his biblical studies)? This is certainly implied. But it is to be noted that in the text itself hardly one of these charges stands alone or has independent significance. If Amos saw that all this striving was condemned and rejected by God, it was because it constituted the folly of what in 6^6 he calls "the affliction of Joseph," for which this society has no concern but which directly or indirectly, consciously or unconsciously, it has helped to cause and to bring about; the situation and fate of those for whom this golden age had no rewards, who were its victims, who were defrauded and oppressed by those who exploited it. Hence: "I abhor the excellency of Jacob, and hate his palaces" (6^8).

No picture is given of the situation of those who are oppressed and in darkness to offset the description of the life of the well-to-do. From the various attacks, however, we can see how they came to be pushed more and more into the darkness by those who enjoyed the light. This is the point which concerns Amos, and, according to his message, *Yahweh* Himself. It is because of this oppression of those who are less favoured, and therefore weaker, by those who further their own interest and in their greater glory constitute a higher society that God looks down in judgment and must bring this whole people under sentence of death. What is the reverse side of all this prosperity and success? What is the foundation of this proud and ambitious structure? A righteous man is sold as a slave because he cannot redeem a debt, and a poor man for the value of a pair of shoes (2^6). They drink the wine which they have purchased with fines on defaulting tenants and they stretch themselves upon pawned clothes (2^8). The innocent are harassed (5^{12}), the weak oppressed, and the needy crushed (for which the fine ladies of 4^1 are rather curiously blamed). The sick are pushed to the wall and their head is rolled in the dust (2^7). A particular occasion for this kind of conduct must have offered itself in the wheat market, which seemed to have been cornered by a few, and in which the consumers were burdened and cheated by all kinds of tricks masquerading as honest dealings ("making the ephah small, and the shekel great, and falsifying the balances by deceit," 8^5), and the small producers by all kinds of exactions (5^{11}). The inhabitants of [450] Assyria and Egypt should come and see all these things, cries Amos: "Assemble yourselves upon the mountains of Samaria, and behold the great tumult in the midst thereof, and the oppression in the midst thereof. For they know not to do right, saith the Lord, who store up violence and robbery in their palaces" ($3^{9f.}$).

And now there follows what is obviously the decisive characteristic of the situation as it is seen in the message of Amos. There is no actual law to restrain the great and protect the poor. There is, of course, a traditional, and perhaps even to some extent a written, code. There are also judges. In every town there is the "gate"—the open place within the city gate where markets were held and where on certain days there was the opportunity for complaints to be laid before leading citizens appointed to hear them. But of what value was this when the "gate" was the very place where the poor were oppressed (5^{12})? when the justice which was sought was turned to wormwood (5^7) and even poison (6^{12})? when those who administered it took bribes (5^{12})? when they were the very ones against whom justice was demanded? or when there was no wish to lose their favour, and it was known only too well that "they hate him that rebuketh in the gate, and they abhor him that speaketh uprightly" (5^{10})? Perhaps 5^{13} refers to a cautious man of this kind who is uneasy about the whole matter: "Therefore the prudent shall keep silent in that time; for it is an evil time." At any rate, there can be no doubt that the voice of righteousness is not heard even, and especially, at the gate; that might takes precedence of right. Who, then, is to help the poor? Amos knows that even in his day there are obviously men of God in Samaria who might be considered in this connexion: "And I raised up of your sons for prophets, and of your young men for Nazirites. Is it not even thus, O ye children of Israel? saith the Lord" (2^{11}). But even this voice has been silenced: "But ye gave the Nazirites wine to drink; and commanded the prophets, saying, Prophesy not" (2^{12})—the very same order as was given to Amos himself. Thus *Yahweh* alone was left as the Friend and Champion and Helper and just Judge of the weak and poor who had suffered through this development—no, through the inhumanity of man to man. It was with His commission and in His name that Amos appeared in Samaria: "The Lord hath sworn by the excellency of Jacob (and therefore by Himself), Surely I will never forget any of their works" (8⁷).

Yahweh Himself! But are there not centres of *Yahweh* worship in Israel—especially the monarchy and the national shrine at Bethel (7¹³)? It is at this point that the accusation of Amos gains its full and final sharpness. It should be noted that his famous polemic against the cult in Northern Israel is hardly directed at all against its obvious syncretistic decadence. He certainly saw this. But it was not his present concern. It is recalled only in the tilt at temple prostitution in 2⁷ (for in 5²⁶: "Siccuth your king, and Chiun the star of your god," we seem to have a later addition, since according to 2 K. 17²⁹ᶠ these were the gods of the foreigners who settled in the country after the fall of Samaria). Even the bull-images of *Yahweh* set up by Jeroboam I do not figure in the attacks of Amos. He took the cult of Northern Israel as a serious cult of *Yahweh* even in the form in which he found it. And he attacked it as such; as *usus*ᴱᴺ³⁹ and not in the light of an *abusus*ᴱᴺ⁴⁰. The truth was that the whole inhumanity and injustice of Samarian society allied itself, not with a worship of gods or idols, but quite decorously with the worship of *Yahweh*; that it was concealed and legitimated by this worship; that it was from the shrine of *Yahweh* that the message of 7¹⁰ could be sent by the high-priest Amaziah to the king: "Amos hath conspired against thee in the midst of the house of Israel: the land is not able to bear all his words," and that Amos himself could be given the command which almost sound like an entreaty: "O thou seer, go, flee thee away into the land of Judah, and there eat bread, and prophesy there: but prophesy not again any more at Bethel" (7¹²ᶠ·).

[451] These were the communications of an ecclesiastic (not a heathen ecclesiastic, but a representative of the Church of *Yahweh*) who obviously regarded as self-evident the union not only of throne and altar (the altar of *Yahweh*) but also of mammon and altar. It is because of this alliance, because of the fact that the evil is masked by the good, the unholy by the holy, that Amos is even more severe in his condemnation of Samarian religion than in that of Samarian worldliness, proclaiming the pitiless judgment of God which will overtake this society not although, but just because, it is so religious a society. "Come to Bethel; and transgress; at Gilgal multiply transgressions; and bring your sacrifices every morning, and your tithes on the third day. And offer a sacrifice of thanksgiving with leaven, and proclaim and publish the free offerings: for this liketh you, O ye children of Israel" (4⁴ᶠ·). What is the verdict of the One in whose worship and to whose glory all this is done? "I hate, I despise your feast days, and I will not smell in your solemn assemblies. Though ye offer me burnt offerings and your meat offerings, I will not accept them: neither will I regard the peace offerings of your fat beasts. Take away from me the noise of your songs; for I will not hear the melody of your viols" (5²¹ᶠ·). *Yahweh* is not dependent on their *Yahweh*-worship; He led Israel in the wilderness without Israel bringing any sacrifices (5²⁵). But their *Yahweh*-worship is dependent upon *Yahweh*. It can be offered only in fulfilment of His will and not to conceal its inversion. If it is offered only for the purpose of this concealment, it would be better not offered at all. This is what is meant when Amos says: "Seek ye me, and ye shall live: but seek not Bethel, nor enter into Gilgal, and pass not to Beersheba" (5⁴ᶠ·). Seek me, however, means "Seek good, and not evil, that ye may live: and so the Lord, the God of hosts, will be with you, as ye have spoken" (5¹⁴). "Hate the evil, and love the good, and establish judgment in the gate: it may be that the Lord God of hosts will be gracious unto the remnant of Joseph" (5¹⁵). "Let judgment run down as waters, and righteousness as a mighty stream" (5²⁴). This is what has to be done, and because it was not done Israel's worship of *Yahweh*, far from compensating the unrighteousness of its life, demanded His wrath and judgment. He did not need the stream of their gifts; what was required was that they should exercise righteousness to their

---

ᴱᴺ³⁹ use
ᴱᴺ⁴⁰ abuse

fellows. "*Yahweh* will not be worshipped, but will destroy, those who have no regard for justice" (Duhm, *op. cit.*, p. 133).

Finally, they hope for a "day of *Yahweh*"; for the fulfilment of His promise as the Lord of the covenant which He has made with them. His people, in the inauguration of a glorious age which will surpass, with God's help, even the prosperity which they already enjoy. Well, God has not forgotten that He is the Lord of the covenant, and that as such His promise must be kept. On the contrary, is He not accusing and threatening "the whole family which I brought up from the land of Egypt" (3¹)?—as He also brought the Philistines from Caphtor and the Syrians from Kir (9⁷). He can say indeed: "You only have I known of all the families of the earth," but it is for this very reason that He must also add: "Therefore I will punish you for all your iniquities" (3²). The very grace which has been addressed to them and which they have rejected will necessarily be their judgment. That day will come, but it will be a very different day from what they think. It will come as a day of the judgment of God which will necessarily fall on them with a final severity just because they are His people. Therefore, "woe unto you that desire the day of the Lord! to what end is it for you? the day of the Lord is darkness, and not light. As if a man did flee from a lion, and a bear met him; or went into the house, and leaned his hand on the wall, and a serpent bit him. Shall not the day of the Lord be darkness, and not light? even very dark, and no brightness in it?" (5¹⁸ᶠ·).

According to Amos, God has no other answer to the inhumanity of man than that it can only be, and has already been, rejected like his stupidity. God would have to be unfaithful to Himself, and to the covenant with man which He has made in His covenant with Israel, if He were to withdraw or even weaken this answer. He maintains the covenant by placing the inhumanity of man under His merciless denunciation and the judgment which remorselessly engulfs it. [452]

3. Again we begin with the statement that in the existence of the man Jesus we have to do with the true and normal form of human nature, and therefore with authentically human life. He lives according to the Spirit even as He is flesh. This means concretely that He lives wholly to God and His fellow-man. He lives, therefore, in one long exaltation, purification, sanctification and dedication of the flesh, i.e., of the human nature which we know only as flesh, only in its abnormal form, only in its decomposition. His life is its normalisation. It is thus the man who has come to himself who encounters us in Him; the man who is at peace with himself as the soul of his body. He lives in the unity intended for the human creature, in the relationship of soul and body ordained in conformity with our nature. He Himself is wholly soul and wholly body. And both as soul and body He is wholly Himself, the soul of His body in its free control, the body of His soul in its free service. He is man as we are, but in this royal freedom: not, of course, in a freedom which He has attained, or which has been lent or given Him; but originally, in His own freedom. He has His life in Himself. He fashions and normalises it. It is thus His own life which He both lives and can and does also offer as a free gift for us men in obedience to the will of God. He makes it a life for God and us, and therefore an incomparable life as His life in His time. He comes from the Spirit and lives according to the Spirit. The Spirit is not, therefore, an alien Spirit, but His own Spirit, in which He is flesh, and exalts and purifies and sanctifies and dedicates the flesh. Again we are forced to say that this is true only of Him, the Son of Man,

who is also the Son of God; and that in this respect He is exalted above all other men. But in this way it is God's valid and effective direction for us which we meet in Him. In a man like ourselves there confronts us the truth of our nature, the sanctity and dignity and right of man, the glory of human life. If, therefore, we receive His Spirit, we know ourselves in Him as those who are elected and created and determined for existence in the truth of His human nature, for an authentically human life.

But in this respect, too, we are those who, confronted by Him, refuse to be those we already are in Him, hesitating to make use of the freedom of the Spirit in the flesh which we are given in Him. Inactive where we ought to be stirred to action, we remain in a being as flesh without spirit, and therefore in a state of disorder, living our lives accordingly. We may describe this—in keeping with the force of the two terms "stupidity" and "inhumanity" which we have already used—as a life of dissipation. This is the third form of the sloth in which we withdraw into ourselves instead of existing as those we already are in and by that One.

[453] Here again, we must first maintain the futility of this form of withdrawal. The normalisation of our nature, the event of the glory of human life, has taken place once and for all in Jesus. This man who in royal freedom is the soul of His body lives—and lives as our Lord and Head and Representative. His direction is issued and it comes to us all. It cannot be reversed. No dissipation of ours can form an absolute contradiction to it. His direction has reference to that to which we are elected and created and determined as men; to ourselves as God irrevocably and from all eternity wills to have us. It summons us to be those we originally are. We cannot be destroyed or expunged as such. We can certainly interrupt God's purpose. But we can do so only as we involve ourselves in self-contradiction. Dissipation involves waste or neglect, and a resultant disorder, discord and degeneration. But we cannot degenerate to such an extent that we cease to be that which God has created us—men. We can live as though we were either mere spirits or mere animals or plants—dissipation involves both—but we cannot actually be spirits or animals or plants. Our souls and bodies constantly proclaim their rights and assert their power, and always in the direction of their original unity in which the soul controls the body and the body serves the soul. Their division, the conflict, the inversion of the order in which man is the soul of his body, is continually shown to be unnatural. As God and our fellow-men are there even though we may ignore and forget and oppose them, and as they show by their existence the falsity and error of our sloth, so we ourselves are there no matter how we may contradict ourselves. We protest, with superior right and greater power, against that which we do to ourselves. What we do is ultimately futile. In this respect, too, our choosing and willing of that which is not can create only a reality of the second order. In our dissipation, too, we cannot do more than practise our sin and reveal our shame. To say otherwise, to ascribe any greater power to the human sloth which has also this distinctive vileness, it would be necessary to call in question

72

the existence of the true man Jesus as the Lord and Head and Representative of all men.

All the same, in all its vileness as man's dissipation it is an undeniable fact. In this form, too, it is not nothing, but something. It is a real disposition of the human will and its decisions and achievements. As man does not will to know God, and as he wills to be without and even against his fellow-men, so he wills himself in the disorder, discord and degeneration of his nature, declining to make use of the freedom to be a whole man which is addressed and given to him in the direction of Jesus, and contracting out of the purifying and sanctifying and reforming movement which derives from Jesus. Our general definition of the sin of man in the form of sloth—that he lets himself fall—is particularly applicable to this aspect of it. Man goes down to ruin when he slips from the place which he is allotted by the grace of God. And he does this by his [454] own choice. He lets himself go. He lets himself be pushed. Where he himself can and should be moving and pushing, he allows himself to be moved and pushed. This means that he falls. He suffers a mishap. But it does not come upon him as a fatality. He brings it about himself by letting himself fall. Sin as sloth, in this particular form of dissipation, is indiscipline. To live as an authentic man would mean to keep oneself disciplined, to remain at the height to which one belongs as a man, to be what one is as a man even at the cost of severity against oneself. But it is here that (from this point of view) the great refusal takes place. In every one of us—and we cannot seek him deep enough in ourselves—there is a vagabond who will not accept discipline, and therefore will not exercise it in relation to himself, however gladly he may do so in relation to others. He prefers to receive permissions rather than commands, and because he regards himself as the supreme court he lives—the basic vagabond—by giving himself permissions rather than commands. But this involves a disruption of the unity in which he is a man. He disintegrates. His soul and body begin to go their separate ways. His soul will no longer control his body, nor his body obey his soul. The two not only contradict one another in their mutual relationship, but also, refusing their distinct function in this relationship, contradict their own essence as the two integrated elements of human nature. If the dissipated man wills, as he does, to be without spirit, he has entered on the irresistible way on which he will finally be soulless and bodiless; the way which can lead only to death.

Here again, we have to do with a decision from which we come in the details of what we do and do not do. It is a matter of the basic perversion of the human will which precedes all the great and little aberrations which are possible, necessary and actual in the light of it, and in which it takes concrete form. What takes place in man's detailed aberrations reflects the dissipation which in its original form, in its bitter root, is nothing other than the disobedience of man, his unbelief, his ingratitude, his enmity against the grace of God directed to him, the transgression of its law. This transgression as such is the law which all his thoughts and words and works will more or less obviously follow.

We do not underline this in order to see the practical dissipation of human life as a perhaps exculpating and atoning destiny. To do so would be particularly inappropriate at a point where it is a matter of our dealings with ourselves, and therefore of the neglect of our most direct responsibility. It has to be realised, however, that the dissipation of what we do and do not do has its efficacy from the fact that we want to be, although we are not, those who can exist only in a profoundly and diversely dissipated activity and inactivity. It was in the same light that we had to understand the ungodliness and inhumanity [455] of man. Everything would be so fine and simple if to set both ourselves and others on our feet we had only to indicate the vileness and guilt of our carnal thought and speech and action, the deep unnaturalness of our enterprises and achievements in that dualism of soul and body, and the dignity of a life lived in the unity and wholeness marked out for us; if we had only to enlighten both ourselves and others, and call us all to order. This enlightenment and call to order is something that we can and should seek both for ourselves and others. But the power of sin in this form is greater than that of any admonition of this kind. The whole history of morality (including Christian morality) has always tried to be a history of this particular appeal, of warfare in the name of the spirit against the flesh (as was thought), of the conflict for man himself, for his exaltation and preservation and against his disintegration and decline. Yet it is a fact that, superior to all morality, his sloth is continually re-enacted in continually fresh manifestations in this form; that the vagabond in us can always merrily escape the discipline which is brought to bear on him; that even the reference to the ruinous nature of his action never seems to make any serious or final impression on him. The appeal is finely made, perhaps, but it does not stick or penetrate. On the contrary, it seems to be defeated already by the power of sin in this form, so that it cannot gain a foothold even with the best of moral teaching. It is an unfortunate and supremely irrational fact, but one which we have obviously to see and to try to understand, that man himself, even as he makes this appeal to himself or others, even as he seriously participates in the history of morality, in that conflict, is the lazy and dissipated creature who sinks back into himself and hates and shuns discipline; that in relation to himself no less than to God and his fellows he is sinful man. That is why his dissipation is so powerful. That is why the appeal against it is so feeble and ineffective. How can human dissipation be arrested when in the first instance it is at work in the man who tries to make the moral appeal to himself and others, when he himself is one who in this respect wills what he ought not to will and does not will what he ought? If we do not realise this, especially in relation to ourselves, then in face of that unfortunate and irrational fact we can only take refuge in illusions or throw up our hands and finally give up in despair. The power of human dissipation, like that of human stupidity and inhumanity, is so great because man himself is no less dissipated than stupid and inhuman. It is from this source, from within ourselves, that our sloth draws its inexhaustible strength in this form too. That which is born of the flesh, and thought and said and chosen and done in the flesh, can only be flesh, and cannot overcome the flesh, even though it may have the character of a most serious and sharp protest against it.

It is to this as the source of evil that we must also look if we are to realise from this standpoint the dangerous nature of sin. We are again asking concerning the inner danger which is the basis of its awful effectiveness. From this standpoint, as we consider it in the form of man's dissipation, we have to say especially that it has a power which is released by man but itself enslaves him. We usually admit with some astonishment that the vagabond in ourselves and others is interesting to us; that he captivates us; that he fascinates and bewitches us; in a word, that he has power over us. If we examine the matter more closely, we find that it is the power of an inclination which we allow ourselves to follow. This is a serious matter because it is actually the case that its power leads to a disarmament of man and therefore to a supreme disinclination. But we are not aware of this. We do not want to be aware of it. More will have to be said about this later. In the first instance it is a power which is at work; the power of a definite inclination. It might be compared to the impulse of many children completely to take to pieces a toy which they are given, to divide it up into its constituent parts, and, of course, to make it quite useless. But do we not have an inclination—an irresistible inclination—to do this? We are all children in this way. It is our pleasure—and this is the awful positive element in what we have called our indiscipline—to decompose our human nature. We promise ourselves a certain satisfaction in doing this. We think that we are particularly human in our desire to do it. It may be that we relieve our soul of its office as the ruler and guardian and preserver of our body so that, freed from the material concerns and problems of the body, it may wander and hover and fly away on its own. Inevitably it seems desirable to us to lead what we consider to be a purely spiritual or inward life; to build a new and, as we think, eternal house in an academic world of thought or an aesthetic or religious world of dreams; to look, if possible, wholly to the things which are invisible, and as little as possible to those which are visible. This possibility can appear very fine and tempting, and the desire to grasp it very noble. It is only if we do not know it that we do not realise its power. When we give way to it, we will not so easily accept the fact that it is the power of an evil desire; that it too is only a particular form of the lust of this world; that it is a form of our dissipation; that it is sloth and therefore sin. Why should it not be holy? On the other hand, it may be that we release our body from the service of our soul and give it free rein to pursue its own impulses and needs. Surely it is desirable that we should grant it its sovereignty and rights, that in a true honesty and realism and self-acknowledgement we should express ourselves confidently and uninhibitedly in this way? This, too, can appear fine and tempting, and the desire to grasp this possibility justifiable, or at any rate strong. If we do not know it, or

[456]

[457] know it closely, we must not conclude too rashly that it has no power. We have only to acquaint ourselves with it to learn differently. Sensual desire, carnal lust, worldliness? Evil lust? The outworking of human dissipation, sloth and sin? A protest may be lodged against defining it in this way. Why should it not be holy even in this form? But, of course, these are only extreme possibilities which are seldom if ever realised in practice. The vagabond within us usually hovers somewhere between the two. One moment he goes off as a liberated soul into the heights; the next as a liberated body into the depths. Indeed, he does not just do one or the other. He does both at once. In what is perhaps the supreme and most refined form of desire, he darts from the one to the other, toying with both at once, denying himself here and confessing himself there, confessing himself here and denying himself there, putting forth his attractions now in the one form and now in the other, and deploying his power to the full in this coquettish dance with its almost innumerable variations. When man has released this power, and is himself enslaved by it, how can he ever be free again? It is dangerous because, in the one form or the other, it is the power of a genuine desire of the heart which exercises a distinctive control over man, but also proceeds from within him. We must also point finally to the fact that in this form too, as the desire of one awakens and inflames that of others, sin is infectious and propagates itself. Rather curiously, this is just because it is so expressly in this form the sin of weakness. To yield on the one side or the other, to let go the reins, and then to take them up again and let them go again, merely for the sake of change and because of a new attraction, is not for nothing the most "popular" form of sin; the one in which it is known to all of us directly. In relation to this form we will all usually confess, if we must, that we too are sinners, and perhaps great sinners. But in relation to it, because it is so common, we think that we can readily find forgiveness, and even that it is assured to us in advance. We are all of us human. We do not realise what we are saying when we talk in this way. We are in the process of denying and destroying and dissipating ourselves as men. We are busily engaged in setting up our own caricature. We are sawing off the branch on which we sit. Yet it is true enough that we cannot reproach one another in this respect. The one can take comfort in the fact that the other is at least not much better and probably much worse. We are all alike at this point. The only trouble is that when we realise this we think that we are justified in doing what we see others do. And so the one calls and draws the other after him.

At this point we are reminded of the host of the damned plunging down in one great clinging mass of flesh as portrayed by Michelangelo and Rubens in their pictures of the Last Judgment. But we may also wonder how they dared so self-evidently to oppose to them a host of saints who were obviously excepted from this attachment to the flesh and its lusts and corruption. Is there any real (and not merely painted) saint who can say that he is free from this attachment and therefore knows that he does not participate in this downward plunge of the mass of all flesh? Is not the true saint distinguished from the false by the fact that—

without taking comfort or finding forgiveness in consequence—he too must confess that he [458] is one with the rest, and that he as little, or even less, deserves anything but this plunge as any habitual sinner, however great or small? Is it not the false saint who thinks that he can so easily separate himself from this mass?

We live indeed in the solidarity before God and with one another in which, fused together by the power of weakness, we do actually live in dissipation, in negligence, in the more spiritual or material desire of the flesh, and therefore in the childish destruction of the dignity of our human nature, but in which we make the foolish boast, as though it made everything good, that we are all of us human. Yet we can see that this is futile, that it merely represents the mortal danger to which we expose ourselves, in which we are indeed already involved, only as we see the origin of our desire, only as we know the source at which it is evil; the place at which it consists in the fact that we are too lazy to follow the movement of God which lifts us up, that instead we let ourselves sink and fall. Fall into what? Into our graceless being for ourselves. It is there in our own heart that death is already enthroned. It is from this point that there necessarily follows our mortal dissipation, just as it is from this point that there necessarily and always follow our stupidity and inhumanity and their deeds.

We cannot properly discuss the problem of sin in this form without here too considering the matter of concealment. Sin in this form seems more open and acknowledged than in its other forms. The obvious reason for this is that we here find ourselves in the most direct and concrete dialectic of the self-contradiction in which we are all involved. It may be presupposed, however, that sin will know how to camouflage itself at this point even more effectively, if anything, than in its other forms. We do not confess it merely by admitting that in relation to it all men and therefore we ourselves are sinners. If we did, we should be involved in a denial and destruction of our dignity as men and therefore of ourselves. We are again prevented objectively from allowing that this is the sum and end of what we will by the good reason that we are in the hand of God, who according to Ez. 18²³ does not will our death but that we should be converted and live. But what do we really know of this reason? It is not in God's hand that we wish to hide. This would mean to will what He wills; to be converted and to live. What we want—and this is not a good reason for not admitting the self-destruction in which we are involved—is simply to live: to live but not to be converted; to live on in the powerful weakness of our evil desire. Here, too, this minus is the very thing that we try to conceal from God, and others, and especially ourselves. The thing we will not accept is the corrupt tendency of the will in which we will not live of God, but only of ourselves. Here, too, hypocrisy arises as a repetition and confirmation and concentration of the sin itself.

And here, too, hypocrisy and therefore the concealment of the sin take [459] place under the title and glory of their opposite. The only thing is that since their work consists in that cleavage of human nature it cannot be reduced to a single denominator. We protect that twofold desire of the flesh with the two-fold pretext of freedom and naturalness. It is so easy on the one hand to pretend that the release of the soul from the link with the body and therefore from the obligation to be its lord and keeper, and the release of the body from the service and control of the soul, the two-sided self-abandonment and self-assertion, is the liberation from a twofold yoke of bondage. Is not the discipline which prevents these releases a kind of foreign rule which man does not need to accept, which—far from exercising—he can and must repudiate? Does he not begin to exist, achieving a genuine vitality, when he sees that this discipline is a superfluous and harmful compulsion; when he resolutely resists it as an attack upon himself; and when, therefore, for his own sake, in expression of his unity and totality as a man, he dares to take the step (from freedom) into freedom, thus undertaking those releases, and granting himself permission, or leave, for either that upward or downward flight, and if we are quite serious for both at once? Can this really be called dissipation, degradation, the work of a man who is without spirit and therefore soulless and bodiless? Surely it is the courageous work of the man who is free in spirit; the work in which he does justice to both soul and body, thus achieving maturity as a man and discovering and maintaining his dignity as such. Can it really be described as sloth? Surely what he thinks and does before this liberation is the true sloth. And sin? Surely sin is to oppose the rule of free spirit, and therefore not to carry through these releases? It is no less easy to regard and expound the results of these releases, the twofold Docetism of a way of existence which is spiritualised on the one side and materialised on the other, as a return to nature, to a being as genuine soul or genuine body in contrast to a supposed spirit which falsifies both. Does not man begin to be an authentic soul and body when he transcends the connexion in which only this so-called spirit can be claimed as human? Does not the discipline which this spirit demands of us, and requires that we should exercise, lead to a paralysis and self-deception in which we are not merely permitted but commanded in the name of reality to consider and seize and enjoy that release? Is this really an existence in antithesis and contradiction, and therefore dissipation, sloth and sin? May it not be that existence in the antithesis and contradiction of these two elements, the dialectic of this powerful weakness, is normal and natural? May it not be that true spirit triumphs in their dualism? May it not be that it is dishonest to try to escape this dualism, to try not to be in the flesh? May it not be that it is the proper thing to be two and not one, and therefore to be in the flesh? Is there [460] not a whole anthropology, bearing the name of Christian, which expressly recognises this dualism, which finds it grounded in necessity, although it then goes on, quite inconsistently, to refuse any serious consideration to the body as the mere prison of the soul, to disqualify its impulses, and in a strange abstraction to describe the life of the soul as the act of its liberation from this prison? Why should we not take seriously this dualism which is confirmed by such ancient testimony? Why do we have to speak of sin when it is merely a matter of giving a proper place to both soul and body, and therefore of freedom in the satisfaction of their specific needs?

We cannot recognise what we have here called the dissipation of man until we have fully heard the ways in which it tries to conceal and vindicate and even glorify itself. We cannot know it until we have considered the show of holiness with which it knows how to invest itself, as we have just indicated. The vagabond in us is not prepared to be depicted as the rogue he really is. He prefers to portray himself as a nobleman, knight and hero. Although he is the very essence of the rule, of ordinary and trivial humanity, he flaunts the banner of freedom and naturalness and pretends to be the interesting exception to the rule. And, of course, we all want to be free and natural and the interesting exceptions. He needs this concealment. Without it, he would be frightened, just as the fool in us would be frightened if he did not pretend to be wise, our inhumanity if it did not espouse some very humane cause. Without this concealment we would stare death in the face. He thus pretends to be the man who is truly alive. And the concealment of our dissipation cannot fail to be effective. It allies itself with the effectiveness which the power of every destructive desire always has. It gives fresh potency to this power. It carries its work to a climax. It gives it radiance and beauty. So long as this concealment is not lacking, the dissipation of man will not merely continue but constantly receive fresh and highly qualified impulses. We can only say, indeed, that our carnal being lives decisively by the impulses which it receives from this concealment.

There is one thing which it cannot do. It cannot arrest or even conceal the destructive outworking of our dissipation. Like our stupidity and our inhumanity, the latter has certain ineluctable consequences. We shall now consider these in relation to the three aspects of our human life and essence.

It is inevitable that the jeopardising of ourselves which is necessarily involved when we abandon and assert ourselves instead of maintaining a disciplined life should mean directly (1) a jeopardising of our being before God and with God. Here, too, we are caught in a vicious circle. As we refuse the knowledge of God, we are involved in a decline into the disorder of our own being as man. And as we become and are men of disorder, God necessarily becomes a stranger and enemy. For He is a God of order and peace. He is the Creator and Guarantor of the peace designed for man in his own nature as the soul of his body. To break this peace is to break with God as its Creator and Guarantor. In our unity and totality as it is constantly renewed by the Holy Spirit we belong to God, and we express the fact in the exercise of the discipline which is simply the obedience that we owe to God. But if we choose the flesh, i.e., one or other form of that dualism, we reject God. We are blind to His work and deaf to His voice. We are no longer able to pray in any true sense. We cannot do so even if our libertinism takes a more spiritual form: perhaps a very pronounced idealism; or a bold inner enthusiasm; or even an intensive religiosity, a very zealous concern for God and His cause. Born of the flesh,

[461]

this will always be flesh. Far from binding us to God, it will separate us from Him—quite irrespective of the fact that we do not give free rein to the physical side but show it all possible severity. It is obvious, of course, that the more flagrant and customary form of libertinage, the so-called emancipation of the flesh in the narrower sense of the term, necessarily has the same result. Primarily, although not exclusively, it is in this sense that the lists of vices in the Epistles of the New Testament speak very emphatically of those who shall not inherit the kingdom of God. How can the debauched and dissipated slaves of their own rampant senses and impulses enter the kingdom of God? Renouncing self-mastery, they have rejected the lordship of God. How, then, can they return to it? But whatever form our debauchery takes, whether it is upward or downward, whether it is the libertinage of thoughts and feelings or that of the appetites, God is not there for the vagabond in us. He may pretend to be free, but he is not free for God. He can neither know Him nor serve Him. Again, he may pretend to be natural, but it can never be natural for Him to be before God and with Him. The habit of self-forgiveness spoils his taste for a life by free grace. Evil desire extinguishes the love of God, and therefore faith and hope in God, first in his heart, then in his thinking and action, and finally in the whole of his life. It may combine itself with the more crude or refined pretence of Christianity, but it can never go hand in hand with a true Christianity which keeps itself in temptation and is powerful in its witness to the world. It disturbs us when we seek God, and come before Him, and call upon Him, and try to do many things with Him and for Him. In the grip of its power, we are not really thinking of God at all, and we need not be surprised if we find that God for His part can make nothing of us and has no use for us. We can only repeat at this point what we said in our discussion of inhumanity as the true reason for the lack of faith, or plight of doubt, both in individuals and on a more general scale. The dissipation of man has to be reckoned as one of the basic reasons for these unfortunate phenomena. This is the first thing which cannot be obliterated by any concealment that it may use.

[462] Again (2) it evokes inhumanity, as it is also its consequence. Here, too, there is a fatal action of cause and effect. How can a man have openness and gladness of heart for others, and plan and achieve the co-ordination of man with man, if he will not keep to the order of human being in himself? How can he respect the dignity of man in others if it escapes him in his own person? What can the dissipated man be for his fellows, or offer to them, apart from the fatal power of a bad example by which he confirms others to their hurt rather than to their salvation, or perhaps, if the other is a little less depraved than he is, the fatal impulse to exalt himself above him, and thus to enter an even more dangerous path. We cannot take the point too seriously that in the measure that we abandon and assert ourselves we are useless for society, refusing our responsibilities in relation to our fellows, our neighbours, our brothers. The destruction of the I in which we are involved necessarily means that there is a vacuum at the point where the other seeks a Thou to whom he can be an I. The

dissipated man becomes a neutral, an It which is without personal activity and with which the other cannot enter into a fruitful personal reciprocity. But we have also to say that the vagabond in me not only causes me to refuse my responsibilities in relation to others, but actually to be a disruptive and harmful influence. My inward unrest necessarily expresses itself outwards. Unable to satisfy myself, I am forced to seek compensation in all kinds of attacks and outrages on that which belongs to my fellows. My conflict with myself necessarily conceals but also reveals itself in disputes with others. The man of disorder is as such a dangerous man. He is potentially a menace to others. As inward and outward peace are indivisible, so too, unfortunately, are inward and outward dispeace. This is the second form in which the dissipation of man always finds expression in spite of every concealment.

It will also work itself out (3) in the fact that our allotted duration of human life will become quite unendurable. The revolt against this limitation, the attempt to escape it, is itself an original form of human sloth. We shall return to this in our final discussion. For the moment, we are concerned with a direct consequence of the destruction and disintegration of human nature, of being in the flesh, as it now concerns us in the form of man's dissipation. The dissipated man is full of anxiety about himself and life and the world. He is not at all the free spirit he pretends to be. He finds no pleasure in the merriness he affects both to himself and others. "Be self-sufficient," he calls to his proud heart. But if everything is going well, why does he need to give this word of encouragement? The truth is that his heart is not at all self-sufficient. He is anxious. He is afraid. He may not be afraid of dying as such. He can neutralise and even explain the thought of dying. We can all do this. What we cannot do is to reconcile ourselves to the fact that all things, and therefore man himself, have their time and are thus limited. It is not a matter of dying. It is a matter of death as the determination of human existence in virtue of which he is finite. [463] And the dissipated man can never come to terms with this determination. He may pretend that he does, but his actions prove the contrary. He is the man who seeks either an upward or a downward flight, or both, from the unity and totality of human life. Either way he condemns himself to an endless and insatiable striving. The aim of every desire is infinity. It is renewed as soon as it finds satisfaction. Satisfaction can only lead it to seek it again. This is just as true of the desire of our thoughts and feelings as of that of our senses. Once unleashed, it can never be appeased. It drives us from desire to satisfaction, and in satisfaction it gives rise to desire. Its essence and beauty consist in the fact that both upwards and downwards it opens up magic casements with unlimited views which give us the thrill either of solemnity or of an arrogant rejoicing. But is not the heart of this thrill a terrible, irrepressible and irresistible longing in face of the infinity opened up on all sides by these casements? Is it not a thrill of horror at the actuality which consists in the fact that we are limited and not unlimited, that our striving can never lead us anywhere in its infinity? *Carpe diem*[EN41] is the word of exhortation and comfort which the dissipated man addresses to himself. But this is simply an expression of the panic in which he lives as he is confronted by a closed door. Do we not always think that we are too late, sometimes even in youth, then in dangerous middle-age, and especially when we are old, and cannot conceal from ourselves the fact that in this or that respect we are indeed and finally too late, and we try to snatch the flowers that may be left, or surprisingly given, by the late autumn? And then it is again too late. In youth or age, the hunt is pointless, because its object does not exist. There is no infinite to satisfy our infinite desires. But this is something which the dissipated man, who has broken loose from the unity and totality of soul and body in which God has created him for existence in the limit of his time, cannot grasp, but must endlessly repudiate in his own endless dissatisfaction. In what he takes to be his successful hunt, he is himself the one who is hunted with terrible success by anxiety. He may try to smother it, but he cannot do so. He may tell himself that he has it under control, but this is not the case. When we consider all the yearnings in what he plans and does, quite apart from his character and achievements, of what man can it not be said that his life-story is one of anxiety? And the same is true of world-history as a whole. The history of the nations, and their politics and cultures, their artistic and scientific and technical achievements, is a history of the great pursuit of man in which he grasps at the infinite and is continually brought up against his finitude, in which he is himself hunted by his anxiety, gripped and controlled by his panic at this closed door, and therefore incapable of any quiet or continuous progress. Is not man so great in all ages just because he is so little in [464] this fear of his own limitation, and this attempt to escape it? And is he not so little in this fear just because he lives in this attempted flight, the dissipated man who is essentially, of course, the slothful man? Engaged in this flight, he necessarily doubts and finally despairs of even the modest success which may come his way. For it is always far too modest. The infinite which is his true goal is still unattainably distant. There can be no modesty in the man who is involved in this upward or downward course of dissipation. For him it is not natural but unnatural to be modest. It is not his glory but his shame. And because he cannot be modest, he inevitably plunges himself (and, as we have seen, his fellows) into one disturbance after another—in utter antithesis to the life for which he is ordained by the divine election and creation, the life which is basically peaceful and inwardly assured, and which therefore radiates peace and creates assurance in others. This is the third thing which our hypocrisy may conceal but cannot alter.

We return to our starting-point. What we have here is a third aspect of the man whom God took to Himself in the man Jesus, exalting him in this One to fellowship with His own divine life. In the light of the existence of this Saviour he is the slothful man; the man who, from the standpoint of what he himself

---

[EN41] Seize the day!

does and does not do, lets himself fall, thinking to attain on all sides this imposing profusion of wild growth. God knows us as men like this when He addresses His mercy to us in this One. He sees us as those who are in the flesh because we wish to be so. What is the plan and purpose of God when he wills and creates and sustains the existence of this One in the mass of men plunging headlong into the depths? Merely to show the law from which we have fallen? Merely to set in relief the fall itself? These are inevitable implicates of the divine work which it is our particular purpose to consider in this context. The sickness of our being as a sinful being in the flesh is undoubtedly revealed in the light of this One. But we must not forget something which is even more true—that "he hath borne our griefs, and carried our sorrows," and that "with his stripes we are healed" (Is. 53$^{4f.}$). We must not forget that it was positively our salvation, our sanctification, that God willed and accomplished as the mighty direction to us all in the existence of the Son of Man, the free and royal man Jesus. Yet we for whom this was done are men like this.

We will again turn to the Old Testament for an illustration, and this time to the strange story of David and Bathsheba in 2 Sam. 11$^{1-12\ 25}$. It is a story which is strange even in relation to its context. It is set at the very heart of an account of the exploits of David after he was instituted king. It therefore forms an intrusive element, and the painful impression which it makes is not removed, although it is perhaps mitigated, by the tragic and yet conciliatory and even hopeful conclusion. If we note how the story of the Ammonite war which was begun in 2 Sam. 10 is taken up again at once in 12$^{26f.}$, we may indeed suspect that the incident was supplied by another source in the redaction of the Book of Samuel, especially as it is not to be found in the corresponding passage in 1 Chron. 19^1–20^3. Is it just a matter of introducing the person of Bathsheba, who according to 12^{24} is the mother of Solomon, and therefore the ancestress of the whole later house of David, reappearing in the New Testament with three other curious women (Thamar, Rahab and Ruth) as one of the ancestresses of Jesus (Mt. 1$^{3f.}$)? If this is really one of the reasons why the story is inserted, it is only with the very different one of the demonstration of David's sin, in the shadow of which this personage is introduced who is so important for the establishment of the house of David. It is to be noted in this respect that the figure of Bathsheba remains rather a colourless one throughout the narrative. In supreme antithesis to Abigail, she seems to be only an object in the whole occurrence. She never has the initiative, and she does nothing to shape the progress of events. The transgression of David is the background which dominates the story of her introduction. And it is this that makes it so strange. In all the previous narratives of the Books of Samuel we have never been told that David sinned, but that he always refrained, or, as in the encounter with Nabal and Abigail, was restrained from doing so. But now, in remarkable contrast to that earlier story, he does not refrain in the very slightest, and there is no one to restrain him. He now does what he could not possibly do earlier as the bearer of the promise. And he does it without any shred of justification, but in a sudden act of wicked arrogance. He can only accept the accusation of the prophet Nathan (who is also introduced for the first time in this story): "Thus saith the Lord God of Israel, I anointed thee king over Israel, and I delivered thee out of the hand of Saul; and I gave thee thy master's house, and thy master's wives into thy bosom, and gave thee the house of Israel and of Judah; and if that had been too little, I would moreover have given unto thee such and such things. Wherefore hast thou despised the commandment of the Lord, to do evil in his sight?" (12$^{7f.}$). Note the sharp contrast between the divine I and David, who now occupies the place which normally

[465]

belongs to all Israel in the message of the prophets; the place of the one who has received nothing but good at the hand of *Yahweh* and has repaid it with evil. To be sure, in and with this evil he has not ceased to be David, the one whom God has elected and called. He proves this at once by the fact that when he is accused by Nathan he freely admits: "I have sinned against the Lord" (12^{13}). It is also proved by the fact that, unlike Saul (1 Sam. 15^{30}), he is given the answer: "The Lord also hath put away thy sin; thou shalt not die." His sin is forgiven. But it has taken place with all its consequences. If the attitude of David on the death of the child of Bathsheba reveals a greatness which is wholly worthy of himself, this cannot alter the fact that the child conceived in the act of his sin had to die. And it is surely intentional that the whole story, embedded in the ultimately victorious war against the Ammonites, constitutes a sombre crisis in what had hitherto been the continually mounting way of David, beyond which he plunges at once into the great catastrophe of the revolt of Absalom. From this point onwards David no longer stands out in contrast to Saul as a figure of unambiguous light. We might almost say—although it would be a consideration which is quite foreign to the account itself—that he becomes a more human character. The whole point of the story, except in so far as it serves as an introduction of Bathsheba, is simply to prove that David too shares in the unfaithfulness of Israel to *Yahweh*, and thus stands with Israel (although not destroying His faithfulness) under the judgment of *Yahweh*.

The decisive content of the story is given with startling swiftness. In the affair in which David becomes a transgressor there is no element of human greatness even in the tragic sense. It is primitive and undignified and brutal, especially in the stratagem by which David tries to maintain his honour. How else can we describe it except as an act of dissipation? When we turn to it from the first Book of Samuel, it surely strikes us that the same cannot be said of the sin of rejected Saul. The offence of Saul was to want to be a *melek* like the kings of other nations. In this perversion he ceased to be a charismatic and was possessed by an evil spirit. But Saul was a whole man even in his transgression (which was so slight from the moral standpoint). He was great even in his demon-possession and tragic end. On the other hand, the elect David who is called and set up in his place is painfully mean and undignified when he transgresses, despising the commandment of the Lord (12^9). Indeed, he is contemptible even to himself. If only he had been caught up in an evil principle and programme! If only he had gone astray and shown his fallibility in a significant entanglement! But as far as he is concerned it is only a trivial intrigue, however savage and evil in its outcome. It amounts only to an almost casual departure from the order which he knows and basically recognises, although one for which he himself is fully responsible. It is a side-step, as it were, in which he takes on a character foreign to himself, and in consequence of which he does that which is equally foreign, almost mechanically involving the greater transgression which is obviously inevitable once he has departed from that order. At every point, both at the outset and in the sequel, it is all below his usual level and petty and repulsive.

The manhood of Israel (with the ark of *Yahweh*, 11^{11}) is encamped under Joab in the open fields. The king has remained behind in Jerusalem, and has just awakened from a siesta (11^2). He is there on the flat roof of his palace. It is not an evil situation, but it is not a very promising one. He gazes indolently at the courtyards of the lower neighbouring houses. "Thou shalt not covet thy neighbour's wife" (Ex. 20^{17}). The gaping David covets the woman—Bathsheba, the wife of Uriah the Hittite, as he is told—whom he there sees washing herself. "Thou shalt not commit adultery" (Ex. 20^{14}). David wills to commit adultery with this woman. He has only to command her as the king, and he does so. Has he not already committed it in his heart (Mt. 5^{28}) as he looks on her and lusts after her—the wife of another? But he does commit that which has already been committed. The woman becomes pregnant. Will he stand by what he has done, not only in her sight, but in that of her husband, of all Jerusalem, perhaps of the child who is yet unborn? The king of Israel an adul-

[466]

terer? The consequences are incalculable. He is afraid of them, not unreasonably, but unjustly. Already, however, he is his own prisoner. It is only by further wrong that he can avert the consequences of the wrong which he has already done. First, he tries to practise a clumsy deception. Uriah is recalled. The ostensible reason is that he should report to David on the progress of the campaign. The real purpose is to restore him to his own house and therefore to Bathsheba. He will therefore think, and even at worst cannot prove a contrary opinion, that the expected child is his own. But this plan is defeated by an unexpected obstacle: "And Uriah said unto David, The ark, and Israel, and Judah, abide in tents; and my lord Joab, and the servants of my lord, are encamped in the open fields; shall I then go into mine house, to eat and to drink, and to lie with my wife? as thou livest, and as thy soul liveth, I will not do this thing" (11^{11}). He will not do it even when he is pressed to do so, and invited to the royal table and made drunk, but sleeps two nights at the entrance to the palace with David's bodyguard. He "went not down to his own house" (11^{13}). David has come up against a man—and it is almost a final appeal to himself—who knows what is right, and who keeps to it even in his cups. His only option therefore—if he is not to retreat, as he is obviously unable to do—is to cause this man to disappear, to die, in order that he may marry Bathsheba and conceal the adultery which he has committed. As king, he has the power to do this. "Thou shalt not kill" (Ex. 20^{13}). Well, he has the power to kill without having to admit it even to himself. And he does it by sending his famous directive to Joab, carried by the returning husband himself, to place him in the fiercest part of the battle against the besieged city of the Ammonites, and then to leave him in the lurch, so that he is killed by the enemies of Israel. His orders were obeyed, involving an unnecessary, imprudent and costly attack which in itself David could only have censured. But he was quite unable to do so. For the report sent by Joab concluded with the news which he desired: "Thy servant, Uriah the Hittite, is dead also." This makes up for everything—even the death of the others who had lost their lives in this futile enterprise. "Then David said unto the messenger, Thus shalt thou say unto Joab, Let not this thing displease thee, for the sword devoureth one as well as another: make thy battle more strong against the city, and overthrow it: and encourage thou him" (11^{25}). He has no real interest now in Joab or the army or the city of Rabbah. The true encouragement is for himself. He can now enjoy the peace which he desires, and which is created by the death of Uriah that he has so skilfully arranged. Bathsheba mourns for her husband. "And when the mourning was past, David sent and fetched her to his house, and she became his wife, and bare him a son" (11^{27}). He could now be born without any scandal. It all belonged to the past. It had all been covered over.

[467]

"But the thing that David had done displeased the Lord." This was the message that the prophet Nathan had to give him. He had done what he should not and could not do as the elect of *Yahweh*. He had contradicted at every point himself, his election and calling, and therefore *Yahweh*. He had allowed himself to stray and fall into lust and adultery and intrigue and murderous treachery—the one following the other by an iron law—and therefore into the sphere of the wrath and judgment of God. "As the Lord liveth, the man that hath done this thing shall surely die," is his own confession when his act is held up before him in the mirror of Nathan's parable. And it invites the crushing retort: "Thou art the man" ($12^{5f.}$). He is the one who has been involved in this incident. No, he is the one who has willed and done it even to its bitter end. He, the bearer of the promise, is also a man of this kind. This is what is revealed with such remarkable frankness in the story of 2 Sam. 11–12. David is now playing the role and aping the style and falling to the level of the petty *melek*, or sultan, or despot of other peoples. David is like all other men. He cannot be relieved of this charge. On the contrary, this is a charge and burden which rests on all Israel and every man. And this has to be brought home by David's very human, yet not on that account excusable, but

85

supremely guilty slip; by what is revealed to be at bottom the normal manner and action even of the heart and life of those who are elected and called.

4. The man Jesus, whose existence forms our starting-point for the fourth and last time, exercised and demonstrated His royal freedom finally and supremely and all-comprehensively in the fact that He gave up His life to God and man, that He allowed it to be taken from Him by men. To lose it? Yes, but also in that way to win and keep it. To perish? To be no more? To belong only to the past? Yes, but to reveal Himself as the One who is incorruptible in the very fact that He perishes and belongs to the past; to live eternally and for all times as the One who was crucified at the conclusion and end of His time. It was in this way, as His life moved towards this coronation and found fulfilment in it, that it became and was and is His life for God and for us: the life of Jesus the Victor, the faithful servant of God, who as such is with the same faithfulness our Lord and Head and Representative; the life of the new and holy and exalted man in whose person we who are still below are already above, we who are still sinners are already sanctified, we who are still God's enemies are lifted up into fellow-

[468] ship with His life; and all this as the life of the man who did not refuse death, and therefore the conclusion and end of His time, but accepted it to find fulfilment in it. We are always unlike Him in the fact that the issue of His life in this fulfilment, His end in the character and significance of this goal, took place once and for all for us, and cannot be repeated in the issue of our lives or our end. But our end or issue is set in the light of His. It can and should reflect it. His end and issue, His crucifixion, i.e., His life as it is fulfilled and triumphant in His crucifixion, because and as it is lived for us, shines as a direction on the existence of us all as it is determined by our finitude. We are not He, nor He we. But as and because He is for us and therefore with us and not without us, we for our part are with Him and not without Him. We are this finally and supremely and all-comprehensively in the very fact that our existence is limited and under sentence of death; an existence in the short space of time which we are pitilessly given. As the Crucified, He lives at the very point where our frontier is reached and our time runs out. He is the Victor there. He not only calls us, then, to look and move forward confidentially and courageously. He gives us—and this is the power of His direction—the freedom to rejoice as we arrive at our end and limit. For He is there. He lives there the life which as eternal life includes our own. He is our hope. And He bids and makes us hope.

But we—again this bitter turn has to be executed—start back at the very place where we should not only be calm and confident but also hope. We fret at the inevitable realisation that our existence is limited. We would rather things were different. We try to arrest the foot which brings us constantly nearer to this frontier. And because we know that we cannot change things, that we cannot cease to move remorselessly towards this place, we look frantic-ally around for assurances on this side of the moment when they will all be stripped away, anxiously busying ourselves to snatch at life before we die. This, too, is a form of our sloth. In this, too, we set ourselves against God and shun His grace; the grace of participation in the movement and exaltation which come from Jesus. In this, too, we fall back and are behindhand. And this, too, is responsible transgression—sin. Our term for this fourth aspect of it is human care. We have met it three times already (under different names) as the fruit and consequence of our stupidity, inhumanity and dissipation. It necessarily entered our field of vision in relation to these aspects of human sloth. But it is also an autonomous form of our sloth, and as such itself the basis and cause of our stupidity, inhumanity and dissipation. All evil begins with the fact that we will not thankfully accept the limitation of our existence where we should hope in the light of it, and be certain, joyously certain, of the fulfilment of our life in the expectation of its end. The root of all evil is simply, and powerfully, our human care.

We must begin, as before, by asserting its emptiness. It is quite futile. Why? Because of the inexorable nature of the destiny, the natural order, in virtue of   [469] which we and all things are corruptible and will perish? This pedestrian thought cannot form a sure foundation for our statement. Always, and rightly, man will struggle against nature or destiny. It is not on this account that he will regard his care as futile. It is futile because our perishing, the terminating of our existence, which we think we should oppose without anxious striving, is the good order of God, one of the tokens of His gracious and merciful and invincible will as Creator. We do not choose something better but something worse, a definite evil, our own rejection and compact with chaos, if we oppose this order when we ought thankfully and joyfully to accept it. Chaos is what God did not will and will never do so. It is, therefore, that which is not. Hence our care is empty and futile. It is for this reason that we have to accept the fact that we cannot add to our life-time (Mt. 6^{27}) and that it is senseless to try to do it. It is for this reason that we have also to accept the fact that our heavenly Father knows what things we have need of (Mt. 6^{32}). There is thus no ground for anxiety on our part. It is empty and futile because we have already been told that this is the case by the earthly Son of our heavenly Father—the One who became and was revealed as the Victor at the very frontier which causes us to start back and retreat and take anxious thought, at the end and issue of His own life. This invasion and destruction of the object of all care (even in its form as destiny and the natural order) has taken place and cannot be reversed. We may continue in care, but this cannot affect the force and validity of the veto which He has laid upon it, not only by His words, but by the act of His life as He sacrificed and fulfilled it on the cross. It cannot alter the fact that He is in fact the hope of the world and our hope. Against what, then, do we seek to assure ourselves? We may be anxious, but we cannot provide for our anxiety the object which it must have if it is to have any final seriousness. We cannot give it an absolute character. We can only deceive ourselves and others if we think that there is good reason for it, and that we achieve anything by it. Our care is empty and futile. By it we can only realise and reveal our sin and shame.

But we do do this, and in this way (even from this standpoint) we create the evil fact of our self-contradiction. We act as though the work and Word of God were nothing; as though Jesus were not risen. We make no use of the freedom which we are granted in Him. The impossible—man's unrest as he tries to reject the ineluctable finitude of his existence—takes place. The negation which he permits himself becomes a "position." The evil of his fear of this frontier, which is the good order of God, acquires historical form and signifi-cance both individually and globally. The life of man becomes an unbroken chain of movements dictated by his anxious desire for assurances: either against possibilities which he fears and tries to avoid because he has to recog-nise in them the approaching shadow of the frontier which he approaches; or in relation to possibilities which he desires because he expects from them ful-filments which for a time at least conceal his certain end, allowing him tempor-arily to forget that which is before him. Care is the remarkable alternation and mixture of this fear and desire against the background of what we think we must regard as a threat rather than our hope. From this angle, the disobedi-ence and unbelief and ingratitude of man consist in his tragic persistence in this opinion, and the evil will which permits it. This opinion is the inexhaust-ible source of care, both as fear and desire, in all its great and little, all its more or less exciting or apparently only incidental and superficial, forms. On the basis of this opinion man is always one who is anxious in some way, although he is the one who ought to be without care, the one from whom all care is removed at the very point where he thinks that he is threatened, at his issue and end which is his appointed future. Because his care has its basis in this opinion, however, it cannot be overcome by a frontal attack. No other man, not even an angel from heaven, can successfully summon me—and I certainly cannot summon myself—to abandon these fears and desires and therefore not to be anxious.

[470]

If we ever take the risk (and it is a risk) of preaching on Mt. 6$^{25-34}$, we at once meet with all kinds of sullen or dispirited or unwilling reprimands (expressed or unexpressed), and most of all, if we are honest, from our own hearts and minds. For how can we help taking care for our life? How can we model ourselves on the fowls of the air and the lilies of the field? How can we seek first the kingdom of God and His righteousness in the assurance that food and drink and clothes will be added to us? How can we leave the morrow and its anxieties—the storm which may mount and break, or the sun which may shine through—and confine ourselves to the troubles (and perhaps the joys) of to-day? How is all this possible?

How can man let go his care when he is of this opinion? We may remove all the things that he fears, or give him all that he desires, but new fears and desires will rise up at once from the inexhaustible source of this opinion and new cares will be his portion. For one day he will inevitably reach his end. If he has no positive joy and comfort, but only anxiety, in relation to this fatal point, if in his approach to this point, this far side of all his fears and desires, he does not see God but nothingness awaiting him, he can only be filled with care. He is a prisoner of the ceaseless movements of care which he himself has to make and has automatically made. We have to see this if we are to realise the power of man's sloth, his culpable negligence, even in this respect; a power which is very real even though the opinion in which this negligence originally consists, and the whole tormented existence to which it gives rise, are quite pointless and therefore empty and futile. Just as inexplicably but in fact man is first a practical atheist, inhuman and a vagabond, and then can only think and speak and act accordingly, so first—how shall we describe him from this final standpoint?—he is the dissatisfied man who necessarily becomes his own slave and lives in the bondage of his need of security. We have to grasp this if we are to be more than indolently surprised at the sea of individual and racial care in which we are all almost submerged. [471]

But when we do see it we recognise the danger. We may again describe this formally by saying that, although like man's dissipation, it seems to consist in a kind of human weakness in face of what is supposed to be an overwhelming opponent, it has power. The distinctive feature of care is that it derives its power from its opponent, from that which causes it and against which man tries to secure himself. It has all the power of the end, of death without God and without hope. This illusionary opponent, who has already been routed, this form of nothingness, is the force which inexplicably but in fact rules in human care and affects the life of man. The thought of it makes man dissatisfied. He thinks that he is menaced by it. Believing this, he can only be anxious. He can only look and move forward to his future with the deep unrest of one who is discontented with his finitude. And it is this illusory picture, the phantasy of a hopeless death, which with great definiteness and consistency dictates the law of his conduct. As he is anxious, he gives life to this phantasy, arming it with its illusory weapons and directing its illusory arm. Care is in fact existence from and to this death, because it is existence which is already smitten and maimed and unnerved and diseased by this death, and therefore a wasting and perishing existence. The care of man increases and deepens and becomes more acute in the measure that he allows it to find expression in that alternation or mixture of fears and desires. As man refuses to find joy and comfort in his end, it thrusts itself (in the form in which he sees it, and therefore without joy and comfort, but menacingly) into his present. He turns to his own grief, constituting it a graceless determination of his existence, that which is full of grace but which he fears as his distant end, the coming of which he tries to avoid, and from which he tries to conceal himself in all kinds of fulfilments. And he is now marked by this phantasy which he has conjured up. He falls victim to it in the present in which he is so concerned to secure his future. From this standpoint, too, he is engaged in that frantic hunt in which he himself is really the hunted. This is the curious power of care. It is only pseudo-creative. But all the same it is a real power even in its impotence. And there can be no escaping its effectiveness. For as man conceives and nourishes that view of his end, the end as he views and empowers it necessarily thrusts itself into his present. We must also mention the fact that it, too, has great powers of expansion and infection. We push one another into these anxious fears and desires and the corresponding joyless present. We mutually increase them, like the panic which spreads like wildfire from one, or a few, to whole masses of people. It may also be recalled in this connexion that many world-situations as [472] a whole can be decisively represented only as states of epidemic anxiety, in which the call and compulsion of hopeless death in one of its forms, manifesting itself either in nervous defence or rapacious attack, and bringing inevitable suffering, constitute the main and universally menacing stream of historical occurrence. When we realise that this is not just something which overwhelms us like an avalanche or an earthquake, but that it derives from ourselves, and takes place in consequence of responsible human decisions, there is every reason to understand care as far more than a regrettable human weakness or an occasional mistake. As man's refusal and negligence it is from the standpoint of his temporality *the* human sin. In its unity and totality the sloth of man has also this form.

Of course, man never thinks of acknowledging what he is and does when he is anxious and therefore the prisoner of care. The self-contradiction in which he is involved is too striking and painful for him to admit that this is what he really intends and wills and does. Care has a merely ludicrous side on which it may be compared to the action of a man who in his desire for a bird in the bush (or for fear of a menacing bird of prey) lets go the bird in his hand. But who of us will admit that he acts foolishly in this way? And in reality this ludicrous folly is suicidal madness. In his anxiety man sets his own house on fire. He bursts the dyke which protects his land from flooding. He torments and crushes himself. In his attempt to find security, he loses it. But who of us will admit this? Behind our reluctance to do this there seriously stands somewhere the will of God in virtue of which what man intends and wills and does in his care is transcended and superseded and made impossible. He, the living God, is really the limit of man, in all His omnipotence and mercy. Is it not inevitable, then, that we should hesitate to confess our care? We are obviously prevented from doing so genuinely by the fact that there is no objective reality to cause us to do it. Objectively, there is only the bitter reality of our ludicrous but demented relationship to the shadow which we ourselves have projected on the wall. Unfortunately, however, it is not a knowledge of this fact which really restrains us from confessing our sin. If we knew this, if we lived with the objective truth that there is no reality in the enemy which threatens us or the abyss before us because we are in the hand and under the protection of God, we should not yield to care in the first place, and then we should not have to confess it and be ashamed of our confession. As we do yield to it, and can only be ashamed of our confession, the only alternative is to try to conceal from ourselves and others and even, as we think, God, the folly and madness of what we do. In a shame which is not authentic we must try to find a cover, a fine pseudonym which will declare the imposing opposite of what we do, an alibi.

The concealment of care will take many different forms because, although care is the same in all men (both as regards its origin in that false opinion and also as regards its outward expression), there are different views as to the [473] imposing opposite by which it may best be covered.

There is the man who by force of circumstances, environment and history is essentially activist; in general terms, the man of the Western world to which we ourselves belong, although it is an open question how near or distant the time may be when the man of the East will bear the same activist stamp. The concealment which this man chooses is the high concept of conscientious work. He defends and justifies and magnifies his anxiety as the work which is laid on man by an inner as well as an outer necessity. He takes the side of that which he desires against that which he fears. He tries to use and exploit the time given and left to him, and in this time his abilities and power and opportunities and possibilities; to pursue his own development within the natural and historical cosmos by which he is surrounded; to make himself his own master both in great things and in small. He sets himself higher or more modest, nearer or more distant, but always binding ends. He can never be too serious or zealous in his efforts to attain them. He is out for success. He must have it. He must achieve something. He creates. And it is by this measure that he assesses himself and others. If he is not creating and achieving, he feels a want; he is restless and fretful. He views with suspicion those who are not creating anything at all or anything worth while. He is happy when he finds himself compelled to work by definite obligations. He is refreshed and comforted by the thought that he is fulfilling his tasks to the best of his knowledge and ability; that in his own place he is a cog which is pushed and pushes, or at any rate rotates, according to a specific plan. All his fears and desires against the background of the great overhanging threat, all his attempts to find security, flow into this canal with its solid banks. His care becomes his glory as it drives the mills and factories—his own or those which are collectively owned—erected by the waterside, so that something is actually achieved for himself and others by the fact that he is anxious. It may be that human care occasionally shines through at the heart of all his activity, but how gloriously transformed it is! How its true character is hidden! When it is translated into conscientious work, who can possibly recognise it as a form of human sloth? The man who is hounded into activity by his care seems to be the very opposite of a slothful man. We need not waste words showing how effective is the concealment of man's denial (expressed as care) when it takes this attractive form.

But there is also the man who is essentially passive. Generally speaking, he is more at home in the tropical East and near the equator than in northern Europe or the United States. And he may not long survive even there—who knows? Yet we must take him into account, for he appears even amongst ourselves. He, too, is a man of care. He, too, knows that human life is threatened

[474]   by that limit, by death. He, too, does not know that this limit or frontier means hope because it is the mercy of God which sets it for man. He, too, has to wrestle with what he knows and does not know. He, too, is concerned to hide his care. But he solves the problem in a different way. He conceals it behind the no less high concept and title of resignation, non-resistance and contemplation. He sees the illusions operative in the zeal and works and morality of the activist. He shakes his head over him no less than the latter does over him. And who is really in the right? He is not the slave of a clock constantly reminding him of what has to be done. He has plenty of time, and for him time is not money, or anything else particularly valuable. He does not find sanctity in work, but in leisure for deliberation and self-adjustment and expectation. His law is not the law of duty but of relaxation. Why should he wish to be a cog which is pushed and pushes? Is not this all empty—a mere snatching at the wind? If in these fortunate territories two days' work are enough to sustain oneself and one's family—why work six? Why create merely for the sake of creating? If the inscrutable will of Allah is done in any case, why not reduce to the very minimum the flame of fear and desire which we cannot altogether extinguish? If we cannot avoid the menacing of our existence by death, why act as though we could prevent it? Why not simply endure it as it declares itself at every moment and at the last definitively? We can only say that this, too, is in its own way a glorious transformation and therefore a concealment of care, and that in many, if not all, its forms it is far superior in dignity to the activity with which the activist usually tries to hide it. Is the passive man really anxious at all? Is it not superfluous, because irrelevant, to speak to him about the fowls of heaven and the lilies of the field? Is he not himself—perhaps too much so—a kind of fowl or lily? a sluggard? a lazybones? He may appear to be so to the activist. But he is also guilty of sloth in the stricter, theological sense. Even with the alternative which he has chosen, he too is the victim of a great illusion. The only thing is that as we say this we have also to recognise that in its own way his illusion too, is a fine one, and even heroic in a way which we do not readily understand, and certainly effective.

How strong the concealment of care is in both forms may best be gauged by the fact that on both sides it is easy not only to reject with a superior gesture the charge that we have here the evil concealment of an evil business but to go over to the counter-attack with the question whether an ethic of work or resignation is not a better antidote to what the Christian message condemns as care than this message itself. The positive content of this message is, of course, overlooked—the assertion of the being and life of God for man at the very point where man thinks he sees only his frontier and the threat this involves. In

[475]   the light of this the assertion seems necessarily to be a mere postulate in the optative. That Jesus is risen and lives has to be heard and grasped if it is to be understood. And if the Christian message does not derive, or does so only uncertainly, from this point, how can the assertion be made with the radical emphasis appropriate to it? How easy it then is either to minimise the serious-

ness of human care, divesting it of its character as sin and representing it as an unfortunate but natural deposit of human weakness, or to show how effectively it can be met with conscientious work or heroic resignation or even a not impossible mixture of the two! How easy it then is to make out that the Christian assertion concerning that frontier is an illusion in face of which these two ways will always commend themselves as more sober and solid methods of bringing poor man release! In line with what we had to say concerning the folly, inhumanity and dissipation of man, we can only say of his care that we have not yet recognised it if we have not paid close attention to what it has to say for itself in its concealment; if we have not seen how powerful it is, not only in itself and as such, but also in its concealment; if we have not realised how excellently it can defend and strengthen and confirm and express itself in the very act of concealment.

One thing, however, it cannot do. It cannot avert its inevitable consequences by any form of concealment. It cannot deny its character as sin, which means ruin, in these consequences. To make this clear, we will look back from this final point in our investigation to the first three. The disruption of the right relationship of man to his temporality, which we have now described as care, appeared already at each of the three earlier points as a consequence of the sin which we then considered from those different standpoints. Our present task is to see it as also a cause of the perversions with which we started.

In this form, as the false view of the threat which causes us anxiety in face of that frontier, it plays (1) a decisive and very special role in the development of what we first described as man's ignorance of God; his unwillingness to honour and love Him as God. The specific operation of care in this respect consists in the fact that already at its root it means not only a general turning away from God but an incomprehensibly desired remoteness from God at the very point where God is nearest to man as God, where He encounters him most impressively and concretely as God: as God in His holy sovereignty as opposed to us and all His creatures; as God in His power to take up our cause with His own distinctive efficacy; as God in the mercy in which He is holy and makes use of His sovereignty. The point where God meets us like this is the limit which is set for us and which finds clear expression in the fact that it is appointed to us once to die. It is not self-evident, but needs the work of His Word and Holy Spirit, that we should know Him at this point where He is our hope in death. But if He is near to us anywhere it is here at this frontier. It is definitely at this frontier that His self-revelation is given, and it consists specifically in the fact [476] that at the very point where we meet our end we are met by our Lord and Creator and Reconciler and Redeemer, and that His being illumines us, in His character as the Lord of life and death, where we think that we can see only the darkness of death. In care, however, man obstinately insists that what he can expect at this point is only darkness and not light, only destruction and not salvation, only an eternal question and not the definitive answer—a menacing opponent whom he must go out to meet, and with whom he must in some way wrestle, prepared either for conflict on the one hand or capitulation on the other. In care man makes his future his own problem. He tries either to avert or to bring about that which it might entail. He presumes to know it and in some way—by his activity or passivity—to master it. His reading of the situation is wrong from the very outset. The God who awaits him at that point, and comes to him from it, is not the opponent of man. He is not man's problem. Man cannot and should not try to strive with God. Man cannot and should not presume to know and master God of himself. Yet it is with this perverted understanding that anxious man looks to the point where God waits for him and wills to encounter him in His self-revelation. In his anxious care man has secured and bolted himself against God from the very outset. He thinks that he can and should deal with God as if He were not God but a *schema*[EN42] or shadow which he has projected on the wall. Is it not inevitable, then, that he should not have hearing ears or seeing eyes for His self-revelation? How can he believe in Him and love Him and hope in Him and pray to Him, however earnestly he may be told, or tell himself, that it is good and right to do this, and however sincerely he may wish to do so? In his care he blocks up what is for him too open access to the fountain which flows for him. Care makes a man stupid. This is the first thing which even the worst of its concealments cannot alter.

But when we turn to the horizontal plane care also (2) destroys human fellowship. It does this in virtue of the unreality of its object. The ghost of the threat of a death without hope has no power to unite and gather. It is not for nothing that it is the product of the man who isolates himself from God. As such it necessarily isolates him from his fellow-men. It not only does not gather us but disperses and scatters us. It represents itself to each one in an individual character corresponding to the burrow from which he looks to the future and seeks to grasp its opportunities and ward off its dangers. Care does not unite us. It tears us apart with centrifugal force. We can and will make constant appeals to the solidarity of care, and constant attempts to organise anxious men, reducing their fears and desires to common denominators and co-ordinating their effects. But two or three or even millions of grains of sand, however tightly they may be momentarily compressed, can never make a rock. Anxious man is a mere grain of sand. Each individual has his own cares which [477] others cannot share with him and which do not yield to any companionship or friendship or fellowship or union or brotherhood, however soundly established. By his very nature he is isolated and lonely at heart and therefore in all that he does or does not do. Even in society with others he secretly cherishes his own fears and desires. His decisive expectation from others is that they will help him against the threat under which he thinks he stands. And it is just the same with them too. Cares can never be organised and co-ordinated in such a way as to avoid mutual disappointment and distrust and final dissolution. And

---

[EN42] pattern

behind disappointment and distrust there lurks, ready to spring, the hostility and enmity and conflict of those who are anxious. It is a rare accident if different cares, although not really uniting, do at least run parallel and thus do not lead to strife. For the most part, however, they do not run parallel for long, but soon intersect. And, unfortunately, they do not do so in infinity, but in the very concrete encounters of those who are anxious. What is thought to be the greater anxiety of the one demands precedence over what is supposed to be the lesser anxiety of the other. The desires of the one can be fulfilled only at the expense of the desires of the other. Or the intersection is because they fear very different things, or—even worse—because the one desires what the other fears, or the one fears most of all what the other desires most of all. It is only a short step from a fatal neutrality to the even more fatal rivalry of different cares and those who are afflicted by them. If care itself remains—and it always does, constantly renewing itself from the source of the false opinion of human temporality—we find ourselves willy-nilly on this way in our mutual relationships, and we have no option but to tread it. There can be no genuine fellowship of man with man. There can only be friction and quarrelling and conflict and war. Care dissolves and destroys and atomises human society. In its shadow there can never arise a calm and stable and positive relationship to our fellow and neighbour and brother. It awakens the inhuman element within us. This is the second ineluctable consequence of care, no matter how fine or strong may be its concealment.

It leads no less necessarily (3) to the disorder which we have called the disintegration of the disciplined unity of man as the soul of his body. So strong is the self-contradiction into which the anxious man plunges himself in his discontent with his finitude that it is inevitable that this unity should be severely jeopardised. We remember the shadow and its power—the hopeless death—which the anxious man portrays on the wall as the picture of the future which supposedly menaces him, in this way summoning and introducing it into his present, and necessarily living with it, or rather dying of it. To do this is radically unhealthy. It pierces his heart and reins. In these circumstances he cannot be a whole man. He can no longer rule as a soul or serve as a body. He reacts against it as a soul by that roving flight into better regions which he himself has [478] selected or invented. And his body reacts against it in the form of all kinds of self-assertion, or in the form of renunciation, or in the form of sickness in all its organs. In this respect, too, care involves the dissolution of humanity. We are describing the process only in its basic form. It will never express itself quite so crudely, or at any rate be revealed quite so abruptly. But there can be no question that care does bring man on to this steep incline. It constitutes a mortal danger. It consumes him. It has the character and effect of hopeless death. It is poison. It cannot serve to build him up, but only to pull him down in what we called dissipation. It introduces not only the atheist and the inhuman man but also the vagabond within us. The man who is dissatisfied with his finitude has all these three within him, as he himself is within all these three. This is the third thing which no concealment of our care can arrest or deny.

We pause and reflect that the man whose reconciliation with God and exaltation, sanctification and purification are at issue when the name of Jesus is proclaimed and believed is this man—the discontented man who in the hopeless attempt to deny his finitude necessarily destroys his peace with God and his fellows and does nothing but harm to himself. God has in mind this man who is slothful, and refuses to act, and rejects the grace addressed to him, in the form also of his care. God knows him, even though he will not and cannot know himself. And God does not love him in spite of the fact that He knows him. He loves him because of this fact. He loves him as His creature who does not cease to be such, and from whom God has not withdrawn His hand and will not do so, because He is true to Himself. It is to him, His creature and covenant-partner in all his corruption, that He has given Jesus to be his Saviour, and saving direction, and Redeemer in and out of his corruption— Jesus, the One who is for him the Victor and Liberator and Redeemer at the very point where in his relationship to the awful picture which he had projected he insults God and treads down his fellows and destroys himself. It is for this man that Jesus lives. The fulness of his eternal life is enclosed in this One. It is to him that this One is given as a promise. It is true that he is the unhappy man of care. But it is even more true that there is said to him with overriding definiteness and all the power of a once-for-all act of God: "The Lord is at hand. Be careful for nothing" (Phil. 4$^{5f.}$).

Once again a biblical passage will give concretion to our analysis. And this time we turn to Num. 13–14—the history of the spies whom Moses sent to investigate the promised land.

We call it a "history," and this calls for a short hermeneutical observation which applies in retrospect to the three preceding *excursi*[EN43] as well. The term "history" is to be understood in its older and naive significance in which—quite irrespective of the distinctions between that which can be historically proved, that which has the character of saga and that which has been consciously fashioned, or invented, in a later and synthetic review—it denotes a story which is received and maintained and handed down in a definite kerygmatic sense. In relation to the biblical histories we can, of course, ask concerning the distinctions and even make them hypothetically. But if we do we shall miss the kerygmatic sense in which they are told. Indeed, the more definitely we make them and the more normative we regard them for the purpose of exposition, the more surely we shall miss this sense. To do justice to this sense, we must either not have asked at all concerning these distinctions, or have ceased to do so. In other words, we must still, or again, read these histories in their unity and totality. It is only then that they can say what they are trying to say. To be sure, the history of the spies does contain different elements. There is a "historical" element in the stricter sense (the persons and cities and localities mentioned). There is also an element of saga (the account of the branch of grapes carried by two men, and of the giants who inhabited the land). There is also the element which has its origin in the synthetic or composite view (fusing past and present almost into one) which is so distinctive a feature of historical writing in Old and New Testament alike. It is to the latter elements that we must pay particular attention in our

[479]

[EN43] digressions

reading of these stories if we are to understand them, for they usually give us an indication of the purpose which led to their adoption into the texts. But in relation to them, if we are discerning readers, we shall not overlook the historical elements or even jettison those which seem to have the character of saga. When the distinctions have been made they can be pushed again into the background and the whole can be read (with this tested and critical naivety) as the totality it professes to be.

The purpose of Num. 13–14 is to show how dreadful and dangerous is the retarding role played by evil anxiety in the transition of Israel from the wilderness to the promised land as an action in the history of salvation. It was perhaps in this way, in the shadow of this particular failing in relation to *Yahweh*, that at a later period—perhaps at the time of the Exile when it was confronted by a dangerous return to its own land—Israel saw its past. Yet this does not mean that at the earlier period of its existence in the wilderness its attitude was not exactly the same, or very much the same, as reported in the story. We shall now consider the picture which it gives.

The wilderness wandering seems to be reaching its end and goal. Israel is on the steppe of Paran (13^1) on the very threshold of the land from which Jacob and his sons had once journeyed to Egypt—the country which their descendants had now left far behind them. The will of *Yahweh* in the great act by the Red Sea, which was their deliverance and liberation, and *Yahweh's* covenant with them, had had as their goal that they should dwell in the land which was now before them. Other nations lived there, but it was still, and already again, their land; for *Yahweh* had promised it to them. In all their march through the wilderness the inhabitation of this land had been their absolutely sure and certain future, guaranteed by God Himself. And now it is to take place. Yet they are not to be brought in blindly and passively. Although led by *Yahweh* at the hand of Moses, they themselves are to act and dare, knowing where they are going, and knowing the land and its inhabitants and soil and cities ($13^{18f.}$). This knowledge is to be given them by trustworthy witnesses who will summon them to joyous action. That is why the twelve spies are selected and sent out, all chosen from among them, one from each of the tribes, and in each case one of the princes or leaders. Caleb from the tribe of Judah and Oshea (whom Moses called Joshua) from the tribe of Ephraim are the representatives of what later become the leading tribes in the south and the north, and they will be particularly prominent later in the story. These spies are to be eyes for the rest of the holy people, and when they have seen they are to be the mouth of authentic witnesses to this people. With this commission they are to enter the land which God has promised Israel, which already belongs to it according to His will and Word, and which has only to be appropriated; and they are then to return and tell. This is all arranged by Moses at the commandment of *Yahweh* ($13^{1–21}$). There will, of course, be a certain element of risk in crossing the frontier, both for them and for the whole people after them. It will be a venture, as we can see from the exhortation of Moses: "Be ye of a good courage." Note that they are also told to bring back some of the fruits of the land: "The time was the time of the firstripe grapes" (13^{20})—not the true grapes, but those of the approaching harvest. The Israelites themselves will actually see these first-fruits. And Moses is confident that these will speak for themselves and kindle the gratitude and joy and courage of the people. In all this we have to remember that there is no question of establishing the glorious content of the promise or the certainty that *Yahweh* will fulfil it and bring them into this good land. On the contrary, the whole being of this people rests on the promise of *Yahweh*. The only purpose, then, is to confirm the promise and to remind the people of its content and certainty. The spies can only be witnesses of the promise, and the people is to hear it attested by them and see it attested by the proofs of fruitfulness which they bring.

[480]

But it is at this point that—quite unexpectedly and incomprehensibly from the standpoint of the story—there comes the invasion of anxious care. It arises first amongst the spies themselves. Ten of these prove to be fainthearts. They have faithfully and eagerly fulfilled the first part of their commission. They have gone through the whole of the south as far as Hebron. At Eshcol they have cut off the great branch of grapes "and they bare it between two upon a staff; and they brought of the pomegranates, and of the figs" (13^{24}). And they return and tell Moses and Aaron and the whole congregation about the land, and show the fruits, and say: "We came unto the land whither thou sentest us, and surely it floweth with milk and honey; and this is the fruit of it. Nevertheless ... " ($13^{26f.}$). After all, there is a serious "But." It is not for nothing that they were told to be of a good courage. And without courage the promise given to the whole people cannot be fulfilled. There was a risk. A venture had to be made. All the spies had been aware of this. But ten of them had obviously not proved to be very courageous on the journey. It is these ten—the overwhelming majority—who, as is only right, act as the spokesmen. And the second part of their report is as follows: "Nevertheless the people be strong that dwell in the land, and the cities are walled, and very great: and moreover we saw the children of Anak there." There then follows a list of all the warlike people they found: the Amalekites, Hittites, Jebusites, Amorites, and Canaanites ($13^{29f.}$). The report is amplified later: "And they brought up an evil report of the land which they had searched unto the children of Israel, Saying, The land which we have gone to search it, is a land that eateth up the inhabitants thereof; and all the people that we saw in it are men of a great stature. And there we saw the giants, the sons of Anak, which come of the giants: and we were in our own sight as grasshoppers, and so we were in their sight" ($13^{32f.}$). Even the milk and honey and great cluster of grapes did not compensate in their eyes for this drawback; what they feared was incomparably greater than what they desired. The truth and power of the divine promise to attest which they had been chosen and now stood before the people could and should have been thrown in the scales against those hosts of people and their strong and secure cities and even the giants. But they themselves had not taken the truth and power of the promise into account, and so their report concluded: "We are not able to go up against the people; for they are stronger than we" (13^{31}). They had not really seen as witnesses of *Yahweh*, and therefore they could not speak as His witnesses. They could not encourage His people, but only attest their own anxious care.

[481]   We remember that they are speaking to the people of *Yahweh*—the people to whom the promise and its content and certainty are not something new, for whom they are only to be confirmed, who are to be summoned by them to resolute action. Surely they will unanimously reject as false witness this report and its conclusion. Unfortunately not. Instead we read that when the people of God heard this report there arose a murmuring; the murmuring of the care engendered in the people too. There were, of course, two witnesses who were not anxious and who were therefore true witnesses, Joshua and Caleb. And we are told (13^{30}) that Caleb "stilled the people before Moses" with the words: "Let us go up at once, and possess it; for we are well able to overcome it." But the continuation of the report of the other ten swept aside this word of encouragement. When the people heard of giants, every restraint was cast aside: "And all the congregation lifted up their voice, and cried; and the people wept that night" (14^{1}). The following day the murmuring was against Moses and Aaron, so that we have good reason to suspect that this was not an accidental but a supremely radical refusal which compromised everything. And indeed: "The whole congregation said unto them, Would God that we had died in the land of Egypt! or would God we had died in this wilderness! And wherefore hath the Lord brought us unto this land, to fall by the sword, that our wives and our children should be a prey?" ($14^{2f.}$). Thus from the future, in which they do not see *Yahweh* and His promise and its fulfilment and His faithfulness and power, but only these people and their strongholds, only these giants, before whom the spies saw

themselves as grasshoppers, death reaches into their present in the form of this mad desire, and even into their past. They are afraid—their poor wives and children!—of what God promises and tells them to do. They would rather have been long since dead—what is the value of milk and honey and clusters of grapes and pomegranates and figs?—in Egypt or in the wilderness. Better this than meet the obviously gigantic danger of their future. But even if they are terribly anxious they are still alive, and can do something to escape the danger. And so there comes the maddest thing of all—a conclusion which far surpasses the purely negative conclusion of the spies: "Were it not better for us to return into Egypt? And they said one to another, Let us make a captain, and let us return into Egypt" ($14^{3f.}$). Absolutely everything is called in question by the care which has now assumed gigantic proportions as a result of this report about giants: their deliverance and liberation; the will and Word of *Yahweh* in this act; His covenant with them; and naturally the authority of Moses and Aaron. Their will is to choose another leader, to set off in the opposite direction, and to return to Pharaoh and slavery—the very thing which, in spite of the protest and warning of Jeremiah, is finally done by the Jewish remnant after the destruction of Jerusalem, "because of the Chaldeans: for they were afraid of them" (Jer. 41^{18}). "No; but we will go into the land of Egypt, where we shall see no war, nor hear the sound of the trumpet, nor have hunger of bread; and there will we dwell" (Jer. 42^{14}). The madness is complete. Panic knows no limits. This is how the people of *Yahweh* proves itself. This is the way in which it treats the divine promise and therefore its own history and election and calling.

What follows in face of this situation is quite majestic: "Then Moses and Aaron fell on their faces before all the assembly of the congregation of the children of Israel" (14^5). They did not try to contradict. They did not speak any word of warning or exhortation. When the people of *Yahweh* holds back, the only hope for this people is *Yahweh* Himself: the absolute prostration of worship before Him; the intercession of those who know Him for those who do not, of those who persist in His calling and the certainty of His promise for those who forget and deny and surrender it. Yet in the first instance we are not told of any intercession, nor is there any express reference to *Yahweh*. We are simply told that they fell on their faces before this crowd in all the madness of its anxiety.

But this is not all. For at a lower level, nearer to the people but resisting their anxious care, [482] representing the true cause of the people because the cause of *Yahweh*, persisting in His calling and promise, there also stand the two faithful and reliable witnesses Joshua and Caleb (the two referred to, perhaps, in Rev. $11^{3f.}$). The first thing that we are told concerning them is that they rent their clothes (14^6) as a sign of their supreme horror at what they recognised to be an act of supreme transgression. There then follows their entreaty in which in all the tumult of that raging anxiety they issue their call, their final appeal, for joy and courage and action: "The land, which we passed through to search it, is an exceeding good land. If the Lord delight in us, then he will bring us into this land, and give us it; a land which floweth with milk and honey. Only rebel not ye against the Lord, neither fear ye the people of the land; for they are bread for us: their defence is departed from them, and the Lord is with us: fear them not" ($14^{7f.}$). Here again we have the clear line of the obedient human action corresponding to the goodness and certainty of the divine promise and sharing *a priori*[EN44] its triumphant character. *Yahweh* is with us. Hence our enemies, even though they be giants, are impotent, and we shall overwhelm them. The only thing is that we must not fear, i.e., we must not be obstinate against *Yahweh* or question and therefore forfeit perhaps his benevolence. But this has already happened. The people is already deaf to this last appeal. It is in vain, therefore, that they recall once more the promise of *Yahweh*. "All the congregation bade stone them with stones" (14^{10}). The two faithful witnesses? Or Moses and

---

[EN44] unconditionally

Aaron as well? Either way, there can be no doubt that raging anxiety now aims to destroy physically the protest made against it in the name of the divine promise, judging its divine Judge in the person of these men, and making this its final word.

It is to prevent this dreadful climax that at this moment the glory of the Lord appears before the tent of revelation in the sight of all Israel, averting the murder of the two witnesses and the irrevocable apostasy of the people, but also as an act of judgment on them. They have made an enemy of the God whose friendship they have despised and rejected. They have evoked death by fearing it. There is now interposed a long section (14^{11-20}) which tells us how God threatens what they have deserved and how it is averted by the explicit intercession of Moses. We see here how extreme is the consequence of their extreme rebellion against *Yahweh*. It is nothing less than their destruction and therefore the annulment of the covenant and promise. But this does not take place. For Moses prays: "Pardon, I beseech thee, the iniquity of this people according unto the greatness of thy mercy, and as thou hast forgiven this people, from Egypt even until now" (14^{19}). And *Yahweh's* answer is: "I have pardoned according to thy word" (14^{20}). This does not mean, however, that what has happened has not happened or has no consequences. The ten false witnesses must die a sudden death (14^{37}). And there can be no question of an entry into the land, and therefore of the fulfilment of the promise, for the whole generation which has been guilty of the anxious care, first in a childish, and then in a raging form. With the exception of Joshua and Caleb, who "had another spirit with him, and hath followed me fully" (14^{24}), "they shall not see the land" (14^{23}). "This evil congregation, that are gathered together against me, in this wilderness they shall be consumed, and there they shall die"—not in Egypt, for the will and act of God cannot be reversed, and the covenant and promise are not annulled, but in the wilderness as they have desired, without experiencing the fulfilment.

The story ends on a dark and unconciliatory note ($14^{39f.}$). "The people mourned greatly" when Moses reported what had happened. They suddenly realise that they have sinned. But it does not appear that they are so very concerned about their sin, their care, their obstinacy against *Yahweh*, and therefore their transgression of the covenant, or that their confession of sin goes so very deep, when early the following morning they come to Moses armed and ready to march northwards into the land: "Lo, we be here, and will go up unto the place which the Lord hath promised." Has their fear of the death which they desired in the wilderness, and which has been ordained for them, suddenly become greater than their fear of the giants? At any rate, they are not ready to accept the destiny which now impends in consequence of their own guilt. They will march out and fight. But they can do this only in defiance of the command of *Yahweh*. The courage of those who are anxious is no more pleasing to Him than their cowardice. "It shall not prosper. Go not up, for the Lord is not among you; that ye be not smitten before your enemies ... because ye are turned away from the Lord, therefore the Lord will not be with you" ($14^{41f.}$). "But they presumed to go up unto the hill top .... Then the Amalekites came down, and the Canaanites which dwelt in that hill, and discomfited them, even unto Hormah" ($14^{44f.}$). *Ubi cessandum est, semper agilis, prompta et audax est incredulitas, ubi autem pergendi autor est Deus, timida est, pigra et mortua*[EN45], is Calvin's observation on this incident (*C.R.*, 25, 209). Their *incredulitas*[EN46] met with the fate which it must always suffer whatever form it takes. The only note of comfort at the end of the story—apart from the existence of the little ones about whom they had been so anxious (14^{31})—is that in this careless enterprise the care-ridden Israelites did not take with them the ark of God, and therefore it was not involved in the catastrophe (14^{44}).

[483]

[EN45] Where it should do nothing, unbelief is always active, quick and audacious. But where God is the author of what is to be done, it is fearful, unwilling and dead

[EN46] unbelief

3. THE MISERY OF MAN

In this sub-section we shall be investigating man as the one who commits sin as we have learned to know it in the form of sloth. Who and what is he in the determination and character which he gives himself and has to bear as he commits it? The starting-point for our answer to this question has already been decided in the first part of this whole section. In relation to the situation which sin creates, as to sin itself, we do not have to think and speak according to our own mind and judgment, but according to the act and revelation and Word of God. Our gaze must be directed on the Son of Man Jesus, on the royal freedom of His existence as exalted and sanctified man, which includes our own true and authentic existence. And it is in the light of this that we must consider our false and inauthentic existence as those who commit acts of sloth. The situation which we create (in our stupidity and inhumanity and vagabondage and discontent) is the misery of man in the sense of his exile as the sum of human woe. To this far country of ours the Son of God has come in order that He may return home as the Son of Man, not in isolation but as our Lord and Head and Representative, bringing us with Him. But instead of being those who are exalted in and with Him, as we are in truth, we are revealed in His light as those who lead a false existence, remaining in exile and therefore in misery as though the true God had come to us in vain, as though He had not taken us up with Him, as though we were not already at home in and with Him, sharing His royal freedom. This is what gives to the human situation the determination and character of human misery. It is the evil fruit of the evil sloth of man. It is the unavoidable fate of the slothful man. Remaining behind instead of going [484] up with Him, he is necessarily the one who is left behind in misery. He prefers his own life below to the divine life above. He chooses to persist in it. He must have it as he himself wills to have it. He must be the one he himself wills to be. He is thus the man who remains below where he does not belong, and is not at home, but where he irrevocably has his place—so long as his corrupt will is not broken by the direction of Jesus. This is, from the standpoint of the sin of man as sloth, what we described as the fall of man from the standpoint of his sin as pride (*C.D.* IV, 1, § 60, 3). It is what the older dogmatics called in its totality the *status corruptionis*[EN47]. Our present term for it is the misery of man.

Even in this *status corruptionis*[EN48] man is not outside the sphere of influence of divine grace. With all his acts of sloth he cannot leave this sphere. When he remains behind, the consequences of this dreadful act are severe, but he does not give God the slip. God does not cease to be the God and Lord and Creator and Covenant-partner even of the stupid and inhuman and vagabond and discontented man, or in the far country which is necessarily the place of this man. And man too, in all his slothful action and the misery which it involves, does

---

[EN47] state of corruption
[EN48] state of corruption

not cease to be the creature and covenant-partner of God. As he has not created himself, he cannot disannul or transform himself. As he has not instituted the covenant, he cannot destroy it or even contract out of it as though it were a free compact. Let us say at once in concrete terms that the descent of the Son of God to our misery and the ascent of the Son of Man to God's glory, the existence of the man Jesus within our slothful humanity, His victory in the crucifixion as our Lord and Head and Representative, the revelation of this victory in His resurrection, the issue of His direction, the outpouring of the Holy Spirit on all flesh—all these are facts. As man has not brought them about, he cannot reverse them by anything that he does. They are facts even in face and at the very heart of his misery. Even in his turning to nothingness and under the overwhelming threat of it, he himself has not become nothing. Even in his misery he belongs, not to the devil or to himself, but to God. The Yes of divine grace is terribly concealed in the No of divine judgment, but it is spoken to him too: even to unhappy Nabal; even to the people of Northern Israel; even to David with his petty sin; even to the murmurers in the wilderness. Jesus lives as very man, and therefore as the very God who humbled Himself to man, who came to him in his misery, who took his misery to Himself. Thus even in his misery man lives as the man for whom Jesus lives. To omit this qualification of man's misery is necessarily to deny Jesus Christ as the Lord who became a servant and the servant who became Lord, and therefore to blaspheme God.

[485] We have to realise, however, that it is these very facts which make the misery of man so severe. The seriousness of the misery which results from the sin of sloth is distinguished from that of a fate by the very fact that the man who is overtaken by it is not in any sense released from the sphere of influence of God and His grace. We can draw the sting from even the worst of fates by not merely suffering but bearing it. It disturbs only so long as we are ourselves unsettled and resist it. In face of it there is a rest in which man can transcend, master and defeat it by surrendering to it. But this is not the case in relation to the hard hand of the living God which is the basis of the misery that results from sloth. Just because God does not let go the man who has plunged into this misery, just because His grace does not depart from him (Is. 54[10]), he cannot find in any opposing rest a way of avoiding unsettlement by it. No surrender can enable him to outmatch it. He cannot, then, transcend or defeat it. He cannot master it. There is no refuge, not even in hell itself, in which he can cease to be in misery. The work and Word of God's grace are still actual and valid for him. Even in this place he himself has not ceased to exist as the creature and covenant-partner of God. But he does so as one who is reluctant, in a perversion of his human creatureliness, as a covenant-breaker whom the Yes of God must strike as His No, who must suffer the grace of God as His disfavour and wrath and judgment. His misery consists in his ill-founded insufficiency, his inexcusable shame, his self-contradiction which cannot be smoothed over. The very thing which limits his misery—the fact that in it he belongs to God—

is also the very thing which makes it so sharp. It is for this reason that we had first to think of its limitation.

But what is this misery which is the ineluctable consequence of his sloth? In reply to this question we shall make three assertions, none of which is to be derived from, or proved by, a supposed empirical observation or conceptual abstraction, but all of which have reference to that which, as the reconciliation of man including his liberation from this misery, is a reality, our living hope, in the being and work of the man Jesus. In the light of this hope we acquire authentic information concerning our exiled present which is already our past in Him, i.e., in the Jesus who lives for us.

1. The liberation of man from the misery created by his sloth is a reality and therefore a living hope for all other men only in the crucified Jesus. To free us He took it to Himself. He made it His own misery. And as the bearer of it He could only die. It was only in His death that He could set this term to it; that He could make an end of it. A sickness which can terminate only with the death of the patient, from which he can be liberated only by death, is an incurable sickness, or one which can be cured only as it reaches its goal and end with the destruction of the sick person, thus coming up against a frontier which even it cannot pass. If Jesus is the patient for us, in our place, burdened with our sickness, it is obvious that we have to say of our sickness that as the misery to which the stupid and inhuman and dissipated and careworn man has fallen victim it is incurable—a fact which emerges with particular impressiveness in all the Old Testament passages to which we referred. Our first proposition is thus that it is a mortal sickness, i.e., that if we ourselves had to bear it, if Jesus had not carried it in our place, it could end only with our death and destruction. [486]

It does in fact end with our death to the extent that Jesus, burdened with our sickness, suffered our death. It is true that in His death, triumphing for us even as He suffered for us, He accomplished our new and healthy birth. But this does not alter its character as a mortal sickness. On the contrary, it reveals its character. The misery of man is of such a kind that an end could be made of it (negatively) only by the death suffered by Jesus and (positively) only in a new life inaugurated by Jesus as He crossed this frontier. By what Jesus has done and is in order to free us from it it is distinguished as "my boundless misery" (Luther), i.e., the misery which has no measure or limit within my human being and thinking and willing and achievement, in the sphere of the whole act in which I exist as a man. There are no reservations, no islands on which and no pauses in which, in relation to myself and apart from what I am in Jesus, I am not in misery. I am wholly and utterly encompassed and penetrated by it. It is co-extensive with my existence. I can toss and turn on my sick-bed. I can transfer or be transferred from one sick-bed to another. When it is particularly severe, I can change hospitals, or, if I prefer, arrange for private treatment. But I am always sick, and my sickness is always the same. It is the incurable misery which dominates my life and always emerges in one form or another.

To what do we refer? We refer simply to the fact that we have no option but to be those we are in the power or impotence of what we do. We refer to the destruction and decomposition of our being which takes place in the fact that we think we can accomplish the actions of our stupidity and inhumanity and dissipation and care. We have seen what is the source of these actions: our groundless and inexplicable but unfortunately real and dangerous turning to that which is not; the perverse love of chaos in which we let ourselves fall where we ought to stand and lift up ourselves. We have also seen where this leads: to the net of our self-contradiction with all its interwoven meshes; to our own devastation; to the perversion of our relationship to God and our fellows and ourselves and our temporality. Coming from the one we are necessarily on the way to the other, hastening towards it. Deriving from the one, our being necessarily bears all the marks of the other, of this whole perversion and devastation. This is the misery of man. It is indeed his being in exile, in the far country. For he is not really at home in his hurrying along this way. The marks of his being on this way do not really belong to him. But it is he who bears them. It is he [487] who must bear them. For it is he who hurries along this way on which he has no future but his own destruction and decomposition, nothingness and himself as its victim.

It is to be noted that we are not yet dealing with death. Man still exists. He still lives. The goal has not yet been reached. Or he himself has not yet been reached by the final thing that comes upon him from this source; just as in the pictures of the headlong plunge of the damned the jaws of hell are only opened and eternal fire is only waiting for them. The misery of man is "only" his being in this plunge into them. It is "only" his being in the movement towards death. Only! As though this were less serious! As though being in death might not even seem to be better! As though the irresistible plunge in this direction, which is the inevitable consequence of man's letting himself fall in his sloth, were not as such—in this qualitative sense—"my boundless misery": the very fact that I cannot be free of it; that I am still there; that I have to accept this situation and can find no release from it. It is here that the sharpness of human misery as grounded in man's limitation works itself out. As God does not abandon him, he cannot abandon himself—not even if he wants to, or tries to realise his desire in what we call suicide. He himself does what he does—the work of sloth. And he himself inevitably is what he does. He can only follow the law of sloth under which he has placed himself. He can only hurry along this way. He cannot do so as his own spectator, as he would like. He can do so only as the active and therefore the suffering person; the one who is not yet in death, but already, and hopelessly, on the way to it.

Note that we are referring to an objective reality which obtains irrespective of our own recognition of it. There is thus no substance in the objection raised by experience, i.e., by a deficient experience of this misery. No man but Jesus has ever known the true breadth and depth, the true essence and darkness, of human misery. What we see and note and know and more or less painfully experience of it is only the shadow of His cross touching us. In all its essence and darkness it is, of course, our misery. It is we who make that headlong plunge. But we can see this only before the passion of Christ, as we hear His cry: "My God, my God, why hast thou forsaken me?" (Mk. 15^{34}). We cannot see it in the terror and doubt and despair which may come on us. Or we can see it in these only as a distant recollection of the misery of which He has made an end in His death; only as a weak echo of His cry; only as a sign that we are truly in Him, and therefore share His sufferings. We have no direct experience of it. We cannot speak of it as though it were an element in our own history. However severely we may be buffeted, there can be no question of repetitions of Golgotha. Not merely quantitatively, but qualitatively, all the content of our experience is completely transcended by Golgotha. But the fact that Golgotha never becomes the content of our own experience and consciousness does not [488] alter the fact that the misery of man as it is there borne and revealed by Jesus and as it may also reflect itself in our experiences is objectively and truly our own misery. Whatever we ourselves may see or not see, God sees us as those who are on the way to death, and we are this in truth. And the fact that we are this is something that we have to let ourselves be told from the place where God has seen us all in the One; from the cross and passion of Jesus. Those who think that they are particularly touched by that shadow in their own lives must not think that human misery is only theirs. And those who are able in their own lives to escape the shadow which reaches them with a certain gaiety and abandon must not think that the misery of man is any the less theirs. It is objectively the case that we are all away from home—exiles. In Jesus we are all back home again. Human misery is behind us. We have passed through the far country. We have died as those who lived there and are born again as new men. We already walk in the light. But it is in the light of Jesus in which we participate that we are accused as those who let themselves sink into their own past and therefore as those who sink in this our past; as those who are still in the far country, still in misery.

We have thought of man's misery as an exile (a sense which used to be borne by the German word *Elend*). But if we take it in the customary sense (as *miseria*^{EN49}) the dreadful feature of this hurrying and plunging to death is that at every point man necessarily exists in a radical perversion. "Perversion" is the term that we must use—not transformation or destruction. Even in that which he is in virtue of his folly in all its forms, he is the good creature of God. Even in his sickness he does not lack any of his members or organs. All the features which make him a man still remain. He has not become a devil or an animal or a plant. Even in his misery he is not half a man, but a whole man. His misery consists in the corruption of this best. The perverted use which he makes of it

---

^{EN49} wretchedness

is followed at once by his corrupt state—the worst. Things which are bright in themselves are all dark for him. Things that he desires all slip out of his grasp. His true glory becomes his shame. The pure becomes impure. The joyful is enwrapped by the deepest sadness. That which uplifts becomes a temptation; every blessing a curse; salvation perdition. We do not see deeply enough if we think and say that there is here *only* darkness, want, shame, impurity, sadness, temptation, curse and perdition. In the strict sense, the misery of man is not a *status*, a *continuum*[EN50], but his being in a history in which there can be no abstract "only." Thus the light is still there, but quenched; the wealth as it slips away; the glory as it turns to shame; the purity to impurity; the joy to sadness. They are all there in this movement from the right to the left, from above to below, in their perversion and corruption; or, strictly, in the event of their

[489] corruption. The slothful man is and exists in the context of this event, in the sequence of such events, in this sinister history. It is the history of his impotent ignoring of the grace of God present to him. It is the history of the opportunities continually offered to him and continually let slip by him. It is his history under the judgments of God. His being in this history is his misery. As he is in this history, he is the *miser*[EN51] who will inevitably be lost and in death without the *misericordia Dei*[EN52].

We emphasise the fact that he is this at every point. This means in the whole fulfilment of his existence and in all the features of his humanity. It does not mean that he is below and in darkness in everything that he is and does. On the contrary, in everything that he is and does he is above. But he is not merely above. He is also engaged in that slipping and sinking and falling on the one-way street from above to below. There is no firm point at which and from which he is involved in any other movement and therefore not in that corruption. He is wholly and utterly caught up in this history. There is no depth of his soul where he is not implicated in this perversion. It is quite futile to talk about a "relic of goodness" which remains to man even as a sinner and which is usually identified rather uneasily with the faculty of reason or a religious or moral *a priori*[EN53] or the like. In answer to this kind of assertion we have to say (1) that the good which remains to man as a sinner is not merely a "relic" but the totality of His God-given nature and its determination, and (2) that in the same totality he exists in the history of the perversion of this good into evil, and is caught up in the movement from above to below. His total being in this movement is his *miseria*[EN54] which has its limit only in the *misericordia Dei*[EN55].

What we call the misery of man corresponds fairly exactly to what the New Testament calls

---

EN50 continuity
EN51 wretch
EN52 mercy of God
EN53 axiom
EN54 wretchedness
EN55 mercy of God

his being in the flesh. As is well known, the term σάρξ^EN56 is ambiguous. On the one side, like the Old Testament *basar*^EN57, it is a term which is simply used to describe man and his person as an existing temporal subject in the totality of his human nature, and especially in the determination in which he is a physical being in this totality. "Flesh and blood" is sometimes used to bring out this sense. To be or live ἐν σαρκί^EN58 or even κατὰ σάρκα^EN59 in this sense is simply to be, to exist, to live as a living human creature in time, with a special emphasis on the physical aspect, on the context of the physico-natural order to which we belong. The fact that this is the special reference is an indication that in it man is regarded, if neutrally, from the standpoint of the lower components of his being. On the other side σάρξ^EN60 has a pejorative sense. It means man in the sphere which is dominated by the power of his own sin. It again means the whole man, but in the corruption which has entered and which works itself out as a result of his sin. It means man as he has turned away from God in his own lust, as he is hostile and opposed to God, as he lacks His Spirit, and as he has fallen a total victim to φθορά^EN61. To be and walk and act ἐν σαρκί^EN62 or κατὰ σάρκα^EN63 in this sense is to be a man—the lower side is no longer neutral but disqualified—in this sphere and therefore under this power, in this perversion, and with desires which are opposed to God and His Spirit, thus falling a victim to φθορά^EN64. In relation to this twofold meaning it is to be noted that the second is already indicated in the first. Even in the first sense σάρξ^EN65 is not unequivocal (like ψυχή, σῶμα^EN66 or νοῦς^EN67). It is not a term used in a normal, but [490] only in a pathological, anthropology. It sees man already as the subject of the history in which he will become σάρξ^EN68 in the second sense. Conversely, however, we must not lose sight of the first sense in the second. The man who lives in the flesh in the pejorative sense is the same as the one who, as described by the same term, simply lives in his humanity in time. We cannot dissolve with a word the tension which there is in the term and which emerges in these changes of meaning. In the various passages we may be pointed more to the one side or more to the other, but the tension remains. In the relationship of the two meanings the term describes the fatal history which confronted the New Testament authors when they looked at man—not others but primarily themselves (Rom. 7)—as he is apart from his being in the one man Jesus, opposing His Spirit and in total need of liberation by Him. To denote his being in the history of the division of his ego, his self-alienation and self-contradiction, they used the term σάρξ^EN69 in its twofold sense. The term describes the ταλαίπωρος ἄνθρωπος^EN70 (Rom. 7^24) who can only cry for redemption—man in his misery.

2. In our redemption from this misery, a new man, the saint of God, has taken our place in the crucified man Jesus in whom our old man died; a new

---

EN56 flesh
EN57 flesh
EN58 in the flesh
EN59 according to the flesh
EN60 flesh
EN61 destruction
EN62 in the flesh
EN63 according to the flesh
EN64 destruction
EN65 flesh
EN66 soul, body
EN67 mind
EN68 flesh
EN69 flesh
EN70 wretched man

man as the subject of new and different acts which are obedient and well pleasing to God. We are freed from our misery to the extent that in Him we too are new men and therefore the subjects of new acts. Less than the new birth of man did not and does not suffice to make him a doer of these new acts in which his sloth is no longer operative and recognisable, in which instead of continually sinking he may lift up himself and stand and be active as a true man. Except as they proceed from the new beginning which has been made in Jesus his acts—and this is our second proposition—will always be the acts of his sloth and misery.

The misery of man as it may be seen in the light of his liberation is a history and not a status or *continuum*^{EN71} in the further sense that it has a life of its own in which it continually confirms and renews itself in an endless circle. We have already stated that what man does he is. But the converse is also true. What he is he does. And he will do it continually to the extent that he does not become another man in Jesus and his action does not become that of the other man who is in Jesus. To use the language of older dogmatics, *peccatum originale*^{EN72} necessarily gives rise to *peccata actualia*^{EN73}. *Peccata actualia*^{EN74} (acts of sin) are *peccata in actione*^{EN75}. The misery of man is characterised by the fact that man not only *is* a sinner. He certainly is, and makes himself, this as he commits sin. But we might accustom ourselves to the fact that he is this. We might learn to master it. We might explain it as a kind of fate—merited, of course, but to be borne and endured by the individual only in solidarity with all history and humanity, in subjection to the sentence pronounced on Adam and on all men in him. But this sentence is already misunderstood. For its reference is to the culpability of the act, the basic act of evil, in which humanity, which has its responsible subject in each individual, was and is implicated from the very first, in Adam. And what characterises the misery of man is that he is evil, not only in his participation in this basic act, not only as a child of Adam, in his heart from his youth up, but also (as this) from moment to moment, "in evil thoughts and words and works from his youth up even to this present," in individual decisions which are wrong decisions in virtue of their source, each of them having its fatal aspect and consequence, each in its own way being an act of unfaithfulness, unbelief, disobedience and ingratitude, each in its own way a work of the sloth for which he is again and no less strictly responsible as for the basic act of his existence. It is true, but it does not release him (for he himself is the one who wills and does it), that as the child of Adam he proceeds continually from the great sloth of man. It is also true, but does not release him (for he himself is again a willing and acting subject), that in the form of

[491]

---

^{EN71} continuity
^{EN72} original sin
^{EN73} actual sins
^{EN74} Actual sins
^{EN75} sins in action

concrete, the most concrete, achievements he continually returns to the sphere of that sloth. The liberation of man as it has taken place in Jesus is his true liberation from this circle. That he (he himself) moves in this circle is his misery.

And to the misery of his being in individual wicked acts there belongs the contradiction that there is no action which is evil in itself and as such, by disposition and constitution, but that the whole action of man is necessarily evil as it takes place in this circle. "For every creature of God is good, and nothing to be refused, if it be received with thanksgiving" (1 Tim. 4⁴). Yet that is the very thing which is lacking. The psychical and physical, spiritual and sensual functions in which the evil acts of men are done can be pure as the functions of the pure (Tit. 1¹⁵). They are this in themselves and as such. The good creation of God persists. We are forced to say this finally not only of the functions of those who are healthy but also of those who are sick in body or soul. The evil does not consist in a disposition of the *psyche* or *physis*[EN76] but in the sloth of their physical and psychic action as it derives from the sloth of their heart. It is in this, and in its service, that that which is not evil in itself becomes evil—the psychic and physical occurrence in which the acts of men are done. Even to the smallest details the slothful man acts in contradiction and conflict with himself. Even to the smallest details he exists in the history of this perversion. In his actual sins it continually acquires new actuality in a whole inter-related sequence of open and secret detailed histories. Apart from his new beginning, apart from the new birth which has already taken place in Jesus, apart from his becoming a different man, and therefore the subject of new and different acts, in the power of His direction, there can be no question of an end of his misery in this respect too.

A dogmatico-historical observation is required at this point. It concerns the locus *De peccato actuali*[EN77] which presents rather a curious picture in older Protestant dogmatics. It consists for the most part in a remarkable and very finely woven net of concepts which are intrinsically antithetical but which are paired off to show how from any particular standpoint the act of sin may take place between two very widely separated points and yet always have the essential character of sin. There are thus, it was taught, *peccata commissionis*[EN78] and *peccata omissionis, peccata infirmitatis*[EN79] or *ignorantiae*[EN80] and *peccata malitiae, peccata voluntaria*[EN81] and *peccata involuntaria, peccata regnantia*[EN82], i.e., sins which dominate a man, or which he allows to master him without a struggle, and *peccata non regnantia*[EN83], those which are not overcome by him, yet which he does not acquiesce in but contests. There is a

[492]

EN76 mind or nature
EN77 On the Act of Sin
EN78 sins of commission
EN79 sins of omission, sins of infirmity
EN80 of ignorance
EN81 malicious sins, voluntary sins
EN82 involuntary sins, reigning sins
EN83 non-reigning sins

peccatum mortuum[EN84], and in some sense latent or potential sin, of which we are not conscious, at least in its full range and extent, and a *peccatum vivens*[EN85], sin living and recognised in the sense of Rom. 7$^{8-9}$. There are *peccata spiritualia*[EN86], of which the soul is particularly guilty (e.g., pride, envy and theological heresy), and *peccata carnalia*[EN87], like gluttony, drunkenness and lechery. There are *peccata clamantia*[EN88], those which cry to heaven, and *peccata tolerantiae*[EN89], those which for all their culpability are endured for a time by the long-suffering of God. The doubtful nature of the whole understanding emerges at once in the obvious difficulty and even impossibility of many of these distinctions. The general purpose was very largely perhaps to differentiate one sin from another as more or less dangerous and disruptive. It is tempting to try to do this, but it constitutes a threat to the presupposition which was sometimes maintained very strongly, that all sins are alike in this, *ut vel minima minimi peccati cogitatio, mortem aeternam millies mereamur*[EN90] (Bucan, *Inst. theol.*, 1602, XVI, 9). Yet if we consider the results rather than the purpose of this whole theologoumen, we have to recognise, not merely that it has a certain practical value as a constituent element in a kind of penitential mirror, but that it helps us to realise that the whole action of man, caught in the cross-fire of the questions put by these distinctions, is unable to avoid the judgment that it is sin, and that it is brought under this judgment, not indiscriminately, but in its differentiation, in its own particular nature and character. If we keep before us the net of these opposing concepts in its totality, we realise that the judgment under which we stand is comprehensive and yet that it is also concrete and specific. If the Word of God pronounces us all guilty, it does not do so generally and amorphously, but with particular reference to each individual in his own place, and again with particular reference to this or that specific action, so that the misery of man is not a night which makes all cats grey, but in it each of us, in each specific action, has his own profile and his own shade of darkness.

One pair of concepts suggested in relation to *peccata actualia*[EN91] was a subject of dispute between the Romanists and Lutherans on the one side and the Reformed dogmaticians on the other. This was the distinction between so-called mortal sins (*peccata mortalia*) and venial sins (*peccata venialia*). According to Roman doctrine there are some sins which are so slight that they do not leave behind any *macula in anima*[EN92] (Thomas Aquinas, *S. th.* II, 1, 89, 1). They are inevitably bound up with human life since the fall. But they are to be compared with what Paul in 1 Cor. 3^{12} calls wood, hay and stubble. They do not prevent the attainment of salvation (89^2) and they are reparable in themselves even apart from the counteraction of divine grace. In contrast, there are the seven deadly sins—according to Thomas (84, 4) *inanis gloria, gula, luxuria, avaritia, tristitia* (*quae tristatur de bono spirituali propter laborem corporalem adiunctum*), *invidia, ira*[EN93]. These are not reparable in themselves. They can be made good only by grace, which means in practice the renewal of baptismal grace by the sacrament of penance. The older Lutheran dogmatics could also speak of a *peccatum*

[EN84] dead sin
[EN85] living sin
[EN86] spiritual sins
[EN87] carnal sins
[EN88] crying sins
[EN89] tolerable sins
[EN90] so that, be it the smallest contemplation of the smallest sin, we deserve eternal death a thousand times over
[EN91] actual sins
[EN92] stain on the soul
[EN93] vainglory, gluttony, luxury, greed, sadness (which is saddened by spiritual good because of the bodily exertion accompanying it), envy, anger

mortale[EN94] as opposed to a *peccatum veniale*[EN95]. "Venial" according to Hollaz (*Ex. theol. acroam.*, 1707, II, 4, *qu.* 20) is *omne peccatum involuntarium in renatis, quod neque gratiam inhabitantem Spiritus sancti excutit, neque fidem extinguit, sed eodem momento, quo committitur, veniam indivulso nexu coniunctam habet*[EN96]. Mortal sin, on the other hand, is that which is committed in transgression of the divine commandment *contra dictamen conscientiae deliberato voluntatis proposito*[EN97] (*qu.* 9). The older Reformed teachers rejected this whole distinction. [493] As they saw it, they can be no resting-place even for the regenerate. On the one side every sin, however slight it may seem to be, is mortal sin. And on the other side every sin can be forgiven by the mercy of God.

In the light of our presuppositions there can be no doubt as to our own position in relation to this controversy. The Roman and Lutheran distinction between mortal and venial sin assumes a quantitative concept of sin which cannot be united with the decisive seriousness of the divine judgment and the human situation under this judgment. It can serve only to veil the depth of human misery and therefore the depth of the free grace of God. On the same ground we have to reject the distinction between voluntary and involuntary sin, and especially the notion that in respect of involuntary sins Christians are more advantageously placed than the unregenerate. Every sin, even the smallest, is mortal sin to the extent that it is worthy of death and involves our mortal sickness. How, then, can we restrict the term to the seven deadly sins, as though a venial sin not in this list could not be just as great as any of these, and even greater than all of them put together? Which supposedly little sin, even the smallest, is not committed in an inner conflict of man and the will of man, so that it is not at one and the same time voluntary sin and involuntary? And what is meant by the idea of a sin which is pardonable in itself, and therefore apart from the merciful God and independently of His pardoning grace? Is there any other forgiveness but that of God? Does not each one of us stand in absolute need of His forgiveness for every sin? Is not His forgiveness promised equally to every sinner for every sin?—excepting only those to whom He is revealed, and by whom He is known, as the merciful God, but who do not keep to His mercy, who try to evade forgiveness and the need of forgiveness in the case of some of their sins, and who thus make themselves guilty of what is indicated in Mk. 3[28] and par. as a limiting concept, the sin against the Holy Ghost. The distinction between lethal and venial sins cannot be sustained. It is quite irrelevant. And in the last resort it is to be rejected because it involves a dangerous tendency in the direction of this terrible limiting concept.

3. The liberation of man from his misery has taken place and is a fact only in the royal freedom in which the man Jesus has accomplished it by giving up Himself, His life as very God and very man, to death for us in obedience to God and as our Lord and Head and Representative. This is the act of free will, the decision of *liberum arbitrium*[EN98], in which the liberation of man from his misery has been once and for all accomplished. Jesus lives. He lives as the Doer of this act of the free and victorious human will breaking the circle of sinful human action and being; the will of the new man, the holy man introduced by God in His person, the man who is free for Him and for us. As such, He lives

---

[EN94] mortal sin
[EN95] venial sin
[EN96] every involuntary sin in those who have been born again which does not drive out the indwelling grace of the Holy Spirit, nor extinguishes faith, but in the same moment in which it is committed, receives a pardon joined by an inseparable bond
[EN97] against the dictate of conscience by the deliberate decision of the will
[EN98] free will

for us. And in Him we also live as men of the same free will, as those who break through that circle, who overcome and conquer our misery, as free men. In Him the mercy of God which limits our misery is really present as the gift of freedom—our own freedom. But this means that in the misery from which we are liberated by Him, i.e., in our own tarrying in our past as caused by our sloth, we are not free apart from Him, nor do we participate in the free and victorious will which breaks through that circle of our sinning. Our third proposition is, therefore, as follows. Our misery, as we have to learn continually from our liberation by Him, is the determination of our will as *servum arbitrium*[EN99].

[494]

It is always a mistake to try to establish or understand the assertion of the bondage of the will otherwise than christologically. It cannot be either proved or disproved by empirical findings or *a priori*[EN100] reflections. As a corollary to the confession of the freedom which has been won for us and granted to us in the man Jesus it is a theological statement—a statement of faith. As such, it has nothing whatever to do with the battle between determinism and indeterminism. It is not a decision for determinism; and the fact that this is not clear in Luther's *De servo arbitrio* is the objection that we are forced to raise against this well-known work and also against the ideas of Zwingli and Calvin. It can take up into itself both determinism and indeterminism to the extent that they are to be understood as the hypotheses of an empiricist or *a priori*[EN101] philosophy. It necessarily excludes both to the extent that they set themselves up, on this or that foundation, as metaphysical dogmas. It describes the perversion of the human situation which results from the sloth of man in his relationship with God. It does not consist at all in the fact that man cannot any longer will and decide, i.e., that he is deprived of *arbitrium*[EN102], that he has no will at all. If this were the case, he would no longer be a man; he would only be part of a mechanism moved from without. This would involve the transformation of man into another and non-human being—an idea which we have exerted ourselves to repudiate from the very outset in this whole context. But the freedom of man does not really consist—except in the imagination of the invincibly ignorant—in the fact that, like Hercules at the cross-roads, he can will and decide. Nor does the bondage of his will consist in the fact that he is not able to do this.

Freedom is not an empty and formal concept. It is one which is filled out with a positive meaning. It does not speak only of a capacity. It speaks concretely of the fact that man can be genuinely man as God who has given him this capacity can in His freedom be genuinely God. The free man is the man who can be genuinely man in fellowship with God. He exercises and has this freedom, therefore, not in an indefinite but in a definite choice in which he demonstrates this capacity. But since this capacity is grounded in His fellow-

---

EN 99 will in bondage
EN100 axiomatic
EN101 axiomatic
EN102 will

ship with God this means in the choice in which he confirms and practises his fellowship with God; in the election, corresponding to his own election and creation and determination, of faith and obedience and gratitude and loyalty to God as the One who is the Creator and Giver not only of his human essence and existence but also of this capacity.

Again, we must not say that this great name is merited by the "freedom" so often described as *posse peccare*[EN103] and *posse non peccare*[EN104]: as though the possibility of *peccare*[EN105] were a genuine possibility offered to man by God and not one which God has forbidden and excluded; as though he could have this [495] possibility in genuine freedom, in his freedom to be genuinely man. The man who has, or can desire, this possibility is already the man who is not free and who must desire it. Of the free man it has to be said: *non potest peccare*[EN106]. His freedom excludes this. It excludes the possibility of sinning. He "cannot" sin in the capacity granted to him by God. In this capacity he can only believe and obey and give thanks and give to the faithfulness of God the response of his own loyalty. He can sin only as he renounces this capacity and therefore, as we have repeatedly maintained, makes no use of his freedom. The sloth of man in all its forms (as stupidity, inhumanity, dissipation and care) and in all its individual acts or omissions consists in his failure to make use of his freedom. And all this is negative. It does not rest on anything that can seriously be called a *posse*[EN107]. It has no basis either in God or in man himself by which it can be explained. It can be described only as a freedom not to be free—which is nonsense. Yet as man's turning to that which is not it does actually take place. It is the grasping of the possibility which is no possibility, but can be characterised only as an impossibility. It is the "choosing" which is not an alternative to the genuine choosing of faith and obedience and gratitude but only the dreadful negation of this genuine choosing. It is the irrational and incomprehensible decision of man. It is a fact only as *peccare*[EN108], ἁμαρτάνειν[EN109], transgression. Yet in this character it is a real fact. It is a sinister fact which is not illumined by any *posse*[EN110]. It is the fact of sin in which man reveals and demonstrates that he is inexplicably the slothful man who does not make any use of his freedom. He can have his freedom only as he uses it, in the choice of the possibility which corresponds to it. If he does not use it, he goes out into the absolute void of a being in unbelief and disobedience and ingratitude, into a being which is no true being. And this means that he loses it. He does not have it. There is no freedom in this unreal being and for those who turn to it. It

---

[EN103] ability to sin
[EN104] ability not to sin
[EN105] sinning
[EN106] he cannot sin
[EN107] ability
[EN108] sinning
[EN109] sinning
[EN110] ability

is *eo ipso*^{EN111} the sphere of bondage. As a sinner man has decided against his freedom to be genuinely man. And in this decision he will necessarily continue to decide against it. "Whosoever committeth sin is the servant of sin" (Jn. 8³⁴). In this briefest of biblical formulations we have the whole doctrine of the bondage of the will. *Non potest non peccare*^{EN112} is what we have to say of the sinful, slothful man. His sin excludes his freedom, just as his freedom excludes his sin. There is no middle position. For the slothful man there is only the first alternative. He has not ceased to be a man. He wills. He is a Hercules, the *arbiter*^{EN113} of what he does. But he does what he does in the corruption of his will. He does not, therefore, do it *libero*^{EN114} but *servo arbitrio*^{EN115}. In a deeper sense than the poet had in mind, it is the curse of an evil deed that it inevitably gives birth to fresh evil. To be sure, the slothful man chooses—in that dreadful negation of true choosing—as he always did. But he chooses only on the path

[496] that he has entered. And on this path, however he may choose, he cannot choose as a true man (for he has turned aside from this genuine possibility), but in all his choices, having yielded to corruption, he can only act corruptly. His starting-point is the repudiation of his freedom. He cannot, therefore, do that which corresponds to his freedom. He necessarily does that which he could not do in the exercise of it. This is the bondage of the human will which is the bitterest characteristic of human misery.

It has its limit in the mercy of God, or concretely in the liberation accomplished for man in Jesus. This limit is set for it in the sanctification of man of which we shall speak in the next section. But as a precaution we must already make the following statement. The concept of limitation (which we are forced to use in relation to the sanctification of man) includes that of a subject of limitation. The liberation of man in Jesus is his new birth and conversion as it has taken place in Him. The freedom which man has and exercises in Him is a new creation. In Him he is free from the committal of sin and for faith, obedience and gratitude. He is, therefore, genuinely free, ὄντως ἐλεύθερος^{EN116} (Jn. 8³⁶). This is the limit which is set to his bondage by his sanctification. But in this life even the sanctified man who partakes of this freedom, even the Christian, is not only in Jesus, not only what he is in Him, and therefore not only free. In solidarity with all other men he is also in himself, in the flesh, in the past which is continually present. He is the one who is limited by this limitation, and as such the one who needs sanctification, liberation. To the extent that he is this, he is not free, and everything that we have said about the bondage of the human will applies in all seriousness to him too. To the extent that he is in the flesh and not in the spirit he is "dead in sins" (Col. 2¹³; Eph. 2¹). He

---

^{EN111} by definition
^{EN112} he cannot not sin
^{EN113} judge
^{EN114} with a free will
^{EN115} with a will in bondage
^{EN116} being free

is not just half-dead, or apparently dead. He is a corpse awaiting the resurrection, and we have to speak in all seriousness of his past which unfortunately is always present. He is engaged in the conflict of the Spirit against the flesh, but also of the flesh against the Spirit (Gal. 5^{17}), and in the last resort he will not refuse to confess with the apostle Paul "that in me (that is, in my flesh) dwelleth no good thing" (Rom. 7^{18}). Conflict does not mean peaceful co-existence, let alone co-operation. Even in the Christian the old man is quite unambiguously the old man. In relation to the new he can be compared only to a rebel whose insurrection is so checked by the power of his sovereign that it cannot work itself out freely but as a limited operation will even serve to promote the general good. Yet even in this way he is a rebel; he is not a servant of his king. The old man, even in the Christian, is not a herald and precursor and partner of the new. In the sense described, he is in bondage. He does not will *libero arbitrio*^{EN117}, but *servo arbitrio*^{EN118}. He does not believe or love or hope or pray—or he does so only in appearance, deceiving himself and others. He is useless, absolutely useless, as far as concerns the good. He is stupid, inhuman, dissipated and discontented. He chooses, but he never chooses the right, only the wrong. All this stands within the limitation, but within it it is just the same as in the case of the non-Christian who does not have a part in that limitation. Within the limitation, as the one who is limited by it, the Christian is himself a practical non-Christian. Freedom and bondage clash in one and the same man: his freedom as a new man in Jesus and in the Holy Spirit; and his bondage as an old man, outside Jesus, in and for himself, in the flesh, in his past which is still present; and both of them total; no *tertium*^{EN119}, no bridge, no mediation or synthesis between them, but only the antithesis of that conflict, life in sanctification, the *militia Christi*^{EN120}. No co-operation, then, between the two! For how can there be co-operation between total freedom and total bondage? How can the Spirit give assistance to the flesh, or the flesh to the Spirit?

[497]

The doctrine which makes this *caveat* necessary is the Romanist doctrine of man's co-operation in the accomplishment of his justification (which as Romanists use the term includes what we call sanctification); his *translatio ab eo statu, in quo homo nascitur filius primi Adae, in statum gratiae ... per secundum Adam Jesum Christum*^{EN121} (*Trid.* VI, *c.* 4). Even on the Roman view this *translatio*^{EN122} cannot, of course, take place without regeneration in Christ, participation in the merits of His passion (*c.* 3) and therefore concretely the sacramental grace of baptism. It cannot take place without the *gratia praeveniens*^{EN123} which in the case of adults at least reaches and calls and supports them even before their baptism (*c.* 5). On the

---

^{EN117} with a free will
^{EN118} with a will in bondage
^{EN119} third
^{EN120} militant Christ
^{EN121} transferral from that state in which man is born as a son of the first Adam, into a state of grace through the second Adam, Jesus Christ
^{EN122} transferral
^{EN123} prevenient grace

other hand, it cannot take place unless they themselves, moved by prevenient grace, are disposed *ad convertendum se ad suam ipsorum iustificationem*[EN124], to a free *assentire* and *cooperari* with this grace. Thus in relation to it man is neither inactive nor active apart from it (*c.* 5) when he comes to the point (we are still in a prior sphere to that of an acceptance of the true grace of justification) of assenting to revelation, of recognising that he is a sinner, of seeking refuge in the mercy of God, of believing in Christ and loving Him, and of beginning to hate his sin, with the ultimate result that he receives baptism and begins a new life and obeys the divine commandments (*c.* 6). All this can and must take place on the Romanist view because even in a state of original sin the *liberum arbitrium*[EN125] of man is *minime exstinctum, viribus licet attenuatum et inclinatum*[EN126] (*c.* 1). In other words, it is not so weakened or perverted that on the presupposition of *gratia praeveniens*[EN127] man is not capable of that *assentire et cooperari*[EN128], of that *se disponere et praeparare*[EN129] (*can.* 4). If this is the case with the man who has not yet participated in the true grace of justification, how much more is it the case with those who have received the grace of baptism (*c.* 7) or its renewal in penance (*c.* 14). This sacramental grace has cleansed away all sin in the strict sense (*totum id, quod veram et propriam peccati rationem habet*[EN130]). What remains is a *concupiscentia vel fomes peccati*[EN131], a painful relic of earth which, although it derives from sin and inclines to it (V, *c.* 5), cannot harm those who do not give place to it, but manfully resist it *per gratiam Christi Jesu*[EN132]. Indeed, those who do this are capable of an *incrementum iustificationis*[EN133] in the form of good works (VI, *c.* 10). They still commit the little, everyday, venial sins in which they do not cease to be righteous. But they also do good works in which they are free even from venial offences (*c.* 11). Even if they fall into mortal sin, and must therefore begin again from the beginning by receiving the sacrament of penance, they will not lose faith (*c.* 15, *can.* 28). In addition, they can merit (*mereri, c.* 16, *can.* 24 and 33) an *augmentum gratiae*[EN134] by good works, and, if they die in a state of grace, the actual reception of eternal life, and ultimately even an *augmentum gloriae*[EN135], a commensurate enhancement of their eternal blessedness.

[498]

These were the statements of Trent as they were drawn up in the year of Luther's death in opposition to Reformation teaching. They had been carefully worked out in a conscientious and critical scrutiny of the development of doctrine in Scholasticism and later Scholasticism, and they were formulated in such a way as to counter at every conceivable point the objection of the Reformers. At the heart of the exposition of the *meritum bonorum operum*[EN136] (*c.* 16) we even come across the sincerely meant statement: *Absit tamen, ut christianus homo in se ipso vel confidet vel glorietur et non in Domino*[EN137]. It is hard to see, however, what force this statement can have in conjunction with a doctrine the whole point of which is to maintain man in an unshaken self-consciousness balancing not only the grace of God but also and

---

[EN124] to the conversion of themselves to their own justification
[EN125] free will
[EN126] in very small measure extinct, although it is weakened and misdirected by powers
[EN127] prevenient grace
[EN128] assent and co-operation
[EN129] disposing and preparing himself
[EN130] all that which has a real and proper ground of sin
[EN131] concupiscence, or tinder of sin
[EN132] by the grace of Jesus Christ
[EN133] increase of justification
[EN134] augment of grace
[EN135] augment of glory
[EN136] merit of good work
[EN137] However, let it not be that the Christian man has confidence or glories in his own self and not in the Lord

primarily his own sin. Both sin and grace are understood as quantities, and on this assumption they are compared and pragmatised and tamed and rendered quite innocuous. The meaning of the conflict between the Spirit and the flesh, of the new man in Jesus and the old in whose form we confront Jesus, of freedom and bondage as totalities which do not complement but mutually exclude one another, is not only unperceived but actually concealed in a whole sea of obliterating formulae and objections and protests which are directed against every kind of quietism and fatalism, which have nothing whatever to do with what has to be said seriously concerning either the *liberum*[EN138] or the *servum arbitrium*[EN139], and which can only secure us against having to see and say what really ought to be seen and said at this point. The teaching office the Roman Church neither willed nor could say this. It will not and cannot say it to-day. Instead it speaks on the one hand of that *assentire* and *cooperari*[EN140] of the unregenerate man in his relationship to the obscure *gratia praeveniens*[EN141] which is arbitrarily invented and cannot be defined with any precision but which results in his capacity for faith and penitence and a turning to grace. And on the other it speaks of the good works of the regenerate man, who is only a little sinner and commits only tiny sins, and who is in the happy position of being able to increase the grace of justification in co-operation with it, and even to augment the degree of his eternal bliss. The practical consequence of all this is that the misery of man is not regarded as in any way serious or dangerous either for Christians or non-Christians. The Reformation communions could not reunite with a Church which held this doctrine, and they cannot accept the call to reunion with it to-day. We ourselves have looked at the matter rather differently from the Evangelical theologians of the 16th century. We have considered the misery of man in the light of the liberation which has taken place and is actually present in Jesus. Our understanding of the enslaved will of sinful man has nothing whatever to do with determinism or pessimism. But for this very reason we cannot accept any more (indeed far less) than they could the mitigation of this misery offered by the Romanist doctrine. "Thanks be to God, which giveth us the victory through our Lord Jesus Christ" (1 Cor. 15[57]). It is a matter of the positive affirmation of this thanksgiving if in substantial agreement with the older Evangelical theology we are committed at this point to a decided negative.

[EN138] free will
[EN139] will in bondage
[EN140] assent and cooperation
[EN141] prevenient grace

§ 66

THE SANCTIFICATION OF MAN

The exaltation of man, which in defiance of his reluctance has been achieved in the death and declared in the resurrection of Jesus Christ, is as such the creation of his new form of existence as the faithful covenant-partner of God. It rests wholly and utterly on his justification before God, and like this it is achieved only in the one Jesus Christ, but effectively and authoritatively for all in Him. It is self-attested, by its operation among them as His direction, in the life of a people of men who in virtue of the call to discipleship which has come to them, of their awakening to conversion, of the praise of their works, of the mark of the cross which is laid upon them, have the freedom even as sinners to render obedience and to establish themselves as the saints of God in a provisional offering of the thankfulness for which the whole world is ordained by the act of the love of God.

1. JUSTIFICATION AND SANCTIFICATION

Under the title "sanctification" we take up the theme which constitutes the particular scope of this second part of the doctrine of reconciliation. The divine act of atonement accomplished and revealed in Jesus Christ does not consist only in the humiliation of God but in and with this in the exaltation of man. Thus it does not consist only in the fact that God offers Himself up for men; that He, the Judge, allows Himself to be judged in their place, in this way establishing and proclaiming among sinners, and in defiance of their sin, His divine right which is as such the basis of a new right of man before Him. It does not consist, therefore, only in the justification of man. It consists also in the sanctification which is indissolubly bound up with his justification, i.e., in the fact that as He turns to man in defiance of his sin He also, in defiance of his sin, turns man to Himself. The reconciliation of man with God takes place also in the form that He introduces as a new man the one in relation to whom He has set Himself in the right and whom He has set in the right in relation to Himself. He has introduced him in the new form of existence of a faithful covenant-partner who is well pleasing to Him and blessed by Him. "I will be your God" is the justification of man. "Ye shall be my people" is his sanctifi-
[500] cation. It is not the final thing that has to be said concerning the alteration of the human situation which has taken place in the reconciliation achieved and revealed in Jesus Christ. In a third part of the doctrine of reconciliation we shall have to consider the whole in relation to the provisional goal of the cov-

enant newly and definitively established in Jesus Christ and therefore in relation to the calling of man. But our present problem is that of his sanctification—his reconciliation with God from the standpoint of his conversion to Him as willed and accomplished by God.

What is meant by sanctification (*sanctificatio*) might just as well be described by the less common biblical term regeneration (*regeneratio*) or renewal (*renovatio*), or by that of conversion (*conversio*), or by that of penitence (*poenitentia*) which plays so important a role in both the Old and New Testaments, or comprehensively by that of discipleship which is so outstanding especially in the Synoptic Gospels. The content of all these terms will have to be brought out under the title of sanctification. But there is good reason to keep the term sanctification itself in the foreground. It includes already, even verbally, the idea of the "saint," and therefore in contradistinction to the other descriptions of the same matter it shows us at once that we are dealing with the being and action of God, reminding us in a way which is normative for the understanding of the other terms as well of the basic and decisive fact that God is the active Subject not only in reconciliation generally but also in the conversion of man to Himself. Like His turning to man, and man's justification, this is His work, His *facere*[EN1]. But it is now seen and understood, not as his *iustificare*[EN2], but as his *sanctificare*[EN3].

In the Bible God Himself is the One who is originally and properly holy, confronting man in his creatureliness and sinfulness, and the whole created cosmos, with absoluteness, distinctness and singularity, with inviolable majesty. "I am God, and not man" (Hos. 11⁹). The seraphim proclaim Him (Is. 6³) as the One who is thrice holy—"holy as it were to a threefold degree" (Proksch in *Kittel* I, 93)—in this sense, in this uniqueness and superiority. But in this as in other respects the biblical teaching about God is not theoretical. It is given in the context of accounts of God's action in the history inaugurated by Him. Nowhere, then, does it look abstractly to this One who confronts us, in His own inner being. He is indeed holy in and for Himself. But he demonstrates and reveals Himself as such in His establishment and maintenance of fellowship with man and his world. The prophet Hosea was the first and, in the Old Testament, the only writer to understand and describe this Holy One as specifically the One who loves His people. But this equation is the implicit declaration of the whole of the Old Testament. In it we have to do with the Holy One who encounters the man who is so very different from Himself, and who does so in that unapproachable majesty, and therefore effectively, but who demonstrates and reveals Himself as the Holy One in the fact that He sanctifies the unholy by His action with and towards them, i.e., gives them a derivative and limited, but supremely real, share in His own holiness. The reference is to the Holy One of Israel, to use the term which dominates both parts of the Book of Isaiah. "God that is holy shall be sanctified in righteousness" (Is. 5¹⁶). It is by His acts of judgment and grace among and to this people that He sanctifies it as its Lord (Ez. 37²⁸) "before the heathen" (Ez. 20⁴¹), "before their eyes" (Ez. 36²³)—and in so doing sanctifies Himself in the world, i.e., activates and reveals Himself in His majesty in the forms and circumstances of human history. This people may and shall and must be "holy to me" (Lev. 10³), i.e., enabled to worship Me, the

[501]

[EN1] doing
[EN2] justification
[EN3] sanctification

119

Holy One, and therefore to attest Me as the Holy One in the world. To use the classical definition of Lev. 19² (cf. 11⁴⁴, 20⁷) quoted in 1 Pet. 1¹⁶: "Ye shall be holy: for I ... am holy." The holiness of this God demands and enforces the holiness of His people. It requires that His own divine confrontation of the world and all men should find a human (and as such very inadequate, but for all its inadequacy very real) correspondence and copy in the mode of existence of this people. It requires this already in and with the election and calling of this people, in and with the fact that He has made Himself the God of this people and this people His people. The imperative: "Ye shall be holy," is simply the imperative indication of the irresistible dynamic of the indicative: "I am holy," i.e., I am holy, and act among you as such, and therefore I make you holy—this is your life and norm. It is not the glory of any man or creature, not even of Israel, but that of *Yahweh* Himself, which sanctifies the tent of meeting (Ex. 29¹³). And at the central point in the New Testament—in spite of all the appeals and exhortations to holiness of life, or rather as their presupposition—there is set as the primary petition (Mt. 6⁹; Lk. 11²): ἁγιασθήτω τὸ ὄνομά σου^EN4. The "name" of God is the holy God Himself, who is present as such in His holiness, present to His people as the Lord, to sanctify it, and in so doing to sanctify Himself. "The name of God is as little hallowed by men as His kingdom comes or His will is done by them" (Proksch, *op. cit.*, p. 113). "It is God Himself who proves His name holy" (p. 91). He proves it in and to men. He sanctifies men. His sanctifying involves a modification of their situation and constitution. They have to deduce the consequences of it. But the sanctifying by which He claims and makes them and their actions usable in His service and as His possession is "a manifestation of His own divine power" (E. Gaugler, *Die Heiligung im Zeugnis der Schrift*, 1948, 13), and as such it is wholly and exclusively His own act, and not theirs. "And the very God of peace sanctify you wholly" (1 Thess. 5²³). He it is who wills and accomplishes, not only His own turning to man, but man's conversion to Him, the claiming of man for His service. And He wills that we should call upon Him daily that this may happen. "I am the Lord which sanctify you" (Lev. 20⁸). In everything that we have to say further on this subject we must exert ourselves always to start from this point.

We must begin, and this is our task in the present sub-section, by glancing back at the first part of the doctrine of reconciliation and making some clarifications concerning the mutual relationship of justification and sanctification as roughly outlined.

For what follows, cf. Alfred Göhler, *Calvins Lehre von der Heiligung*, 1934, 81 f., 107 f., and G. C. Berkouwer, *Faith and Sanctification*, 1952, with which I am particularly happy to record my general agreement.

1. As we now turn to consider sanctification in and for itself, we are not dealing with a second divine action which either takes place simultaneously with it, or precedes or follows it in time. The action of God in His reconciliation of the world with Himself in Jesus Christ is unitary. It consists of different "moments" with a different bearing. It accomplishes both the justification and [502] the sanctification of man, for it is itself both the condescension of God and the exaltation of man in Jesus Christ. But it accomplishes the two together. The one is done wholly and immediately with the other. There are also different aspects corresponding to the different "moments." We cannot see it all at

---

EN4 hallowed be Thy name

once, or comprehend it in a single word. Corresponding to the one historical being of Jesus Christ as true Son of God and true Son of Man, we can see it only as the movement from above to below, or the movement from below to above, as justification or sanctification. Yet whether we look at it from the one standpoint or the other our knowledge can and may and must be a knowledge of the one totality of the reconciling action of God, of the one whole and undivided Jesus Christ, and of His one grace.

In its later stages the older Protestant dogmatics tried to understand *iustificatio*[EN5] and *sanctificatio*[EN6] as steps in a so-called *ordo salutis*[EN7], preceded by a *vocatio*[EN8] and *illuminatio*[EN9], and followed by the separate processes of *regeneratio*[EN10] and *conversio*[EN11], and then (in the Lutherans) by a *unio mystica*[EN12] and *glorificatio*[EN13]. For the most part this *ordo salutis*[EN14] was thought of as a temporal sequence, in which the Holy Spirit does His work here and now in men—the outworking of the reconciliation accomplished there and then on Golgotha. This temporal sequence corresponded only too readily to that of the temporal relationship between the humiliation and exaltation of Christ as it was viewed in the Christology of the older dogmatics. A psychologistic pragmatics in soteriology corresponded to the historicist pragmatics of Christology. Psychologistic? This was not the primary intention, and it was indeed the fear of slipping into psychology, into a mere recording of the spiritual experience of the Christian, which for a long time restrained the older orthodoxy from constructing an *ordo salutis*[EN15] in the sense of a temporal sequence. The original aim was to describe the order of the *gratia Spiritus sancti applicatrix*[EN16], of the appropriation to the needy human subject of the salvation objectively accomplished in Jesus Christ—that which is summed up in the title of the third book of Calvin's *Institutes*: *De modo percipiendae Christi gratiae et qui inde fructus nobis proveniant, et qui effectus consequantur*[EN17]. But if this *percipere*[EN18] consists in a series of different steps, how can it better be made apprehensible than as a series of spiritual awakenings and movements and actions and states of a religious and moral type? The greater and more explicit the emphasis on the *ordo salutis*[EN19] understood in this way—and this was the tendency in the 17th century—the more clearly it was revealed by the uncertainties, contradictions and exegetical and conceptual arbitrariness and artificiality in which those who espoused it were entangled, that they were on the point of leaving the sphere of theology. And the nearer drew the time—the time of the Enlightenment which dawned already with Pietism—in which a religious and moral psychology would take over the leadership and suppress theology, first at this point, and then everywhere. Certainly there are rays of light, as when we suddenly read in Quenstedt (*Theol. did. pol.*,

---

[EN5] justification
[EN6] sanctification
[EN7] order of salvation
[EN8] vocation
[EN9] illumination
[EN10] regeneration
[EN11] conversion
[EN12] mystical union
[EN13] glorification
[EN14] order of salvation
[EN15] order of salvation
[EN16] gracious application of the Holy Spirit
[EN17] On the means of obtaining the grace of Christ, the benefits for us which proceed therefrom, and the effects resulting from it
[EN18] obtaining
[EN19] order of salvation

1685, III, *c.* 10, *th.* 16) that all these ἀποστελέσματα EN20 of Jesus Christ and the Holy Spirit, and particularly justification and sanctification, take place *tempore simul, et quovis puncto mathematico arctiores adeo ut divelli et sequestrari nequeant, cohaerent*EN21. This is inevitable if we are really thinking of the act of God as it comes to man in Jesus Christ by the Holy Spirit. If Quenstedt and that whole theology had taken this insight seriously, it would have meant that they could not have understood that *ordo*EN22 as a series of different divine actions, but only as the order of different "moments" of the one redemptive occurrence coming to man in the *simul*EN23 of the one event. This would perhaps have led to a collapse of the historicist prag-

[503]   matic, and even perhaps to the dualism between an objective achievement of salvation there and then and a subjective appropriation of it here and now, in favour of a recognition of the simultaneity of the one act of salvation whose Subject is the one God by the one Christ through the one Spirit—"more closely united than in a mathematical point." The God who in His humiliation justifies us is also the man who in His exaltation sanctifies us. He is the same there and then as He is here and now. He is the one living Lord in whom all things have occurred, and do and will occur, for all. Unfortunately, however, the recognition of this *simul*EN24 did not lead even to a serious consideration of the relationship between justification and sanctification, let alone to any general advance in this direction. We cannot escape to-day the task of taking this recognition seriously.

2. When, however, we speak of justification and sanctification, we have to do with two different aspects of the one event of salvation. The distinction between them has its basis in the fact that we have in this event two genuinely different moments. That Jesus Christ is true God and true man in one person does not mean that His true deity and His true humanity are one and the same, or that the one is interchangeable with the other. Similarly, the reality of Jesus Christ as the Son of God who humbled Himself to be a man and the Son of Man who was exalted to fellowship with God is one, but the humiliation and exaltation are not identical. From the christological ἀσυγχύτως EN25 and ἀτρέπτως EN26 of Chalcedon we can deduce at once that the same is true of justification and sanctification. As the two moments in the one act of reconciliation accomplished in Jesus Christ they are not identical, nor are the concepts interchangeable. We are led to the same conclusion when we consider the content of the terms. In our estimation of their particular significance we must not confuse or confound them. Justification is not sanctification and does not merge into it. Sanctification is not justification and does not merge into it. Thus, although the two belong indissolubly together, the one cannot be explained by the other. It is one thing that God turns in free grace to sinful man, and quite another that in the same free grace He converts man to Himself. It is one thing that God as the Judge establishes that He is in the right

---

EN20 works
EN21 at one and the same time, and as in any mathematical point, they cohere too closely to be divided or separated
EN22 order
EN23 at the same time
EN24 at the same time
EN25 inconfusably
EN26 immutably

1. Justification and Sanctification

against this man, thus creating a new right for this man before Him, and quite another that by His mighty direction He claims this man and makes him willing and ready for His service. Even within the true human response to this one divine act the faith in which the sinful man may grasp the righteousness promised him in Jesus Christ is one thing, and quite another his obedience, or love, as his correspondence, to the holiness imparted to him in Jesus Christ. We shall speak later of the indestructible connexion between these. But it is a connexion, not identity. The one cannot take the place of the other. The one cannot, therefore, be interpreted by the other.

It is a *duplex gratia*[EN27] that we receive in the *participatio Christi*[EN28] (Calvin, *Instit.* III, 11, 1). Similarly, its reception in faith and penitence is twofold: *etsi separari non possunt, distingui tamen debent. Quamquam perpetuo inter se vinculo cohaerent, magis tamen coniungi volunt quam confundi*[EN29] (3, 5). For: *Si solis claritas non potest a calore separari, an ideo dicemus luce calefieri terram, calore vero illustrari*[EN30] (11, 6)? [504]

Sanctification is not justification. If we do not take care not to confuse and confound, soteriology may suffer, allowing justification (as in the case of much of Roman Catholicism in its following of Augustine, but also of many varieties of Neo-Protestantism) to merge into the process of his sanctification initiated by the act of the forgiveness of sins, or by allowing faith in Jesus Christ as the Judge judged in our place (this is in my view the most serious objection to the theology of R. Bultmann) to merge into the obedience in which the Christian in his discipleship has to die to the world and himself. The "I am holy" is not merely a kind of preface or unaccented syllable introducing the really important statement: "Ye shall be holy." In all the thinking along these lines about the justifiable emphasis on the existential relevance of the atonement, where is the regard for the God who accomplishes it, the bowing before the freedom of His grace, the adoration of the mystery in which He really says an unmerited No to sinful man, the joy of pure gratitude for this benefit? Where is the presupposition of a sanctification worthy of the name? Is it not better to make justification, even in its significance for sanctification, genuinely justification, instead of trying to understand it from the very outset merely as the beginning of sanctification?

On the other hand, justification is not sanctification. If we do not take care not to confuse and confound, soteriology may also suffer by allowing sanctification to be swallowed up in justification. It may be because of the overwhelming impression of the comfort of the grace which is effective and has to be understood as justification. It may be in view of the true consideration that justification is in any event the dominating presupposition of sanctification. It may be with the correct insight that even in his best works the sanctified man still stands in continual need of justification before God. It may be in a justifiable anxiety that under the name of sanctification a prior or subsequent self-justification may creep in to the detriment of the sovereignty of grace. These are all legitimate considerations which can be traced back to the younger Luther and Zinzendorf and H. F. Kohlbrügge; and with the help of some of the more pointed statements of these writers, and an exaggeration (and therefore distortion) of their basic teaching, they can easily lead to a monism of the *theologia*

[EN27] twofold grace
[EN28] participation in Christ
[EN29] even if they cannot be separated, they ought nevertheless to be distinguished. Although they cohere with one another by a perpetual bond, nevertheless they should be more joined than confused
[EN30] If the light of the sun cannot be separated from its heat, should we then say that the earth becomes warm by its light, and is illuminated by its heat?

crucis[EN31] and the doctrine of justification. In this monism the necessity of good works may be maintained only lethargically and spasmodically, with little place for anything more than rather indefinite talk about a life of forgiveness, or comforted despair, or Christian freedom, or the love active in faith. If we do not give any independent significance to the problem of sanctification, do we not necessarily obscure in a very suspicious way the existential reach of the atonement, the simple fact that justification always has to do with man and his action, and that faith in it, even though it is a work of the Holy Spirit, is still a decision of man? Can we ignore the fact that in the Bible the work of the sovereign grace of God as a work of Jesus Christ and the Holy Spirit includes the sanctification of man as distinct from his justification? Is it not a serious matter to miss the sovereignty and authority of grace in this form? If we do not understand it as sanctifying grace, we not only do despite to its richness, but far too easily, and indeed inevitably, we begin to look for the indispensable norm of the Christian way of life elsewhere than in the Gospel (in which we think we have only the consoling word of justifying grace), and are forced to seek and grasp a law formed either by considerations drawn from the Bible or natural law, or by historical convenience. But this means that we are involved in double book-keeping, and either tacitly or openly we are subjected to other lords in a kingdom on the left as well as to the Lord Jesus Christ whose competence extends only, as we think, to the forgiveness of sins. Is it not advisable to make sanctification, even in its connexion with justification, genuinely sanctification, instead of trying to understand it from the very outset merely as a paraphrase of justification?

[505]

3. Yet it is even more important to remember, and the warning we have to give in this respect must be correspondingly sharper, that since justification and sanctification are only two moments and aspects of one and the same action, they do belong inseparably together. We have had to draw attention to the unavoidable dangers of confusion which threaten on both sides, and which have actually overwhelmed the Church and theology with very serious consequences. But we have to say that to ignore the mutual relationship of the two can only lead at once to false statements concerning them and to corresponding errors in practice: to the idea of a God who works in isolation, and His "cheap grace" (D. Bonhoeffer), and therefore an indolent quietism, where the relationship of justification to sanctification is neglected; and to that of a favoured man who works in isolation, and therefore to an illusory activism, where the relationship of sanctification to justification is forgotten. A separation of justification and sanctification can have its basis only in a separation within the one actuality of Jesus Christ and the Holy Spirit; in an isolation of the self-humiliating Son of God on the one side, and of the exalted Son of Man on the other. If we have also to accept the $\dot{\alpha}\chi\omega\rho\dot{\iota}\sigma\tau\omega\varsigma$[EN32] and $\dot{\alpha}\delta\iota\alpha\iota\rho\dot{\epsilon}\tau\omega\varsigma$[EN33] of Chalcedonian Christology, justification and sanctification must be distinguished, but they cannot be divided or separated. We have only to ask ourselves: What is the forgiveness of sins (however we understand it) if it is not directly accompanied by an actual liberation from the committal of sin? What is divine sonship if we are not set in the service of God and the brethren?

[EN31] theology of the cross
[EN32] indivisibly
[EN33] inseparably

1. *Justification and Sanctification*

What is the hope of the universal and definitive revelation of the eternal God without striving for provisional and concrete lesser ends? What is faith without obedience? And conversely: What is a liberation for new action which does not rest from the very outset and continually on the forgiveness of sins? Who can and will serve God but the child of God who lives by the promise of His unmerited adoption? How can there be a confident expectation and movement in time without the basis of eternal hope? How can there be any serious obedience which is not the obedience of faith? As God turns to sinful man, the conversion of the latter to God cannot be lacking. And the conversion of man to God presupposes at every point and in every form that God turns to him in free grace. That the two are inseparable means that the doctrine of justification has to be described already as the way from sin to the right of God and man, and therefore as the way from death to life, which *God* goes with him. And it means for the doctrine of sanctification that it has to show that it is really with *man* that God is on this way as He reconciles the world with Himself in Jesus Christ.

It was Calvin who saw and expressed this point with particular clarity. There is hardly a passage in which we have any doubt whether the reference is to justifying or sanctifying grace, and yet he everywhere brings out the mutual relationship of the two moments and aspects. His primary statement and starting-point is as follows: *Sicut non potest discerpi Christus in partes, ita inseparabilia sunt haec duo, quae simul et coniunctim in ipso percipimus: iustitiam et sanctificationem. Quoscunque ergo in gratiam recipit Deus, simul Spiritu adoptionis donat, cuius virtute eos reformat ad suam imaginem*[EN34]. (*Inst.* III, 11, 6).

There is thus no justification without sanctification. *Sola fide et mera venia iustificatur homo, neque tamen a gratuita iustitiae imputatione separatur realis (ut ita loquar) vitae sanctitas*[EN35]. The proclamation of forgiveness has as its aim *ut a tyrannide satanae, peccati iugo et misera servitute vitiorum liberatus peccator in regnum Dei transeat*[EN36]. Thus no one can apprehend the grace of the Gospel without *meditatio poenitentiae*[EN37] (3, 1). It is certainly not in virtue of our holiness that we enter into fellowship with God. We have to stand in this already if, engulfed by His holiness (*eius sanctitate perfusi*), we are to follow where He calls. But it belongs to His glory that this should take place, for there can be no *consortium*[EN38] between Him and our *iniquitas*[EN39] and *immunditia*[EN40] (6, 2). We cannot, therefore, glory in God without *eo ipso*[EN41]—and this is for Calvin the basic act of penitence and the new life—renouncing all self-glorying and thus beginning to live to God's glory (13, 2). Thus the righteousness of

[506]

[EN34] Just as it is not possible to divine Christ into parts, so also there are two inseparable aspects, which we perceive at the same time, joined in him: righteousness and sanctification. Therefore, whomever God receives into his grace, at the same time he gives the Spirit of adoption, by whose power he restores them to his own image

[EN35] Man is justified by faith alone, and by pure forgiveness, but real (so to speak) holiness of life is not to be separated from the free imputation of righteousness

[EN36] in order that the sinner may be freed from the tyranny of Satan with its yoke of sin, and the miserable slavery of vice, and cross over into the Kingdom of God

[EN37] the meditation of repentance

[EN38] fellowship

[EN39] iniquity

[EN40] impurity

[EN41] by definition

§ 66. *The Sanctification of Man*

God calls for a *symmetria*[EN42], a *consensus*, which must be actualised in the obedience of the believer. It calls for a confirmation of our adoption to divine sonship (6, 1). For this reason the one grace of God is necessarily sanctifying grace as well. *In Christi participatione, qua iustificamur, non minus sanctificatio continetur quam iustitia .... Inseparabiliter utrumque Christus in se continet. ... Nullum ergo Christus iustificat, quem non simul sanctificet*[EN43] (16, 1, and we find the same *simul* in 3, 19). *Fatemur dum nos .... Deus gratuita peccatorum remissione donates pro iustis habet: cum euismodi misericordia coniunctam simul esse hanc eius beneficentiam, quod per Spiritum suum sanctum in nobis habitat, cuius virtute nos sanctificamur, hoc est consecramur Domino in veram vitae puritatem*[EN44]. (14, 9). There can thus be no doubt that, as Calvin saw it, the Reformation did not wish to give to the problem of the *vita hominis christiani*[EN45], of penitence and good works, any less but a much greater and more serious and penetrating attention than was done either by the Humanists (who followed Erasmus) on the one side or contemporary Romanists on the other. In the context in which it was set by him the *sola fide*[EN46] obviously could not become a comfortable kiss of peace.

On the other hand, of course, there is no sanctification without justification. *An vera poenitentia citra fidem consistere potest? Minime!*[EN47] (3, 5). There is no *spatium temporis*[EN48] between the two in which the man who is righteous before God in faith is not also holy and obedient to Him. But it is only this man who can and will be obedient and holy. How could he be seriously penitent if he did not know: *se Dei esse? Dei autem se esse nemo vere persuasus est, nisi qui eius gratiam prius apprehenderit*[EN49]. (3, 2). How can there be a free and happy conscience towards God in penitence and therefore in the life of the Christian without the certainty of the righteousness before God which he is given, and has to be given continually, by God? (13, 3). Even the obedient and holy and loving man who penitently lays hold of this righteousness still lives in the flesh and therefore as a sinner before God. Hence it follows: *Nullum unquam exstitisse pii hominis opus quod, si severo Dei iudicio examinaretur, non esset damnabile*[EN50] (14, 11) and: *nec unum a sanctis exire opus, quod, si in se censeatur, non mereatur iustam opprobrii mercedem*[EN51] (14, 9). Even the regenerate and converted stand in absolute need of forgiveness and justification in all their works of penitence and obedience, which of themselves cannot possibly justify them (14, 13). Good works, which God has promised to reward (18, 1 f.), in which we have to progress, and in the doing of which we may find confidence (14, 18 f.), can be present only as God of His free goodness justifies not only our persons but also our works (17, 5 f.), as *assidua peccatorum remissione*[EN52] (14, 10; 12) He

---

[EN42] reflection

[EN43] In the participation in Christ, by which we are justified, sanctification is contained no less than justification ..., Christ holds each inseparably in himself ..., Therefore Christ justified no-one whom he does not at the same time sanctify

[EN44] While we admit ..., God reckons us whom he has given free forgiveness of sins as righteous, that his goodness is at the same time conjoined with mercy, because by his Holy Spirit he lives in us, by whose power we are sanctified, that is, we are consecrated to the Lord for true purity of life

[EN45] life of the Christian man

[EN46] by faith alone

[EN47] Or could true repentance exist without faith? By no means!

[EN48] duration of time

[EN49] that he belonged to God? But no-one is truly persuaded that he belongs to God, unless he has beforehand grasped his grace

[EN50] There has not been one work of a pious man which, if examined by the severe justice of God, would not be damnable

[EN51] not one work goes forth from the saints which, if considered in itself, would not merit the righteous recompense of reproach

[EN52] by a constant forgiveness of sins

assesses and recognises and accepts as good, on the basis of the righteousness of Jesus Christ [507] ascribed to us, that which we do in supreme imperfection and even guilt and corruption (14, 8 f.). There can be no doubt that Calvin—the reformer at the time of the reconstruction of the Evangelical Churches and the developing Counter-Reformation, and therefore with different interests from Luther—stands squarely on the basis of his predecessor. The notion of *duplex gratia*[EN53] was not his own. Even the older Luther (cf. *C.D.* IV, 1, 525 f.), in passages which are, of course, rather remote and obscure, had referred in the same sense as Calvin, and with the same conjunction and distinction, to justification and sanctification, healing, purification, etc. And Calvin for his part had not surrendered one jot of the decisive insight of Luther concerning justification. The only distinctive features—and they were not really un-Lutheran, or prejudicial to the content and function of the doctrine of justification—were the formal consistency with which he spoke of this *duplex gratia*[EN54] and the material emphasis which he laid on the doctrine of the *novitas vitae*[EN55] based on justification.

4. It remains only to ask whether there is perhaps an *ordo (salutis)*[EN56] in the relationship of justification and sanctification and therefore a superiority and subordination, a *Prius*[EN57] and *Posterius*[EN58], in the one event of grace and salvation. We presuppose that there is no such order in the temporal sense. The *simul*[EN59] of the one redemptive act of God in Jesus Christ cannot be split up into a temporal sequence, and in this way psychologised. The justification and sanctification of man, manifest in the resurrection of Jesus Christ and effective in the Holy Spirit, are an event in this *simul*[EN60], and not therefore in such a way that his justification first takes place separately (as though it could be his justification by God if it did not also include his sanctification), and then his sanctification takes place separately (as though it could be his sanctification by God if at all its stages and in all its forms it were not based upon and borne by the event of his justification). No, they both take place simultaneously and together, just as the living Jesus Christ, in whom they both take place and are effective, is simultaneously and together true God and true man, the Humiliated and the Exalted. Yet this does not mean that we can lay aside the question of their order. It has to be raised and answered because it is necessary that we should dissipate the last remnants of the monistic and dualistic thinking which occupied us under (2) and (3). If there can be no question of a temporal order, the only order can be that of substance. And it is not quite so easy to answer the question of this order as might at first sight appear.

From our deliberations under (2) and (3) it is clear in what sense justification has to be understood as the first and basic and to that extent superior moment and aspect of the one event of salvation, and sanctification as the

---

EN53 twofold grace
EN54 twofold grace
EN55 newness of life
EN56 order (of salvation)
EN57 before
EN58 after
EN59 at the same time
EN60 at the same time

second and derivative and to that extent inferior. It is indeed in virtue of the condescension of God in which the eternal Word assumed our flesh that there takes place the exaltation of man in the existence of the royal man Jesus. It is in virtue of the forgiveness of his sins and his establishment as a child of God, both fulfilled in the gracious judgment and sentence of God, that man is called and given a readiness and willingness for discipleship, for conversion, for the doing of good works, for the bearing of his cross. It is in virtue of the fact that he is justified in the presence of God by God that he is sanctified by Him. Surely it is obvious that if we ask concerning the structure of this occurrence justification must be given the priority over sanctification.

[508]

Yet is this the end of the matter? Do we not have to recognise that the existence of the royal man Jesus, and therefore the true answering of the question of obedience, the summoning and preparing of man for the service of God, have a radiance and importance in the Bible which are not in any way secondary to those of justifying grace? Is the first the only possible answer? In the question of the material order of this whole event do we not have to take into account—irrespective of the question of its inner movement—its meaning and purpose and goal? And does it not seem that that which is second in execution (*executione posterius*), i.e., sanctification, is first in intention (*intentione prius*)? What is it that God wills and effects in the reconciliation of man with Himself? By the incarnation of His Word does He not will and effect the existence of the royal man Jesus and His lordship over all His brothers and the whole world? By His humiliation to be the Judge judged for us, and therefore by the justification of man before Him, does He not will and effect the existence of a loyal and courageous people of this King in covenant with Himself, and therefore the sanctification of man? And even this may not be the ultimate, or penultimate, word concerning the *telos* of the event of atonement. Yet in relation to the relationship between justification and sanctification are we not forced to say that teleologically sanctification is superior to justification and not the reverse? It is obvious that we cannot help putting and answering the question in this form too.

Yet there are still good reasons for the first answer; and it is not without its significance. This being the case, is it really necessary or wise to choose between them at all? In so doing, might we not be encroaching on the actuality of the one grace of the one Jesus Christ? And this is something which cannot be permitted merely out of a desire to systematise. In any case, are we not asking concerning the divine order of the divine will and action revealed and effective in Jesus Christ? Might it not be that in this—in this particular function and respect—the *Prius*[EN61] is also the *Posterius*[EN62] and *vice versa*? This would mean that both answers have to be given with the same seriousness in view of the distinctive truth in both—intersecting but not cancelling one

---

[EN61] before
[EN62] after

128

another. In the *simul*[EN63] of the one divine will and action justification is first as basis and second as presupposition, sanctification first as aim and second as consequence; and therefore both are superior and both subordinate. Embracing the distinctness and unity of the two moments and aspects, the one grace of the one Jesus Christ is at work, and it is both justifying and sanctifying grace, [509] and both to the glory of God and the salvation of man. Where else does God (the God known in Jesus Christ) seek and create His glory but in the salvation of man? And yet who can say that the glory of God to the salvation of man is greater or smaller in man's justification or sanctification? Again, where is the salvation of man (the man known in Jesus Christ) to be found but in the glory which God prepares for Himself in His action to and with man? Yet who is to say that the salvation of man to the glory of God is greater or smaller in the fact that man is justified by God or sanctified by Him? If we start at this point, and therefore at the grace of the covenant effective and revealed in Jesus Christ, we have the freedom, but we are also bound, to give to the question of the order of the relationship between justification and sanctification this twofold answer. There is no contradiction. As a twofold answer, it corresponds to the substance of the matter.

The question of the order of this relationship was one which claimed Calvin's attention, and it will help to elucidate what we have just said if we briefly recall his answer. We might almost say that this question poses *the* great problem of method in the third book of the *Institutio*[EN64]. Is it on justification or sanctification that the emphasis must fall in what is to be said concerning the grace of Jesus Christ and its fruits and effects? When we read Calvin we may still—although not necessarily—be baffled by this question.

There can be no doubt that in practice his decisive interest is primarily in the problem of sanctification. Those who come to him from Luther will be almost estranged when right at the beginning of the third book (1, 1), although not without justification in the linguistic usage of the Bible, he lays all the emphasis on the sanctifying power of the Holy Spirit, and it is not for a long time (only in chapter 11) that he comes to speak of justification at all. According to his own explanation (11, 1), he first wishes—and the whole sequence of chapters 3–10 is subservient to this aim—to show (1) that the faith by which alone, through the mercy of God, we attain the grace of righteousness before Him, is not a faith which is indolent in relation to good works, a *fides otiosa*[EN65], and (2), and more positively, *qualia sint sanctorum bona opera*[EN66]. It is for this reason that he describes faith itself as regeneration, the regeneration which is realised in penitence (chapters 3–5), and then goes on to portray the Christian life in its character as self-denial, as the bearing of the cross, as *meditatio futurae vitae*[EN67], and as a right relationship to earthly and temporal possibilities and possessions (chapters 6–10). It is only at this point—we might almost say at a first glance as a great qualification and corrective—that he introduces the doctrine of justification (chapters 11–18). Then in what follows concerning Christian freedom (19) and prayer (20) we seem to have a continuation and completion of the interrupted theme. And since this can be

---

[EN63] at the same time
[EN64] Institutes
[EN65] idle faith
[EN66] what the nature is of the good works of the saints
[EN67] reflection on the future life

abandoned only after a retrospective glance at its origin in God's election (21–24) and a prospective glance at its final goal in the resurrection of the dead (25), it obviously seems to constitute the true and proper substance of Calvin's teaching. *Ad colendam iustitiam renovat Deus quos pro iustis gratis censet*[EN68] (11, 6). In the light of this sketch, and what constantly emerges as the admonitory tenor of the whole, we might regard it as established beyond any doubt that, as distinct from Luther, Calvin must be called the theologian of sanctification. He is this to the extent that the sharp underscoring of the new life and altered conversation of the believer in Jesus Christ, the reference to his essential inner and outer transformation was the particular concern which he took up in practice against the excesses which sometimes gained the upper hand in his own epoch (not without some support from the Reformation Gospel), and in answer to the humanistic and Romanist criticism of the *sola fide*[EN69] of Reformation teaching. And quite apart from the contemporary background and occasion, his question was one which has also a true biblical foundation: What is it that God in His grace wills of man and achieves in his life? In this—we might almost say, strategic—respect there is good reason for the primacy of sanctification in Calvin.

[510]

But the picture undergoes a curious transformation when we turn our attention from the practical intention to its execution. For we then have to say that it is on the doctrine of faith developed in the great second chapter of the book that he bases everything that follows as seen from the dominating standpoint of regeneration in conversion. But Calvin could not speak of faith (cf. especially sections 16, 23, 24, 29, 30 and 32 of chapter 2) without anticipating the decisive content of the doctrine of justification. Faith is a sure and certain knowledge grounded in the truth of the promise of grace given in Jesus Christ, and revealed in our understanding (*mentibus*) and sealed in our hearts by the Holy Spirit. The regeneration of man, and therefore his sanctification in all its stages and forms (2, 7), does not take place except in this faith; in the faith whose *proprius scopus*[EN70] is the *promissio misericordiae*[EN71], the evangelical Word concerning the free divine *benevolentia*[EN72] to man (2, 29). Thus at the very beginning of the doctrine of justification (11, 1)—rather surprisingly, but not really so in view of this second chapter—we are told that this *iustificatio* which has hitherto been touched on only lightly is the *cardo praecipuus sustinendae religionis*[EN73] to which we must give particular care and attention (*maior attentio curaque*[EN74]) and in relation to which sanctification is only the *secunda gratia*. *Primum omnium*[EN75] is necessarily to be found *quo sis apud Deum loco et quale de te sit illius iudicium*[EN76]. Without this foundation there is neither assurance of salvation nor *pietas in Deum*[EN77]. It should be noted with what extreme precision that which, in the light of so many Old Testament verses and passages, Calvin can say about the importance of the good works of the believer even in justification (especially chapters 13–14 and 17–18) is qualified by the most urgent recollections of the continuing freedom of justifying grace, and by a constant recall to the rest of faith in the promise which alone enables us to speak of the goodness and comfort and reward of the works of the believer. And it is to be noted finally that even in the description of the *novitas vitae*[EN78] (chapters 3–10 and 19–20) which

---

[EN68] God renews those whom he freely reckons as righteous for the cultivation of righteousness
[EN69] by faith alone
[EN70] proper scope
[EN71] promise of mercy
[EN72] goodness
[EN73] main pivot which upholds religion
[EN74] greater attention and concern
[EN75] second grace. The first matter of all
[EN76] in the place where you stand before God and how his judgment is concerning you
[EN77] piety towards God
[EN78] life of the Christian man

so strongly characterises the third book he not only does not lose sight of the totally unmerited establishment of man in a state of grace by the act of majesty of the divine mercy, but obviously sets that which he describes in the reflection of this act. His real subject is self-denial and the cross, the orientation to the life beyond, Christian freedom and prayer. And in the strict sense these are all critical and limiting determinations of the *vita hominis christiani*[EN79]. Even in chapter 10, where the emphasis falls on the this-worldly qualification and responsibility of the Christian life, there is little real trace of the fabled activism of calvinistic ethics. This reserve in the portrayal of sanctification is connected with the fact that in Calvin this is not only related to the simultaneous justification of man but in this relationship and from justification it acquires the character of a submission to this act of majesty. When all this is taken into account we may well ask whether Calvin was not primarily a theologian of justification.

In fact we can and should learn from the classical example of his mode of treatment that we can give only a twofold answer to the question of priority in the relationship of these two moments and aspects. Calvin was quite in earnest when he gave sanctification a strategic precedence over justification. He was also quite in earnest when he gave the latter a tactical precedence. Why could he be so free, and yet so bound, in relation to the two? Because he started at the place which is superior to both because it embraces both, so that in the light of it we can and must give the primacy, now to the one and now to the other, according to the different standpoints from which we look. The basic act in which they are a whole, in which they are united and yet different, and in which—without any contradiction—they have different functions according to which they must each be given the primacy, is as Calvin sees it (and as he describes it in the first chapter of the third book) the *participatio Christi*[EN80] given to man by the Holy Spirit. What this involves calls for separate consideration. [511]

2. THE HOLY ONE AND THE SAINTS

The reconciliation of the world with God in its form as sanctification takes place as God fashions a people of holy men, i.e., those who in spite of their sin have the freedom, which they have received from Him to live in it, to represent Him among all other men and to serve Him in what they are and do and suffer. "God so loved the world" is relevant in this connexion too. The sanctification of man, his conversion to God, is, like his justification, a transformation, a new determination, which has taken place *de jure*[EN81] for the world and therefore for all men. *De facto*[EN82], however, it is not known by all men, just as justification has not *de facto*[EN83] been grasped and acknowledged and known and confessed by all men, but only by those who are awakened to faith. It is the people of these men which has also known sanctification. Only God Himself knows the extent of this people, and its members. The invitation to belong to it is extended to all. Certainly it is not co-extensive with the human race as such.

[EN79] newness of life
[EN80] participation in Christ
[EN81] as a matter of right
[EN82] As a matter of fact
[EN83] as a matter of fact

131

Certainly it is a special people of special men who are marked off from all others because they are set aside by God from among all others. Yet its special existence is not an end in itself. It is marked off from the race, from others, in order that it may make "a provisional offering of the thankfulness for which the whole world is ordained by the act of the love of God." It is the living promise of the positive meaning which in the act of atonement God has restored not only to its own existence but to that of all men. It is the witness of the love with which God has loved the world. What has come to it *de facto*[EN84] has come to all men *de iure*[EN85]. But in so far as it is only to it that it has come *de facto*[EN86] (with the provisional task which this involves), it is concretely differentiated and separated from the world and all other men. To this extent it is a holy people of holy men. Among those who *de facto*[EN87] are not holy it is the creaturely reflection of the holiness in which God confronts—not indolently but actively—both itself and the world, addressing it even as He is distinct from it. It is with this God who in His holiness acts to and with His people—the people of His saints—that we have to do in our present deliberations. His action is man's sanctification.

[512] The phrase "holy people" is an obvious one, but it is used with astonishing infrequency in the canonical Old Testament. The most striking example is in Ex. 19⁶ (quoted in 1 Pet. 2⁹), where Moses is charged by *Yahweh* to tell the Israelites that they of all peoples are to be His possession ("for all the earth is mine"): "and ye shall be unto me a kingdom of priests, and a holy nation, *goy*[EN88] (a word which is usually applied only to the Gentiles) *qadosh*[EN89]. We find *am qadosh*[EN90] in Deut. 7⁶ and 28⁹, Is. 62¹² and Dan 7²⁷. For the most part, however, it is only the worshipping congregation (or more exactly its convening) which is called "holy," and not the people as such. In many cases (as in the combination *qahal q'doshim*[EN91] in Ps. 89⁵ and in the Book of Daniel) the *q'doshim*[EN92] are the angels. The word *ḥasidim*[EN93], which Luther regularly translated as "saints" in the Psalter, denotes the pious in Israel. On one occasion Aaron is called "the saint of the Lord" (Ps. 106¹⁶), but the reference here is to his office rather than his person. In the history attested in the Old Testament many words and things are called "holy" in virtue of their meaning and function. It is in this sense that we have to understand the "holy princes" of Is. 43²⁸. When the remnant of destroyed Israel is called a "holy seed" in Is. 6¹³ the drift is obviously eschatological. The only other genuine references as far as I can see are Ex. 22³¹: "Ye shall be holy men unto me," Ps. 16³: "The saints that are in the earth," Ps. 34⁹: "O fear the Lord, ye his saints," and Deut. 33³: "All his saints are in his hand." There seems to be no doubt that the restrained use of the term is deliberate. The history attested in the Old Testament clearly has to do with the sanctification of this people and these men. But since the references to their sanctity are so few and inciden-

---

EN84 as a matter of fact
EN85 as a matter of right
EN86 as a matter of fact
EN87 as a matter of fact
EN88 nation
EN89 holy
EN90 holy people
EN91 congregation of the holy ones
EN92 holy ones
EN93 the pious

tal the main emphasis is obviously on the sanctification itself, or rather on the One who as the Holy One is the active subject who sovereignly confronts the holy people and the men who belong to it.

Even more surprising and complicated are the results of an investigation of the New Testament. We are forced to say at once that the number of texts from which we can deduce the important credal formula *sancta ecclesia*[EN94] is even less than that of passages which describe Israel as the holy people. This does not mean that the formula is mistaken. But in our interpretation of it we must pay attention to the sense in which the New Testament does seem very occasionally to speak of a kind of *sancta ecclesia*[EN95]. As far as I can see, there are only two passages which call for consideration. The first is the Old Testament quotation in 1 Pet. 2[9]: "Ye are ... an holy nation" ($\xi\theta\nu os$ $\xi\gamma\iota o\nu$[EN96]). But the $\xi\sigma\tau\epsilon$ is lacking which would make this an analytical statement. The meaning obviously seems to be that those who are addressed (in contrast to the rejected of the preceding verse) are elected and called to execute as a holy people the commission which is described immediately afterwards. The other passage is Eph. 5[24f.], and this, too, does not say directly that the Church is holy but that Christ has loved the $\xi\kappa\kappa\lambda\eta\sigma ia$[EN97] and given Himself for it in order that, cleansing it with the washing of water by the word, He might sanctify it and "present it to himself a glorious church ($\xi\nu\delta o\xi o\nu$[EN98]), not having spot, or wrinkle, or any such thing; but that it should be holy and without blemish." In this passage it is quite obvious that the holiness of the community is the goal and intended result of the sanctifying action of Jesus Christ, not as an inherent quality but as the character which He will give it in the fulfilment of this action. And it may well be asked in all seriousness whether the $\iota\nu a$ $\pi a\rho a\sigma\tau\eta\sigma\eta$[EN99] does not refer to the form of the community as it will be in the future, when this action is completed, and the last time in which it lives now is over. At any rate we can speak only of considerable reserve in describing the Church as holy (as in the corresponding Old Testament references to Israel). As against this, however, the men who compose the Church (unlike the Israelites) are not only described with astonishing frequency as holy but are actually called "the saints." The term $\xi\gamma\iota o\iota$[EN100] or oi $\xi\gamma\iota o\iota$[EN101] does not figure in the Gospels, and only infrequently in Acts, but in the earlier and later strata of the Epistles and Revelation it has become almost a technical term for Christians, and in many passages (1 Cor. 16[1]; 2 Cor. 8[4], etc.) it is used specifically of the members of the original community at Jerusalem. Yet rather strangely no individual Christian is ever called a saint. John the Baptist is called "a just man and an holy" in Mk. 6[20], but this does not constitute a genuine exception. The saints of the New Testament exist only in plurality. Sanctity belongs to them, but only in their common life, not as individuals. In this plurality they are, of course, identical with the Christian community, so that the term "holy community," although it is only thinly attested, is not in any sense foreign to the New Testament. Indeed, in 1 Cor. 14[33] the congregations are generally referred to as "churches of the saints." Yet we must not imagine that their holiness derives from that of the individual members who constitute them, for as we have seen these are not called "saints" as individuals. The truth is that the holiness of the community, as of its individual constituents, is to be sought in that which happens to these men in common; in that which comes to it and them in the course of this happening. We may hazard the provisional definition that the

[513]

EN94 holy church
EN95 holy church
EN96 you are
EN97 church
EN98 glorious
EN99 so that he may present it
EN100 saints
EN101 the saints

ἅγιοι EN102 are the men to whom ἁγιότης EN103 comes in a common history which constitutes them an ἔθνος ἅγιον EN104. Thus the linguistic usage of the New Testament, for all its important differences from that of the Old, points us basically in the same direction. In other words, we are required to consider the history in which there takes place the sanctification, the ἁγιασμός EN105, of these men and therefore their unification as a community. But this means automatically that we are required to consider the One who as the Holy One is the acting Subject in this history. The Holy One constitutes the saints.

In the original and proper sense of the term, the Holy One who is the active Subject of sanctification, and who constitutes the saints in this action, exists only in the singular as the saints do only in the plural. None of those who are outside Him is different as God is; none is high and distant and alien and superior as He is. There is, of course, difference, gradation, and therefore holiness even within the visible and invisible, the material and spiritual world which is outside God. But with the exception of that which God Himself creates as He sanctifies this can always be transcended and the distance which it involves bridged. And if the final mark of the holiness of God is that, without destroying or even denying His own superiority, He can not only bridge but cross the distance which separates Him from that which He is not and which is therefore unholy, and that He does in fact do this in a genuine exercise and revelation of His superiority, this only means that no other holiness can be compared with His even in respect of this quality. For outside God there is indeed a superiority of one thing to another. And the distance may be bridged, the relationship reversed, the superiority of that which is superior destroyed. But there can be no crossing the gulf in such a way that that which is superior not only does not lose but exercises and reveals its superiority. To put it more simply, as the One who is always holy in His mercy, in virtue of His revelation as Creator, Reconciler and Redeemer, God the Father, Son and Holy Spirit is the only Holy One in the true sense. If there is any other holiness, it is the special work of His special act, the fruit of the action in which He, the Holy One, makes saints in reflection of His own holiness.

Saints! We are not yet this by a long way. Sanctification, the action of the God [514] who is always holy in His mercy, the activity in which He crosses this gulf, does indeed involve the creation of a new form of existence for man in which he can live as the loyal covenant-partner of God who is well pleasing to and blessed by Him. But these are far-reaching and pregnant words if we take them literally. They sound like "idle tales" (Lk. 24¹¹)—no less strange (since they refer to man and therefore to us all) than the report of the resurrection of Jesus Christ. Where is man in this new form of existence, as the loyal covenant-partner of God? Who of us is this man? Yet less sweeping words (and even these words if we do not take them literally) are quite insufficient to describe what is

---

EN102 saints
EN103 holiness
EN104 holy nation
EN105 making holy

at issue in man's sanctification by God. Even if it is only a matter of creating a copy of His own holiness, its reflection in the world which is distant from Himself, the reality of this reflection can be no less than that of a man who is marked off from the rest of the world, not as a second God, but as a man who can live the life of a true covenant-partner of God, i.e., not disloyal but loyal, not displeasing but well pleasing, not cursed but blessed, and in this freedom able to exist in a form which is different from that of all others. At any rate, this is not too strong an expression for the content of sanctification as it is understood in the Bible. Later, we shall have to find even stronger expressions. At the very least we have to say of sanctification that its aim is the man who does not break but keeps the covenant which God has made with him from all eternity. The man who is awakened and empowered by the action of the holy God does this. He is sanctified. He is a saint of God. But who and where are the men of whom this can be said? We shall certainly speak of them, but we are well advised not to speak of them too quickly or directly.

For if, as the Subject of the occurrence in the course of which there arises the existence of saints, God alone is originally and properly holy, this necessarily means that even human holiness, as the new human form of existence of the covenant-partner of this God, cannot originally and properly be that of many, but only of the one man who on the human level is marked off from all others (even the holy people and its members) as sanctified by God and therefore as the Holy One. It is with a view to Him that the people Israel exists as the people of God, and from Him that the community of the last time derives as the community of God. The sanctification of man which has taken place in this One is their sanctification. But originally and properly it is the sanctification of Him and not of them. Their sanctification is originally and properly His and not theirs. For it was in the existence of this One, in Jesus Christ, that it really came about, and is and will be, that God Himself became man, that the Son of God became also the Son of Man, in order to accomplish in His own person the conversion of man to Himself, his exaltation from the depth of His transgression and consequent misery, his liberation from his unholy being for service in the covenant, and therefore his sanctification. This is the divine act of [515] sanctification in its original and proper, because direct, form; in its once-for-all uniqueness. All its other forms, the sanctification of Israel and the community with the distant goal of that of the whole of the human race and the world, are included in this form, by which they are all conditioned. We look into the void if in respect of everything that takes place as sanctification on the circumference of Jesus Christ (whether in the Old Testament or the New), and in exposition of all its forms (discipleship, conversion, good works and the cross), we do not fix our gaze steadfastly on this centre as the place where alone it is a direct event, reaching out with the same reality (but only in virtue of the reality of this centre) to all the other places. How much false teaching, and how many practical mistakes, would have been avoided in this matter of sanctification if in direct analogy to the doctrine of justification by faith alone we had been bold or modest enough basically and totally and definitively to give precedence and all the glory to the Holy One and not to the saints; to the only One who is God, but God in Jesus Christ; and therefore to the royal man Jesus, as the only One who is holy, but in whom the sanctification of all the saints is reality!

According to 1 Cor. 1³⁰ Jesus Christ Himself is made unto us sanctification as well as justification. As E. Gaugler rightly observes (*op. cit.*, p. 76), this saying expresses in the shortest possible compass the truth that even sanctification has to be thought of in terms of the history of salvation. Sanctification takes place as history because and as this man who is directly sanctified by God is its acting Subject in the royal authority thereby given Him by God, God Himself being the One who acts through Him. In Jn. 10³⁶ He calls Himself the One "whom the Father hath sanctified." But being man as the Son of God He can equally well say: "I sanctify myself" (Jn. 17¹⁹). For according to Heb. 10²⁹ it is He Himself who in the first instance is sanctified by His blood as the blood of the covenant. He certainly addresses God: "Holy Father" (Jn. 17¹¹). And He prays: "Sanctify (thou) them through thy truth" (Jn. 17¹⁷). But He Himself is the fulfilment of this request as the Son of the Father. In Ac. 4²⁷⁻³⁰ as the One who is directly sanctified, He is called "the holy servant Jesus," and in Ac. 3¹⁴ "the Holy One and the Just" whom the Jews denied. He was recognised as such by the demons who cried after Him (Mk. 1²⁴; Lk. 4³⁴): "I know thee who thou art, the Holy One of God." And according to Jn. 6⁶⁹ this was also the confession of Peter: "And we believe and are sure that thou art ... the Holy One of God." As such He is the One of whom it is said (1 Pet. 1¹⁵): "He which hath called you is holy." Heb. 2¹¹ is even stronger: He is the ἀγιάζων EN106, the One who sanctifies, by whose existence and action there are also ἀγιαζόμενοι EN107, saints. Everything that follows flows from this source and is nourished by this root. It is on this basis that the call goes out to others that they can and should and must "be holy in all manner of conversation" (1 Pet. 1¹⁵).

For this One is no more holy in isolation than the holy God. He is what He is in this unique and incomparable and inimitable fashion as the One who is elected by God and Himself elects as God, the One in whom the decision has been made concerning all men, in whom they have been set in covenant with God and therefore ordained for conversion to Him. He is thus the Lord and Head and Shepherd and Representative of all men, but primarily of His own particular people, of His community in the world. It has not always been taken with sufficient seriousness that He took our place and acted for us, not merely as the Son of God who established God's right and our own by allowing Himself, the Judge, to be judged for us, but also as the Son of Man who was sanctified, who sanctified Himself. Far too often the matter has been conceived and represented as though His humiliation to death for our justification by Him as our Representative were His own act, but our exaltation to fellowship with God as the corresponding counter-movement, and therefore our sanctification, were left to us, to be accomplished by us. "All this I did for thee; What wilt thou do for me?" The New Testament does not speak in this way. It knows nothing of a Jesus who lived and died for the forgiveness of our sins, to free us as it were

[516]

EN106 Sanctifier
EN107 sanctified

retrospectively, but who now waits as though with tied arms for us to act in accordance with the freedom achieved for us. It is natural that He should be thought of in this way when it is overlooked and forgotten that He is not only the suffering Son of God but also the victorious and triumphant Son of Man. He is this, too, in our place and favour. This too, declared in His resurrection from the dead, is a moment and aspect of the mighty reconciling action of God which has taken place in Him. This, too, is the free and freely disposing grace of God addressed to us in Him. This means, however, that in and with His sanctification ours has been achieved as well. What remains for us is simply to recognise and respect it with gratitude in that provisional praise, the offering of which is the reason for the existence of His people, His community and all its individual members. We are not sanctified by this recognition and respect, by the poor praise that we offer. We are not saints because we make ourselves such. We are saints and sanctified because we are already sanctified, already saints, in this One. Already in Him we are summoned to this action. And the fact that this is so—not in ourselves but supremely in this One—is the reason for this action and the object of our recognition, respect and praise. The creation of man's new form of existence as God's covenant-partner is not, therefore, something which is merely before us, even as concerns ourselves. We have not to achieve it by imitation. Even if we could do this—and we cannot—we should be too late; just as we should be far too late in any attempted creation of heaven and earth. All that we can do is to live under the heaven and on the earth which God has created good. Similarly, our only option is to see and accept as an accomplished fact man's new form of existence, our sanctification, and to direct ourselves accordingly. He Himself has accomplished it in a way which is effective and authoritative for all, for His whole people and all its individual members, and ultimately for the whole world. The fact that it is accomplished in Jesus as our Lord and Head means that we are asked for our obedience, or supremely our love; just as the fact that our justification is [517] accomplished in Him means that we are asked for our faith. There is no prior or subsequent contribution that we can make to its accomplishment. As we are not asked to justify ourselves, we are not asked to sanctify ourselves. Our sanctification consists in our participation in His sanctification as grounded in the efficacy and revelation of the grace of Jesus Christ.

In this respect, too, the New Testament is quite unambiguous. "And for their sakes ($\dot{v}\pi\grave{\epsilon}\rho$ $a\dot{v}\tau\hat{\omega}\nu$) I sanctify myself, that they also might be truly sanctified" (Jn. 17^{19}). Curious saints, we might think, especially in view of the warning of 1 Cor. $6^{9f.}$: "Know ye not that the unrighteous shall not inherit the kingdom of God? Be not deceived: neither fornicators, nor idolaters, nor adulterers, nor effeminate, nor abusers of themselves with mankind, nor thieves, nor covetous, nor drunkards, nor revilers, nor extortioners, shall inherit the kingdom of God. And such were some of you." How will Paul continue after this solemn statement? With the demand that there should be no backsliding in this direction? that there should be a destruction of every remnant of this type of conduct? that there should be a concern for restitution and a corresponding new beginning in the opposite direction? Is there not every occasion for this? Is it not the natural drift of what he says? Yet he himself develops his "Be not deceived" and his charge very differently. For in the immediate continuation in v. 11 he says: "But ye are washed, but ye are sanctified, but ye are justified in the name of the Lord Jesus, and by the Spirit of our God." To oppose to the raging flood of human vice a barrier by which it is set effectively in the past all that is needed is the ἀλλά^{EN108} of recollection of what has taken place in Jesus Christ, and in Him for them and to them. It is exactly the same in Col. 1$^{21f.}$, where the readers are addressed as those who "were sometime alienated and enemies in your mind by wicked works," but whom Christ "hath reconciled in the body of his flesh through death, to present you (cf. Eph. 5^{27}) holy and unblameable and unreproveable in his sight." So, too, in Heb. 13^{12}: "Wherefore Jesus also, that he might sanctify the people with his own blood, suffered without the gate." The meaning of all these ἵνα^{EN109} sentences is not that—by His own example maybe—He should offer them the possibility or chance or opportunity of sanctification, or that He should set them in a decision which they themselves have to make, but that in His death and passion He should make the decision and accomplish their sanctification in their place, laying the foundation on which they actually stand and are called and ordained to be ready to stand and go. This comes out most clearly in Heb. 10$^{5f.}$, where Ps. 40$^{7-9}$ is quoted and expounded as follows: The true High-priest Jesus has taken away the first, the gifts and offerings of men which God did not desire, in order to establish the second, the: "Lo, I come to do thy will, O God" (v. 9). Hence we can be told in v. 10: "By the which will we are sanctified through the offering of the body of Jesus Christ once for all." Note the use of ἐφάπαξ^{EN110} in this context and with this reference. In substance, the statement is repeated in v. 14: "By one offering he hath perfected for ever (εἰς τὸ διηνεκές) them that are sanctified (by it)." And note that according to v. 5 the replacement of the "first" (the gifts and offerings of men) by the "second" (His own doing of the will of God) was accomplished by Jesus already εἰσερχόμενος εἰς τὸν κόσμον^{EN111}, i.e., by His entry into the world as first concealed in the Old Testament promise. And we are taken even further back in 2 Thess. 2^{13}, where Paul thanks God that he "hath from the beginning (ἀπ᾽ ἀρχῆς) chosen you to salvation through sanctification of the Spirit and belief of the truth"; and also in Eph. 1^4, where the great opening hymn begins with the words: "According as he hath chosen us in him before the foundation of the world, that we should be holy and without blame before him in love." It is at this height that the decision concerning our sanctification was resolved—and since the resolve is God's already taken. It is at this depth that Jesus Christ is and acts for us as our Lord and Head even as concerns our own conversion to God. In so far as this is its meaning and content, the history of the royal man Jesus crowned in His death at Calvary had this dimension from the eternity of the will of God fulfilled by Him on earth and in time. That is why Paul can hazard a statement like that of 1 Cor. 3^{17}: "The temple of God is holy, which temple ye are." That is why those gathered into the community can and must be called "saints." They are sanctified and therefore "saints in Christ Jesus" (1 Cor. 1^2; Phil. 1^1); in and with the One who originally and properly is alone the Holy One. For He is their Head and Lord and King. They do not belong to themselves, but to Him. They are saints, not *propria*^{EN112}, but *aliena sanctitate; sanctitate Jesu Christi*^{EN113}. They are holy in the truth and power of His holiness. It is not in defiance but in virtue of this fact that we can never take too literally the New Testament statement about the existence of sanctified men and therefore saints. Where has the New Testament to be taken more literally than in the passages where it speaks of the power and authoritativeness of the new form of

[518]

EN108 but
EN109 so that ...
EN110 one for all
EN111 coming into the world
EN112 with their own holiness
EN113 with the holiness of another, with the holiness of Jesus Christ

human existence achieved in Jesus Christ and therefore created by God? The realism with which it speaks about the existence of saints (in Jesus Christ) may be gathered from the fact that incidentally, but quite categorically, Paul hazards the statement in 1 Cor. 7^{14} that the existence of these men involves the sanctification of those around them who in themselves are not sanctified: "For the unbelieving husband is sanctified by the (believing) wife, and the unbelieving wife is sanctified by the (believing) husband: else were your children (also) unclean; but now (in the New Testament this $\nu\hat{\nu}\nu$ $\delta\acute{\epsilon}^{\text{EN114}}$ recalls the christological reference with which all this is said) are they holy." That it is given to men to be saints (only, but with supreme reality) in their participation in the sanctity of the One who alone is holy means that there is created in the world a fact by which the world cannot be unaffected but is at once—wittingly or unwittingly—determined and altered. It is now the world to which there belongs also the existence of these men, this people. And it has to contend with this fact.

In the participation of the saints in the sanctity of Jesus Christ there is attested the sanctity of man as it is already achieved in this One who alone is holy. We shall have to ask later, in the specifically Christian ethics which will form the subject of the fourth and concluding part of the doctrine of reconciliation, what is the practical result of this self-attestation of man's accomplished sanctification in what he does and does not do. Our present concern is with this self-attestation as such. This consists in the participation of the saints in the sanctity of Jesus Christ; in what Calvin called the *participatio Christi*$^{\text{EN115}}$.

We must first speak about its presupposition. It consists in the fact that the sanctification of man attested in it is actually accomplished in the one Jesus Christ in a way which is effective and authoritative for all, and therefore for each and every man, and not merely for the people of God, the saints. Not a little depends on our realising and considering this. In the participation of the saints in the sanctity of the one Jesus Christ, we are not dealing with the conclusion of a private arrangement between Him and them, but with His cause as the King, and the execution of His office as such. In their sanctification He attests that He is the Lord of all men. In all its particularity their sanctification [519] speaks of the universal action of God, which has as its purpose and goal the reconciliation of the world, and therefore not merely of this group of individuals in the world. As it creates the fact of the existence of these men, this people, within the world, their sanctification attests the great decision of God which in Jesus Christ has been made not only concerning them but concerning all the men of every time and place. This takes away from the particular existence of these men any appearance of the accidental. It gives it the stamp of supreme necessity and obligation. It removes its declaration and expression from the atmosphere of the pride of religious self-seeking and self-sufficiency. It sets it in the larger sphere of the creation of God. It gives it a solidarity even with secular things with which it is contrasted. Even in its antithesis to these it is characterised as a humble rendering of service. This is the basis of both the

---

EN114 but now
EN115 participation in Christ

dispeace and the peace of the saints in their relationship to others. They know that the sanctification of man, of all men, is already fulfilled (like their justification) in the one man Jesus, that it is effectively and authoritatively fulfilled in Him, and that it calls for their faith and love.

But this knowledge is the knowledge of the man Jesus as the "firstborn among many brethren," as He is called with magnificent breadth in Rom. 8²⁹, or "the firstborn of every creature" (Col. 1¹⁵). The one who in Him is elected by God and has elected Him is man; man as such in this One. Thus the humanity of Jesus in the particularity in which He is this one man is, as the humanity of the Son of God, humanity as such, the humanity for which every man is ordained and in which every part already has a part in Him. What took place in Him—the exaltation of man, and therefore His sanctification for God—took place as the new impression of humanity as such. It was accomplished in the place of all others. In the exercise of His kingly office it took place for them too: with all the mercy of the love which seeks all; with all the seriousness of the will which extends to all; with all the power of the act which is done for all; with all the authoritativeness of the decision which has been taken for all. In all His singularity Jesus Christ never was or is or will be isolated. For in this singularity He was and is and will be, and worked and will work, from and to all eternity for all. We do not see Him at all if we do not see Him in our place; if we do not therefore see the direct relevance of His being and action for ours; if we do not therefore see ourselves as determined by His being and action. But all this is not a private arrangement between Him and us. He is not merely our Lord and Representative. As He takes our own place He takes also that of our fellows and brothers. The relevance of His being and action is for ours, but also for that of others who are beside and around us in likeness with us. They no less than we are determined by Him. The knowledge of the man Jesus includes the [520] knowledge and enclosure of our own and every other human existence in His. There are, therefore, no saints (and saints are those who know the man Jesus) to whose participation in the sanctity of this One there does not also belong a knowledge of the all-embracing character of His existence in its comprehension not only of themselves but also of the children of the world.

Calvin's doctrine of the *participatio Christi*[EN116] has one weakness which we can never too greatly deplore and which we can never forget in all his thoughtful and instructive presentation of justification and sanctification. This consists in the fact that he found no place—and in view of his distinctive doctrine of predestination he could not do so—for a recognition of the universal relevance of the existence of the man Jesus, of the sanctification of all men as it has been achieved in Him. The eternal election which according to Eph. 1⁴ has been made in Jesus Christ was referred by Calvin only to those who in God's eternal counsel are foreordained to salvation and therefore to reconciliation, justification and sanctification in Jesus Christ, while His existence has no positive significance for those who are excluded from this foreordination, for the reprobate. The consequence is that when Calvin describes the work of the Holy Spirit in which Christ illuminates and calls men to faith (in the first chapter of

---

[EN116] participation in Christ

the third book), he restricts it from the very first to the circle of the elect. Thus the *participatio*^{EN117} or *communicatio Christi*^{EN118}, and the justification and sanctification of man grounded in it, is a divine action which has only particular significance. For the reprobate, Jesus Christ did not die. For them He neither humbled Himself to be man as the Son of God, nor has He been exalted to fellowship with God as the Son of Man. Neither in the one way nor the other has He acted representatively for them as their Lord and Head and Shepherd. We will not now develop either the serious distortion of the biblical message which this involves (cf. *C.D.* II, 2, §§ 32–35) or its inhumanity. We need only say that it carries with it (1) a dissolution of the strict correlation between the glory of God and the salvation of man. For Calvin the glory of God triumphs only in the salvation of specific men, although it is served by the perdition of the rest. It carries with it (2) the fact that the final and proper ground of election even of the elect is not to be sought in Jesus Christ, but in the inscrutable and immovable decision by which it is decided whether or not they belong to the elect in Jesus Christ. It carries with it (3) the fact that, although their election on the basis of this fore-ordination, and therefore their *participatio Christi*^{EN119}, and therefore their justification and sanctification, do serve the glory of God, they are also an end in themselves, and are thus pointless and unprofitable, since in their realisation they have no positive function in relation to the rest of God's creation. It carries with it (4) the fact that they can serve only to attest the holiness of a God whose mercy is limited to them, and whose love is restricted by a limit which He Himself has arbitrarily and inscrutably set. But since this is not a total love it cannot be accorded a total confidence. Even for those who are just and holy in Jesus Christ this seriously compromises what appears to be their exalted position. In Calvin's conception of the *participatio Christi*^{EN120} there is lacking that which we have described as the objective presupposition of the participation of the saints in the sanctity of Jesus Christ—the sanctification which has come to man *a priori*^{EN121} in Him, which is absolutely sure to the saints, and which gives to their existence teleological meaning among other men. In place of it there yawns the abyss of the absolute decree of a God who is absolutely hidden and anonymous, who does not act in Jesus Christ, who cannot be seen or known in Him, who is God, not in His merciful omnipotence, but in a very different mystery. This means that Calvin's doctrine of sanctification does not have the foundation which is finally needed to carry it. At this point, therefore, we have to look resolutely beyond his conception.

What has to be said about the sanctification which comes *de facto*^{EN122} on the [521] saints in virtue of their participation in the sanctity of Jesus Christ acquires its weight from what has to be said concerning the sanctification which has already come on man—on the saint, but also on every other man—*de iure*^{EN123} in Jesus Christ. But now that we have referred to this presupposition we must turn to the question how the transition is made from this presupposition to the participation of the saints, of the particular people of God in the world, to the sanctification which has come on them *de facto*^{EN124}. How do they become witnesses of that which has come on the whole world and all men in the one

---

^{EN117} participation
^{EN118} communion with Christ
^{EN119} participation in Christ
^{EN120} participation in Christ
^{EN121} unconditionally
^{EN122} as a matter of fact
^{EN123} as a matter of right
^{EN124} as a matter of fact

Jesus Christ? What is the happening which constitutes it this particular people of God armed and commissioned with this witness? The development of the answer to this question is the task of this whole section. In this basic sub-section we must first indicate its general features and scope.

There can be only one point of departure. These saints, the people of God in the world, are men whom the Holy One, the royal man Jesus Christ exalted in His death to fellowship with God, does not confront only in a certain object-ivity, as the "historical Jesus," as a problem set for them, as a possibility and chance offered them, or in such a way that they have still to actualise the relevance of His existence for themselves (and for all men). Do they not have to "wrestle" with Him? Later they do, and this in all seriousness. This is the problem of Christian ethics. But they have to do so only on the basis of the fact that there is no separation between Him and them, but only a companionship in which He Himself has set them as the One who has been raised again from the dead and lives, who was and is and will be in the power of the eternal will of God triumphing in His death, the crucified Lord of all men and therefore their Lord, and now their Lord in particular because it is not hidden from them, but revealed to them, that He is the Lord of all men and therefore their Lord. In the particularity of their existence it is not (or only subsequently) a matter of their understanding and interpreting His existence and its relevance. It is a matter of its self-interpretation as this is not now concealed from them but revealed to them. This is not without its effect on their existence. In it the basic decision is revealed which has been taken concerning them. It compels them at once to a reinterpretation of themselves in accordance with the truth concerning them which has hitherto been suppressed. If He lives, this royal man, and if He does so as the Lord, their Lord, this means even for their own self-understanding that they are His, the people of His possession. They for their part cannot, then, confront Him neutrally as those who are remote and alien—which would really mean hostile, for there is no such thing as neutrality at this point. They belong *to* Him, and in such a way that they belong to *Him.* They are not identical with Him, and never will be. He and He

[522] alone is the Holy One of God, who originally and properly is the Holy One among them and at their head, for He alone is true God, and therefore the true and royal man. But He, the Holy One, being revealed to them as such and not hidden, present as their living Lord, has laid His hand on their creaturely and sinful being and thinking and action and inaction, claiming it for Himself as such, making them witnesses of His sanctity, and therefore and to that extent fellow-saints with Him, even as the sinful creatures they are. He has placed them and their whole being and thinking and action and inaction—we must now take up again the main statement of our christological basis (§ 64, 4)—under His direction. As the New Testament puts it, He has reached and touched them in the quickening power of His Holy Spirit. The Holy Spirit is He Himself in the action in which He reveals and makes Himself known to other men as the One He is, placing them under His direction, claiming them

as His own, as the witnesses of His holiness. The Holy Spirit is the living Lord Jesus Christ Himself in the work of the sanctification of His particular people in the world, of His community and all its members.

At this point we rejoin Calvin. We cannot overlook the weakness introduced by his doctrine of predestination into his establishment of the *participatio Christi*[EN125]. Much less, however, can we overlook the exemplary determination and power with which, in the first chapter of the third book (within this limit), he asserted the Christ-created participation of the saints in the sanctity of Jesus Christ, and therefore their membership in Him as their Lord, as the basis of all soteriology. It is because of this, as the result of his thinking from this centre, that he has the clear insight into the relation between justification and sanctification which we had cause to admire in our first sub-section.

It would not be Christ, we are told in 1, 1, if He existed *extra nos*[EN126], as a *Christus otiosus frigide extra nos, procul a nobis*[EN127] (1, 3); as though He were the subject of the divine act of redemption in *privatum usum*[EN128]; or as though He were One about whom, as those separated from Him, and believing that He exists outside us, we thought that we could "speculate." Our task is to be "graffed in" to Christ (*insert*, Rom. 11[17]), to put Him on (Gal. 3[27]), to form with Him a single whole (*in unum coalescere*). But it is He Himself who does this by the Holy Ghost. Without the Holy Ghost the promise of salvation would be quite empty. It would reach only our ears (1, 3), and all human teachers would cry in vain (1, 4). The Holy Spirit is the bond (*vinculum*) by which Christ binds us effectively to Himself (1, 1). His work consists in the fact that He enlightens us as *magister* or *doctor internus*[EN129], as *Spiritus intelligentiae*[EN130], as the Spirit of truth. That is, He brings us to the light of the Gospel, giving us eyes to see, causing us to grasp the heavenly wisdom, and thus giving us the faith in which the *communicatio Christi*[EN131] with us as His own, and therefore our justification and sanctification, become a concrete event (1, 3 and 1, 4). Since the Holy Ghost is the Spirit of the Son as well as the Father, all this is, of course, the work and gift of Jesus Christ Himself. It is not for nothing that as the second Adam (1 Cor. 15[45]) Jesus Christ Himself is called the *Spiritus vivificans*[EN132] (1, 2).

We must now take some further steps from this starting-point in an attempt to gain an acquaintance with the most general features of the specific event in which the sanctification of man becomes an event *de facto*[EN133]. From what we have seen, the "saints" are those whose existence is affected and radically [523] altered and re-determined by the fact that they receive direction in a particular address of the One who alone is holy. He creates saints by giving them direction. This expression might seem to be too weak and external and therefore ineffective in relation to what it is meant to describe. But even in itself the word "direction" speaks meaningfully and dynamically enough of man's indication to a particular and new situation, of the correction which he must

---

[EN125] participation in Christ
[EN126] outside us
[EN127] idle Christ, coldly outside us, far from us
[EN128] his own private sphere
[EN129] master or internal teacher
[EN130] Spirit of understanding
[EN131] communion with Christ
[EN132] life-giving Spirit
[EN133] as a matter of fact

receive in it, and of the instruction which he is thereby given to adopt a particular attitude. Nor is this direction merely the type that one man may give to another. It is the direction of the royal man Jesus, who is the one true Son of God. And it is given by Him as the Lord as in the work of His Holy Spirit He is revealed and present to these men as the One who is risen and lives, as their Head and Shepherd. Thus, unlike any direction which one man may give to others, it falls, as it were, vertically into the lives of those to whom it is given. It is thus effective with divine power. It is the sowing and the developing seed of new life. It crushes and breaks and destroys that which resists it. It constitutes itself the ruling and determinative factor in the whole being of those to whom it is given. As is brought out by the German word *Weisung*—and it is in this sense that we are using it—it becomes their wisdom. We do not use the word in any restrictive sense. We use it merely for the sake of precision. It reminds us that the power or sowing which proceeds from the existence of the royal man Jesus, the critical and constructive force with which He invades the being of men and makes them His saints, is not a mechanical or organic or any other physical operation, nor is it in any sense a magical. It is the power of His Word spoken with divine authority and therefore in illuminating fruitfulness and power. The sanctification of the saints by *the* Holy One takes place in the mode appropriate to the being of the Son of the God who is the eternal Logos, and to the relationship of the Son of Man to other men. He speaks. He does so forcefully, not merely in words but in acts, in His whole existence, and all-comprehensively in His death. Yet He speaks. And others hear Him. They do not hear Him only with their ears, or as they hear other men, but effectively—as a call to obedience. Yet they hear Him. Hence the sanctification of man as the work of the Holy Spirit has to be described as the giving and receiving of direction. It is in this way that the Holy One creates the saints. It is in this way that He shares with them, in supreme reality, His own holiness; man's new form of existence as the true covenant-partner of God.

Again in the most general terms we ask how this impartation is to be understood, and our best plan is to begin from the bottom upwards. These saints are indeed at the very bottom. They themselves are not royal men, nor are they exalted to fellowship and cooperation with God, as has to be said of this One.

[524] He indeed is enthroned at the right hand of God the Father. But this means that, as in virtue of His direction they recognise Him as theirs and themselves as His, He confronts them within the world as God confronts the whole world. They are not merely creatures. They are slothful, stupid, inhuman, dissipated and careworn sinners. And as His direction is given them, they have to see and confess that this is the case. They are still sinners—these saints, these recipients of the direction of the exalted man, of the Son of Man who is also the Son of God. They are still below. The direction given and received is one thing; they themselves in comparison with it are quite another. What, then, differentiates them from the world, from other men, from those who are not saints? There can be no doubt that they are differentiated from the world; that as the

Word is spoken to them and heard by them they are saints; fellow-saints with the Holy One, His people. But in what sense is this true and can it be said concerning them?

To describe their sanctity—in view of the fact that they are undoubtedly still sinners—we must first use a very modest and restrained, yet quite significant expression. They are disturbed sinners. Their sleep as such is broken. Their course as such is slow and lame and halting. Their activity as such is hemmed in by qualifications and doubts. They are no longer happy in the cause that they have espoused. Now it is not at all self-evident that man should be a disturbed sinner in this way. The unreconciled man, the man to whom the reconciliation of the world with God, which comprehends his own sanctification, is concealed, is an undisturbed sinner. Naturally, he too has his own restraints and periods of unrest. But he is able to surmount and master them. It is his conscious or unconscious, primitive or refined art of living to be able to master them, and thus in peace and harmony with himself to pursue his sleep and course and activity. These, and his whole activity below, are possible, necessary and natural in spite of all his unrest. And he cannot genuinely disturb himself. There is, therefore, no point in accusing him, or treating him ironically. He does not understand what we are talking about if we tell him that he ought to be seriously disquieted. The only disturbance that he knows is one which can be overcome, not one which cannot be overcome. The direction of the Son of Man, the work of the Holy Spirit, is needed if he is to be disturbed in a way which cannot be overcome. The saints are sinners who are disturbed in this way. As the sinners they still are they are confronted by the existence of *the* Holy One and therefore by the name and kingdom and will of God. It is not concealed from them that the kingdom has drawn near. It has approached others as well as themselves. But as distinct from others they are aware of the fact, and they have to live with the fact that it is the case. But the kingdom of God is the contradiction of all sloth, and therefore of their own. It is an active protest against what they do and do not do here below. They have to accept this protest. As it is made and revealed to them, it applies to their own being. They themselves are still sinners, and they have to recognise and confess that this is so. But there is now no room for complacency. They cannot happily pursue their course. They do what they do. But they do it as those to whom it has been said, and who have heard, that it is wrong. They have been deprived of all authorisation to do it; of every possibility of extenuating or excusing it. They can no longer continue to do it with confidence. Why not? Because in the exalted Son of Man, the royal man Jesus, they have perceived and have before them their Brother, and themselves as His brothers. It is He who disturbs them in their activity here below. And He continues effectively to disturb them. They are His saints as those who are effectively disturbed. Sanctification is a real change even in this restricted sense—the creation of a new form of existence in which man becomes the true covenant-partner of God. As an undisturbed sinner he is always a covenant-breaker, unreconciled with God

[525]

and unusable by Him. The better he succeeds in achieving inner harmony, the less he can be reconciled with God and used by Him. But when, although he is a sinner and here below like all others, he meets and has to accept, in virtue of the direction of the incarnate Son of God, the name and kingdom and will of God, and therefore that active protest, even here below he is already placed where he belongs, at the side of God, made a partisan of God even against himself and the world, and radically and definitively separated from the unholy, who may not be so great sinners as he, but who are still undisturbed sinners. It makes a tremendous difference whether a man is on the one side or the other; whether in his person the sin of the world is arrested sin or unarrested. The people of God in the world are those who still stand in daily need of forgiveness but upon whose hearts and consciences there has been written, not their own or a human, but the divine contradiction of their sinning.

We will now choose another less restricted and rather more penetrating term to describe the men of this people. They are not merely disturbed in their sinful will and action. A limit is set to their being sinners by the direction which they are given. Within this limit their being is still that of sinners. They still live in the flesh. In relation to this "within" everything that has to be said about the misery of man, and especially about his lack of freedom to do the will of God, applies to them too. But this "within" is not infinite. On the contrary, a definite limit has been set for it. And this is their sanctification. It is from this limit that there comes on man that which we have already described as the disturbance of his sinful action. There can be no reducing the seriousness with which he has still to recognise himself as a creature which is slothful towards God, and which constantly reproduces its sloth. Nor can there be any reducing the seriousness of the fact that he stands under the accusation and [526] condemnation of God. Yet we have also to recognise that this being is overwhelmingly limited (not merely *de iure*[EN134] but *de facto*[EN135]) by the direction which he is given. It is limited to this "within." It is, therefore, relativised. Its continuance is radically threatened. What limits it is again the revealed name of God, His imminent kingdom, His will which is done for man, claiming him as His creature, negating his being as a sinner, and destroying the force which binds him and reduces him to misery and bondage. The limitation which thus comes to him is his sanctification. Because it is God's act, it is an overwhelming limitation. It is not at all the case, then, that the being of saints is compromised by their being as sinners. On the contrary, their being as sinners, their life in the flesh, is overwhelmingly and totally compromised by their being as saints. As God enters their life actively and concretely in virtue of the direction which they are given, in the act of lordship of the Son of Man, in the truth of His Word and the actuality of the Holy Spirit, their being as sinners, however ser-

---

EN134 as a matter of right
EN135 as a matter of fact

iously it may still assert itself, is pushed into a corner. It may still intrude into the present, but it belongs to the past. The "within" is in this corner, and is itself the past. It no longer counts. What really counts is its limitation. For the reality of this limitation has its basis in the exaltation of Jesus Christ. It is, therefore, divine reality. The being of man as a sinner, on the other hand, has its reality only in virtue of that which is not. The people of God in the world are those to whom it is revealed, and who may live in and by the knowledge, that their being as sinners is one which is assailed by God, and therefore basically and definitively; that the ground on which they are sinners has been taken away from them, even though they are still sinners. This is what distinguishes the recipients of the direction of the Son of God from the world which does not share this knowledge—although the ground has already been cut from under its sinful being as well.

The word "disturbance" which we used first to describe sanctification as *participatio Christi*[EN136] refers to its critical character, although it is not on that account only a formal term. We must now take a further step. As sinners, the recipients of the direction of the One who alone is holy are disturbed in their sinful will and action by the fact that their existence is positively placed under a new determination. In other words, they are called. In their totality they are the ἐκκλησία[EN137], a gathering of those to whom the Son of Man has spoken and who have heard His voice. In this sense they are set aside by Him. Or better, here below, within the world which is not yet aware of its reconciliation with God accomplished by Him, its sanctification in Him, they are set at His side, in order that they may be there His witnesses, the witnesses of the Holy One. As such they are disturbed sinners; sinners who are disturbed by the fact that He has made clear to them the divine No to their own sinful will and action, and that of all men. Because it is His No, it is effective. It thus involves [527] for them an irresistible and invincible disturbance. But again, because it is His No it is not an empty or abstract No. It is concretely filled out with the Yes of His direction. This is not merely correction. It is also instruction. As those who are called by Him, they are not merely called out; they are also called in. They are called into the fellowship of their existence with His. It is to be noted that they are called as those they are, in their action here below, which still has all the marks of sinful action. They still exist here below. "Whilst we are at home in the body, we are absent from the Lord" (2 Cor. 5⁶). For we are not above where He, the royal man, exists. But there above He is our Lord and Head and Representative: the Son who is sanctified by the Father, and who sanctifies Himself, for us and for all men; the true Covenant-partner of God in fellowship and co-operation with Him. He is all this, not for Himself, but for the saints, as theirs, as their Brother. It disturbs them below that they have this Brother above, bone of their bone and flesh of their flesh. For as the One who, exalted

---

[EN136] participation in Christ
[EN137] church

in this way, is theirs, their Brother, He is not concealed from them as He is from others of whom it may also be said that He is theirs, their Brother. He is not distant, a mere historical Jesus. He is revealed and near to them, their living Lord. As such He attests Himself to them, imparting Himself in the truth and power of His, the Holy Spirit. As such, and speaking to them as such, He disturbs them in their slothful sleep and course and activity. Awakening them as such, He startles them out of the peace in which they think that they can continually express their sinful being as others do. But calling them out in this way. He calls them to Himself. As those who still live below He calls them to fellowship with Him as the One who is exalted above. This does not mean only the critical disturbance but in and with it a positive alteration of their being below. They may and can and must lift up themselves as those who are summoned by Him."Lift up your heads"(Lk. 21^{28}), is the call. What is meant is that they should look to Him, the exalted, royal man, who has come to them as their own, their Brother, and will come again, and is now present with them below even though He is above; that they should look to Him, the Holy One, and in this looking to Him as their Lord and Representative be His saints. This looking to Him, not with bowed but uplifted head, is the setting up of these men. It is their positive sanctification—in contrast to others upon whom this has come *de iure*[EN138] but not *de facto*[EN139]. "Looking unto Jesus, the author and finisher of our faith" (Heb. 12^2), they live. This looking is their sanctification *de facto*[EN140]. As they are called by Him, and look to Him and therefore lift up themselves, they have a part here below in the holiness in which He is the One who alone is holy.

[528] We speak of men who are always sinners like others; who at every moment and in every respect need forgiveness, the justification before God which is sheer mercy. Their sanctification takes place here below where there is no action that does not have the marks of sloth or can be anything but displeasing to God. This is true even of their lifting up of themselves, even of their looking to the Lord, which is their action as saints. Who is there who really lifts up his head, and looks directly and steadfastly at the One who is the Holy One for us, as we must do if our action is to be well pleasing to God and to show that we are true covenant-partners of God? How painfully we lift up ourselves! How basically compromised is our attempt to do so by so much indolent and wilful slouching! Is it really more than the eddy which may arise and be seen in a powerfully flowing stream but which cannot alter the course of the stream as a whole? These men are saints as they lift up themselves in obedience to the call which comes to them. But they are not saints in virtue of the seriousness or consistency with which they make this movement, or look to the One who calls them. They are saints only in virtue of the sanctity of the One who calls them

---

EN138 as a matter of right
EN139 as a matter of fact
EN140 as a matter of fact

and on whom their gaze is not very well directed. He alone on whom they look takes from that which they do, their lifting up of themselves, the doubtful and questionable character from which it is never free in and for itself. He alone takes from it the powerlessness and insignificance, the inability to bear witness, which it inevitably shares with the action of all other men. He alone sanctifies it by accepting it as perfect, and therefore by continually justifying it. He alone gives to it here below in the world, where these men also exist, the power and significance of a right answer to His self-attestation and therefore of a witness to the sanctification of man as accomplished in Him.

More important for our present purpose, however, is the fact that He does actually do this. It is not just any call which comes to them and which they obey as they lift up themselves and look to Him. It is His call. If we accept the picture of the stream and the eddy, to make it true to the facts we shall have to say that the eddy does not arise through the inter-play of forces within the stream, but by the operation of an alien factor—perhaps a powerful wind which comes sweeping across it. The lifting up of man effected by his sanctification is his own act, and it is similar to all his other acts. Yet it is different from all his other acts to the extent that the initiative on which he does it, the spontaneity with which he expresses himself in it, does not arise from his own heart or emotions or understanding or conscience, but has its origin in the power of the direction which has come to him in these spheres. It is necessary and indispensable that he should rouse himself and pull himself together and find courage and confidence and take and execute decisions, but this is only the spiritual and physical form of a happening which does not originate in himself and is not his own work, but the gift of God. It is not as his own lord but as the recipient of this gift that he carries through the movement which we call his [529] lifting up of himself. He executes it as the answer to a call which does not come from himself but from the One who encounters him, and is present and revealed to him, as the Lord and therefore as his Lord. No matter how similar this movement may be to those of all other men—for he has no other means to hand than those common to all men—it is absolutely dissimilar in the fact that it is his correspondence to the life-movement of his Lord as produced, not by his own caprice, but by the will and touch and address and creation and gift of this Lord. Those who receive Him, who are given the power to become the children of God, who believe in His name, are not born of blood, or of the will of the flesh, or of the will of man, but of God (Jn. 1[12f.]). Their action is nourished by the mystery of the life-giving Spirit by whom the Lord has united these sinful human creatures to Himself. Their action attests this mystery, and therefore the One who has united them to Himself. This is what has to be said of them, and can be said only of them. This is their sanctification.

Because and as and to the extent that it comes to them from Him, and is His work, it is a real alteration of their being, They are still sinners. Their action is still burdened with all the marks of human sloth. It still stands in need of the forgiveness, the justification, which they cannot achieve of themselves, and which God does not owe them. All this is true. But even more true is the fact that as they lift up themselves they fulfil a movement in which their being—however questionably they may fulfil it—becomes and is conformable to His being, the being of their Lord. Yes, their being below is conformable to His above. Their painful lifting up of themselves in the flesh, in the world from which they are not yet taken, is conformable to his enthronement at the right hand of God the Father Almighty. "I, if I be lifted up from the earth, will draw all men unto me" (Jn. 12^{32}). The constitution of His people on earth takes place in the power of His drawing unto Himself. This drawing unto Himself is His kingly work fulfilled in divine power. It cannot, then, be called in question. But if this is the case, the same is true of the existence of His people, His saints, and the lifting up of themselves in which they are drawn to Him. As that which corresponds to His exaltation, as the attestation of the elevation of man accomplished in Him, it is a historical event. In what takes place to them as He calls them to lift up themselves, His exaltation has its concrete consequence in the world and its continuing and not yet arrested development. The eddy arises and is visible in the stream, first in the lives of these men, but then—seeing that they have their fellows—as a fact in the common life of all men. It is now not merely human sloth which rules here below. As it is given to these men to lift up themselves, in opposition to human sloth and defiance of it (in its sphere and not unhampered by it) we find also a willingness and readiness,

[530] a courage and joyfulness, to be the new man who is loyal to His covenant-partnership with God and therefore loyal to his human brothers. The stream flows on, and all men—even the saints, for they are still here below—flow with it. But the powerful wind is blowing from above. And stirred up by it there is obedience as well as disobedience. It is highly unsatisfactory obedience. It stands in constant need of forgiveness. But it is obedience. To that extent there is the sowing seed of new life in the field which is the world. It is only a sowing. It is only seed. And this seed must die if it is to bear fruit. But it is genuine seed—seed which while it is sown below does not come from below, but from above. This is sanctification, the actual sanctifying of the saints by the Holy One. Its dignity and reality are no less than those of justification, but the same. The human situation does not remain unchanged, as it would necessarily do in itself, and as it seems to do to those who do not have eyes to see. The change is only relative. For sanctification is not an ultimate, only a penultimate, word. Like justification, it is not redemption or glorification. Yet for all its relativity it is a real change. For there are now men who lift up themselves and raise their heads.

We must now return, however, to the second word which we used to describe the critical character of sanctification as *participatio Christi*^{EN141}. We called it the limit which is set for man in his being as a sinner. And in the case of this term, too, we must now step on to the positive significance. We have said that

---

^{EN141} participation in Christ

the name and kingdom and will of God limit the corrupt and miserable being of man, pushing it into a corner, making it his past, thoroughly relativising it. It is the act of lordship of the Son of Man, His direction, which in this way cuts as it were right across the existence of man and draws this frontier. Now obviously we do not exhaust the meaning of this event by saying that in it the being of man as a sinner is attacked and limited and made a thing of the past. As we learn from 2 Cor. 5^{17} there has also come into being something new. The space which the Holy Spirit makes outside the sinful being of man which He limits cannot be an empty space. He Himself fills it. For "where the Spirit of the Lord is, there is liberty" (2 Cor. 3^{17})—the liberty for being on behalf of God and one's brothers which the sinful man does not have as such, and the lack of which is the deepest woe in which he finds himself plunged as a sinner. In his sinful activity he should not merely find himself disturbed by the direction which comes to him but awakened to lift up himself, to look to Jesus, and in so doing to be sanctified and holy. But he needs the capacity, the ability, the freedom, to do this. It has to take place here below, in the flesh, in the world. But in this sphere there is no freedom for it. He exists *servo arbitrio*[EN142]. He is a prisoner of sin who continually commits new sins. No true Christian has ever suffered seriously from the illusion that within the limit set by the divine direction he does not still live in this bondage in which he cannot even think of this lifting up of himself, of this looking to Jesus, let alone accomplish it. Yet as his sinful being is limited in the power of the divine direction he is given a total freedom in face of this total bondage. And in the New Testament sense of the term this freedom does not mean the possibility of either lifting up himself or not, of perhaps looking to Jesus and perhaps looking elsewhere to other lords. No, the One who has accomplished this powerful limitation could not be the Lord if He had merely opposed to the sinful being of man this paltry freedom of choice. What He imparts to man when He gives him His direction is not a possibility but the new actuality in which he is really free in face of that bondage: free in the only worthwhile sense; free to lift up himself in the sense described. He can do this, not because he should, but because he may. The imparting of this capacity is the liberation of man—his sanctification. In this capacity he is set in sovereign antithesis to his being as a sinner. He is not compelled continually to commit new sins. He may refrain from doing so. He may do the opposite. In the capacity which is imparted to him, on the basis of the permission which he is given, he will—if he makes use of it—do the opposite. He cannot do anything else. Whether he makes use of it is, of course, another matter. Our present concern is with the permission which he is given; the sovereignty in which he is set in opposition to his own being as a sinner. And to this as such there is no limit.

We say this even of the saints who are all very obviously and palpably sinners, in whose lives there is continually to be found much that is very different from

[531]

[EN142] in a will in bondage

this lifting up of themselves, who clearly continue to make use of very different freedoms and permissions from those given them by the divine direction; of all kinds of supposed freedoms and permissions which they think they can and should give themselves, but which are in fact illusory. The total, unlimited, sovereign freedom of the Spirit is given them even though they are still in the world like all other men. Their being as sinners is radically assailed, but not destroyed. They still think and speak and act as those who are not free, but who, according to the classical formula of the *Heidelberg Catechism,* are "inclined by nature to hate God and my neighbours." What would become of the freedom of the saints if it had to be guaranteed by the use they make of it; if its possession were dependent on the power with which they exercise it? They do indeed have to use and exercise it. How can they receive it if they do not do this? But the freedom of the saints is grounded and enclosed, not in the dignity and power of this reception, but in the dignity and power of the gift made, or rather of the Giver of this gift, in the freedom of the royal man Jesus to whom they are summoned to look. They do not look to Him very well. But they are made free, and are free, only in the fact that it is He to whom they look. They are saints only in the fact that He sanctified them. What Paul says in Gal. $4^{25f.}$ with reference to the Synagogue may rightly be applied to every form of the people of God on earth—that "the Jerusalem which is above is free, which is the mother of us all."

[532]

Here again, however, the emphasis must fall on the other aspect. The Holy One does actually give it to His saints to be free: free to lift up themselves and look to Him; and therefore freed from the compulsion to sin which results from their being as sinners. Even here below, as those who live in the flesh, they need never again bewail the fact that they have to sin: that they have therefore to make use of other ostensible freedoms and permissions; that they have therefore in certain respects to persist in the general sloth of man which characterises them too; that they cannot therefore lift up themselves. They have no time either for the arrogance of the indeterminists or the pusillanimity or melancholy or idle dissuasions of the determinists. In view of the One to whom they look—however well or badly—in their *participatio Christi*[EN143], everything is in good order as regards their freedom. Their sovereignty over their being in the flesh and in sin is unequivocally established and secured against every assault. There may often be good cause to bewail both new and old connexions with that which is below. They may often do things which apart from the forgiveness of sins would inevitably involve their ruin. But they cannot ascribe this to the incompleteness of impotence of the freedom which they are given. They lack it as they fail to make use of it. But it is still given, and in their fellowship with the Holy One they still have it. As they are called, so they are also equipped to be a brave people of their Lord. They make themselves equivalent to the children of this world, to whom they are supposed to be His

---

[EN143] participation in Christ

witnesses, if they leave this in any doubt, accepting in relation to themselves the general deploring of human incapacity instead of resolutely doing what they are well able to do. The fact is that they *are* able to lift up themselves and look to Jesus and be what they are—His saints. For, as they well know, He has stooped down to them and looked on them. The positive element concealed in the limitation of their unholy being, the freedom which has become a factor in their life, has also to be thought of as real. Otherwise there would be no place for the apostolic admonition given in the New Testament to Christians. This is not given as a law or ideal proclaimed in the void. It is not given as though the question whether or not they can obey were still open and to be answered. It is obviously given on the assumption that they are free, and that they can make use of the freedom in which they have been made free in Christ (Gal. 5^1). Without this assumption there would be no such thing as Christian ethics even for us. All the things that we have to develop in ethics in relation to the command of the God who reconciles the world with Himself can only be concretions of the lifting up of themselves, the looking to Jesus, of which Christians are capable because they have been given the freedom for them. It is true that in its original and proper form they have this freedom, not in themselves, but in the One who is above. But called by Him to fellowship with Himself, placed in it, united with Him by His Holy Spirit, they are free here and now in correspondence to His kingly rule at the right hand of God the Father Almighty. To their salvation they are free only for this. But they are genuinely free for this. They can look to Him and be His saints in everything that they do in this look. 2 Cor. 5^{17} is true of them: "If any man be in Christ, he is a new creature"; and especially Heb. 12^{10}: they are "partakers of his holiness" and above all Jn. 8^{36}: "If the Son therefore shall make you free, ye shall be free indeed"—ὄντως ἐλευθεύροι EN144. It is all provisional, for the saints are still captives. But it is all very real, for they are already liberated. If it is true that they are still prisoners, it does not count. The captivity is behind them, freedom before them. And all this is in their fellowship with the Holy One. All this is in virtue of the fact that they are called by Him. "Now ye are clean through the word that I have spoken unto you" (Jn. 15^3).

[533]

3. THE CALL TO DISCIPLESHIP

"Follow me" is the substance of the call in the power of which Jesus makes men His saints. It is to this concretion of His action that we must now turn. The lifting up of themselves for which He gives them freedom is not a movement which is formless, or to which they themselves have to give the necessary form. It takes place in a definite form and direction. Similarly, their looking to Jesus

---

EN144 being free

as their Lord is not an idle gaping. It is a vision which stimulates those to whom it is given to a definite action. The call issued by Jesus is a call to discipleship.

We must not waste time describing and criticising that which, in adoption of very earlier traditions, the later Middle Ages and certain Evangelical trends understood and attempted as an *imitatio Christi*EN145. The matter is well enough known. It involves a programme in which we try to shape our lives by the example of the life of Jesus as sketched in the Gospels and the commandments which He gave to His own people and to all men generally. And the objections to it are obvious, and therefore facile. It will be more instructive for our present purpose if we turn at once to the problem which is unavoidably posed by these movements, and especially by the New Testament itself. The discussion of this problem will enable us to weigh both critically and positively the doctrine and exercise of the *imitatio Christi*EN146.

Easily the best that has been written on this subject is to be found in *The Cost of Discipleship*, by Dietrich Bonhoeffer (abridged E.T., 1948, of the German original *Nachfolge*, 1937). We do not refer to all the parts, which were obviously compiled from different sources, but to the opening sections, "The Call to Discipleship," "Simple Obedience" (omitted in the E.T.) and "Discipleship and the Individual." In these the matter is handled with such depth and precision that I am almost tempted simply to reproduce them in an extended quotation. For

[534]

I cannot hope to say anything better on the subject than what is said here by a man who, having written on discipleship, was ready to achieve it in his own life, and did in his own way achieve it even to the point of death. In following my own course, I am happy that on this occasion I can lean as heavily as I do upon another.

Before we take up the problem as such, it may be as well to consider briefly what is to be learned linguistically from the biblical use of the decisive term ἀκολουθεῖνEN147. In this respect I am indebted to G. Kittel's article in his *Wörterbuch*.

Ἀκολουθεῖν means to go after or behind someone. Rather strangely, the Old Testament used the corresponding word mostly as a kind of technical term for the sinful pursuit of others gods. This gave to the word a pejorative sense, and Jer. 2² is perhaps the only occasion that we read of a following of *Yahweh*: "I remember thee, the kindness of thy youth, the love of thine espousals, when thou wentest after me in the wilderness, in a land that was not sown." The Rabbis doubted, indeed, whether there could be any following of God at all in the sense of a following of God Himself, of His *shekina*EN148. For God is far too transcendent. As they saw it (in a striking parallel to the Greek idea of the similarity which man achieves with God by ἕπεσθαιEN149 as he acts like Him), it is a matter of following the qualities or acts of God: of planting the land as God did the Garden of Eden; of clothing the naked as God clothed Adam; of visiting the sick as God did Abraham; of comforting the sad as God did Isaac; of burying the dead as God did Moses. In this we have almost an early form of the later Christian idea of *imitatio*EN150. For the rest, the Old Testament and Rabbis offer us only the "following" (which has no theological significance) of honoured leaders. The warrior follows his captain, the wife her husband, the bride her bridegroom, the son of the prophet his master, the scholar the rabbi who goes or rides before him on an ass. It is this that leads us to the New Testament with its thought of following Jesus. This occurs only in the Four Gospels (with the exception of Rev. 14⁴); and in the first instance it envisages an external going after him, the word being apparently limited to this sense in such passages as Mk. 3⁷, etc., where

---

EN145 imitation of Christ
EN146 imitation of Christ
EN147 following
EN148 presence
EN149 following
EN150 imitation

we are told that "a great multitude followed him." Following as they practised it had both an inward and an outward limit. Yet there were others—and it is here that the word acquires its pregnant meaning—who are called by Jesus and follow Him in the sense that they accompany Him wholeheartedly and constantly, sharing His life and destiny at the expense of all other engagements and commitments, attaching themselves to Him, placing themselves in His service, and thus showing that they are qualified to be His disciples; not as though the Messianic salvation is ascribed only to them, or even to them in particular, but as those who particularly attest and proclaim it. Their qualification as disciples, and therefore for discipleship in this pregnant sense, is a gift, a $εὔθετος$ $εἶναι$ EN151 for the kingdom of God (Lk. 9^{62}), a capacity with which they are endowed. Normally the fact that they are endowed in this way means also that they accompany Him. Yet there are some qualified disciples who do not do so, and on the other hand there are others who accompany Him but are not qualified disciples in this sense. It is worth noting in conclusion that the New Testament never uses the substantive "discipleship" ($ἀκολούθησις$ EN152) but only the verb $ἀκολουθεῖν$ or $ὀπίσω$ $μου$ $ἔρχεσθαι$ EN153. This is a warning that in our consideration of this question we must always remember that we are dealing with what is obviously on the New Testament view an event that cannot be enclosed in a general concept. The further implications of discipleship must be developed from concrete passages within this wider context.

1. We will again begin by stating that the call to discipleship is the particular form of the summons by which Jesus discloses and reveals Himself to a man in order to claim and sanctify him as His own, and as His witness in the world. It has the form of a command of Jesus directed to him. It means the coming of grace, for what is disclosed and revealed in Jesus is the reconciliation of the [535] world with God as his reconciliation and therefore the fulness of salvation. But as it encounters him in this summons, grace has the form of command, the Gospel the form of the Law. The grace which comes to him requires that he should do something, i.e., follow Jesus. It is thus a grace which commands. Jesus is seeking men to serve Him. He has already found them to the extent that He has elected them as ordained to this end. They are already His people even as He claims them. He thus establishes His particular relationship to them by commanding them. He does this in His authority as the Son of Man who is their Lord, who can thus dispose concerning them, who has already done so, and who addresses them accordingly. Both Jeremiah and Paul understood that even from the mother's womb they were ordained for the action commanded. Jesus is already the Lord of those whom He calls to follow. He calls them as such. He commands them as those who already belong to Him. This is what constitutes the overwhelming force of His command. This is why there can be no legitimate opposition to it. This is why there can be no question of any presuppositions on the part of those who are called: of any capacity or equipment for the performance of what is commanded; of any latent faith; of any inward or outward preparation. This is why there can be no question of self-selection on the part of those who follow. This is why those who are called

EN151 being fit
EN152 to follow
EN153 to follow or coming after me

cannot think of laying down conditions on which they are prepared to obey His command. Just because the command of Jesus is the form of the grace which concretely comes to man, it is issued with all the freedom and sovereignty of grace against which there can be no legitimate objections, of which no one is worthy, for which there can be no preparation, which none can elect, and in face of which there can be no qualifications.

Disobedience to the command of Jesus: "Follow me," as in the case of the rich young ruler in Mk. 10$^{17f.}$ and par., is a phenomenon which is absolutely terrifying in its impossibility. It provokes the question of the disciples: "Who then can be saved?", for in it there is revealed the far too common rule of the natural, or unnatural, attitude of man to this command. In the light of the command of Jesus given to a man, disobedience is inconceivable, inexplicable and impossible. On the other hand, we might ask who is the man Levi that when Jesus sees him at the receipt of custom (Mk. 2$^{14f.}$) He should at once issue the same command: "Follow me"? How much we should have to read into the short account if we were to try to explain from Levi himself, and his moral and religious qualifications, why it is that he is given this command and proceeds at once to execute it. We can only abandon the attempt. The secret of Levi is that of the One who calls him. Again, we are told in Lk. 9$^{57-58}$ about a man who met Jesus in the way with the offer: "I will follow thee whithersoever thou goest." He is obviously one who has presumed to do this on his own initiative. And his answer is the terrible saying about the foxes which have holes, and the birds of the air nests, "but the Son of man—whom he is going to follow—hath not where to lay his head." He does not realise what it is that he thinks he can choose. He does not know how terrible is the venture to [536] which he commits himself in the execution of this choice. No one of himself can or will imagine that this is his way, or take this way. What Jesus wills with His "Follow me" can be chosen only in obedience to His call. We can see this from the saying of Peter in Mt. 14^{28}: "Lord, if it be thou, bid me come to thee on the water." Without being bidden by Christ, he could not do this. It has also been noted that there can be no conditions. The man mentioned in Lk. 9$^{61-62}$ lacked true discipleship, not merely because he offered it to Jesus as a matter for his own choice, but because he also made a condition: "But let me first go bid them farewell, which are at home at my house." Those who offer themselves to be disciples are obviously bound to be of the opinion that they can lay down the conditions on which they will do this. But a limited readiness is no readiness at all in our dealings with Jesus. It is clear that this man, too, does not really know what he thinks he has chosen. It is certainly not the following of Jesus. This is commanded unconditionally, and therefore it cannot be entered upon except unconditionally. The answer of Jesus makes it quite plain that this man cannot be considered as a disciple: "No man, having put his hand to the plough, and looking back, is fit for the kingdom of God."

2. The call to discipleship binds a man to the One who calls him. He is not called by an idea of Christ, or a Christology, or a christocentric system of thought, let alone the supposedly Christian conception of a Father-God. How could these call him to discipleship? They have neither words nor voice. They cannot bind anyone to themselves. We must be careful that we do not conceal the living Jesus behind such schemata, fearing that the One who can issue this call, who has the words and voice to do it, and above all the right and authority and power to bind, might actually do so. Again, discipleship is not the recognition and adoption of a programme, ideal or law, or the attempt to fulfil it. It is not the execution of a plan of individual or social construction imparted and

commended by Jesus. If the word "discipleship" is in any way used to denote something general and not a command is that this or that specific man to whom it is given should come to, and follow, and be with, the One who gives it. In this One, and the relationship which it establishes between Him and the one He calls, a good deal more is involved. But there is nothing apart from Him and this relationship. That a man should come to Him is the one complete work which he is called to do. We may say, therefore, that in practice the command to follow Jesus is identical with the command to believe in Him. It demands that a man who as such brings no other presuppositions than that he is entangled like all other men in the general sloth of man, and has to suffer the consequences, should put his trust in God as the God who is faithful to him the unfaithful, who in spite of his own forgetfulness has not forgotten him, who without any co-operation or merit on his part wills that he should live and not die. In the call of Jesus he is met by the fulfilled promise of God as valid for him. In and with the command of Jesus, solid ground is placed under his feet when he is on the point of falling into the abyss. What the command requires [537] of him is simply, but comprehensively, that in practice as well as in theory he should regard it as able to bear him, and stand on it, and no longer leave it. This is what we do when we trust; and in so doing we do all that is required of us. To do this is to believe. But in the faith here required we do not have a trust *in abstracto*[EN154] or in general, nor do we have the rash confidence of a hazardous journey into space. It is demanded by Jesus—the Son of Man who as the Son of God speaks in the name and with the full authority of God. And what Jesus demands is trust in Himself and therefore, in the concrete form which this involves, trust in God. He demands faith in the form of obedience; obedience to Himself. This is the commitment to Him which constitutes the content of the call to discipleship. We cannot separate any one moment of this happening from any of the others. That He, the Son of Man who is the Son of the Father, lives and rules as the Lord of all men; that as the Saviour of all men He comes to a particular man, who is as little worthy of it as any others, to make Himself known to him as the One who is also his Saviour; that in so doing He simply claims him for Himself as one of His, and for His service; that He thus demands of him faith in God and trust in Himself; that the faith demanded of this man includes the obedience which has to be rendered to Jesus: all these are inseparable moments of the one occurrence. There is no discipleship without the One who calls to it. There is no discipleship except as faith in God as determined by the One who calls to it and frees for it. There is no discipleship which does not consist in the act of the obedience of this faith in God and therefore in Him.

It is with these contours that the call to discipleship goes out as recorded and attested in the Gospels. Everything depends upon the fact that Jesus Himself is there and lives and calls men to Himself. We are never told what His will is for Levi or Simon Peter, or the others

[EN154] in the abstract

whom He calls. Nor is any attempt made to establish or explain His authority to call them. It is enough for the Evangelists in their description of the origin of the disciple-relationship, and it must obviously be enough for us too in our understanding of it, that Jesus does actually call them, and call them to Himself. He summons them. They are to give to Him the faith of which God is worthy and which is owed to Him; the faith and therefore the confidence that they are helped by Him and therefore by God; that within the world of human sloth and its consequences they are helped to overcome these and to be set up: "He that followeth me shall not walk in darkness, but shall have the light of life" (Jn. 8¹²). Or, as we are told of the 144,000 who "follow the Lamb whithersoever he goeth," they are the firstfruits of the redeemed from among men, and they bear His name and the name of His Father in their foreheads, and they sing a new song before the throne (Rev. 14¹ᶠ·). His summons is, however, that they should give to Him and therefore to God a true and serious and total faith: not a mere acceptance of the fact that He is their Lord nor an idle confidence that they are helped by Him; but this acceptance and confidence as a faith which is lived out and practised by them; a faith which is proved to be a true and serious faith by the fact that it

[538] includes at once their obedience—what Paul called the ὑπακοὴ πίστεως[EN155] in Rom. 1⁵ and 16²⁶, and the ὑπακοὴ τοῦ Χριστοῦ[EN156] in 2 Cor. 10⁵. "Why call ye me, Lord, Lord, and do not the things which I say?" (Lk. 6⁴⁶). There can be no doubt that what moved those who were called to be disciples as they followed the call of Jesus was simply their faith in Him as the Lord, and therefore in God. But it was a faith which at once impelled them to obedience. There is nothing in the accounts of the call of the disciples to suggest a kind of interval, i.e., that they first believed in Him, and then decided to obey Him, and actually did so. It is never an open question whether, when and how obedience has to begin if faith is presupposed. Faith is not obedience, but as obedience is not obedience without faith, faith is not faith without obedience. They belong together, as do thunder and lightning in a thunderstorm. Levi would not have obeyed if he had not arisen and followed Jesus. The fishermen by the lake would not have believed if they had not immediately (εὐθύς) left their nets and followed Him. Peter on the lake (Mt. 14²⁹) would not have believed if he had not obeyed Jesus' call to come, and left the boat and gone to Him on the water. But Peter and all of them did believe, and therefore they did at once and self-evidently that which was commanded. It is true that in the continuation of the story Peter looked at the raging wind instead of Jesus, and was afraid, and doubted, and could go no farther, but could only sink, and would have sunk if he had not been gripped by the hand of the One in whom he had so little faith. But this only shows that the disciple cannot obey without believing, or conversely that when he believes he must and can obey, and actually does so.

3. The call to discipleship, no matter how or when it is issued to a man, or whether it comes to him for the first time or as a second or third or hundredth confirmation, is always the summons to take in faith, without which it is impossible, a definite first step. This step, as one which is taken in faith, i.e., faith in Jesus, as an act of obedience to Him, is distinguished from every other step that he may take by the fact that in relation to the whole of his previous life and thinking and judgment it involves a right-about turn and therefore a complete break and new beginning. To follow Jesus means to go beyond oneself in a specific action and attitude, and therefore to turn one's back upon oneself, to leave oneself behind. That this is the case may and will not always be equally

---

[EN155] obedience of faith
[EN156] obedience of Christ

perceptible from the particular step, the particular action or attitude, which is demanded as the act of faith. But—however imperceptible that which we do may be—it can never be a question of a routine continuation or repetition of what has hitherto been our customary practice. It always involves the decision of a new day; the seizing of a new opportunity which was not present yesterday but is now given in and with the call of Jesus. Inevitably the man who is called by Jesus renounces and turns away from himself as he was yesterday. To use the important New Testament expression, he denies himself.

Where it is used in a pregnant sense, and not merely of a simple denial, $\dot{a}\rho\nu\epsilon\hat{i}\sigma\theta a\iota$ EN157 always denotes in the New Testament the renunciation, withdrawal and annulment of an existing relationship of obedience and loyalty. Peter denies that he was ever with Jesus of Nazareth: "I know not, neither understand I what thou sayest" (Mk. 14^{68} and par.). The Jews deny Jesus, their own Messiah, the Servant of God, in the presence of Pilate (Ac. 3^{13}). There are also ostensible, but in reality anti-Christian, Christians who deny the Lord who bought them (2 Pet. 2^1). In particular, they deny that Jesus is the Christ, thus making themselves [539] guilty of a denial of the Father and the Son (1 Jn. 2^{22}). John the Baptist denies that he himself is the Messiah (Jn. 1^{20}), and in so doing he does not deny, but indirectly recognises, that Jesus is. Denial is the opposite of confession ($\dot{o}\mu o\lambda o\gamma\epsilon\hat{i}\sigma\theta a\iota$), in which a man stands both in word and deed to a relationship of obedience and loyalty in which he finds himself. The disciple who does not do this to others in respect of his relationship to Jesus—" whosoever therefore shall be ashamed of me and of my words in this adulterous and sinful generation " (Mk. 8^{38})—denies Him as Peter did; and this automatically means that so long and to the extent that he does this the relationship of Jesus to him, His advocacy for him before God, is dissolved:" Him will I also deny before my Father which is in heaven "(Mt. 10^{33}, cf. 2 Tim. 2^{12}). This is the objective factor in the bitterness experienced by Peter in consequence of his denial. In the same sense, and with the menace of the same dreadful consequences, there is a denial of the name of Jesus (Rev. 3^8) or of His $\pi\iota\sigma\tau\iota s$ EN158 (Rev. 2^{13}). It is remarkable that the same verb which in this pregnant sense denotes the most dreadful thing of which the disciple can conceivably be guilty in his relationship to Jesus is also used (although this time with reference to himself) to describe the peak point in this relationship, the characteristic turning of obedience. In 2 Tim. 2^{13} the culminating reason for the impossibility of denying Christ as the Christian sees it is the fact that" he cannot deny himself "—for how can the Son of Man deny that He is the Son of God? But at the decisive point in the Synoptists (Mk.8^{34}) the very opposite is true of ourselves:" Whosoever will come after me, let him deny himself " ($\dot{a}\pi a\rho\nu\eta\sigma\dot{a}\sigma\theta\omega$ $\dot{\epsilon}av\tau\dot{o}v$). The idea is exactly the same. The man who is called to follow Jesus has simply to renounce and withdraw and annul an existing relationship of obedience and loyalty. This relationship is to himself. When he is called to discipleship, he abandons himself resolutely and totally. He can and must say of himself instead of Jesus: "I know not the man" (Mt. 26^{72}). He cannot accept this man even as his most distant acquaintance. He once stood in a covenant with him which he loyally kept and tenderly nurtured. But he now renounces this covenant root and branch. He can confess only Jesus, and therefore he cannot confess himself. He can and will only deny himself.

But in the context of discipleship to Jesus, which is a definite happening, this is a very definite step. It is not merely a new and critical and negative mind

---

EN157 to deny
EN158 faith

and attitude in relation to himself. This will also be involved. But in and for itself, in the uncommitted sphere of inwardness, this might be present without the definite loosing of a man from himself, and therefore without a definite act of obedience. In this case discipleship would only be theoretical. It would not be an actual event. The call to discipleship would not have really reached and affected the man, or he would have imprisoned and tamed and rendered it innocuous in the sphere of emotion or reflection. An inner withdrawal from oneself is not by a long way a breach of the covenant or denial of acquaintance with oneself, and therefore self-denial in the sense of discipleship. In itself and as such, if this is the whole of the matter, it might be the most radical and obstinate denial of this breach or renunciation. Indeed, where this is the whole of the matter, it will certainly be such. Self-denial in the context of following Jesus involves a step into the open, into the freedom of a definite decis-

[540] ion and act, in which it is with a real commitment that man takes leave of himself, of the man of yesterday, of the man he himself was; in which he gives up the previous form of his existence, hazarding and totally compromising himself without looking back or considering what is to become of him, because what matters is not now himself but that he should do at all costs that which is proposed and demanded, having no option but to decide and act in accordance with it—cost what it may. "For God's sake do something brave," was once the cry of Zwingli to his contemporaries. Not feel, or think, or consider, or meditate! Not turn it over in your heart and mind! But *do* something brave. If it is to this that Jesus calls man in His discipleship, there can be no avoiding genuine self-denial.

To be sure, we have not merely to do anything that is brave, or that smacks of bravery. Even though we might find precedents for it in history, or Church history, or the Bible, a mere act of bravery might well be performed without self-denial. Indeed, it might even be an act of supreme self-assertion. For all his sloth, the old Adam whom we have to leave behind loves sometimes to emerge in great acts. It is a matter of doing that which is proposed to us by Jesus. It may be great or it may be small. It may be striking or it may be insignificant. But its performance is laid upon us, not by ourselves, but by the One who has called us to Himself, who has willed and chosen us as His own. And we are to perform it in the act of that obedience which cannot be separated from faith in Him. As a man renders this obedience, he will certainly not be able to assert himself. He can only deny himself. The call with which Jesus calls and binds him to Himself means that he should leave everything that yesterday, and even yet, might seem self-evident and right and good and useful and promising. It also means that he should leave a merely inward and mental movement in which he does not really do anything, but only speechifies in an idle dialectic, in mere deliberations and projects concerning what he might do but cannot and will not yet do, because he has not yet reached the point of action in his consideration of it and of the situation in which it is to be done. He takes leave of both, for in both the old Adam is enthroned—the self whom he has to deny in the discipleship of Jesus. This Adam is denied in the new act demanded by the call of Jesus, and the brave thing demanded of His disciples consists in what D. Bonhoeffer calls "simple obedience." Obedience is simple when we do just what we are told—nothing more, nothing less, and nothing different. In simple obedience we *do* it, and therefore we do not finally not do it. But what we do is literally and exactly that which we are commanded to do. The only possible obedience to Jesus' call to discipleship is simple obedience in these two senses. This alone is rendered in self-denial. This alone is the brave act of faith in Jesus.

Bonhoeffer is ten times right when at this point he inveighs sharply against a theological interpretation of the given command and the required obedience which, is to the effect that the call of Jesus is to be heard but His command may be taken to mean that the obedience required will not necessarily take the form of the act which is obviously demanded but may in certain cases consist in the neglect of this act and the performance of others which are quite different. [541]

This interpretation may be stated as follows. The command of Jesus is naturally to be heard and accepted and followed with joy. It is the commanding grace of God, and therefore the salvation of the whole world and of man, entering his life as a free offer. How can he resist it? But what does it mean to follow? What is commanded is obviously that he should come to Jesus; that he should believe in Him as God; that he should believe in God by believing in Him; that he should trust Him wholly and utterly; that he should be willing and ready, therefore, for every hazard or venture or sacrifice that in a given situation might prove to be necessary to confirm this trust. Yet as concerns the concrete form of the command of Jesus, in which we have to do with something definite that we are commanded to do or not do, this concrete thing is only designed more sharply to describe and emphasise the totality and depth with which the command requires faith, and with faith the willingness and readiness for what may in certain circumstances be the supreme and most perfect sacrifice. Obedience to it means an inward liberation from everything in which we might otherwise put our trust; the loosening of all other ties to the point of being able to sever them at any moment. We need not do precisely what the command of Jesus explicitly demands. The point of the explicit command is the implicit—that we should believe, and that in our faith we should be alert to do either that which is explicitly commanded or something similar and along the same lines. When we have accepted that which is implied in the command, we have already obeyed in the true sense. We have "as though we had not." By what is meant in the command, and the willingness and readiness we bring to it, everything else that we have is radically called in question. We do everything only "as though we did it not." Inwardly, therefore, we are free. We are free even perhaps to do that which is explicitly commanded. But do we have to do it? No, for that would be a legalistic interpretation of the command, which even in what seems to be its concrete demand that we should do this or that is really calling us only to the freedom in which we may do it but do not have to do so. On a true and proper interpretation the command of Jesus does not command us to do this specific thing. There is no question of having to do it. In obedience to the command we may just as well do something else and even the very opposite. For example, instead of giving all that we have to the poor, we may maintain and increase our possessions; or instead of turning the other cheek, we may return the blow which we have received. All, of course, "as though we did it not"! All in a willingness and readiness one day perhaps—when the opportunity and situation offer—to do that which is concretely demanded! All on a true and spiritual understanding, and in a genuine exercise, of the obedience of faith! All in a grateful appropriation of the salvation which comes with Jesus' call to discipleship! But with the result that for the moment that which Jesus literally asks remains undone, and the outward state and course of affairs remains unchanged by His command and our obedience.

Bonhoeffer's commentary on this line of thought and its result is as follows (*Nachfolge*, p. 35): "Where orders are given in other spheres, there can be no doubt how matters stand. A father says to his child: Go to bed, and the child knows what has to be done. But a child versed in this pseudo-theology might argue as follows. My father says: Go to bed. He means that I am tired. He does not want me to be tired. But I can dissipate my tiredness by going out to play. Therefore, when my father says: Go to bed, he really means: Go out to play. If this were the way in which children reasoned in relation to their fathers, or citizens in relation to the state, they would soon meet with a language that cannot be misunderstood—that of punishment. It is only in relation to the command of Jesus that things are supposed to be different."

[542]

The ghost of this interpretation cannot be too quickly laid. The commanding grace of God, and therefore salvation as Jesus' call to discipleship, never come into the life of a man in such a way that he is given leave to consider why and how he may best follow the command given. The command given is recognisable as the command of Jesus by the fact that it is quite unambiguous. It requires to be fulfilled by him only as it is given—and his reception or non-reception of salvation depends upon whether this is done or not. The faith which Jesus actually demands is not just a radical readiness and willingness for all contingencies—a kind of supply which is there to draw upon as required but is stored up for the time being. It is distinguished as trust in Jesus, and therefore as genuine trust in God, by the fact that as it is given to man and grasped by him it at once takes on the form of the definite resolve and act indicated by the call of Jesus. The command given to a man by Jesus is not given to the one who receives it in such a way that he may freely distinguish between what is meant and what is willed, between the implicit content and the explicit form, the former being accepted but the latter provisionally ignored. It has its content only in its specific form. Only as it turns to the latter can it keep seriously to the former. Again, it is not the case that in obedience to the call of Jesus we can and should and even (in all prudence) must postpone a full inward and outward rendering of it until we find a favourable opportunity and situation; the psychological, historical, economic or political situation indispensable to its integral achievement. To be sure, we for our part have not to create a situation of this kind. But we have to realise that the command of Jesus given us itself creates the situation and all the conditions of the situation in which we have to obey, so that there is no place for any further waiting for a developing situation or suitable moment, nor for any further consideration, appraisal or selection of different possibilities, but only for instant obedience. In obedience we are not about to leap. We are already leaping.

The line of argument which we have been reconstructing has, of course, a ring of profundity. It seems to give a triumphant answer to monks and fanatics and other legalists. But this is an illusion. It is not simple obedience that is legalistic, but the arbitrarily discursive and dialectical obedience which evades the command. It is the disobedience, disguised as obedience, of a flight into inwardness at the point where the inward man can and should express himself outwardly. It is the disobedience of the flight into faith at the point where faith as the obedience of the heart relentlessly involves the obedience of action. It is not from the concrete command of Jesus that there comes the threat of the Law to whose dominion we must no longer subject ourselves; it is from the forced conceptions in the light of which we think we can arbitrarily release ourselves from concrete obedience to the concrete command of Jesus. Those who acted legalistically were not the fishers by the lake who at the bidding of Jesus left the nets and followed Him, but men like the rich young ruler who when he heard what he had to do "was sad at that saying, and went away grieved: for he had great possessions" (Mk. 10²²). If we will not bear the yoke of Jesus, we have to bear the yoke which we ourselves have chosen, and it is a hundred times more heavy. The attitude corresponding to that line of argument has nothing whatever to do with the true flight to Jesus. On the contrary, it is a flight from Him. We refuse to take the first step towards Him, and therefore we cannot take any further steps. Where we undertake the flight to Him, it is inevitable that in and with the first step demanded not merely the outer but the inner state and course of our lives and therefore our surroundings will be affected and in some way basically altered. The call of Jesus makes history when it is heard and taken seriously. It is by this that we may know whether or not it is heard; whether or not it is heard and taken seriously as a call to self-denial.

4. The call to discipleship makes a break. It is not the obedient man who [543] does it, not even with his simple obedience. What he does in this obedience can only be an indication of this break. If he is not to be disobedient, what option has he but to do as he is told? But good care is taken—and he has to realise the fact—that in his action he can never accomplish more than an indication, demonstration and attestation of this break. It is the call of Jesus, going out into the world and accepted by him, which makes the break; which has already made it. The kingdom of God is revealed in this call; the kingdom which is among the kingdoms of this world, but which confronts and contradicts and opposes them; the *coup d'état* of God proclaimed and accomplished already in the existence of the man Jesus. The man whom Jesus calls to Himself has to stand firm by the revelation of it. Indeed, he has to correspond to it in what he himself does and does not do. His own action, if it is obedient, will always attest and indicate it. It will not do this in accordance with his own judgment or pleasure. It will do it in the way commanded. But because it is the man Jesus who causes him to do what he does it will attest and indicate only this revelation. It may do so to a smaller or lesser degree. It may do so in strength or in weakness. But always it will set forth the kingdom of God drawn near, and therefore the greatest, the only true and definitive break in the world and its history as it has already taken place in Jesus Christ and cannot now be healed.

It is with this that we have to do in the discipleship of Jesus exercised in self-denial. While it is a matter of the personal self of the individual called by Jesus, of the dissolution of the covenant with himself, the self-denial of the disciple is only a kind of culminating point in the great attack in which he is called to participate as His witness, and which he has to recognise and support as in the first instance an attack upon himself. If we are not ready to deny ourselves, of what use can we be as witnesses of the great assault which is directed against the world (for the sake of its reconciliation with God) in and with the coming of the kingdom? Our self-denial, and the first step which we are commanded to make by Him who calls us, are not ends in themselves. They stand in the service of this great onslaught.

But in this onslaught it is a matter of God's destruction, accomplished in the existence of the Son of Man, of all the so-called "given factors," all the supposed natural orders, all the historical forces, which with the claim of absolute validity and worth have obtruded themselves as authorities—mythologically but very realistically described as "gods"—between God and man, but also between man and his fellows; or rather which inventive man has himself obtruded between God and himself and himself and his fellows. The dominion of these forces characterises the world as the world of the slothful man. It continually makes it the world which strives against God, but which is for this very reason in a state of hopeless disintegration and in need of reconciliation with God and of His peace. When they are posited absolutely, possessions (which are significantly described as the "mammon of unrighteousness" in Lk. 16^9) and worldly honour, the force which defends them, the family with its claims and even the law of a religion (and worst of all a religion of revelation) are all gods which are first set up by man, which are then worshipped in practice and which finally dominate him, interposing themselves between God and him, and himself and his fellows, and maintaining themselves in this mediatorial position. It is not men, or any one man, who can make the break with these given factors and orders and historical forces. What man does of himself may take the form of an attempted repudiation but it will always serve to confirm and strengthen them, continually evoking new forms of their rule. The little revolutions and attacks by which they seem to be more shaken than they really are can never succeed even in limiting, let alone destroying, their power. It is the kingdom, the revolution, of God which breaks, which has already broken them. Jesus is their Conqueror.

[544]

If we are His disciples, we are necessarily witnesses of this fact. We are awakened by Him from the dream that these forces are divine or divinely given actualities, eternal orders. We can no longer believe, and therefore we can no longer think or accept, that men, including ourselves, are indissolubly bound and unconditionally committed to them. In their place there stands for us the Conqueror Jesus, the one Mediator between God and man, and man and his fellows; He who is the divine reality; He who decides what can and cannot be, what is and is not, a divinely given reality for us. If we are His disciples we are freed by Him from their rule. This does not mean that we are made superior, or set in a position of practical neutrality. It means that we can and must exercise our freedom in relation to them. It must be attested in the world as a declaration of the victory of Jesus. The world which sighs under these powers must hear and receive and rejoice that their lordship is broken. But this declaration cannot be made by the existence of those who are merely free inwardly. If the message is to be given, the world must see and hear at least an indication, or sign, of what has taken place. The break made by God in Jesus must become history. This is why Jesus calls His disciples. And it is for this reason that His disciples cannot be content with a mere theory about the relativisation of those false absolutes; a mere attitude of mind in which these gods no longer exist for them; an inward freedom in relation to them. It is for this reason that in different ways they are called out in practice from these attachments, and it is a denial of the call to discipleship if they evade the achievement of acts and attitudes in which even externally and visibly they break free from these attachments. They can never do this, in any respect, on their own impulse or according to their own caprice. It is not a matter of our own revolt, either as individuals or in company with those likeminded. It is a matter of the kingdom of God and God's revolution. But the disciple of Jesus is always summoned to attest this in a specific way by his own act and attitude. He has no right, nor is he free, to avoid the concretely given command. This is where we see the relevance of what we said about simple obedience in 3. There can be no question in self-denial of a soaring and tranquillising mysticism of world-renunciation and freedom and conquest in which the obligation to the godless and hostile orders already broken in Christ is not only maintained but if anything validated and sanctified. If this is all that is involved, then no matter how profoundly or attractively it is present it is a highly irrelevant enterprise. No, it is important only as, in obedience to the One who demands it, it is an indication of His attack and victory, and therefore a concrete step out into the open country of decision and act; of the decision and act in which, even though he can only indicate what is properly at issue, man can only seem to be strange and foolish and noxious to the world around him. Is it not inevitable that in the first instance he will have this appearance even to himself? He must and will run the risk of being an offence to those around him—and in so far as he sees with their eyes, to himself. He will not seek or desire this. But he cannot avoid the risk that it will be so. In relation to the world he cannot, then, restrict himself to an attempted "inner emigration" in which he will not be offensive, or at least suspicious, or at the very least conspicuous, to those who still worship their gods. It is not merely a matter of saving his own soul in the attainment of a private beatitude. He loses his soul, and hazards his eternal salvation, if he will not accept the public responsibility which he assumes when he becomes a disciple of Jesus. It is more than doubtful whether he is doing this if his existence does not force those around him to take notice—with all the painful consequences this may involve for him. But they will not take notice, nor will they be disturbed or annoyed by his existence, if he does not come out into the open as the one he is, doing what they do not do, and not doing what they do; if in his attitude to the given factors and orders and historical forces which they regard as absolute there is no difference between him and them, but only uniformity and conformity. This may have for him the advantage that he will not be disturbed or assailed by them, but can live by his faith, and find joy and even secret pride in what may perhaps be a very radical opposition in inward attitude. The only trouble is that he will be quite useless as a witness of the kingdom of God. As a quiet participant in the cause of this kingdom he will avoid giving offence to anyone, but he will also evade the

[545]

obedience which he is required to render. For this obedience necessarily con-

sists in the fact that publicly before those around him he takes what is in a specific form a new path which leads him out of conformity with them to a place to which he specifically is pointed, so that to those who still persist in conformity he involuntarily but irresistibly makes himself conspicuous and suspicious and offensive, and can expect to meet with serious or petty forms of unpleasantness from them. He will not provoke them. Like Daniel in the lions' den, he will be cautious not to pull the lions' tails. But he will encounter what he must encounter if God does not unexpectedly decree otherwise. He will have to endure it. It is better not to describe him as a warrior. If he is in his right senses, he will not think of himself as such. He does not go on his way out of conformity in opposition to any other men, but on behalf of all other men, as one who has to show them the liberation which has already taken place. The *militia Christi*[EN159] will arise of itself, although there can, of course, be no question of Christian contentiousness against non-Christians, let alone of violence, crusades and the like. And even the *militia Christi*[EN160] will not really consist in conflict against others, but decisively in conflict against oneself, and in the fact that one is assailed, and in some way has to suffer, and to accept suffering, at the hands of others. It is certainly not our commission to add to the sufferings of others, and therefore to fight against them. Even for the sake of the kingdom of God which we are ordained to serve we need fight only by indicating, in what we do and do not do, the fact that it has dawned, that it has broken into the old world, so that visibly—and not just invisibly—we refuse respect and obedience to all the generally recognised and cultivated authorities and deities, not lifting our hats to the different governors set over us. We know that the battle against them is already won; that the victory over them is already an accomplished fact; that their power is already broken. Our task is perhaps offensive to others, but intrinsically it is the friendly and happy one of giving a practical indication of this fact. In its discharge we are concerned with the release and liberation of these others too. And we cannot escape this task.

At this point we must think of the concrete form of the demand with which Jesus in the Gospels always approached those whom He called to discipleship. It is common to every instance that the goal is a form of action or abstention by which His disciples will reveal and therefore indicate to the world the break in the human situation, the end of the irresistible and uncontested dominion of given factors and orders and historical forces, as it has been brought about by the dawn and irruption of the kingdom. It is common to every instance that the obedience concretely demanded of, and to be achieved by, the disciple, always means that he must move out of conformity with what he hitherto regarded as the self-evident action and abstention of Lord Everyman and into the place allotted to him, so that he is inevitably isolated in relation to those around him, not being able or willing to do in this place that which is generally demanded by the gods who are still fully respected in the

---

EN159 conflict of Christ
EN160 conflict of Christ

world around. At this particular place he is freed from the bonds of that which is generally done or not done, because and as he is bound now to Jesus.

We must emphasise the "because and as." Except as he is directly bound to Jesus, a man is [547] never called out of conformity with those around, and therefore loosed from the bonds of that which is generally done or not done. And this binding to Jesus must be thought of as a very particular matter—something which comes to each individual in a highly particular way in his own particular time and situation. To *this* man He *now* gives—and this man now receives—*this* command as the concrete form of the call to discipleship now issued to him. It is not the case, then, that he is loosed from one general form of action, from the legalism of the world as determined by the dominion of those gods, only to be bound to the legalism of another generality, which simply consists in a radical, systematic and consistent penetration and destruction of the first. In face of the solid front of the action which is normative for the man of the world the commanding of Jesus does not establish what we might call the counter-front of an action which is normative for all His disciples in every age and situation. His bidding—and this is rather different—is that in accordance with the direction which He gives to each disciple in particular there should be different penetrations of this front and the establishment of signs of the kingdom in the world which is ruled by the gods and subject to their legalism. Thus, apart from Himself as the Lord, there is no new and revolutionary law to which His disciples are no less subject than others are to the old law of the cosmos dominated by these false absolutes. There is no such thing as a party which is rallied by this law and which has to contend for it as the parties of the divided world have to fight for their different conceptions of the laws which rule the world. There is only the new commanding of Jesus in its relationship to this particular man elected by Him and in this particular time and situation which He has fixed. This new commanding of His is the concrete form in which He calls these men, here and now, to discipleship, and therefore sanctifies them.

It is clear that in the directions to discipleship embodied in the Gospel tradition we have to do with collective accounts, even (and especially) where the call is generally addressed to a majority of His disciples or it may be to all of them. The fact that this was very quickly obscured led to the mistaken attempt to create out of these directions a *nova lex*[EN161], a general mode of Christian action in opposition to that of worldly action. The truth is, however, that what the Gospel sayings about the following of His disciples really preserve are certain prominent lines along which the concrete commanding of Jesus, with its demand for concrete obedience, always moved in relation to individuals, characterising it as His commanding in distinction from that of all other lords. And these sayings are read aright by individuals who accept their witness that they too are called to obedience to the Lord who may be known as this Lord by the fact that His commanding, while it does not require the same thing of everyone, or even of the same man in every time and situation, always moves along one or more of these prominent lines. And the lines recorded in the Gospel all agree that man is always called to make a particular penetration of the front of the general action and abstention of others; to cut loose from a practical recognition of the legalism determined by the dominion of worldly authorities. Everything depends upon the fact that it is Jesus who demands that we make this penetration and cut loose in this way. If this is not demanded, we can be sure that it is not the command of Jesus. And if it is not effected, we can be sure that there is no obedience to Him. Even in action along the main lines of the concrete forms of His demands there can be no true action apart from a commitment to Him, i.e., except as it is done for His sake. Conversely, however, there can be no commitment to Him if the action of the disciple is not along one or more of the great lines and if the

---

EN161 new law

freedom of the kingdom of God is not attested—this is the common element in every case—to the imprisoned world in a visble concretion.

For us Westerners, at any rate, the most striking of these main lines is that on which Jesus, according to the Gospel tradition, obviously commanded many men, as the concrete form of their obedient discipleship, to renounce their general attachment to the authority, validity and confidence of possessions, not merely inwardly but outwardly, in the venture and commitment of a definite act. We do not have here the realisation of an ideal or principle of poverty as it was later assumed into the monastic rule. Nor do we have the basis of a new society freed from the principle of private property. It is simply, but far more incisively, a question of the specific summons to specific men, as in Mt. 5^{42}: "Give to him that asketh thee, and from him that would borrow of thee turn not thou away" (severely sharpened in Lk. 6^{35}: "Lend, hoping for nothing again"); or in Mt. 5^{40}: "And if any man will … take away thy coat, let him have thy cloke also"; or 6^{31}: "Therefore take no thought, saying, What shall we eat? or, What shall we drink? or, Wherewithal shall we be clothed? For after all these things do the Gentiles seek"; or 6^{19}: "Lay not up for yourselves treasures upon earth, where moth and rust doth corrupt, and where thieves break through and steal"; or 6^{24}: "No man can serve two masters …. Ye cannot serve God and mammon"; or in the charge to the disciples in Mt. $10^{9f.}$: "Provide neither gold, nor silver, nor brass in your purses, nor scrip for your journey, neither two coats, neither shoes, nor yet staves"; or the demand, illustrated in the parable of the unjust steward, that we should make friends with the mammon of unrighteousness as long as we have it (Lk. 16^9), and in this sense be "faithful" to it; or the radical command addressed to the rich young ruler whom Jesus loved: "One thing thou lackest: go thy way, sell whatsoever thou hast, and give to the poor" (Mk. 10^{21}); and the echo in the words of Peter (Mk. 10^{28}): "Lo, we have left all, and have followed thee." The line along which all this is said is obviously the same, although it cannot be reduced to a normative technical rule for dealing with possessions. On the contrary, it is palpable that these are specific directions given to specific men at specific times and to be specifically followed, not in a formalised or spiritualised, but a literal sense. The drift of them all is clearly that Jesus' call to discipleship challenges and indeed cuts right across the self-evident attachment to that which we possess. The man to whom the call of Jesus comes does not only think and feel but acts (here and now, in this particular encounter with his neighbour) as one who is freed from this attachment. He not only can but does let go that which is his. By doing exactly as he is commanded by Jesus he successfully makes this sortie, attesting that the kingdom of mammon is broken by the coming of the kingdom of God.

Along a second line the instructions given by Jesus have to do no less directly with the destruction by the coming of the kingdom of what is generally accepted as honour or fame among men: "Blessed are ye, when men shall revile you, and persecute you, and shall say all manner of evil against you falsely for my sake" (Mt. 5^{11}). For "if they have called the master of the house Beelzebub, how much more shall they call them of his household" (Mt. 10^{25}). And therefore "whosoever shall smite thee on thy right cheek, turn to him the other also" (Mt. 5^{39}). Or according to the parable of the wedding-guests (Lk. $14^{7f.}$): "Sit not down in the highest room … but in the lowest room …. For whosoever exalteth himself shall be abased; and he that humbleth himself shall be exalted." Or again: "Whosoever will be great among you, let him be your minister" (Mt. 20^{26}). Or again, in the presence of a real child whom Jesus called and set in the midst when His disciples were concerned about the question of the greatest in the kingdom of heaven: "Except ye be converted, and become as little children, ye shall not enter into the kingdom of heaven" (Mt. $18^{1f.}$). Or again, in direct contrast to those who love and claim the uppermost rooms at feasts and the chief seats in the synagogue and greetings in the market, we are not to be called Rabbi or father or master (Mt. $23^{6f.}$). "How can ye believe, which receive honour one of another," is Jesus' charge against the Jews

3. The Call to Discipleship

(Jn. 5^{44}), and by way of contrast He demands that the disciples should wash one another's feet: "For I have given you an example, that ye should do as I have done to you" (Jn. 13^{14f}). To come to Jesus is to take a yoke upon oneself like a gallant ox (Mt. 11^{29}). All this can hardly be formulated, let alone practised, as a general rule for improved social relationships. It is again clear that these sayings assume the existence of men who are freed by the concretely given command of Jesus from the universal dominion and constraint of ordinary conceptions of what constitutes social status and dignity and importance. It is not concealed from these men that all such conceptions are transcended and outmoded by the incursion of the kingdom of God; that there is a transvaluation of all values where the grace of God rules. They can and should reveal this in their action and abstention, in which they are no longer concerned with what those around regard as honour or dishonour. The disciple of Jesus can descend from the throne—the little throne perhaps—which even he may be allotted in human society. He does not do this wilfully or of his own choice, but as he is commanded. Yet as he is commanded he *does* it.

Along a further line the command of Jesus, and the obedience which has to be shown to it, takes the concrete form of an attestation of the kingdom of God as the end of the fixed idea of the necessity and beneficial value of force. The direction of Jesus must have embedded itself particularly deeply in the disciples in this respect. They were neither to fear force nor to exercise it. They were not to fear it as brought to bear against themselves, for at the very worst their enemies could kill only the body and not the soul. Their true and inward selves would remain inviolate. Why should they not fear, and to what degree? Because the very hairs of their head which might be hurt, and they themselves as they might be subjected to mortal attack, are all under the care of the fatherly assistance and protection of God, apart from which not even a sparrow can fall to the ground. And they are of more value than many sparrows. They may have to suffer force as it is used against them, but they are secure in face of it. Hence they are commanded: "Fear not" (Mt. 10^{28f}). On the other hand, those who have no need to fear the exercise of force against them by others because it cannot finally harm them can hardly expect to apply force against others. Ought fire from heaven to be called down on the Samaritan village which would not receive Jesus (Lk. 9^{52f})? According to one variant only a tacit answer was given in His turning and "threatening" them. According to the other He said explicitly: "Ye know not what manner of spirit ye are of. For the Son of man is not come to destroy men's lives, but to save them." And the story ends with the short statement that "they went to another village." To this there corresponds the direction given in Mt. 10^{13f} that where they are not received the disciples are to shake off the dust from their feet and move on. The peace which they aim to bring to those who for the moment are obviously unworthy of it will then return to themselves (whereas they would clearly lose it if they adopted any other attitude). Again, when the multitude came from the high-priests with swords and staves as against a robber (Mt. 26^{47f}), and one of the disciples "stretched out his hand, and drew his sword, and struck a servant of the high-priest's, and smote off his ear," he was commanded by Jesus to put the sword back into its scabbard: "For all they that take to the sword shall perish with the sword." Jesus might have had twelve legions of angels from His Father. But He does not ask for them. For He does not need this protection and is not prepared to make use of it. Hence the disciple who draws his sword must be delivered from this vicious circle. Nor does the exercise of force begin with killing. It begins when we are angry with our brother, when we call him *raca* or fool, when there are judicial proceedings (Mt. 5^{21}). The disciple of Jesus will have nothing to do with this kind of behaviour, let alone with retaliation for the sake of glory or possession (Mt. 5^{38f}). It is to be noted that in all these sayings there is no reference to the greater or lesser atrocities usually involved inescapably where force is exercised. The decisive contradiction of the kingdom of God against all con cealed or blatant kingdoms of force is to be seen quite simply in the fact that it invalidates the whole friend–foe relationship between man and man. Either way, force is the *ultima ratio*[EN162] in this relationship. If we love only those who love us again, the publicans and sinners can do the same. If we show humanity only to our brethren, the heathen do likewise (Mt. 5[46f.]) Of what avail is this? In spite of it, force is everywhere exercised because friend–foe relationships are not affected by it. What the disciples are enjoined is that they should love their enemies (Mt. 5[44]). This destroys the whole friend–foe relationship, for when we love our enemy he ceases to be our enemy. It thus abolishes the whole exercise of force, which presupposes this relationship, and has no meaning apart from it. This is attested by the disciple in what he does or does not do. Quite seriously and concretely he himself now drops out of the reckoning in this twofold relationship. Once again, there can be no question of a general rule, a Christian system confronting that of the world, in competition with it, and in some way to be brought into harmony with it. But again, for the one whom Jesus, in His call to discipleship, places under this particular command and prohibition, there is a concrete and incontestable direction which has to be carried out exactly as it is given. According to the sense of the New Testament we cannot be pacifists in principle, only in practice. But we have to consider very closely whether, if we are called to discipleship, we can avoid being practical pacifists, or fail to be so.

If along the third main line of the texts in question we have to do with the overcoming, proclaimed with the incursion of the kingdom of God, of the false separation between man and man revealed in the friend–foe relationship and concretely expressing itself in the exercise of force, along a fourth line we have, conversely, the dissolution of self-evident attachments between man and man. It is a matter of what in popular usage, although not in that of the Bible, is usually described as the family. The relationships between husband and wife, parents and children, brothers and sisters, etc., are not questioned as such. Man would not be man if he did not stand in these relationships. What is questioned is the impulsive intensity with which he allows himself to be enfolded by, and thinks that he himself should enfold, those who stand to him in these relationships. What is questioned is his self-sufficiency in the warmth of these relationships, the resolving of their problems and the sphere of their joys and sorrows. What is questioned is his imprisonment in them, in which he is no less a captive than in other respects he may be to possessions or fame. The message of liberation comes to him in this captivity to the clan. Thus the excuse of the invited guest: "I have married a wife, and therefore I cannot come" (Lk. 14[20]), is seen to be on exactly the same level as those of others who had bought land or oxen which claimed their prior interest. And in the same connexion Jesus gives the remarkable reply to the man who was ready to be a disciple but first wanted to bury his father: "Let the dead bury their dead: but go thou and preach the kingdom of God" (Lk. 9[59f.]). To the same series belong all the provocative sayings of Jesus about the leaving (ἀφεῖναι), dividing (διχάζειν), disuniting (διαμερίζειν) and even hating (μισεῖν) which are involved in the discipleship of Jesus—not destroying the relationships as such, but certainly dissolving the connexions which continually arise and obtain in them. According to Mk. 10[29] we have not only to leave house and lands but even brother or sister, mother or father or children (the "or" shows us that we are dealing with individual cases), for His sake and for the sake of the Gospel. Jesus also warns us against the view that He has come to bring peace on earth (Mt. 10[34f.]). He has not come to bring peace, but a sword. And if a man loves father or mother, son or daughter, more than Him, he is not worthy of Him. Or, according to the parallel passage in Lk. 12[52]: "For from henceforth there shall be five in one house divided, three against two, and two against three." The strangest possible expression is used in Lk. 14[26]: "If any man come to me, and hate not his father, and mother, and wife, and children, and brethren, and sisters, yea, and his own life also, he cannot be my

[551]

[EN162] last resort

disciple." Hate? It is not the persons that are to be hated, for why should they be excluded from the command to love our neighbours? It is the hold which these persons have and by which they themselves are also gripped. It is the concentration of neighbourly love on these persons, which really means its denial. It is the indolent peace of a clannish warmth in relation to these persons, with its necessary implication of cold war against all others. The coming of the kingdom of God means an end of the absolute of family no less than that of possession and fame. Again, there is no general rule. No new law has been set up in competition with that of the world, which points so powerfully in the opposite direction. But there is proclaimed the freedom of the disciple from the general law as it is given to him, and has to be exercised by him, in a particular situation (by the particular direction which he receives). There can be no doubt that in its fear of the bogy of monasticism Protestantism has very radically ignored this proclamation of Jesus Christ, as also that of other freedoms. To a very large extent it has acted as though Jesus had done the very opposite and proclaimed this attachment—the absolute of family. Can we really imagine a single one of the prophets or apostles in the role of the happy father, or grandfather, or even uncle, as it has found self-evident sanctification in the famous Evangelical parsonage or manse? They may well have occupied this role. But in the function in which they are seen by us they stand outside these connexions. In this respect, too, no one is asked to undertake arbitrary adventures. But again, no one who really regards himself as called by Jesus to discipleship can evade the question whether he might not be asked for inner and outer obedience along these lines. The life of the new creature is something rather different from a healthy and worthy continuation of the old. When the order is given to express this, we must not refuse it an obedience which is no less concrete than the command.

Along a fifth line, to which we can never devote too much attention, the required obedience consists finally in a penetration of the absolute *nomos*[EN163] of religion, of the world of piety. It is worth reflecting that what Jesus has in mind was not the piety of heathen religion, but that of the Israelite religion of revelation. He has not, of course, come to deny or destroy or dissolve it (Mt. 5$^{17f.}$). He Himself accepts it, and He does not require His disciples to abandon or replace it. But He does demand that they should go a new way in its exercise; that they should show a "better righteousness," i.e., not better than that of the people, the common herd, but better than that of its best and strictest and most zealous representatives, the scribes and Pharisees; better than the official form which it had assumed at the hands of its most competent human champions. This better righteousness is not more refined or profound or strict. It is simply the piety which the disciple can alone exercise in face of the imminent kingdom of God. It has nothing whatever to do with religious aristocracy. On the contrary, the kingdom knocks at the door of the sanctuary of supreme human worship. The disciple must act accordingly. According to two groups of sayings (both contained in the Sermon on the Mount) Jesus summoned to this advance on two different fronts. It is a matter of morality on the one side and religion on the other. Morality is dealt with in Mt. 5$^{21-48}$. The commandment: "Thou shalt not kill," is universally accepted. But what does it mean? There is something worse than killing because it is the meaning and purpose in all killing. This is anger against one's brother; a state of contentiousness and strife. And it is here that the obedience of the disciple must begin. Again, what is meant by adultery? The real evil, from which the disciple refrains, is to be found much further back than the actual deed. It consists in the evil desire which is present prior to the act. And it is at the point of desire that we either refrain or do not refrain. Again, what is false swearing? It is all swearing because this as such is an illegitimate questioning of God. The disciple renounces this

---

EN163 law

[552] because it is enough for him if according to the best of his knowledge and with a good conscience he says either Yes or No, and not secretly both at once. What is meant by just retribution? The disciple does not exercise it in any form. What is neighbourly love? There is enjoined upon the disciple a love which includes the enemy. But, of course, when we talk like this, what becomes of the whole structure of practicable morality? And how will its representatives and adherents react to this interpretation? Religion is dealt with in the sayings concerning almsgiving, prayer and fasting (Mt. 6$^{1-18}$), and the main drift in all of them is that these things are not to be done publicly but secretly. Where, then, is the witness?—we might ask. The answer is that the witness of the disciple consists in the fact that he refrains from attesting his piety as such. If he is to display the kingdom of God, and proclaim it from the housetops (Mt. 10^{27}), he will not make a show of his own devoutness but keep it to himself, allowing God alone to be the One who judges and rewards him. This restraint will be a witness to the pious world with its continual need to publicise itself, and perhaps even to the secular world. It will speak for itself—or rather, it will speak for that which does seriously and truly cry out for publicity. No official religiosity will readily acquiesce in the silent witness of this restraint. But here too, of course, it is not a matter of formulating and practising principles. Nor does this twofold invasion of the sphere of common sanctity mean that a clear line of demarcation is drawn. How can we fail to see that here, too, His command refers to particular men in particular situations, demanding from them a no less particular obedience, the obedience of discipleship.

(There is another equally prominent line of concrete direction which we have not yet touched upon, and shall not do so in this context. In many of the New Testament records the call to discipleship closes with the demand that the disciple should take up his cross. This final order crowns, as it were, the whole call, just as the cross of Jesus crowns the life of the Son of Man. In view of its outstanding significance we shall reserve this aspect for independent treatment in the final sub-section.)

Looking back at what we have said about the concrete forms of discipleship, we may make the further general observation that the general lines of the call with which Jesus made men His disciples in the Gospels enable us in some sense to envisage the situations in which these men were reached by His call and how they had to obey it concretely. Indeed, the New Testament *kerygma* not only permits but commands us to do this. The picture of these men and the way in which they were concretely ordered and concretely obeyed is one which ought to impress itself upon us. In this respect it forms, with the call issued by Jesus, the content of the New Testament *kerygma*. The reason why we have to bring out these main lines along which it takes concrete shape is that the call to discipleship as it comes to us will always be shaped also by this correlated picture. Yet as it was for them, it will be a call which here to-day is addressed directly and particularly to each one of us, so that its specific content is not fixed by the specific content of His call there and then as we have learned it from the Gospels. To be sure, the call of Jesus will be along the lines of the encounter between the kingdom of God and the kingdoms of the world. And it will have to be accepted in this form. But this does not mean that the living Son of Man is confined as it were to the sequence of His previous encounters, or that His commanding moves only in the circle of His previous commanding and the obedience which it received. It is not for us simply to reproduce those pictures. That is to say, it is not for us to identify ourselves directly with those who were called then, and therefore to learn directly from what they were commanded what we are necessarily commanded, or from their obedience what our own obedience must be. We will always know that it is His voice which calls us from the fact that in what is demanded of us we shall always have to do with a break with the great self-evident factors of our environment, and

[553] therefore of the world as a whole. which will have to be made in fact, both outwardly and inwardly, along the lines indicated in the New Testament, corresponding to, and attesting,

the irruption of the kingdom of God. In other words, we shall always have to do with a form of the free activity which Paul described in the imperative of Rom. 12²: μὴ συσχηματίζεσθε τῷ αἰῶνι τούτῳ EN164. But from what the New Testament tells us of His commanding, and of the obedience demanded from these particular men and rendered by them, we have to hear His voice as He speaks to *us*, calling us in the particular situation of obedience determined by His Word. It is not enough, then, merely to copy in our activity the outlines of that in which these men had to obey His demands. This of itself is not an entry into discipleship. As we have to remember in relation to every "rule," we might try to copy everything that Jesus demanded and that these men did, and yet completely fail to be disciples, because we do not do it, as they did, at His particular call and command to us. There is, of course, no reason why He should not ask exactly the same of us as He did of them. But again—along the same lines—He may just as well command something different, possibly much more, or the same thing in a very different application and concretion. In these circumstances it might well be disobedience to be content to imitate them, for if we are to render simple obedience it must be to the One who, as He called them then, calls us to-day. It is now our affair to render obedience without discussion or reserve, quite literally, in the same unity of the inward and the outward, and in exact correspondence to the New Testament witness to His encounter with them. There can certainly be no question of a deviation from these main lines. What we find along these lines can never be a mere *consilium evangelicum* EN165. It is always a binding *mandatum evangelicum* EN166 which demands the response of a corresponding decision and action. And there will always be reason for distrust against ourselves if we think that what may be required of us along these lines will be something less, or easier, or more comfortable than what was required of them. Grace—and we again recall that in the call to discipleship it is a matter of grace, of the salvation of the world, and therefore of our own salvation— cannot have become more cheap to-day (to use another expression of Bonhoeffer's). It may well have become even more costly. Or, to put it another way, it may well be that the freedom given in and with obedience to the call to discipleship has not become less but greater. But however that may be, the freedom given in this way was then, and still is, our sanctification.

4. THE AWAKENING TO CONVERSION

Our starting-point is again the conclusion of our second sub-section—that the sanctification of man consists in fellowship with Jesus the Son of Man, in the power of His call, and in the freedom which we are given in the strength of His Holy Spirit to look to Him and thus to lift up ourselves in spite of the downward drag of our slothful nature. We are now dealing with this lifting up of ourselves in and for itself—or, let us say quite plainly from the very outset, with the divine mystery and miracle of this lifting up of ourselves. It characterises sanctification as a real happening which takes place to men here and now in time and on earth. It is real, of course, not because it takes place as human and earthly history, but because it takes place in fellowship with the life of the

---

EN164 do not be conformed to this age
EN165 evangelical advice
EN166 evangelical command

§ 66. *The Sanctification of Man*

holy Son of Man. For all that it is so provisional and limited, the sanctification
[554] of man as his lifting up of himself is a work which is eternally resolved and
seriously willed and effectively executed by God. In this divine reality, however,
it takes place in time and on earth. It consists in the fact that as men may lift up
themselves they acquire and have here and now, in all their lack of freedom, a
freedom to do this of which they avail themselves. We must now turn our attention to this happening as such. How does it come about that men become
Christians in fulfilment of this divinely real work.

The theme of our third sub-section was itself, of course, an answer to this question. It
comes about as Jesus calls them to discipleship. We can never go beyond this answer. But we
can and must put the counter-question: How does it come about that they are actually
reached by this call in such a way that they render obedience, becoming the disciples of Jesus
and doing what they are ordered to do as such? We shall see at once—as already in our
opening sentence we have taken up again and repeated from our earlier discussions—that it
is a matter of the freedom which they are given by the One who calls them, by Jesus. How can
it really take place except in freedom? But we must now see how it takes place in the freedom
which is given by Jesus to these particular men. Our present questions concerns the inward
movement in which they are the men to whom this freedom is given and who may and must
at once exercise it in the obedience of discipleship as we have described it. To put it meta-
phorically, we are investigating the source from which this living water has its direct and
unimpeded flow.

The first thing that we have to say is that Christians (and therefore those
who are sanctified by *the* Holy One) are those who waken up. This, too, is a
picture. But it is a biblical one, and it tells us more clearly than any abstract
term that we might substitute what is really at issue. As they awake they look up,
and rise, thus making the counter-movement to the downward drag of their
sinfully slothful being. They are those who waken up, however, because they
are awakened. They do not waken of themselves and get up. They are roused,
and are thus caused to get up and set in this counter-movement. Thus strictly
and finally this awakening as such is in every sense the source in whose irresistible flow they are set in the obedience of discipleship. But we will leave this
point for the moment.

Where someone is awakened and therefore wakes and rises, he has previously been asleep, and has been lying asleep. Christians have indeed been
lying asleep like others. What distinguishes them from others is that this is now
past; that they have been awakened and are awake. Or is it not the case that
they are still asleep, or fall asleep again? Is there not still a Christianity which
sleeps with the world and like it?

"Therefore let us not sleep, as do others; but let us watch and be sober" (1 Thess. 5⁶).
"Now it is high time to awake out of sleep" (Rom. 13¹¹). "Awake thou that sleepest, and arise
from the dead, and Christ shall give thee light" (Eph. 5¹⁴). This is not missionary preaching—or it is so only in the sense that the call is also and primarily to the Christian community. How the eyes of the disciples were overcome by sleep in Gethsemane (Mk. 14⁴⁰)! And did
[555] not all the virgins become sleepy and sleep—the wise as well as the foolish—according to Mt.
25⁵? "Blessed are those servants, whom the lord when he cometh shall find watching" (Lk.

174

12^{37}). But is not this the highly exceptional case? Do we not all need continually to be reawakened?

We cannot, therefore, define Christians simply as those who are awake while the rest sleep, but more cautiously as those who waken up in the sense that they are awakened a first time and then again to their shame and good fortune. They are, in fact, those who constantly stand in need of reawakening and who depend upon the fact that they are continually reawakened. They are thus those who, it is to be hoped, continually waken up.

The sleep from which they awaken is the relentless downward movement consequent upon their sloth. Like all others, they participate in this movement, dreaming many beautiful or bad dreams but not really knowing what is happening to them. When they waken, or are wakened, they experience a jolt which both arrests them in this movement and sets them in the counter-movement. They realise where their way was leading, that they must not tread it any further, and that they now can and must take the opposite direction. In this event and realisation—which are both included in the shock that they receive—they wake up for the first time—which will certainly not be the last. In this awakening they become Christians—men who are now free, and who make use of their freedom, to look up and raise themselves. The verse 2 Cor. 5^{17} is true of them as this happens: "Old things are passed away; behold, all things are become new." For in this awakening they are "in Christ" in the narrower sense of the term as it applies only to them.

But this awakening is also—and here the metaphor breaks down—an awakening and therefore a rising from the sleep of death; the sleep from which there can be no awakening except in the power of the mystery and miracle of God. This is the real truth about the descent, the downward plunge, of sinful and slothful man, and the unawareness with which he makes and suffers it. We can waken ourselves from the sleep of all kinds of errors and phantasies and falsehoods. The very violence of the dream in which we surrender to them may rouse us. Or we may be wakened from these states of slumber or drowsiness by an accident, an external event or fate, or the intentional or unintentional intrusion of others. But from the sleep of covenant-breaking humanity, of the world in conflict with God, there can be no awakening, not even by the greatest catastrophes, by the crashing in ruins of whole cities, by the imminent threat of the worst personal evils, by the thunderous voices of the very greatest prophets. Certainly none of us can of himself supply the jolt which will awaken from this sleep. No salvation or perdition affecting man from without can reach him in this sleep, and startle and illuminate him, and fetch him to his feet. Nor are there any impulses, or emotional movements, or [556] deep-burrowing reflections, in which he can reach and awaken himself in this sleep. The sleep which he sleeps is the sleep of death, and what is needed is that he should be wakened and waken from death. There is thus required a

175

new and direct act of God Himself if there is to be the awakening in which a man becomes a disciple, a Christian.

At this point we may recall the saying at the conclusion of the story of the rich young ruler (Mk. 10²³ᶠ·), which is the same in all the parallel accounts. It tells us how hard it is—harder than for a camel to go through the eye of a needle—for a rich man to enter into the kingdom of God. And it causes the disciples the greatest astonishment (περισσῶς ἐξεπλήσσοντο ᴱᴺ¹⁶⁷), for they rightly perceive that it is not just a matter of the rich but of all men and even of themselves, the rich young ruler being the general rule rather than an unfortunate exception. "Who then (in these circumstances) can be saved (at all)?" they say one to another. "And Jesus looking upon them saith, With men it is impossible, but not with God: for with God all things are possible." That a man should follow Jesus, and therefore enter into the kingdom and become a fellow and witness of the kingdom is quite possible with God, but only with Him. Hence the saying at the end of the story of the Prodigal Son: "This thy brother was dead, and is alive again; and was lost, and is found" (Lk. 15³²). Hence the call of Eph. 5¹⁴: "Arise from the dead." Hence the statement in Eph. 2¹ᶠ·: "And you hath he quickened, who were dead in trespasses and sins; wherein in time past ye walked according to the course of this world, according to the prince of the power of the air, the spirit that now worketh in the children of disobedience …. But God, who is rich in mercy, for his great love wherewith he loved us, even when we were dead in sins, hath quickened us together with Christ (by grace are ye saved;) … and that not of yourselves: it is the gift of God: not of works, lest any man should boast." We have really passed (μεταβέβηκεν ᴱᴺ¹⁶⁸) from death to life if we hear the Word of Jesus, and believe in Him that sent Him, and love the brethren (Jn. 5²⁴; 1 Jn. 3¹⁴). Nothing less than this transition, which cannot be initiated by ourselves or any experience of our own but has its analogy only in the resurrection of Jesus Christ from the dead, can even be considered when it is a matter of the awakening and rising up to the obedience of discipleship.

The awakening to which we refer belongs to the order and takes place according to the law of divine action. This does not exclude, but includes, the fact that it takes place in the context and under the conditions of human action. How could it be the real sanctification of real man if man himself were not present in his inner and outer activity, if it took place at some supernatural height or depth without him? It certainly does not take place without him. It takes place to and in him. It involves the total and most intensive conscription and co-operation of all his inner and outer forces, of his whole heart and soul and mind, which in the biblical sense in which these terms are used includes his whole physical being. Otherwise it would not be his awakening. And his fellow-man, who is also indispensable if he is to be a man, is certainly not absent, or present only as a passive spectator, but also takes part in his awakening, perhaps as one who is himself waking, perhaps in some other way. As we have stated already, his awakening is an event on earth and in time. It has, therefore, a historical dimension. The narrower and wider social circles in [557] which he lives are deeply implicated in it. It does not in any sense lack creaturely factors of every kind. Taking place wholly and utterly on the earthly and

---

ᴱᴺ¹⁶⁷ they were utterly amazed
ᴱᴺ¹⁶⁸ he has gone over

creaturely level, it does not merely have an aspect which is wholly and utterly creaturely, but it is itself wholly and utterly creaturely by nature. But, while all this is true, it has its origin and goal in God. It belongs to the order of that action which is specifically divine. It is a subordinate moment in the act of majesty in which the Word became flesh and Jesus Christ rose again from the dead. On this aspect—its true and proper aspect—it is a mystery and a miracle. That is to say, the jolt by which man is wakened and at which he wakens, his awakening itself as the act in which this takes place and he rises, is not the work of one of the creaturely factors, co-efficients and agencies which are there at work and can be seen, but of the will and act of God who uses these factors and Himself makes them co-efficients and agencies for this purpose, setting them in motion as such in the meaning and direction which He has appointed. We are thus forced to say that this awakening is both wholly creaturely and wholly divine. Yet the initial shock comes from God. Thus there can be no question of co-ordination between two comparable elements, but only of the absolute primacy of the divine over the creaturely. The creaturely is made serviceable to the divine and does actually serve it. It is used by God as His organ or instrument. Its creatureliness is not impaired, but it is given by God a special function or character. Being qualified and claimed by God for co-operation, it co-operates in such a way that the whole is still an action which is specifically divine.

For the moment we will postpone our investigation of the jolt or shock which initiates it, thus making it in its totality a divine action which seizes and dominates, while it does not exclude, all creaturely factors and their motions. Our first question must be simply concerning the awakening as such, and the meaning and content of this event. No matter what may be its origin and goal, which factor may be first and which second, or where the preponderance may lie, it does at any rate take place. And it takes place all at once. It does not take place in stages. It does not take place in such a way that first one thing happens with its own particular meaning and content, and then another with a different meaning and content; the divine on the one side and the human on the other. Nor does it take place on two different levels, so that we are forced to look first at what happens on the top deck as it were, and then at what happens on the lower; the gift and work of God in the one case, and the task and action and abstention of man in the other. This awakening and waking of man is one event with one meaning and content. In the first instance, therefore, it must concern us in its unity as such. We call it the awakening of man to conversion.

The Christian Church counts on the fact that there is such a thing as the [558] awakening of man to conversion. If it did not do so, it would not believe in God the Father; in the Son of God who became flesh and who in the flesh was the holy Son of Man, the royal man; or in the Holy Spirit. In its supposed confession of God it would be thinking of a mere idea and staring at a dead idol. If we believe in God in the sense of the Church we believe in an awakening of man to conversion. We count on the fact that there is such a thing. No, we count on the fact that God Himself gives and creates and actualises it. We do not, therefore, count only on the chance or possibility of it. We do not count merely on the fact that there may be such a thing. To do this is itself quite impossible without faith in God. For we have to do here with the awakening which has the character of an awakening from the dead, with the conversion to which a man is awakened in this way, with his wakening and rising from the dead. How can we count on this apart from faith? But in faith in God we do not count only on the fact that it may be so, or that God may give it. We count on the fact that God does actually give it. We count on the awakening of man to conversion as an actuality. As truly as God lives and is God, so truly this awakening takes place. To say God the Father, Son and Holy Ghost is to say also the awakening of man to conversion. This is the first nail that we have to drive in securely. The reality of this event depends wholly on the reality of God. And it depends on it so seriously and unconditionally and indissolubly that we can also say that the reality of God stands or falls with the reality of this event. Only for us? It is perhaps better *not* to make this restriction. God would not be God if this awakening did not take place. For He would not be the God of the covenant; of His free grace. He would not be the God who is true to this covenant as the Reconciler of the world which has fallen from Him, and therefore as the One who awakens man from the sleep of death and calls him to Himself. He would not, then, be God at all. As truly as He is God, so truly He does this. The basis of Christian existence lies as deep as this. It is not the Christian who guarantees it. It is God Himself. God Himself takes responsibility for its reality. We are thus given a simple test. Do we believe in God? We do so only if we believe in the awakening of man to conversion. Conversely, do we believe in the awakening of man to conversion? We do so only if we believe in God.

The Christian Church also counts on the awakening of man to conversion because it cannot conceal the fact that the Scriptures of the Old and New Testament count on it and call on the Church to do so. It is true that the Bible is one long account of the great acts of God which have their centre in Jesus Christ and which still have their hidden goal of which they are themselves the hidden beginning. But these acts of God take place, and the One in whom they have their centre and goal and beginning exists, among and in relation to [559] many men. They are God's dealings with these men. They are God's revelation in the power of which these men become its witnesses. As we have already established incidentally at an earlier point, they also have their place in the biblical account to the extent that the divine speech and action has reference to them and constitute them its witnesses. As witnesses to it they form an integral part of the biblical witness to God's work and revelation. The totality of the biblical account thus includes the fact that, grounded in the acting and self-revealing God, in the promised and incarnate and expected Jesus Christ, the awakening to conversion is a reality among these men. It is just as real as God, or Jesus Christ, is real. For our present purpose it makes no odds with what degree of clarity or confusion, of perfection or imperfection, it impresses itself upon these men and finds expression in them. Either way, it is a reality. In and with the history of God and Jesus Christ there also takes place the history whose meaning and content is the awakening of men to conversion. There are men whose existence is positively or negatively or critically determined by this reality. It is determined by it because it is determined by the judicial and gracious speech and action of God, which is judicial as and because it is gracious. It is determined by it because it is determined by the existence of Jesus Christ. The whole weight of the witness about God and His Holy One carries in and with it, for those who let Scripture speak for itself, the witness which is less perhaps, but inseparably connected with the greater: the witness not only of the Holy One but also of the saints; the witness concerning Abraham and Moses and David and the people Israel and its major and minor prophets and the community and the apostles as they are determined by the One to whom they themselves bear witness. In all its distinctness and indistinctness, *hominum confusione et Dei providentia*[EN169], this is the witness concerning this reality. When the Church allows Scripture to speak to it, even if it wished, it could not help counting on the reality of the awakening to conversion in view of these men. It could not prevent this reality from impinging upon it as a problem posed for itself—not merely the reality that there is such a thing, but that it is God who gives and creates and effects it. The witness of Holy Scripture is that God does this. We should have to reject its witness altogether if we were to deny that it is also the witness to this reality. What the Church makes of it is another question. It has made of it many things—some good and some bad. It has often seemed not to know how to make anything of it at all. But it can never, or never altogether, set it aside or ignore or forget it. The Church? We are the Church. It is thus our turn to tackle it as we try to understand and explain the sanctification of man, and especially the way in which the men who lie asleep as slothful sinners look up and lift up themselves and become obedient instead of disobedient.

Let us go right to the heart of the matter at once and say that this rising up of man takes place in his conversion. The sleep from which man is awakened according to Scripture consists in treading a wrong path on which he is himself perverted, and can never be anything else. Thus awakening from this sleep, and the rising which follows, is far more than a vertical standing up. It makes no odds whether we go this false path erect or stooping. As Scripture sees it, waking and rising from sleep is turning round and going in the opposite direction. That God awakens us to this is the problem set for the Church, and therefore for us, by Holy Scripture. It cannot be exchanged for the (in themselves) very interesting problems of improvement or reformation or more noble effort in our further progress along the same path. It is not a question of improvement but alteration. It is not a question of a reformed or ennobled

[560]

[EN169] by the confusion of men and by the providence of God life, but a new one. And the alteration and renewal mean conversion—a term which we cannot avoid for all its doubtful associations. As it emerges in Holy Scripture, the human reality which is inseparably connected with, and determined by, the reality of God and Jesus Christ is the awakening of man to convert. The movement which we see made by the men of the Bible, or which is always aimed at, is *this* movement. We cannot say—for it simply would not be true—that we see in the Bible converted men. What we can and must say is that we see men caught up in the movement of conversion. If conversion is not behind them, it is also not in the mists before them. They are at the very heart of the movement. They had moved away from God. And it is saying too much to claim that they have moved right back to God. But what we must say is that they can no longer proceed without God. On the contrary, they are compelled to rise up and come to Him, and are now in the process of doing so. This is the movement of conversion. And the awakening to this movement which in some way comes to these men and characterises them is the reality which impinges upon us, and becomes our own problem, in and with the reality of God and of Jesus Christ.

Conversion, and therefore life in this movement, means renewal. In relation to a life which is not engaged in this movement, it is the new life of a new man. Conversion means the turning on an axis. The life of the old man, which is not engaged in this conversion, also involves movement. But it has no axis—and that is why it is not engaged in conversion. It moves straight ahead, and this means straight ahead to the descent—the plunge—to death. It is a life which is encircled by death. The difference between the life of the one who is engaged in conversion and that of others is not that the former moves itself, but that it has an axis on which to turn. It is properly this axis which makes this man a new man, giving him a part in its own movement. But the axis which makes his life a movement in conversion is the reality which is not concealed from him, but revealed as the truth, that God is for him and therefore that he is for God. God is for him as a proprietor is for his possessions, protecting and guarding and cherishing them but also controlling them, answering for them but also disposing them according to his own purposes. And he himself is for God as possessions stand under the protection and control, the responsibility and disposition, of their owner. This is the axis which, when it is established in his life, makes it a life in conversion. For with this twofold "for"—the second grounded in the first—he is told both to halt and to proceed. His former movement is halted; and he is told to proceed in the opposite direction. And the two moments, which belong together in an indissoluble unity, constitute his conversion. Revealed to him as truth, the reality that God is for him and he for God sets him in this movement, in the *conversio*[EN170] which is as such his *renovatio*[EN171]. In the dynamic of this twofold principle—because God is for

[561]

[EN170] conversion
[EN171] renewal

him and he for God—he can and may cease to proceed in the old direction and turn round and begin to move the other way.

Calvin summed up this principle of conversion and renewal with masterly brevity and comprehensiveness in the short statement: *Nostri non sumus, sed Domini*[EN172] (*Instit.* III, 7, 1). In this way God's Yes to man and man's Yes to God, and the consequent turning from and to, are brought together in a single formula. We do not belong to ourselves. When we did belong to ourselves, when we knew only that we belonged to ourselves, we were old men involved in that descent and headlong plunge on the old way. But we now belong to God as our Lord. As we belong to Him we are free, and it is for us only to cease proceeding on the old way and to enter on the way appropriate to where we now belong. *Nostri non sumus, sed Domini*[EN173]. As we follow the movement of this axis, we become new men.

The establishment of this axis in human life—or better, the establishment of human life on this axis—and the change of direction in human life which this inaugurates, is obviously the theme of the petition in Ps. 51[10f.]: "Create in me a clean heart, O God; and renew a right spirit within me. Cast me not away from thy presence; and take not thy holy spirit from me." The same principle of conversion and renewal is also the subject of Jer. 31[33] with its promise of the new covenant: "I will put my law in their inward parts, and write it in their hearts; and will be their God, and they shall be my people." It is also at issue in Jer. 32[39]: "And I will give them one heart, and one way, that they may fear me for ever, for the good of them, and of their children after them"; and of the parallel in Ezek. 36[26f.] (cf. 11[19f.]): "A new heart also will I give you, and a new spirit will I put within you: and I will take away the stony heart out of your flesh, and I will give you an heart of flesh. And I will put my spirit within you, and cause you to walk in my statutes, and ye shall keep my judgments, and do them." These are the passages to which Paul referred in the much misunderstood words of Rom. 2[14f.] (cf. Felix Flückiger, *Die Werke des Gesetzes bei den Heiden nach* Röm. 2[14ff.], Th. at Basel, 1952, 17 f.), when he contrasted the disobedience of the Jews with those Gentiles—the Gentiles who are called to the God of Israel by the Gospel—who do not have the Law but who φύσει[EN174], of themselves, do what the Law demands and are thus a law to themselves, showing that "the work of the law is written in their hearts, their conscience also bearing witness, and their thoughts the meanwhile accusing or else excusing one another."

We can see what is meant by the passages in Jeremiah and Ezekiel if we note that they are developments of the promise and summons which we find so often and so urgently in the prophets Amos, Hosea, Isaiah and Jeremiah himself that Israel should and must return to *Yahweh*, i.e., to an unconditional and obedient trust in Him in contrast to any trust in man or in strange gods, and therefore to a no less unconditional renunciation of everything that is evil, i.e., that opposes the lordship of *Yahweh*. It is on the basis of the reality of the covenant, which includes the "I will be your God" as well as the "Ye shall be my people," that the imperative call is sounded to seek *Yahweh* and live (Am. 5[4]), to return to *Yahweh* instead of fleeing from Him (Jer. 4[1]), to break up the fallow ground instead of sowing thorns, and to circumcise to the Lord, taking away the foreskin of the heart (Jer. 4[3f.]). But who does this? In all the ancient prophecies the actual or even possible fulfilment of this demand is never really envisaged. They do not know of any people which actually converts to *Yahweh*. Even in the passionate Hosea we find the pointed saying (5[4]): "They will not frame their doings to turn unto their God: for the spirit of whoredoms is in the midst of them, and they have not known the Lord." And in Isaiah (1[3f.]): "The ox knoweth his owner, and the ass his master's

[562]

[EN172] we are not our own, but the Lord's
[EN173] we are not our own, but the Lord's
[EN174] by nature

crib: but Israel doth not know, my people doth not consider. Ah sinful nation, a people laden with iniquity, a seed of evildoers, children that are corrupters: they have forsaken the Lord, they have provoked the Holy One of Israel to anger, they are gone away backward. Why should ye be stricken any more? ye will revolt more and more: the whole head is sick, and the heart faint. From the sole of the foot even unto the head there is no soundness in it." And again in Isaiah ($30^{15f.}$): "For thus saith the Lord God, the Holy One of Israel; In returning and rest shall ye be saved; in quietness and in confidence shall be your strength. But ye said, No; for we will flee upon horses ... we will ride upon the swift." And again in Jeremiah (13^{23}): "Can the Ethiopian change his skin, or the leopard his spots? then may ye also do good, that are accustomed to do evil." That a remnant will return in a not very closely delineated future (Is. 10^{21}) is significantly emphasised by the name *sh'ar Yashub*[EN175] which the prophet gave to his son (7^3), but this is the most that can be said in this direction. For when we read in Is. $30^{20f.}$ about the teacher of Israel who will no longer be concealed, "but thine eyes shall see thy teacher, and thine ears shall hear a word behind thee, saying, This is the way, walk ye in it, when ye turn to the right hand, and when ye turn to the left," it may be suspected that what we have here is a voice from the later prophecy which dared to speak of the new spirit and heart and conversation given to Israel, and therefore of a fulfilment of the unfulfilled and unfulfillable demand of earlier prophecy which was not achieved by Israel itself but achieved on it, i.e., the actuality of the covenant as the truth revealed to man and forcefully changing his life; the dynamic principle: *Nostri non sumus, sed Domini*[EN176].

We have to remember the dark folly attested in the older prophecy if we are to appreciate what is really meant by coming to conversion and renewal in the sense of the Old and New Testaments; by the establishing of the life of man on that axis so that it is set in that movement. The order in which this takes place is defined once and for all in Is. $48^{6f.}$: "I have shewed thee new things from this time, even hidden things, and thou didst not know them. They are created now, and not from the beginning; and previously thou heardest them not; lest thou shouldest say, Behold, I knew them. Yea, thou heardest not; yea, thou knewest not; yea, thine ear was not previously opened." It is a matter of seeing the kingdom of God (Jn. 3^3), of entering into it (Jn. 3^5). But this is possible only for the man who is newly conceived and born of God (Jn. 1^{13}; 1 Jn. 3^9). It is "a new creation" (2 Cor. 5^{17}), and "the wind bloweth where it listeth, and thou hearest the sound thereof, but canst not tell whence it cometh, and whither it goeth: so is every one that is born of the spirit." The question of Nicodemus is not really so stupid as it may sound: "How can a man be born, when he is old? can he enter the second time into his mother's womb, and be born?" (Jn. 3^4). We may well ask: "How can [563] these things be?" (Jn. 3^9). There can be no question of any $\delta\dot{\nu}\nu\alpha\sigma\theta\alpha\iota$[EN177], of any general possibility, of this $\gamma\epsilon\nu\dot{\epsilon}\sigma\theta\alpha\iota$[EN178]. The fact is that the reality of this twofold "for" is revealed as the truth; that it takes place in its own possibility, as a "birth from above" (Jn. 3^3). Thus, in relation to everything that man previously was or otherwise is, it is a beginning newly posited by God. The walking $\dot{\epsilon}\nu\,\kappa\alpha\iota\nu\dot{o}\tau\eta\tau\iota\,\zeta\omega\hat{\eta}s$[EN179] (Rom. 6^4) which corresponds to the resurrection of Jesus Christ is a transformation ("metamorphosis," Rom. 12) which comes over man in the form of a $\dot{\alpha}\nu\alpha\kappa\alpha\dot{\iota}\nu\omega\sigma\iota s\,\tau o\hat{\upsilon}\,\nu o\acute{o}s$[EN180]. In Tit. 3^5 it is described by the very word ($\pi\alpha\lambda\iota\gamma\gamma\epsilon\nu\epsilon\sigma\dot{\iota}\alpha$[EN181]) which in Mt. 19^{28} is used to describe the Messianic renewal of the cosmos which concludes the last age. We have to think in this order if we are to realise what is

---

[EN175] a remnant will return
[EN176] we are not our own, but the Lord's
[EN177] 'can'
[EN178] being
[EN179] in newness of life
[EN180] renewing of the mind
[EN181] regeneration

involved in man's conversion. *Conversio*[EN182] and *renovatio*[EN183], applied to the actual sancti-fication of man, are nothing less than *regeneratio*[EN184]. New birth! The man involved in the act of conversion is no longer the old man. He is not even a corrected and revised edition of this man. He is a new man.

We continue at once that in conversion we have to do with a movement of the whole man. There are in his being no neutral zones which are unaffected by it and in which he can be another than the new man involved in this pro-cess. By the establishment of his life on this axis everything that he is and has is brought under its influence. If anything is not brought under its influence, and thus remains in the continuity of his previous being as the old man, he can be and have and do it only *per nefas*[EN185]. This is the case because in the prin-ciple of his conversion and renewal, at the centre where his life is bound to this axis, we have to do with God. That God is for him, and he for God, is a total reality which asserts itself in his life in the power of total truth, setting him wholly and not merely partially in this movement, placing him wholly under the call to halt and proceed. We will try to see what is meant by the totality of this movement in some of its most important dimensions.

1. We cannot interpret the conversion and renewal of man merely in terms of a relationship between him and God, to the exclusion of any relationship with his brother. To be sure, we are dealing with the fact that God is for him, and he for God; with this reality as a revealed truth which forcefully sets him in motion. But he is not a man without his fellow-men. How can this truth set him in motion if, as he makes this movement, it does not encroach at once upon his relationship with his fellows, necessarily involving the perishing of the old and the emergence of a new thing in this relationship? It would not be the conversion of the whole man if it did not commence and work itself out at once in this relationship.

Calvin was on good biblical ground—that of the Old Testament prophets from Amos onwards—when in his detailed explanation of the main proposition, under the title *De abnegatione nostri*, he did not keep to the sphere of *Deus et anima* preferred by Augustine, but followed up his general development of the theme of self-denial, and his (rather cold) eluci-dation of the terms *sobrietas, iustitia*[EN186] and *pietas*[EN187] (which he took from Tit. 2[11f.]), by showing (*Instit.* III, 7, 4–7) how *abnegatio nostri*[EN188] expresses itself in the community and society generally as humility, gentleness, a readiness to serve, responsibility, and loyalty; how this cannot be refused to any man, however mean his estate may be, however little he may [564] mean to us, and however unworthy he may be of it; and how finally and supremely it consists in the acts of an affectionate love which does not humiliate or bind others but exalts and liberates them—and all this just because it is a matter of the *gloria Dei*[EN189] in the life of the

---

[EN182] conversion
[EN183] renewal
[EN184] regeneration
[EN185] wrongly
[EN186] sobriety, righteousness
[EN187] piety
[EN188] denial of ourselves
[EN189] glory of God

new man, *ut sibi in tota vita negotium cum Deo esse reputet*[EN190] (7, 2). It was in exactly the same way, and just because they understood it in the strictest sense, not merely in terms of ethics or reformation but as a return of Israel to its God, that at once and most emphatically the prophets interpreted it as a conversion and renewal in the practical, cultic, economic and political conduct of Israel, as a radical alteration of the ruling social relationships, so that Israel's great unwillingness for conversion was seen by them above all in its obstinacy in respect of human relationships.

2. Again, we cannot try to see and realise the conversion of man in a new movement and activity (whether purely inward or purely outward). Because God is for him, and he for God, it is a matter of his heart, his thinking, his will, his disposition and also of his consequent action and abstention on the same ultimate basis. It is a matter of his disposition and action together; of the two as a totality. Conversion in a separate inner or religious sphere, or conversion in a purely cultic or moral, political or ecclesiastical sphere, is not the conversion of man as it is set in motion by God. The conversion in which he returns to this peace embraces in this sense too the whole man.

In explanation of the term μετάνοια [EN191] we may take as our starting-point the fact that literally it speaks first of a change of mind, of a shift of judgment, of a new disposition and standpoint. But we must be careful not to leave it at that. For this would be to reduce the term from its biblical meaning to that of a mere change of mind, possibly linked with repentance, which it bore in the Greek world. As against this, the ἀνακαίνωσις τοῦ νοός [EN192] of Rom. 12² takes place within the comprehensive movement which is described in Rom. 12¹ as a παραστῆσαι τὰ σώματα ὑμῶν θυσίαν ζῶσαν ἁγίαν τῷ θεῷ εὐάρεστον. τὰ σώματα ὑμῶν [EN193] means your bodies, i.e., your whole persons. Even the μετανοεῖν [EN194] proclaimed by John the Baptist is a tree which at once brings forth fruits (Lk. 3⁸). It extends (Lk. 3¹⁰ᶠ·) to the performance of very concrete acts in practical alteration of a prior human attitude. But again, it cannot exhaust itself merely in the performance of these or any other acts. It is here that the criticism of the prophets was brought to bear against an ostensible conversion supported by all kinds of practice. We have only to think of the well-known prophetic criticism of sacrifice, noting the context in which it appears, e.g., in Hos. 6¹ᶠ. In this passage there is first quoted a pilgrim song of exemplary beauty, inviting to a penitential service: "Come, and let us return unto the Lord: for he hath torn, and he will heal us; he hath smitten, and he will bind us up. After two days will he revive us: in the third day he will raise us up, and we shall live in his sight. Let us seek earnestly to know the Lord. As soon as we seek him, we shall find him; and he shall come unto us as the rain, as the latter and former rain which refresheth the earth." How often this passage has served as a text even for Christian ministers on days of fasting and penitence! The only thing is that we often overlook the continuation, the answer given by the prophet, which is as follows: "O Ephraim, what shall I do unto thee? O Judah, what shall I do unto thee? For your love is as a morning cloud, and as the dew it goeth away. Therefore have I hewed them by the prophets; I have slain them by the words of my mouth; and thy judgments are as the light that goeth forth. For I desired love, and not sacrifice; and the knowledge of God more than burnt-offerings." What is lacking?—we might ask. There is

---

[EN190] so that he might consider that his duty is with God his whole life
[EN191] repentance
[EN192] renewal of the mind
[EN193] presenting your bodies as a living sacrifice, holy and pleasing to God. Your bodies
[EN194] repentance

obviously no lack of deeds, nor of willingness, nor religious zeal, in the performance of them. But there is lacking in this case, not the outward but the inward thing which makes the [565] movement in which they are engaged conversion—the true and radical and persistent love in which this willingness and its achievements must have their basis if they are to have any meaning. For a more radical and extended version of this passage we might well think of 1 Cor. 13³: " And though I bestow all my goods to feed the poor, and though I give my body to be burned, and have not love, it profiteth me nothing"—it has nothing to do with conversion.

3. We cannot make the conversion of man into a purely private matter, as though it were only a concern of the individual, the ordering of his own relationship to God and his neighbour, of his inward and outward life, of his own achievement of pure and essential being. It is right to emphasise its personal character, its singularity, and the isolation in which this individual must perish as the man he was, and can and may become new. But we must remember at this point the basis on which alone, if it takes place, it is an affair of the individual. The biblical individual is not selfishly wrapped up in his own concerns. It is a matter of God—that God is for him and he for God. But to say God is to make mention of the name of God which is to be hallowed, the kingdom of God which is to come, the will of God which is to be done on earth as it is done in heaven. That God, the Subject of this universal mystery, and in this action, is for him, and that engaged in this action he for his part is for God—this is the axis on which the individual moves as he turns from his own way to God. His conversion and renewal is not, therefore, an end in itself, as it has often been interpreted and represented in a far too egocentric Christianity. The man who wants to be converted only for his own sake and for himself rather than to God the Lord and to entry into the service of His cause on earth and as His witness in the cosmos, is not the whole man. When we convert and are renewed in the totality of our being, we cross the threshold of our private existence and move out into the open. The inner problems may be most urgent and burning and exciting, but we are not engaged in conversion if we confine ourselves to them. We simply run (in a rather more subtle way) on our own path headlong to destruction. When we convert and are renewed in the totality of our being, in and with our private responsibility we also accept a public responsibility. For it is the great God of heaven and earth who is for us, and we are for this God.

The saying of Jesus to Peter: "When thou art converted ... " (Lk. 22³²), is one of the few passages in the New Testament which brings out directly the personal character of this movement, although it is to be noted that it thus continues: "Strengthen thy brethren." Ac. 3²⁶ is also, of course, striking in this respect (cf. Jer. 25⁵; Jon. 3⁸) "Unto you first God, having raised up his servant, sent him to bless you, in turning away every one of you ($\H{\epsilon}\kappa\alpha\sigma\tau\sigma\varsigma$ EN195) from his iniquities." In the Old Testament it is especially in Ezekiel (e.g., 3¹⁶ᶠ·, 18⁴ᶠ· ²⁰ᶠ·) that we find an "existential" application of the promise and call to the individual—that he should turn from his former way and live. Self-evidently, that which becomes explicit in Ezekiel is the meaning of both Testaments. The proclaimed conversion to God is an action

---

EN195 each

and being ascribed and promised personally to each individual. It is a happening which applies particularly to him; which reaches to the heart and veins, the bones and marrow, of this or that particular man. And there is biblical precedent in the Book of Proverbs for what becomes so important in the later Church as the individual cure of souls. In general, however, we cannot overlook the fact that in the Bible the call for conversion is usually addressed—even when it is in the singular—to a plurality of men, to the people Israel, to Jacob-Israel in its totality, to Jerusalem or Ephraim. We have to remember this especially in Deutero-Isaiah, where many statements are formulated in the second person singular and seem to call for an understanding in terms of an individual application. To be sure, they can and should be read in this way too. But in so doing, we must not lose sight of the original meaning in which they are addressed to a people. The preaching of the Baptist opens with a general μετανοεῖτε^EN196, as does also that of Jesus Himself. There is obviously no fear that the collective will weaken the seriousness of the decision demanded from the individual. Far from weakening it, it is the plural which constitutes it a genuine seriousness. Behind this plural there stands the seriousness of the great cause of God in the world, of His name and kingdom and will which the community and all its members have to serve; the seriousness of His decision as in each individual it reaches and affects all men. The conversion of man is his conversion to God when in and with it he adds himself as *sanctus*^EN197 to the *communio sanctorum*^EN198.

4. We cannot understand the conversion of man as a matter for only one period in his life, which others will follow in which he can look back on what has happened *quasi re bene gesta*^EN199, or in which he might have to repeat it at this or that specific point, the prior or intervening times being periods in which he does not live in conversion, either because he is already converted, or is in need, and capable, of conversion but is only moving towards it. If it is the revealed truth that God is for him and he for God which necessitates his conversion and sets him in this movement, the movement is one which cannot be interrupted but extends over the whole of his life. It is neither exhausted in a once-for-all act, nor is it accomplished in a series of such acts. Otherwise how could it be an affair of the whole man? It becomes and is the content and character of the whole act of his life as such. Certain moments in the totality of the fulfilment of this act, certain impulses and illuminations, disturbances, changes and experiences which we undergo at particular times, may have the meaning and character of a particular recollection of its total content. But sanctification in conversion is not the affair of these individual moments; it is the affair of the totality of the whole life-movement of man. To live a holy life is to be raised and driven with increasing definiteness from the centre of this revealed truth, and therefore to live in conversion with growing sincerity, depth and precision.

As seen by contemporaries the Reformation of the 16th century began on October 31, 1517, when Luther nailed his theses on indulgences to the door of the Castle Church, Wittenberg. The first two of these theses were as follows: (1) *Dominus et magister noster Jesus*

EN196 repent
EN197 holy
EN198 communion of saints
EN199 as a deed well done

4. The Awakening to Conversion

Christus dicendo "penitentiam agite, etc.," omnem vitam fidelium penitentiam esse voluit[EN200]; (2) *quod verbum de penitentia sacramentali (id est confessionis et satisfactionis, que sacerdotum ministerio celebratur) non potest intelligi*[EN201]. We have substituted the word conversion for what Luther [567] called penitence because the latter term almost inevitably evokes associations which link the matter under discussion with a momentary event (whether once-for-all or repeated). Now momentary events of this kind—either in the Romanist form of the reception of the sacrament of penance, or in the Pietist and Methodist form of a simple or more complex experience of conversion—are not identical with conversion to God, because the latter is the totality of the movement of sanctification which dominates and characterises human life—a movement in which there can be no breaks or pauses when conversion is no longer needed or only needed afresh, but when he might also propose to fulfil it for the second or third, or hundredth time. No matter whether they are understood sacramentally, emotionally or ethically, individual moments of this kind, and all the specific liturgies and experiences and conflicts and confessions and achievements of penitence, can be understood only as particularly prominent moments in the whole life-movement from the old to the new man. If we can hardly lack such moments, none of them can be fixed, let alone estimated, with such precision that its specific content can be responsibly identified with the happening in which we become saints of God; with our conversion as it is set in motion from this centre. If the latter takes place only in these moments, and not in the whole context of human life, it does not take place at all.

To convert, μετανοεῖν[EN202], in the sense of the Baptist and the synoptic Jesus does, of course, include the new beginning of human life at a particular time. It also includes all kinds of action commanded at a particular time. In this respect we have already recalled Lk. 3[10f.] in relation to John, and we may also refer to what we said on the subject of discipleship. But New Testament μετανοεῖν[EN203] is differentiated from the well-known and highly estimated "penitential" (t'shubah) of current Jewish theology and piety, which consisted essentially in a once-for-all or repeated individual movement, by the fact that it is "a radical change in the relationship of God to man and man to God" (J. Behm, in *Kittel* IV, 995), of which it is a distinctive feature that it is not in the background as something that has happened, nor is it present in isolation as something which has to be repeated from time to time, but it controls and characterises the whole life of man from this beginning. In New Testament μετάνοια[EN304] man moves forward steadily to continually new things in the same movement. "Though our outward man perish, yet the inward man is renewed day by day" (2 Cor. 4[16]).

In this respect, we have to note the call to conversion as it is sounded in the letters of the Apocalypse to Christian communities which have behind them a "first love" (Rev. 2[4]), and "first works" (2[5]), and even sometimes later works which were more than the first (2[19]), but which seem to have come to a standstill, and therefore in practice to have given up, at one point or another. Μετανόησον[EN205] is demanded of them almost with some degree of menace. And over against all of them—even the community of Philadelphia (3[7f.]) whose failure is least apparent—there is set ὁ νικῶν[EN206], he that overcometh, to whom Jesus gives to eat

---

[EN200] Our Lord and Master Jesus Christ, in saying 'do penitence etc.' wanted the whole life of the faithful to be penitence
[EN201] this word cannot be understood in terms of sacramental penance (that is, of confession and satisfaction, which are celebrated in the ministry of priests)
[EN202] to repent
[EN203] to repent
[EN204] repentance
[EN205] 'Repent!'
[EN206] the one who conquers

of that tree of life (2^7), who shall not be hurt by the second death (2^{11}), who is given the white stone with the name which no one knows but he who receives it (2^{17}), who is granted power over the nations (2^{26}), whom He will confess before the Father and His angels (3^5), whom He will make a pillar in the temple of His God (3^{12}), who is allowed to sit with Him on His throne as He Himself overcame and is set down with His Father in His throne (3^{21}). "He that hath an ear, let him hear what the Spirit saith unto the churches," is what we read at the end of each of the letters. Who, then, is the contrasted "overcomer" in all the glory ascribed to him? The content of the μετανόησον[EN207] is clear in these passages. The first love must not be left behind, nor the first works left undone ($2^{4f.}$). "Be thou faithful unto death, and I will give thee a crown of life"(2^{10}). "Remember how thou hast received and heard, and hold fast" (3^3). "Be watchful" (3^2). "Behold, I come quickly: hold fast that which thou hast, that no

[568]

man take it from thee" (3^{11}, cf. 2^{25}). Note the present tense in the well-known verse: "Behold, I stand at the door, and knock: if any man hear my voice, and open the door, I will come in, and will sup with him, and he with me" (3^{20}). It is he who does this now, to-day, that is the "overcomer" who shares His glory. And the Spirit tells the communities that they are to do this, and to be overcomers, victors, in so doing. He tells them then—and in this consists their μετανοεῖν[EN208]—that the content of the present day can only be that of the first day; that it can consist only in a steadfast and responsible moving forward from this beginning.

It is a strangely eloquent fact that Paul uses the terms μετανοεῖν[EN209] and μετάνοια[EN210] with comparative infrequency, and John not at all. We may rightly suspect that the words were allowed to drop in view of their association with the Jewish theory and practice of penance. If Paul prefers to describe the same thing as ἀνακαίνωσις[EN211], or παλιγγενεσία[EN212], or the dying of the old and rising of the new man; if in John πιστεύειν[EN213] is defined from the very first in such a way that it includes conversion; and if in the language and thought of 1 John especially there is a constant antithesis of light and darkness, truth and error, love and hate, life and death, God and the world, these are only expressions for the radical things which the Synoptics mean by μετανοεῖν[EN214] as opposed to the Rabbinic call to penitence, and they serve to bring out its character as an act, and an act which is constantly renewed.

In this context we ought perhaps to consider what has always been regarded as a difficult passage, Heb. 6^{1-10}. It tells us plainly and sharply that there can be no repetition of conversion because, once it has taken place, it determines the whole life of man in a process which brooks of no interruption. It is instructive to consider how this is established and explained in the passage. The section opens in v. 1a with a summons that Christians should leave behind (ἀφέντες) the problem (λόγος) of the ἀρχὴ Χριστοῦ[EN215], of the beginning which Christ has made with us, as one which has already been solved and decided. We must not act as if we had still to make a beginning with Him. Instead, we should resolutely and decidedly allow ourselves to be carried by Him from this beginning made with us to the end which He has appointed. In other words, we should be constantly in movement, ἐπὶ τὴν τελειότητα φερώμεθα[EN216]. We should thus refrain (vv. 1b–2) from trying to lay a fresh

---

[EN207] 'repent!'
[EN208] to repent
[EN209] to repent
[EN210] repentance
[EN211] renewal
[EN212] regeneration
[EN213] believing
[EN214] repentance
[EN215] beginning of Christ
[EN216] we are being carried to perfection

foundation with answers to questions which grope back beyond this beginning, as though it had not been made, as though we did not come from it, and as though we had still to posit it. Some of these questions are mentioned: How is it that I have turned away from dead works? How can I believe in God? What is the meaning of my baptism? Is there a resurrection of the dead? What is meant by eternal judgment? In themselves these are all possible and justifiable questions—and it is not for nothing that that of μετάνοια EN217 is the first to be mentioned. But they can be raised only as questions which have been answered already. And they must be set aside as idle and unprofitable to the extent that they represent the attempt to lay a fresh foundation; to the extent that they are posed in the void, where the ἀρχὴ Χριστοῦ EN218, and therefore our own conversion, and faith, and baptism, and the resurrection and judgment are seen only as future possibilities. "This will we do" (καὶ τοῦτο ποιήσομεν) is the resolute continuation in v. 3. We will leave behind us the attempt to lay a fresh foundation, which is in any case a futile attempt, since we did not lay it and do not have to do so. We will set all this in the past and move constantly towards the goal, "if God permit." We will do it. But of ourselves we have no freedom to do it. If we have the freedom, we have it only as it is given us by God. But according to vv. 4–6 we can count on this freedom because the alternative of falling behind is quite impossible. For who are we? In vv. 4–5 it is boldly assumed that we are among those who have been enlightened once and for all, who have tasted heavenly gifts, who have been made partakers of the Holy Ghost, who have tasted the good Word of God and the powers of the world to come. We may and must understand ourselves as such. For us as such it is quite impossible (v. 6) that as those who have fallen   [569] behind or away (παραπεσόντες) we should come afresh to conversion (ἀνακαινίζειν εἰς μετάνοιαν) as though nothing had happened. Would not this be to crucify afresh, and put to an open shame, the Son of God, the Victor, who has made this beginning with us, and set us in the movement from which we come so gloriously endowed? Would it not mean that we go behind Him as well as ourselves, striking out not only the gifts but Himself the Giver? We are not free to do this. We are free, therefore, to leave behind that which can only be behind as an enterprise foredoomed to failure. We are free to move forward. In vv. 7–8 the same lesson is enforced by a metaphor. The earth has drunk in the rain which frequently falls on it, and it brings forth useful vegetation for those for whom it is tilled (v. 7). If thorns and briers do also grow, of course, they quickly show themselves to be worthless, and the only option is to "curse" and burn them (v. 8). Christians, however, are to be compared to the good crop rather than the bad. The moral is drawn in vv. 9–10. The direction given in v. 1a is in force. It can and must be followed (v. 3). There can be no doubt that vv. 1–8 do include a good deal of anxiety and admonition and even warning. The readers do not seem to be readily identifiable with those who are freed for this action as described in vv. 4–6. May it be that *per nefas* EN219 they find themselves in the fatal sphere *ante Christum* EN220? May it be that they are not engaged in that movement to the goal? May it be that they are occupied instead with those idle questions, and therefore with laying a fresh foundation? May it be that they are denying Christ the Victor? May it be that they are producing a crop of thorns and briers which can only be destroyed by the consuming fire? It is evident that this question seriously engages the author: otherwise why should he have raised the issue? He had already brought up the question in 3¹²ᶠ: "Take heed, brethren, lest there be in any of you an evil heart of unbelief, in departing from the living God. But exhort one another daily, while it is called To-day." And he will later (12¹⁷) recall the case of Esau who when he had sold his birthright

---

EN217 repentance
EN218 beginning of Christ
EN219 wrongly
EN220 before Christ

found no τόπος μετανοίας EN221, though he sought it carefully with tears. The whole tenor of the Epistle is that of a warning against this danger, of a most urgent "To-day, To-day." But in the particularly serious passage 6¹⁻¹⁰ the author does think of his readers as actually overwhelmed by the impending threat. On the contrary, he says: "We are persuaded better things of you, and things that accompany salvation—εἰ καὶ οὕτως λαλοῦμεν, though we thus speak" (v. 9). The basis of his certainty is that God is not unrighteous, but righteous; that He does not forget but remembers that they are at work, and love His name, and have ministered to the saints, and do minister (v. 10). The danger may thus be discounted, for there is something far more certain than the danger in which the author obviously sees his readers stand and to which he earnestly draws their attention. They are in fact engaged in the movement described in v. 1a. And God knows and recognises that they are those who are engaged in it. In the passage which follows (v. 11 f.) there is required only the exhortation appropriate to the direction there given—that they should persevere, and not become slothful, in the movement initiated once and for all by their once and for all μετάνοια EN222.

The post-apostolic and early catholic Church failed to take note of these warnings in the Gospels, Paul, John and Hebrews. Relapsing into the ways of thinking of later Judaism, it again made the conversion which rules the whole life of Christians into a matter of particular acts, and later of a special penitential discipline. This led finally to the special "sacrament of penance" which Luther contrasted so sharply with the μετανοεῖτε EN223 of Jesus. As Luther perceived, sacramental penitence is not the conversion demanded by Jesus. True conversion, or penitence, can take place only in the whole life of believers. Calvin's view was exactly the same. In opposition to the Anabaptists and their companions (*sodales*) the Jesuits, [570] he found it necessary to state: *poenitentia in totam vitam proroganda est homini Christiano* EN224 (*Instit.* III, 3, 2). Believers know that this warfare (*militia*) will end only with their death (3, 9).

We may sum up as follows. By the revealed truth that God is for him and he for God, the whole man is set in the movement of conversion. It is for this that he is awakened in sanctification, and it is in this that his raising of himself consists. In every dimension we have to do with the whole man, as already explained in detail. In the light of this conclusion, we must now go on to make a second main proposition—that in this movement we have to do with a warfare, or, to put it a little more precisely and less dramatically, with a quarrel, or falling-out.

It is a pity that there is no English or French equivalent for the very useful German word *Auseinandersetzung*, which exactly sums up what we have in mind. Of course, it is a word that has to be used very cautiously and selectively in theology. We cannot wish to fall out with God, with Jesus Christ, with the Holy Spirit. We can only be glad and thankful that God is on our side. It is also better not to fall out with Holy Scripture or the Church as the communion of saints. And it is better that there should be no falling out in our relationship with our neighbours. But there is every cause—and it is with this that we are concerned in the present context—to fall out with oneself. It is just this that the man engaged in conversion can never cease to do. It can and must be said that his conversion consists in the fact that he is seriously at odds with himself.

EN221 place of repentance
EN222 repentance
EN223 repent!
EN224 penitence is required of the Christian man his whole life

4. *The Awakening to Conversion*

We cannot overlook the fact that in the fulfilment of this movement a man finds himself under a twofold determination.

The first consists in the powerful summons to halt and advance which is issued, and by which he is set in this distinctive movement, in virtue of the fact that God is for him and he for God, and that this fact is clearly and powerfully revealed to him. In this determination he is the new man; the man who is impelled by the Spirit of God, to use the phrase of Rom. 8[14]. In this determination he repents and renounces what he previously was and did, leaving his old way, abandoning himself as he was, boldly enterprising a completely new and different being and action, entering a new way, affirming and apprehending himself in the future which thereby opens up for him—and all this, commensurate with the powerful cause which sets him in this movement, in the unqualified totality of his existence and being as a man.

But the second determination under which he finds himself consists in the fact that it is still he himself who is wholly placed in this movement and constituted the one who makes it. It is he himself, i.e., the one for whom this call to halt and advance previously had no meaning or power. As he gives himself to enter this way, he comes from the old way. He repents, but he does so as the one who previously knew nothing of repentance. He boldly enterprises a new being, but he does so as one who previously had no boldness to do so. He affirms and apprehends himself in the future indicated by this cause which effectively moves him, but he does so as the one who has also his past. Even in [571] the turn which he executes, at the very heart of the present of this happening he is never without his past. To-day, already impelled by the Spirit, he is still in the flesh of yesterday. He is already the new man, but he is still the old. Only in part? Only to a limited extent? Only in respect of certain relics? The older theology was right when in relation to the sinful past of man as it still persists in the present of conversion it referred to the remains or relics of the old man, of the flesh and its sinful action. It is only as sorry remains that the being and action of man under this second determination can be seen and understood in the light of the first determination. But it was an unfortunate delusion if this remnant was regarded as fortunately smaller in relation to something other and better. On the contrary, if we are just a little honest with ourselves (as we will be in serious conversion), we cannot conceal the fact that it is again the whole man with whom we have to do in this residuum; that it is still the whole man who under this second determination is in puzzling contrast with himself under the first. The man who to-day is confronted by that call to halt and advance, who to-day is set in that movement, in the totality of his existence and being, by the powerful truth that God is for him and he for God, is also to-day, and again in the totality of his existence and being, the sinful man of yesterday. Thus in the to-day of repentance we have not only to do with the presence of certain regrettable traces of his being and action of yesterday. No, the one who is under the determination and in the process of becoming a totally new man is in his totality the old man of yesterday.

191

The situation can be understood, therefore, only in the following terms. In the twofold determination of the man engaged in conversion we have to do with two total men who cannot be united but are necessarily in extreme contradiction. We are confronted with two mutually exclusive determinations.

It is worth pointing out that Calvin did not perceive this relationship between the new and the old in the 1539 edition of the *Institutes*, but had obviously come to do so by 1559. In the former case he spoke of a *pars nostri*[EN225] which in regeneration remains subject to the yoke of sin. In it we cling to an *aliquod de vetustate*[EN226]. The soul of the believer is thus divided into two parts which confront each other like two wrestlers (*duo athletae*), the one being stronger than the other, although attacked and hampered by him. *Praecipuo cordis voto et affectu*[EN227] the believer strives after God, his *superiores partes*[EN228] following the Spirit. He hates and condemns the evil which *per imbecillitatem*[EN229] he still commits. He can sin consciously only in face of the opposition of his heart and conscience. And it is by this fact that the regenerate is differentiated from the unregenerate. At the corresponding point in 1559, however, this whole interpretation has been abandoned (III, 3, 9 f.). The old and the new, sin and grace, are no longer two parts in the being of the regenerate. The Romanist ideas of *fomen mali*[EN230], a mere *infirmitas*[EN231], still present and active in the believer have now disappeared. In opposition even to Augustine, and in strict agreement with Paul, Calvin now

[572]

speaks of the *pravitas*[EN232] peculiar even to the regenerate, of the sin which dwells in him too, and which can obviously be met, not by something higher (the *superiores partes*[EN233]) in himself, but only by the new man as such, who is begotten of the Spirit. It is clear that on this basis—but only on this basis—what Calvin said about the justification and forgiveness needed by even the regenerate is possible and necessary and cogent in the strict sense intended. If, on the other hand, the saints are in some degree not sinners, we can hardly avoid the conclusion that to this degree, in respect of the stronger of the two wrestlers, they no longer stand in need of justification.

Luther's *simul*[EN234] (*totus*[EN235]) *iustus, simul*[EN236] (*totus*[EN237]) *peccator*[EN238] has thus to be applied strictly to sanctification and therefore conversion if we are to see deeply into what is denoted by these terms, and to understand them with the necessary seriousness. It is certainly hard to grasp that the same man stands under two total determinations which are not merely opposed but mutually exclusive; that the same man, in the *simul*[EN239] of to-day, is both the old man of yesterday and the new man of to-morrow, the captive of yesterday

---

[EN225] part of us
[EN226] something of our old self
[EN227] by a particular commitment and affection of the heart
[EN228] superior parts
[EN229] as a result of weakness
[EN230] tinder of evil
[EN231] weakness
[EN232] depravity
[EN233] superior parts
[EN234] at once
[EN235] wholly
[EN236] righteous, at once
[EN237] wholly
[EN238] a sinner
[EN239] at the same time

and the free man of to-morrow, the slothful recumbent of yesterday and the erect man of to-morrow. But there is no easier way of seeing and understanding the matter. Static and quantitative terms may seem to help, but they are not adequate to describe the true situation. They involve a separation into constituent elements. It is true that the situation seems to cry out for this separation. It seems to be much more illuminating if, instead of saying that the whole man is still the old and yet already the new, in complete and utter antithesis, we say that he is still partially the old and already partially the new. But if we put it in this way we mistake the matter. For the new man is the whole man; and so too is the old. And conversion is the transition, the movement, in which man is still, in fact, wholly the old and already wholly the new man. We are badly advised if we abandon this statement because we fear the severity of the antithesis. To do so, and thus to proceed to transform and divide the *simul*[EN240] into a *partim-partim*[EN241], in which the old man of the past is sharply and a little triumphantly separated from the new man of the future, is to leave the sphere of the *vita christiana*[EN242] as it is actually lived for a psychological myth which has no real substance. The *vita christiana*[EN243] in conversion is the event, the act, the history, in which at one and the same time man is still wholly the old man and already wholly the new—so powerful is the sin by which he is determined from behind, and so powerful the grace by which he is determined from before. It is in this way that man knows himself when he is really engaged in conversion.

But now we must go on to emphasise no less sharply that the conversion in which he is simultaneously both, is an event, an act, a history. The coincidence of the "still" and "already" is the content of this *simul*[EN244]. Because this "still" and "already" coincide in him, it is not the *simul*[EN245] of a balancing or co-ordination of two similar factors. Nor are the positions of the two moments which are simultaneously present—the old and the new man—in any sense [573] interchangeable. On the contrary, they are wholly and utterly dissimilar. There is an order and sequence in this *simul*[EN246]. There is direction—the movement to a goal. The old and the new man are simultaneously present in the relationship of a *terminus a quo*[EN247] and a *terminus ad quem*[EN248]. Thus conversion, in which at one and the same time we are still the old man and already the new, and both wholly and altogether, is neither a juggling nor a movement in a circle. In accordance with the fact that it is initiated by the divine command to halt and advance, the man engaged in it finds that—with no possibility of

---

[EN240] at the same time
[EN241] partly ... partly ...
[EN242] Christian life
[EN243] Christian life
[EN244] at the same time
[EN245] at the same time
[EN246] at the same time
[EN247] starting point
[EN248] ending point

interchange—he is wholly denied as the old man of yesterday and wholly affirmed as the new man of to-morrow; that he is wholly taken out of identity with the former and wholly set in identity with the latter; that he is in no sense taken seriously by God as the former but taken with unqualified seriousness by God as the latter; that as the former he is wholly given up to eternal death and as the latter wholly taken up into eternal life. When he is simultaneously the old and the new man, and both in totality, he is not only forbidden to be this in neutrality, in a static equipoise of the two; he finds that this is quite impossible in practice. He can be the two only in the whole turning from the one to the other. We speak of this turning when we speak of his conversion. And we emphasise the serious and radical nature of it when we speak of the twofold, total determination of the man engaged in it.

In these circumstances the thought of falling-out is perhaps the best to describe the situation. To begin with, it indicates that the coincidence of the "still" and the "already," of the old man and the new, of the *homo peccator*[EN249] and the *homo sanctus*[EN250], cannot remain. It is true that there is no present in which we can look beyond this *simul*[EN251], in which the man engaged in conversion is not wholly under the power of sin and wholly under that of grace. Yet he is not merely not authorised by the content of the two determinations coinciding in this *simul*[EN252], nor is he merely prohibited, but he is positively prevented from understanding this *simul*[EN253] as something lasting and definitive. To his own salvation, he has no continuing city. If it is true that we can never at any time see beyond this *simul*[EN254], it is equally true that this *simul*[EN255], in virtue of its dynamic as a moment in the history of God with man and man with God, points beyond itself, impelling to the only possible decision between the two total determinations which now coincide in man. He cannot remain what he still is *in toto*[EN256]. He can no longer be this in face of what he already is *in toto*. And what he already is *in toto*, he may become and be in such a way that he is this alone (excluding what he still is *in toto*). What in this *simul* is still present in conjunction as a twofold determination of one and the same man cannot by its very nature remain in this conjunction. Its whole will and movement and impulse is to fall out or to fall apart, and to do so in the direction unequivocally characterised by the radically different content of this twofold determination; not dualistically in a division or re-stabilised co-existence of an old man and a new, a sinner and saint; but monistically in the passing and death and definitive end and destruction of the one in favour of the development and life and exclusive, uncompromised and inviolable existence of the other. In the quar-

[574]

EN249 sinful man
EN250 holy man
EN251 at the same time
EN252 at the same time
EN253 at the same time
EN254 at the same time
EN255 at the same time
EN256 as a whole

rel in which a man finds himself engaged in conversion—as he who is still wholly the old and already wholly the new man—he has not fallen out with himself partially but totally, in the sense that the end and goal of the dispute is that he can no longer be the one he was and can be only the one he will be.

The great antinomies in John (light–darkness, etc.), and the alternative expressions of Paul (the putting off and death of the old and putting on and rising of the new, or the opposition and conflict between the Spirit and the flesh), may again be recalled in this connexion. We have to reflect that the New Testament speaks in this way of the present of the community and its members (the members of the body of Christ). The references are all to the life of believers, the regenerate. We are never given to understand that the one deter- mination of the man engaged in conversion, the Christian man, is seen and regarded only as his heathen or Jewish past, and the other only as his future. On the contrary, it is the life of believers, the Christian present, which is here pitilessly but resolutely set in the light of this twofold determination, as illustrated by the concrete admonitions and promises of the Epis- tles. Again, however, we are nowhere given to understand that there will arise even moment- arily a state of rest or equipoise as between two co-ordinated factors. Christians are forcefully ejected from any fancied equipoise or co-ordination by the fact that in this *simul* there are addressed to them very concrete warnings and promises concerning their present. They are not placed before or in a choice or decision, but under a choice which has been already made, a decision which has been resolved and executed, concerning them. They have been brought face to face with a powerful summons to halt and advance. And it is a divine sum- mons which has a total reference in both cases to death on the one side and life on the other; in the power of which what they still are in their totality cannot continue but only cease and disappear; in which therefore the old thing, their being in the flesh, cannot be completed, but only replaced, by that which they already are in their totality, their being in the Spirit. They can now walk only as those they already are, not as those they still are; in the Spirit and not in the flesh. But this means that what they still are is now behind them, and it is only what they are already that is before them. We are not engaged in conversion, nor are we Christians in the New Testament sense, if we are not involved in this falling-out with ourselves in which it is not merely a matter of this or that on the one side or the other, but of death on the one side and life on the other—in this order and with this teleology.

Calvin was right, therefore, when he praised as scriptural the traditional description of repentance as *mortificatio*[EN257] and *vivificatio*[EN258] as Melanchthon and M. Bucer had intro- duced it into Reformation doctrine (III, 3, 3). But he added that it needs to be properly understood. He was obviously dissatisfied with the Scholastic understanding of *mortificatio*[EN259] as a mere *contritio cordis*[EN260]; a *dolor*[EN261] and even a *terror animae*[EN262] on the ground of the knowledge of sin and ensuing judgment; a basic self-dissatisfaction in which man sees that he is lost and wants to be different; the inward shattering of man in self- despair. He was no less dissatisfied with the understanding of *vivificatio*[EN263] as merely the comforting of man by faith in the light of the goodness and mercy and grace of God; his lifting up of himself, and coming to himself, in relation to the promised salvation in Christ. [575] There is nothing wrong with these descriptions, in which the psychological aspect of conver-

---

[EN257] mortification
[EN258] vivification
[EN259] mortification
[EN260] contrition of the heart
[EN261] sadness
[EN262] fear of the soul
[EN263] vivification

sion is considered and perspicaciously and on the whole accurately represented. But we may learn from Calvin himself (3, 8) why they are inadequate. This is obviously because they have to do only with the subjective and psychological side of the process, and therefore cannot do justice to the objective content of the weighty words *mortificatio*[EN264] and *vivificatio*[EN265]—no matter how strong may be the expressions used (*consternatio, humiliatio*[EN266] and even *desperatio*[EN267]), or how fine the description of the *consolatio*[EN268]. By *mortificatio*[EN269], Calvin tells us in his own language, we have to understand *totius carnis, quae militia et perversitate referta est, interitus*[EN270]. This involves the *res difficilis et ardua*[EN271] of an action in which we have to put off ourselves like a garment, being forced to take leave of our *nativum ingenium*[EN272]. If everything that we have of ourselves is not done away (*abolitum*), we can only suppose that *interitus carnis*[EN273], and therefore *mortificatio*[EN274], has not really taken place. Thus the first step to obedience is the *abnegatio naturae nostrae*[EN275]; the *abnegatio nostri*[EN276] which later supplies a title for the decisive chapter in his doctrine of sanctification. This, he believes, is what the Old Testament prophets meant by conversion. And by *vivificatio*[EN277]—again in the sense of the prophets—we have to understand the fruit of righteousness, justice and mercy which grows out of the heart and soul and mind of a man who has been filled by the Holy Spirit with what may rightly (*iure*) be called a new thinking and willing. But Calvin returns at once, almost anxiously and with striking emphasis, to the first point. Because by nature we are turned aside from God, we will never do the right *nisi praecedat abnegatio nostri*[EN278]. There can be no awakening to the fear of God, no *initium pietatis, nisi ubi gladio Spiritus violenter mactati in nihilum redigimur*[EN279]. There is needed the *interitus communis naturae*[EN280] (the nature common to all men) in the above sense if God is to be able to reckon us His children.

Is not the impression left by this presentation strangely mixed? There can be no doubt that Calvin brings out with great clarity the literal seriousness of the biblical terms, and therefore the radical sharpness, the objective and strictly antithetical character, of the dispute with himself in which the man engaged in conversion finds himself, of the resolute falling-out or falling-apart which is involved (as opposed to a mere tension of two opposing spiritual states, in respect of which terms like *mortificatio*[EN281] and *vivificatio*[EN282] might appear to be only rather exaggerated metaphors). Calvin was quite right when, renouncing all attempts at plastic representation, he spoke so inexorably of *interitus, abnegatio*[EN283] and

---

[EN264] mortification
[EN265] vivification
[EN266] consternation, humiliation
[EN267] desperation
[EN268] consolation
[EN269] mortification
[EN270] the death of the whole of the flesh, which has been crammed full of conflict and perversity
[EN271] difficult and arduous task
[EN272] natural mind
[EN273] the death of the flesh
[EN274] mortification
[EN275] the denial of our own nature
[EN276] denial of ourselves
[EN277] vivification
[EN278] unless denial of ourselves first take place
[EN279] beginning of piety, except where we be put to death by the sword of the Spirit, and reduced to nothing
[EN280] death of the common nature
[EN281] mortification
[EN282] vivification
[EN283] death, denial

reductio ad nihilum[EN284], of the slaying sword of the Spirit, and then of the Spirit as the only principle of what may be seriously called a new life. There can be no objection to the radical nature of his presentation. Calvin points us most significantly to the height beyond all psychologising where the conversion of man is real and all the spiritual processes which attest it have their basis and superior truth. On the other hand, it cannot be denied (and the explanation is to be found in an even more deep-seated defect in his teaching) that the doctrine of Calvin obviously suffers (cf. A. Göhler, *op. cit.*, p. 41 f.) from a curious overemphasising of *mortificatio*[EN285] at the expense of *vivificatio*[EN286] which might be justified to some extent from the older but not from the later prophets of the Old Testament, and certainly not from what is understood by μετάνοια[EN287] in the New. What we have called the divine call to advance is in Calvin so overshadowed by the divine summons to halt that it can hardly be heard at all. The result is that his presentation is not merely stern, as is inevitable, but sombre and forbidding. And this is quite out of keeping with the themes presented. It does not enable us to see the decision operative in the *simul peccator et sanctus*[EN288], the teleology of man's falling-out with himself. Man seems almost to be left in the air. The truth is that in the New Testament the real dying and passing and perishing of the old man is matched by a no less real rising and coming and appearing of the new, and that it is in the power of this,   [576] the *vivificatio*[EN289], that there can be also the *mortificatio*[EN290]. To take only one example, note the emphasis in statements like those of Col. 3[1f.] and Eph. 2[1f.]. It is in view of the Yes pronounced to man in the omnipotence of the divine mercy that there arises this falling-out with ourselves and we hear the inexorable No to our being in the flesh. But this aspect is not given its proper place, and does not clearly emerge, in the presentation of Calvin. The impression is left that the *interitus*[EN291] of the old man is what really matters in this happening, and in contrast to this the *vivificatio*[EN292] is introduced only as a pale and feeble hope. It is not for nothing that in the description of the latter we miss the realism which is so impressive in the presentation of the *mortificatio*[EN293], and that—contrary to Calvin's true intention—the emphasis falls on the rise of new *cogitationes et affectus*[EN294]. Why is it that Calvin could not speak of the life of the new man in terms no less radical and categorical—indeed, more so—than those which he used in relation to the death of the old?

The same question has to be addressed (in an even sharper form) to the doctrine of conversion advanced by H. F. Kohlbrügge (cf. on this point W. Kreck, *Die Lehre von der Heiligung bei H. F. Kohlbrügge*, 1936, esp. 90 f.). It must never be forgotten that in the great pietistic, rationalistic and romantic twilight of the 19th century Kohlbrügge was one of the few who revealed a precise knowledge of the height where the conversion of man has its actuality and origin. In the light of this he gave powerful advocacy to the proposition (more than once explicitly stated in Calvin) that the renovation of man consists decisively in a growing and deepening knowledge of sin. In the light of the Law (Kreck, p. 98 f.) he becomes "more and more corrupt, and more and more sinful, until he finally realises that he is altogether man." "He is a great saint before God, and the best doctor and professor,

---

[EN284] reduction to nothing
[EN285] mortification
[EN286] vivification
[EN287] repentance
[EN288] at once a sinner and holy
[EN289] vivification
[EN290] mortification
[EN291] death
[EN292] vivification
[EN293] mortification
[EN294] thoughts and feelings

who knows of himself only that he is a great transgressor." God dislocates the hips of His saints, so that they walk with a limp. "That which is of God acquires an attitude and gait like Jacob's, whereas Esau strides powerfully through the world." "The saints of God can do nothing in advance; everything is taken out of their hands ... they have no capacity of themselves, no wisdom, and even no faith when it is needed, but are full of fear and trembling and hesitation and anxiety." The pious are those who "do not hide the fact that they are not pious, and are prepared to live only by the pious God." "Even when you are a hundred years old in His service, you will be the same fool, and God will be the same merciful God" (p. 94). "All my own work and activity and faith is of such a kind that even if I were clothed with all the faith and works of all saints and patriarchs and prophets and apostles, and stood before you with an unvarnished faith, I should cast it all from me and shake it off like refuse in the presence of my God. For there is grace only for the naked" (p. 95). Can we read all this without assenting from the very depths of our hearts—and yet without also having to ask whether it is really true? Are not these propositions different from those of Calvin (to their disadvantage) to the extent that the *mortificatio*[EN295] of which they plainly speak is obviously conceived of again—for Kohlbrügge was a child of his age—on the psychological level, being understood and described as a process of awareness of an extremely negative type? And the result is that Kohlbrügge can take up again a rather doubtful qualification that Calvin had abandoned: "You may indeed sin like a worldling; you may sink below the level of cattle and demons" ... but there is still the possibility of repentance and sorrow; we cannot persist in it; we cannot remain in it; we have the means to deal with it; we are to hate it and flee it (p. 99 f.). And this has the further result that conversely Kohlbrügge can describe the *vivificatio*[EN296] which begins beyond this self-humiliation in terms which make it difficult for us (because they are still on the psychological level) not to catch suddenly the ring of perfectionism: "Yet I live, says the believer. I live in the sight of God. I live before His judgment

[577]

throne in His grace. I live in His favour, light and love. I am perfectly redeemed from my sins. The ledger contains no debt against my name. The Law no longer demands, accuses, or condemns. I am holy as my Father in heaven is perfect. The whole good-pleasure of God embraces me. It is the ground on which I stand, the rock by which I am sheltered. All the blessedness and rest of God lifts and bears me. I breathe in it, and am eternally whole. I have no more sin; I commit no more sin. I know with a good conscience that I am in the ways of God and do His will, that I am wholly in accordance with His will—whether I go or stand, sit or lie, wake or sleep. Even what I think and say is according to His will. Wherever I may be, at home or abroad, it is according to His gracious will. Whether I work or rest, I am acceptable to Him. My guilt is eternally expunged, and I cannot incur new guilt which will not be eternally expunged. I am well kept in His grace, and cannot sin. No death can kill me. I live eternally like all the angels of God. God will no longer be incensed against me and chide me. I am redeemed for ever from future wrath. The world will no longer touch me, nor the world entangle me. Who will separate us from the love of God? If God is for us, who can be against us?" (quoted from Bonhoeffer, *Nachfolge*, 205 f.). Even though it is conceivable that *in extremis*[EN297] a Christian may use the extravagant language of Kohlbrügge both negatively on the one side and positively on the other, the fact remains that with him as with Calvin the emphasis falls on the negative side, on the destruction of all our own holiness even as Christians, on the annihilating attack on all forms of self-righteousness, even the most refined, even those which appeal to the grace of God, to Christ, and to the Holy Spirit. Once we have read Kohlbrügge, we can never again forget this attack, and we shall be grateful that he has

---

[EN295] mortification
[EN296] vivification
[EN297] in desperate straits

conducted it so radically. In some of his disciples the matter was pressed almost to the point of becoming a triumph for the publican and sinner, who almost jubilantly flaunts his self-consciousness as such and looks down on the poor pietists and others. This would never have happened, and the attack itself would have been more serious and lasting in its effects, if Kohlbrügge had been in a position to offset his exposition of *mortificatio*[EN298] by a no less (and even more) powerful exposition of the corresponding *vivificatio*[EN299]. Not, of course, in the form of "a depiction of Christian character" (Kreck, p. 102) and the like, which rather strangely he did attempt on one or two occasions, and rather pregnantly in the passage quoted above, but in the form of an exposition of the law of life under the rule of which a man finds himself when his own autonomy is irrevocably brought to an end. It is the power of this law which distinguished the attack from the mere assault of a half-despairing, half-complacent defeatism which it might easily seem to be as represented by Kohlbrügge. It is this power which makes it serious, effective and helpful, leading man to the humility of the genuine publican, not the arrogance of the false publican who is really in his own way a Pharisee. It is because and as God issues the command to proceed that He also issues the command to halt, and not conversely. He kills the old man by introducing the new, and not conversely. It is with His Yes to the man elected and loved and called by Him that He says No to his sinful existence, forcing him to recognise that we are always in the wrong before God.

This is what is obscured, or at any rate does not emerge clearly, in the discussions of both Calvin and Kohlbrügge, where the accent is placed on the other side. Both of them knew the superior place from which alone there can be conversion, and therefore a serious dispute with oneself. But both failed to allow its origin—in Jesus Christ—to speak for itself with sufficient force and clarity, and therefore to bring out the teleology of the dispute, i.e., the fact that *vivificatio*[EN300] is the meaning and intention of *mortificatio*[EN301].

We must now speak more specifically of the basis and origin of conversion, of man's awakening to it, and of the power which sets and keeps it in motion as his falling-out with himself. At the beginning of this discussion we described it as an axis which establishes itself in the life of man, or on which his life is established, so that he has to follow its movement in his own life and being, its turning automatically making his life a life in conversion. We called this dynamic principle the power of the reality that God is for him, and he for God, as this reveals itself to him and shows itself to be the truth. Some elucidations are now needed in respect of this centre of the problem. [578]

We must (1) abandon the figure of the axis with the magical or mechanical or automatic associations which it might conjure up, and call the thing intended by its proper name. When Paul speaks of a man led to conversion by the Spirit of God, it is not at all the case that he is betrayed into the sphere and influence of an overwhelming impulse with the alien movement of which he has to co-operate and by which he *nolens volens*[EN302] sets himself in totality under that twofold determination as an old and new man, and therefore in that dispute with himself. It is true, of course, that it is by the omnipotence of

---

[EN298] mortification
[EN299] vivification
[EN300] vivification
[EN301] mortification
[EN302] willing or not

God that he is awakened to conversion and set in this movement. But the omnipotence of God is not a force which works magically or mechanically and in relation to which man can be only an object, an alien body which is either carried or impelled, like a spar of wood carried relentlessly downstream by a great river. It is a matter of God's omnipotent mercy, of His Holy Spirit, and therefore of man's liberation, and therefore of his conversion to being and action in the freedom which he is given by God. To be sure, there is a compulsion. He *must* pass from a well-known past to a future which is only just opening up, "to a land that I shall shew thee"; from himself to the old man to himself as a new man; from his own death to his own true life. There is necessarily a compulsion. No question of a choice can enter in. He is not merely set in, i.e., before a decision. He makes the decision, looking neither to the right hand nor to the left, nor especially behind. But the compulsion is not a mere compulsion. It is not abstract. It is not blind or deaf. We have to realise that a mere compulsion is basically evil and demonic. The compulsion obeyed in conversion is not of this type. It is the compulsion of a permission and ability which have been granted. It is that of the free man who as such can only exercise his freedom. The omnipotence of God creates and effects in the man awakened to conversion a true ability. He who previously vegetated to death under a hellish compulsion, in a true comparison with the driftwood carried downstream, may now live wholly of himself and be a man. The coming, the opening up of this "may" is the revelation of the divine summons to halt and proceed; the power which makes his life life in conversion. Because and as he is given this permission and ability, he necessarily stands at this point. He *must* leave those things which are behind, and reach forth unto those things which are before, pressing toward the mark (Phil. $3^{13f.}$). It is for this that he is freed, [579] and free. In this freedom there has been taken from him once and for all any mere choosing or self-deciding. In the exercise of this freedom—still as the man he was, already as the man he will be—he fulfils his conversion.

Calvin was well aware of this (III, 3, 21): *singulare esse Dei donum poenitentiam*[EN303]. He rightly recalled that when the Christians in Jerusalem heard what Peter had to say in Ac. 11, "they glorified God, saying, Then hath God also to the Gentiles granted repentance unto life" ($\mu\epsilon\tau\acute{\alpha}\nu o\iota\alpha\nu$ $\epsilon\emph{i}s$ $\zeta\omega\acute{\eta}\nu$, v. 18); and 2 Tim. $2^{25f.}$, where Timothy is exhorted to instruct in meekness those that oppose themselves, hoping that God may give them "repentance to the acknowledging of the truth, and that they may recover themselves (lit. become sober) out of the snare of the devil, who are taken captive by him to do his will." He also observes with justice that it would be easier to create ourselves as men than *proprio marte*[EN304] to assume a new nature. But this is what is at issue in Eph. 2^{10}. We are created by God unto good works. *Quoscunque eripere vult Deus ab interitu, hos Spiritu regenerationis vivificat*[EN305]. Penitence is inseparably connected with the faithfulness and mercy of God. According to Is. 59^{20}, He is the Redeemer of Zion, who comes in and with conversion from transgression in Jacob. But if

---

[EN303] that repentance is the single gift of God
[EN304] by one's own exertion
[EN305] Whomsoever God wills to snatch from death, those he makes alive by the Spirit of regeneration

the case is as Calvin saw and stated it, it is hard to see why his penitential teaching as a whole could and should become that sombre picture in which the main features are the thunderings and lightnings of *mortificatio*[EN306]. On his own presuppositions, ought he not to have described *vivificatio*[EN307] as God's *opus proprium*[EN308], and *mortificatio*[EN309] only as its reverse side, God's *opus alienum*[EN310]? Why did he not do this? Who authorised him almost completely to conceal what is from its very basis and origin the clear and positive meaning and character of conversion as liberation by giving to *vivificatio*[EN311] only a minor position as the reverse side of *mortificatio*[EN312] (A. Göhler, *op. cit.*, p. 43)? Or who forbade him to understand the relationship as it is truly established by the basis and origin of the whole?

But as we enquire (2) concerning the specific character of the basis and origin of conversion, and therefore the particular nature of the awakening of man to it, we must take a step backwards. The dynamic principle of this movement is the truth, revealing itself to man, that God is for him, and that—in virtue of the fact that God is for him—he is for God. It is this truth which frees him for God, and therefore for that dispute with himself. It is this truth which kills and makes alive. Thus in its origin and basis, at the superior place where it is set in motion, the conversion of man is a decision of God for him which not only makes possible a corresponding decision of man for God, the free act of his obedience, but makes this act and obedience real, directly causing it to take place. If in this basis and origin the order were different, and the truth revealed to man were that man is for God, and therefore God for man, the truth would not make us free. It would simply be a demand that man should be what he is not free to be. It would then have nothing to do with *vivificatio*[EN313]. For how can the man who is against God become a new man merely by being asked to make a decision which is quite alien to him and to be for God? But it could also have nothing to do with *mortificatio*[EN314]. It might startle and frighten man, but it could not and would not in any way raise him out his existence as a sinner, or even affect this existence. It would simply be an abstract law—a law without any *locus*[EN315] in a life fulfilling and embodying it, [580] but merely advancing the arid claim that it is the law of God, and that as such it has the right to demand that man should be for God, and thus fulfil the condition under which God will also be for him. This abstract law has never yet led a man to conversion, even by killing him, let alone by making him alive. It has no power to do either. For it is not the living God, nor His quickening Spirit, who places man under this law. The revealed truth of the living God in His quickening Spirit has its content and force in the fact that it is He first who is for man,

---

EN306 mortification
EN307 vivification
EN308 proper work
EN309 mortification
EN310 alien work
EN311 vivification
EN312 mortification
EN313 vivification
EN314 mortification
EN315 place

and then and for that reason man is for Him. God precedes therefore, and sets man in the movement in which he follows. He says Yes to him when man says No, and thus silences the No of man and lays a Yes in his heart and on his lips. He loves man even though he is an enemy (Rom. 5¹⁰), and thus makes him the friend who loves Him in return. As it is revealed to man that this is how matters stand between him and God—and this is what is revealed to him by the Holy Spirit—he comes to have dealings with the living God and the quickening Spirit. He is awakened to conversion. He is plunged into the dispute with himself in which he dies as an old man and rises again as a new. In short, it is unequivocally and exclusively by the Gospel, the revealed grace of God, that conversion is effectively commanded as a radical termination and a radical recommencement. But effectively means as a gift of freedom, and therefore as the law of his own free act apart from which he has no freedom to choose any other. The law which he obeys has its *locus*[EN316] in his life as it is freed by the Gospel. As the "law of the Spirit of life" (Rom. 8²), it frees us, but in so doing it genuinely binds and engages us. It makes the divine summons to halt and advance quite unavoidable. It makes quite natural and self-evident the being in transition from what we still are to what we are already.

This brings us to the deep reason for the difficulty which we have in following Calvin's doctrine of penitence—for all our admiration for its many excellent features—and for the similar difficulty which we experience in relation to that of Kohlbrügge. Was it not Calvin himself who told us that conversion has its origin in faith (III, 3, 2), that no one can seriously repent unless he knows God, and no one can know God unless he has first laid hold of His grace, that the preaching of repentance by John as well as Jesus derives its weight from, and has to be understood in the light of, the approaching kingdom of God? If only we could keep him to his statement about *mortificatio*[EN317] and *vivificatio*[EN318] (3, 9): *utrumque ex Christi participatione nobis contingit*[EN319], or to the section (3, 19) where he returns to the same truth: *per evangelii doctrinam audiunt homines suas omnes cogitationes, suos affectus, sua studia corrupta et vitiosa esse!*[EN320] But we cannot do this. He certainly does state unequivocally that it is the free and liberating grace, goodness and mercy of God revealed in the Gospel, His mighty Yes to man, which leads man to the Yes to God and to life according to His promise, and therefore to a No to self and to his previous life. But this line is continually crossed by another which tells us (3, 7) that the fear of God, the thought of impending judgment, the dread of sin, the obligation to give God the glory which is owed, is the true *principium*[EN321], the *exordium poenitentiae*[EN322], and therefore that which leads us to the knowledge of Christ (3, 20). Is not this the very opposite of the earlier view? And unfortunately, in face of the striking overemphasis on *mortificatio*[EN323], we can hardly maintain that in practice it was the first view which shaped his understanding of penitence. Why did he so morosely argue that

[581]

[EN316] place
[EN317] mortification
[EN318] vivification
[EN319] that each comes to us through our participation in Christ
[EN320] through the teaching of the Gospel, men hear that all their thoughts, their feelings and their desires are corrupt and wicked!
[EN321] beginning
[EN322] outset of repentance
[EN323] mortification

vivificatio[EN324] is not to be regarded as a joy (*laetitia*), but consists rather in the *studium sancte pieque vivendi*[EN325]?—as though there were any necessary antithesis between the two, or as though this *studium*[EN326] could have any other origin than in a great joy, the joy of the one who has been made free for this zeal! Why does the chapter which had begun so finely by relating faith and repentance end in sections 22–25 with a rather irrelevant discussion of the threatening sin against the Holy Ghost, and finally with a grim reminder of king Ahab and similar examples of a hypocritical and therefore useless repentance? In so far as Calvin's teaching is shaped by these considerations, finding the *principium poenitentiae*[EN327] in fear of God and its primary fulfilment in *mortificatio*[EN328], and thus acquiring a predominantly sombre character, we can only say that, contrary to his own initial statements, he develops his doctrine in the light of a concept of law which cannot be regarded as identical with the "law of the Spirit of life" of Rom. 8². And it could easily be shown that the same is true of Kohlbrügge, who in this context (with similar results for his total view) made explicit use of the concept of the law which kills as that which initiates the movement of conversion. That conversion is really a liberation, and how this is the case, is something which does not emerge with adequate clarity either in Kohlbrügge or in Calvin. And how can it possibly do so if we do not see and say that it has its basis and origin in the Gospel, or if we do not take this fact with true seriousness?

Finally (3), we have to ask concerning the superior place itself and as such where it is a real fact, and can thus emerge as potent truth in the work of the Holy Spirit, that God is for man and man for God. Everything that we have so far said depends ultimately upon whether we can say that this is not a mere suspicion, or hypothesis, or construct, or axiom of philosophical metaphysics, or dogma of theology, but that it is really the case with unassailable objectivity. In other words, the event of revelation which has been our starting-point in all these discussions must be merely the manifestation of a real event which takes place with incontestable objectivity. It is in relation to this climax that—to look back for a moment from the point we have just reached—all our previous statements have been made: about the primacy of the Gospel in virtue of which the decisive work of that event of revelation is the new life, the *vivificatio*[EN329], of man; about the liberation imparted to him in it; about the force and depth and teleology of the dispute in which he fulfils this liberation; about the totality with which, awakened to repentance, he finds himself claimed and impelled. How do we know all these things? How is it that we can treat them as a reality, and interpret this reality only as has actually been the case? On what basis have we thought and spoken about the totality of conversion, and reached our detailed decisions, partly for and partly without and even against Calvin, by whom we have especially tried to orientate ourselves in this field?

[EN324] vivification
[EN325] desire to live in holiness and piety
[EN326] desire
[EN327] beginning of repentance
[EN328] mortification
[EN329] vivification

[582]

The answer is quite simple. We have merely taken seriously what Calvin called the *participatio Christi*[EN330], making it the ultimate foundation of his whole doctrine of sanctification. The actual event which is an event of revelation in virtue of the enlightening work of the Holy Spirit, and as such sets in motion the conversion of man, is the Christ-event. Jesus Christ is the climax, the superior place, where it is properly and primarily and comprehensively real, where it originally takes place, that God (*vere Deus*[EN331]) is for man, and man (*vere homo*[EN332]) is for God. If the conversion of man is the movement which is initiated and maintained from the point where this is primarily and comprehensively real, this is only to say that it has its basis and origin in this climax, in Jesus Christ.

We ask how it may really come about that the divine summons to halt and advance breaks into the life of man, our life. And the answer is simply that when it comes about, then in the power of the Holy Spirit it is in virtue of the one man who is like us and near us as our Brother, but unlike and quite above us as our Lord, seeing that He has not merely received this summons to halt and advance primarily and properly and directly from God, but has properly and immediately and perfectly fulfilled it as a man, accomplishing it in the act of His own life and death. He, and in the strict sense He alone, is the One who hears and does what God summons us to do with His call to halt and advance.

We ask where and when there has taken place, takes place and will take place, as an actual event, this movement of man in the totality and with the radical dispute in which the old man dies and the new arises, this liberation by God's free grace. And the answer is simply that in the strict sense it is an actual event only in Him, in His life, in His obedience as the true Son of God and true Son of Man. In Him it is an event which is effective and valid for many in the power of the truth of the Holy Spirit. But properly it is an event only in Him.

We ask who is the man of whom we have spoken continually as one who is engaged in conversion. And the answer is simply that in the true sense it is He alone. It is not He without those to whom He is revealed as such in the power of the Holy Spirit. It is He as their Head. But it is He, and He alone, as the origin and basis of the conversion of the many.

Let us be honest. If we relate to ourselves, to you and me, to this or that Christian (even the best), that which is said about the conversion of man in the New Testament, and which we have to say with the New Testament, it will have the inevitable smack of hyperbole and even illusion—and the more so the more we try to introduce it, either by way of analysis or assertion, in the form of statements about the psychico-physical conditions or impulses or experiences of individual Christians or Christians generally, or in the form of general or

---

[EN330] participation in Christ
[EN331] truly God
[EN332] truly man

specialised pictures of the Christian life. What are we with our little conversion, our little repentance and reviving, our little ending and new beginning, our changed lives, whether we experience them in the wilderness, or the cloister, or at the very least at Caux? How feeble is the relationship, even in the best of cases, between the great categories in which the conversion of man is described in the New Testament and the corresponding event in our own inner and outer life! How can we say, in relation to our own persons or those of others, that we or these others have come out of darkness into light, that we have passed from death to life, that the old man has died and the new is risen, that we are in a state of *mortificatio*^{EN333} and *vivificatio*^{EN334}, or merely that we are converted or in the process of being converted? If all this is to be referred directly to ourselves, are we not condemned to vacillate between a heaven-soaring spiritual optimism and a mortally despairing spiritual pessimism (both perhaps in the astonishingly exaggerated form in which they meet us in the thought of Kohlbrügge), and therefore between legalism under the banner of the one and libertinism under that of the other?

[583]

But everything is simple, true and clear when these statements are referred directly to Jesus Christ, and only indirectly, as fulfilled and effectively realised in Him for us, to ourselves. It is to be noted that they are indirectly, and therefore genuinely, to be referred to us: in virtue of the fact that He is the Head and we the members; in virtue of our being in and with Him; in virtue of the fact that by His Holy Spirit He has clothed us with that which properly He alone is and has; in virtue of the fact that He allows us to have a share in that which belongs to Him. What more do we want? We should have much less, indeed nothing at all, if we tried to demand and seize more. It is in His conversion that we are engaged. It is in His birth, from above, the mystery and miracle of Christmas, that we are born again. It is in His baptism in Jordan that we are baptised with the Holy Ghost and with fire. It is in His death on the cross that we are dead as old men, and in His resurrection in the garden of Joseph of Arimathea that we are risen as new men. Who of us then, in relation to our own conversion or that of others, can seriously know any other terminus for this event than the day of Golgotha, in which He accomplished in our place and for us all the turning and transforming of the human situation, and as He did so was crowned as the royal man He was, our Lord? It is because this is the case, because everything is actual and true in the light of this climax, that the awakening to repentance is the power of the Gospel, a liberation, and that it has the force and depth and teleology which are proper to it, and claims man in his totality.

What remains, then, for us? Jesus Christ remains, and in and with Him everything, in and with Him the whole reality and truth that God is for us and

---

^{EN333} mortification
^{EN334} vivification

[584]

we for God, and therefore the whole power of our conversion. And the knowledge of faith remains, that He is the man in whose existence all this is true, and that the movement fulfilled in Him is therefore really ours. And there then remain the little movements of our own inner and outer life, our hearts and hands, which we have to make and judge modestly and soberly, of which we have not to boast, in which the great critical and positive movement which He has made for us and with us must and will be reflected, but in which we can only attest this (in the measure of seriousness and fidelity which we are given and which we have to exercise). It remains for us to know that in the whole capacity of our Christian existence we are borne by the great movement which He has fulfilled, and which far transcends all the measures of our movements; and therefore as those who are His to love Him as the One who is ours—always and wholly and exclusively in response to the fact that He has first loved us.

5. THE PRAISE OF WORKS

Works are primarily the acts and fruits of human operation in contrast to the processes and products of organic nature. The term thus refers to history in the strict sense. As man exists as such, he works. His life is a sequence of conscious or unconscious, greater or smaller, important or less important, imposing or negligible works. And where can we define with any certainty or precision even the limits indicated by these distinctions, let alone say that the sequence of his works is ever broken? "Oh may the soul do good e'en as we slumber!" To our works there also belong, of course, the things we refrain from doing, with all the consequences involved. The sequence of works in which our lives consist can and will be broken only with our death. In the present context we are speaking of the life, and therefore of the works, of Christians according to our previous statements; of those who are sanctified in the Holy One, called to His discipleship, and awakened by Him to conversion.

There is a praise of their works—and this will be the theme of our fifth and shorter sub-section. We use the term "praise" in the general sense of affirmation, acknowledgment, approval and applause. In relation to the works of Christians, the praise of these works necessarily refers in some sense to their particular relationship to God, or concretely to Jesus Christ, who as the true Son of God and Son of Man is their Lord and Head, to whom they belong, and by whom they and the works are measured. In this context the "praise" of works can have a twofold meaning. It can mean (1) that God praises them, affirming and acknowledging and approving them; and it can mean (2) that their works praise God, affirming and acknowledging and approving Him.

For a New Testament illustration of the first sense of "praise" we may think of the conclu-

5. *The Praise of Works*

sion of I Cor. 4⁵, where, in relation to the judgment which he also may personally expect at the hands of God, Paul says: τότε ὁ ἔπαινος γενήσεται ἑκάστῳ ἀπὸ τοῦ θεοῦ—"then shall every man have praise of God." An example of the second sense is to be found in Eph. 1¹², [585] where it is said of Christians that they are elected and called and ordained of God εἰς τὸ εἶναι ἡμᾶς εἰς ἔπαινον δόξης αὐτοῦ, "that they should be to the praise of his glory." Both passages envisage only that the Christian with his action and its fruits will either receive praise from God, or be to God's praise. This is the more striking in 1 Cor. 4⁵ because in this verse the context is that of future judgment. It might have been expected that Paul would speak of receiving praise or blame. But it seems to be taken as axiomatic that we have all to expect only praise. And in Eph. 1¹² the possibility is never even considered that the works of Christians might serve the very opposite of the praise of God.

If we are to speak of the praise of works, we have to keep this twofold use of the term constantly before us. The two meanings converge in the fact that the works to which they refer are obviously good works. If they were not good—in a sense still to be fixed—they would not be praised by God, nor praise Him. If He praises them, this includes the fact that He finds pleasure in them as good works. And if they praise Him, this includes the fact that as good works they are adapted and able to do this. We might well have given to this sub-section the more usual but hotly debated title "Good Works." We prefer "The Praise of Works" because (in this twofold sense) it at once tells us something definite and even decisive concerning what constitutes the goodness of works: that God can and will and actually does praise them; and that they for their part can and may and actually do praise Him.

We may begin by saying in a very general way, and without detailed elucidation, that it is obligatory that Christians should do good works in this twofold sense. They cannot be Christians, and belong to Jesus Christ as their Lord and Head, to no purpose. If they are sanctified in Him, and called to His discipleship, and awakened to conversion, and engaged in conversion under His powerful rule, and if they are all these things in their lives and therefore in the sequence of their works, inevitably there will be in their works some element of the praise of God (in this twofold sense), and therefore of goodness. Otherwise the whole event of reconciliation, to the extent that it consists also in the conversion of man to God and therefore in his sanctification, would be quite futile. It would be in vain that the true Son of God became the true and royal man among all others, their living Lord. And we would have to add that the event of reconciliation would be futile even as God's gracious turning to man, even as the justification of man before Him; and that it would be all for nothing that even as true God Jesus Christ had taken our place and given Himself up for our sins. If there are no human works which are praised by God, and praise Him in return, and are thus good, in what sense can we speak of a real alteration of the human situation effected in the death of Jesus Christ and revealed in the power of His resurrection by the Holy Spirit? And how can our attestation of it fail to be pointless and empty?

But we may dismiss this hypothesis. The scriptural testimony to the great acts [586] of God includes the witness to what has come and comes and will come to men in and with these acts of God. And to this clearly attested work there undoubtedly belongs also the existence of men who do in fact do good works (whatever we mean by this); who do works in which God takes pleasure, which have therefore a share in His praise and which also serve to praise Him. It is the case according to the Old and New Testament that words are not only required of specific men but spoken by them, that acts are not only demanded but achieved, that attitudes are not only expected but adopted: words and acts and attitudes which God can affirm, which for their part indicate an affirmation of God, and in which the turning of man to God takes place no less than the turning of God to man; good works which as such are clearly and sharply distinguished from other words and acts and attitudes as bad works.

It is also the case according to the Old and New Testaments that a reward is promised for these works. The concept is eschatological, and we cannot discuss it in this context. We mention it only to emphasise the definiteness with which Scripture counts on the occurrence of good works.

The divine judgment on all men is very sharply formulated in the Bible—that all are sinners (even and especially the saints). The absolute dependence of all on the free grace of God is unconditionally recalled. Yet while this is the case, what man does and does not do is never described, either in a recognition of the universal sinfulness of man or an acknowledgment of the sovereign mercy of God, as a night which makes all things dark. Just because God alone is righteous and holy, not remotely but in His acts among and to men, there are also righteous and unrighteous, holy and unholy men, goodness and evil, good works and bad, in the life of each individual man (including the holy and righteous). We have dealt with the evil works of men in the previous section. Our present concern is with their sanctification. We are thus concerned with the fact that there are also good works—good because they are praised by God and done to His praise. If we are to accept the witness of Scripture, we cannot ignore this, let alone deny it. Scripture not only trusts the God of the covenant, Jesus Christ and the Holy Spirit, that this will be the case. It attests it as a reality within its witness to God the Father, Son and Holy Spirit and His works. This must be our starting-point.

In all that we say (following the example of the Epistle of James) we presuppose the Pauline and Reformation doctrine of justification by faith alone without the works of the Law, as already understood and developed in *C.D.* IV, 1, § 61. This gives rise to certain delimitations which we have consciously to bear in mind.

No works, however good (even the best), have the power to justify before God the man who does them; to reinstate him in the right to exist before Him which he has forfeited, and continually forfeits, as a sinner; to make him a child of God; to earn for him the promise of eternal life. Works which we may try to do with this intention and claim are as such works of an unbroken pride, and are not therefore good works but bad. Man can be righteous before God, the child of God and heir of eternal life, only by the pardon which he can grasp in faith alone and not in any work, and which is that of the grace of the God active and revealed in Jesus Christ—a grace which consists in the unmerited forgiveness of sins.

It thus follows that there is no man—even the doer of good (or the best) works, even the most saintly—who does not stand in lifelong need of the forgiveness of sins and therefore of that pardon, and is not referred wholly and utterly to the faith which grasps that pardon. "The truth is that we are beggars" (Luther).

It follows further that because man exists in the sequence of his works, each of his works, as well as he himself, stands in need, as the work of a sinner, of justification, and therefore of forgiveness, and therefore of the unmerited recognition of God. His boast, as the man who does it, is grounded only in the free grace of God turned to Him—a grace which can be related only in faith to man and his works and acts and the fruits of his acts. Any other glory ascribed to himself or his works immediately disqualifies the latter as bad works, even though they may be the best.

Finally, since it is only in faith and not by direct perception or appropriation that we can seize our righteousness and that of our works (as the forgiveness of our sins, even of those which we commit in the best of our works), the final word concerning our right and wrong, and that of our works, is reserved for the universal and definitive revelation of the judgment of God—a revelation which we now await but in which we do not yet participate. "For we must all appear before the judgment seat of Christ; that every one may receive the things done in his body, according to that he hath done, whether it be good or bad" (2 Cor. 5^{10}). Our only confidence and peace in face of this reservation is "that I expect the Judge who has exposed Himself for me to the judgment of God, and taken away all the curse from me" (*Heid. Cat. Qu.* 52). Yet we walk by faith, not by sight, even in respect of our certain knowledge of the pardoning sentence of this Judge.

All this is behind us as we now go on to speak of good works. This does not mean that it is forgotten or set aside. On the contrary, it is the frontier which we cannot cross again. It is the ground which we must always have beneath us if we are to read securely. Yet it is a frontier from which we may now move away, so that it need not cramp or confuse us. It is the ground on which we may securely advance. Our question does not relate to good works in general but to the good works of the Christian, and therefore to works which can be seriously called good on the presupposition of justification by faith alone. As a special form of the question of the sanctification of man, this question has to be recognised in its own right, and put and answered, in view of the fact that Scripture so blatantly counts on the existence of good works.

It is a step forward if we note that in the Bible the concept of work or works is applied in the first instance, and decisively for all that follows, to the acts of God and their consequences. Primarily it is God who is at work. And this shows us what is meant by the fact that man is also at work. But the works of God are good. It is said primarily and properly of God Himself that "He saw everything that He had made, and, behold, it was very good" (Gen. 1^{31}). And primarily and properly it is His works which praise their Master. If there are human works of which this can be said, we have to seek them in the context of the work or works of God.

That this is no mere surmise is proved by the fact that according to the witness of Scripture the work of God stands in a primary and basic relationship to man. It is, of course, a work which embraces all creation, heaven and earth and all that therein is. But it binds it together. It directs it to a specific goal— His covenant with man, His own glory in this covenant and the salvation of man. It is His work in the history of this covenant, in which the history of the

[588]

209

whole cosmos participates, and which constitutes the meaning and true content of the history of the whole cosmos. As creation, according to Gen. 1, is the outward basis of this covenant, and this covenant the inward basis of creation, there begins at once in and with creation the history of this covenant, and therefore the proper work of God to which all His other works are subordinate. This history, and therefore the proper work of God, emerges with the election, calling, preservation and over-ruling of the people Israel, in which, according to the witness of the Old Testament, there is heralded the actualisation of the glory of God and the salvation of man. It attains its goal in the fact that God Himself becomes man and as such performs that which is promised, actualising His own glory and man's salvation. That this has taken place in Jesus Christ, that all human history and that of the whole cosmos can only hasten to the direct and universal and definitive revelation of this completed work of God, is what the community which has derived from Israel in its Lord and Head now has to proclaim, according to the witness of the New Testament, in the last time which is still left to itself and the world. This happening in its totality, beginning with creation, proceeding by way of the reconciliation resolved and accomplished in Jesus Christ, and culminating in the redemption awaited with its manifestation; this history of the covenant is the work of God which all His other works serve and to which they are subordinate. It is the good work of God. He proves Himself to be good by nature, and therefore the source and norm of all goodness, by the fact that this is His work and therefore His will. It is the will of His goodness which is here at work. God ordains that in all His holiness, righteousness and wisdom, in all His omnipresence, omnipotence and glory, He Himself should be active in this work which has man as its aim and goal. He did not need to do so. He does not do it for Himself. He gives Himself up to it. In this work He is good in Himself only as He is good to man, actualising His own glory only with man's salvation. He has to do with man in this work. He has turned wholly to man. He has even given Himself up to him. In a relentless compromising of His own case, He has addressed Himself wholly to the cause of man.

[589]

We have first to consider again the work, the act and acts of God as the Lord of His covenant with man; and Jesus Christ as the One who completes this work. "Come, behold the works of the Lord, what astounding things he hath done in the earth" (Ps. 46⁸). Or, as a summons to the whole earth: "Come and see the works of God: he is terrible in his doing toward the children of men" (Ps. 66⁵). The complaint lodged against the careless in Jerusalem (Is. 5¹²) is that "they regard not the work of the Lord, neither consider the operation of his hands." There can, of course, be no question, as we are told in Eccles. 8¹⁶⁻¹⁷, of fathoming and understanding and explaining this work in its totality, in relation to everything that takes place under the sun by day or by night. But it may be known—it makes itself known—at its heart and centre, as the history of the covenant of grace. "The works of his hand are verity and judgment; all his commandments are sure. They stand fast for ever and ever, and are done in truth and uprightness. He sent redemption unto his people: he hath commanded his covenant for ever: holy and reverend is his name" (Ps. 111⁷ᶠ·). It is of this heart and centre of God's work, and therefore of the true and proper work of God, that Jesus speaks

5. The Praise of Works

according to the Johannine saying (Jn. 5^{17}): "My Father worketh hitherto, and I work," doing the work of my Father (Jn. 10^{37}), and He Himself working as He dwells in me (Jn. 14^{10}). The meat of Jesus—His very life—is to do the will of Him that sent Him, "and to finish his work" (Jn. 4^{34}). According to Jn. 17^1 He had already finished it, thus glorifying on earth the One who sent Him. The divine work in question is the actualisation of the covenant between God and man, the achievement of reconciliation, as heralded in Israel and proclaimed by the community. We must start with this as the completed good work of God if we are to see what is the possibility and actuality of good works on the part of man.

If there are good works on the part of man—and the Bible says that there are—we can state (without defining the matter more closely) that it is only in relation to this good work of God. What man does and achieves is thus in some sense bright and powerful in the light and power of what God does and achieves. The distinction of a human work is to declare the occurrence of the good work of God. A human work can do this, because God in His work always has to do with men and what He does does not take place at a distance from men, but among them. From first to last it is God's history with men and among them. Why, then, should it not be declared and, as it were, reflected in a human work? The works of the man Jesus show that human works are capable of doing this. The inner quality of man, not only by man's judgment but God's, is another question the answer to which is not decisive for the present question whether there can be a good human work which declares the good work of God. The man Jesus did the good works of His Father as He lived and died in our stead, in the place of sinners, in the flesh, in our character. We conclude that even a sinful man in his sinful work—and we are all sinners and all our works are sinful—may declare the good work of God, and therefore, even as a sinner and in the course of sinning, do a good work.

"I shall not die, but live, and declare the works of the Lord. The Lord hath chastened me sore: but he hath not given me over unto death" (Ps. 118$^{17f.}$). The people are chastened—the reference seems to be to Israel chastened for its sins—but even as such they are rescued from the death they have deserved, and may live, in order that they may proclaim the works of the Lord. The Lord is their strength and song, and has become their salvation, they have been told (v. 14). And so they are those who according to Ps. 107^{31} "praise the Lord for his goodness, and for his wonderful works to the children of men"; who have seen His wonders in the deep and whose soul melted because of trouble: "They reel to and fro, and stagger like a drunken man, and are at their wits' end" (v. 24 f.). And so we may but should not be surprised that after Paul has had to bring so many warnings and accusations against the Corinthians he can finally address to them the supremely natural summons: "Therefore, my beloved brethren, be ye stedfast, unmovable, always abounding in the work of the Lord" (1 Cor. 15^{58}); and then again: "Watch ye, stand fast in the faith, quit you like men, be strong" (16^{13}). Even in relation to the Corinthians the ground of the work of the Lord and faith in it is obviously assumed to be strong enough to bear this curious people, so that Paul has only to summon them to stand fast on it and they will be a strong and manly people always abounding in God's work. There is absolutely no question of any work of their own, but only of what the ἔργον τοῦ κυρίου^{EN335} may do concerning them, and of their own capacity for it as

[590]

EN335 work of the Lord

granted by this work. We may appeal in elucidation to Tit. 2^{14}, where it is said of Jesus Christ that He gave Himself for us to purify for Himself a people for His own possession, zealous of good works. Whatever else it may mean for a people, the completed work of the Lord can cleanse it, thus making it a people which in spite of its sin may be used in His service.

It is evident that there can be no question of any meritoriousness of works, or of any glory in their achievement which can either be claimed by or ascribed to the one who performs them. This is equally the case even when we are dealing with the less sinful and to that extent better works of someone who is not so notoriously a sinner. Works can be good only as they declare what God has done and accomplished—the goodness in which He has turned to man and given Himself for him. That works are capable of this declaration does not alter the fact that they are the sinful works of great or little sinners. It is with such men and their works that God has to do in His good work. If He is good to them, why should they not be able to declare His goodness as the men they are?—not, of course, with a capacity that they have brought, but because there is something to declare, i.e., because the good work of God takes place, God being good to men (to these men who with their corresponding works are not good), turning to them and interposing and offering Himself up for them. It is only in this context and relationship that there can be, and are, good works on the part of men. All the works which are called good and described as good in the Bible take place in this context. Their goodness comes down from above into the human depths. It is imparted to them from above. And in the human depths it can only magnify the majesty of God to which it originally and properly belongs.

Only that which comes down from above, from the divine work of the fulfilled covenant, of completed reconciliation, into the human depths, is according to Jas. 1^{17} "a good and perfect gift." There can be no good human work unless it has this divine work as its basis and source. Bad works—those which Eph. 5^{11} calls "unfruitful" and Heb. 6^1 and 9^{14} "dead" (which may include a dead faith, Jas. $2^{17f.}$)—are simply works which do not have this divine work as their basis and origin. They are blind mirrors which do not reflect or declare the work of God. They do not in fact take place, as they might, in this context and relationship. Conversely, the good action demanded by God in the Law—action on the way continually proposed to Israel especially in the Book of Deuteronomy —is simply action which takes place in relationship to the work of *Yahweh* and corresponds to the grace of His covenant. Without this, and without recognising it, Israel could not even choose let alone perform this action. If it does choose and perform it, if it does works which are described as good and demanded by the Law, it does not do anything extraordinary but simply declares in its own works the work of the God who is gracious to it, confessing that it is His work and possession: "It is he that hath made us, and not we ourselves; we are his people, and the sheep of his pasture" (Ps. 100^3). Is there any trace here of a meritoriousness of its action? What can this people earn that has not been given already as a work of the hands of God? Is there any trace of glory in achievement? How can they glory when they do only the good works which are expected and with which they can only declare that which they are by the goodness of God? "When ye shall have done all those things which are commanded you, say, We are unprofitable servants: we have done that which was our duty to do" (Lk. 17^{10}). Why is the Law of God so glorious as described in Ps. 119? Certainly not because it shows Israel, and sets in its hand,

[591]

212

an instrument to make God gracious, and to assure itself by its own corresponding achievements of His faithfulness and assistance. The glory of the Law is that it gives Israel a direction
which it gladly hears and obeys because, as it is continually given, it is continually aware that
the power and mercy of God are already present, and that it knows already, and increasingly.
His faithfulness and assistance. Where the will and command of God are not understood as a
demonstration of His free goodness and favour to man, but as a demand the fulfilment of
which is the condition on which God's goodness and favour will be addressed to Him, or on
which he may direct them to himself; where, then, man believes that he must earn merit and
achieve self-glory in his relationship with God, there can be no question of true obedience
or good works. He does not do that which he ought to do. Everything that he does is perverted from the very first. And according to the witness of the Old Testament it was the sin of
Israel, as of all nations, not to recognise the grace of God, and therefore not to be capable of
obedience, but only of bad, unfruitful and dead works. It is not insignificant that in these
circumstances it continually turned to the gods of the surrounding nations. Only for very
brief periods was Israel grateful to God, and therefore self-evidently faithful and promptly
obedient. For the most part it was only in the life and words and works of individuals, of the
prophetic men of the remnant, that the relationship between divine and human goodness
was kept alive and maintained as a witness to the rest of the people as they continually fell
into fresh transgression. In their protest against Israel's transgression they merely announced the fulfilment of the good work of God, and therefore the actualisation of good human
works, which had been from the very first the goal of *Yahweh's* covenant with Israel. The
witness of the New Testament proclaims the fulfilment of the good work of God and the
actualisation of good human works as the message concerning Jesus Christ and the summons to faith in Him. It regards Himself, and faith in Him, as the right way which has already
been chosen for us men; the way on which we already find ourselves in Him: "For by grace
are ye saved through faith; and that not of yourselves; it is the gift of God; not of works lest
any man should boast. For we are his workmanship ($\pi o i\eta\mu a$), created ($\kappa\tau\iota\sigma\theta\acute{\epsilon}\nu\tau\epsilon\varsigma$) in Christ
Jesus unto good works, which God hath before ordained that we should walk in them" (Eph.
$2^{8f.}$).

We have now established that it is the good work of God which alone makes
possible the good works of man. But the good work of God itself assumes
always a special form as good works are done by man, and man's work declares
the good work of God. What is meant by "declare" but to participate in the
annunciation of the history of the covenant in the New Testament or its proclamation in the New, and, therefore, because this history is the work of God, in
the attestation of this work? But even if our work has a part only in its attestation, in so far as this is possible for a human work it has a part in the divine
work itself. It takes place in its service. And it is as it is done in its service that it
is a good work. It is not self-evident that a man should really stand in the service of the good work of God, or that his own work should really be done in
this service. It is not at all the case that all the works of all men are the work of
God simply because it is done among them, and that they thus declare it and
take place in its service and are therefore good works. Since all men are sinners and their works sinful, is it not more reasonable to suppose that there can
never be any declaration of the work of God by human works, that it cannot be
said of any human work that it takes place in the service of God's work and
therefore as a good work? We do not need to be particularly pessimistic to

[592]

come to this melancholy conclusion. We might say that it is shaped by the common rule which is broken when good works do in fact take place. But the rule is not broken from below by better sinners and their less sinful works. Even the best man cannot place himself and his work in the service of the work of God, or make his work a declaration of God's work and therefore a good work. When this takes place, it is obviously because God's own work assumes a special form. This work itself—and it is of this that the Old and New Testaments speak when they speak of good human works—takes place in a very special way to particular men, declaring and indicating and attesting and making itself known to them, and in so doing impressing them into its service, empowering them for it, giving them a willingness and readiness to take part themselves in its declaration. We can put it in this way. The work of God which has taken place *for* them as for all men also takes place *in* them in the form of this illumination, with the result that as the men they are they have a share in it—only as its witnesses, but as such a real share. The history of the covenant, whose acting Subject is God, now takes place in its relationship to them in such a way that their personal history, whose subjects they themselves are, can no longer be alien or neutral in its relationship to it, but necessarily takes place in actual correspondence with it. To the extent that this is the case, they and their works are declarations of the work of God, having a part both in the annunciation of Jesus Christ in the Old Testament and His proclamation in the New, and thus being good works. It is to be noted that the men in relationship to whom the good work of God has this particular form are sinners like the rest—possibly to a less degree, possibly to a greater, but still sinners. They are not differentiated from others by the fact that they are not transgressors in the judgment of God, or that even their good works are not full of transgression.

[593] They are differentiated only (but genuinely) by the fact—and here we return to the controlling concepts of the previous sub-sections—that they are sanctified in and by the Holy One; that they are called to His discipleship; that they are awakened to conversion by His Holy Spirit; and that they are engaged in conversion. To the extent that they are this, and exist as such, their works are taken into service by God and are good works, quite irrespective of what they might be apart from this relationship in the eyes of men and above all in the eyes of God, and quite irrespective of the fact that even as good works they are full of transgression. What these men do as those who are in Jesus Christ, and in love to Him, and correspondence with the work of God, is well done.

According to the Old and New Testaments it is an absolutely new and astounding fact that a man may be a co-worker (συνεργός) with God (1 Cor. 3⁹), and that his works, as an attestation of the work of God, may stand under the promise of being well done and therefore good works. Of none of us is this the case by nature. And none of us can take it upon himself. If it is true of us, it is true only on the basis of a special attitude of God within the covenant between Himself and man. It is true only as we are elected by God for His service, and called out to the side of God, quite apart from any fitness or value of our own. From us as such good works are expected. As such we can and should and may and will do them. We ourselves! For our calling is to obedience, to our own free action as the men we are. Our good works can and should and may and will be our very own. Hence the saying of Jesus to His disciples in Mt. 5$^{16f.}$: "Let your light so shine before men that they may see your good works, and glorify your Father which is in heaven." But the fact that they have or are this light—"ye are the light of the world," "a city that is set on a hill," the candle which is not "put under a bushel, but on a candlestick"—is not something that they have snatched or resolved of themselves, but something that they have become in virtue of His calling. It is in the power of this calling that their works are good works even as their own. It is as *Yahweh* stretches out His hand, and touches a man's lips, and puts His words in his mouth, and sets him here and now over the nations and kingdoms, that already in the Old Testament (Jer. 1$^{9f.}$) the prophet becomes the man he is—the one whom *Yahweh* has chosen for this work even before he was fashioned in the womb (Jer. 1^5). And it is in exactly the same way that the New Testament apostle (Gal. 1^{15}) understands his existence and his freedom to speak and work. The people of God works out its salvation in a certain willing and doing, but it does so because God is the One who works (ὁ ἐνεργῶν) His own willing and doing (Phil. 2$^{12f.}$). Paul speaks, but he "will not dare to speak of any of the things that Christ has not wrought by him to make the Gentiles obedient, by word and deed" (Rom. 15^{18}). He hastens to apprehend (Phil. 3^{12}), but he does so only as he is already apprehended by Christ. He works and fights according to His working (ἐνέργεια) which works in him mightily (Col. 1^{29}). It is true also of other believers that the word spoken to them "worketh effectually" in them (1 Thess. 2^{13}). "What hast thou that thou didst not receive?" (1 Cor. 4^7). Where men are active in the community as awakened and endowed by the Spirit, it is God "which worketh all in all" (1 Cor. 12^6). And not in spite of this fact, but because of it, they are all engaged in the full and manifold activity which can only praise Him, and which can be good only as it declares His work. In all this God is the δυνάμενος, the One who empowers (Eph. 3^{20}). He is this in His power which works in us (δύναμις ἐνεργουμένη ἐν ἡμῖν) impelling us to action. This power which works in us far exceeds anything that we can ask or think. How, then, can we fail to trust it, or trust it only to a limited degree, in our own action? When we do trust it we can only affirm: "Unto *him* be glory in the church and in Christ Jesus." A good work as Scripture understands it is one which is set in motion by Him, which finds itself in this motion, and which understands and demonstrates that this is the case. [594]

We can now repeat with greater emphasis our previous statement that it is in the particular goodness of the work of God that a man may participate with his own good works. It is God's free gift if he finds that he and his life-history are set in this distinctive relationship with the history of the covenant, and impressed into the service of the work of God and used to declare it. And in each individual instance of working it is again God's free gift if His work is a real declaration of God's work, and in the performance of it he may genuinely share in the annunciation or proclamation of Jesus Christ. As he cannot make himself one of the particular men of whom this is true, he cannot assume that any specific work really takes place in this correspondence, in the light and power of the divine work, and therefore that it is well done. He can only believe in the grace of God encountering and and revealed to him. Even when he is supremely enlightened and filled and impelled by it, he can only be thankful that—as it is not hidden but revealed—it has come to him in this particular way. He can only pray that God will not hide His face or let him fall, as he must recognise each passing moment that he has deserved a hundred times. He can only dare to make use of the freedom given; to keep before him, in all that he does, the fact that both in the totality and in specific works he may and must be thankful. He will then act calmly and resolutely and vigorously, but always knowing that he must lay himself and what he wills and does and achieves wholly in the hand of the God who has so graciously chosen and called him to participate in His work. He will constantly commend it to Him, that He may forgive that in which it is sinful, that He may receive it like himself, that He may sanctify it, that He may use it and order it, that He may give it the character of a service rendered and acceptable to Himself—which is something that can never be given by the man who performs it. None of the true saints of God can ever imagine that in his works he is really doing something outstanding in the sense of putting God under an obligation or earning His grace and favour. If he succeeds in restraining this foolish idea for a short time, or even inures himself to some extent against falling into it again, this is a sure criterion—though not a guarantee—that what he does is well done. He cannot create any such guarantee by his own humility of disposition in what he does. It can only be given by the God who elects and calls him, and grasped in faith. But in faith he can and may and will grasp it. And by the faith in which he does this, and the divine guarantee which he grasps in faith, there will be created the radical claimlessness, but also the calm and resolution and vigour, the free humour, which distinguish the work that is well done, the good work, fairly distinctly if not quite unequivocally from others. And he will do this work confidently. It will even be legitimate and possible for him to derive confidence, and the assurance of his freedom and therefore his holiness, from the fact that he lives cheerfully and gaily strides to work as one whom God has endowed with freedom.

[595]

He does it in the same way as a good tree (to use a favourite New Testament comparison) produces and bears good fruit. He does it as the work (Ac. 26^{20}) or fruit (Mt. 3^8) of his conversion, corresponding to its occurrence. He does it as the work of love (Heb. 6^{10}) or faith (1 Thess. 1^3; 2 Thess. 1^{11}). In Jn. 6$^{28f.}$ we have the extremely succinct answer of Jesus to those who asked Him: "What shall we do, that we might work the works of God (ἐργαζώμεθα τὰ ἔργα τοῦ θεοῦ)?" "This is the work of God, that ye believe on him whom he hath sent." Is there not included in this all human work in its relationship to the work of God? Similarly, there has always rightly been derived from the well-known negative formula of Rom. 14^{23}: "For whatsoever is not of faith is sin," the positive truth that what is of faith, and is the work of faith, is well done. But is it the work of faith? The fact that in the doing of good works we have to do with works of conversion, love and faith makes it clear that even in detail the doing of good works is not something which is subject to the caprice or control of man (even of the man who stands in sanctification); that the freedom for it has to be continually given even in detail. It is not the case, then, that God has begun something in and with him which he himself has now the authority and power to continue and complete. "He which hath begun a good work in you will perform it (ἐπιτελέσει) until the day of Jesus Christ" (Phil. 1^{16}). God is powerful enough (2 Cor. 9^8) to pour out the fulness of His grace on His own "that ye, always having all sufficiency (lit. autarchy) in all things, may abound to every good work." It is God, and He alone, who has the power to give them the freedom to do such works of themselves. As it is given by Him, it will constantly be expected and hoped and asked of Him. Paul presupposes in 2 Thess. 1^{11} that in the community we can count on the occurrence of the ἔργον πίστεως[EN336], and therefore, as we have seen, on an εὐδοκία ἀγαθωσύνης[EN337] (on the divine good-pleasure in the good which takes place). Yet this does not prevent but seems to cause him to pray for the fulfilment of this ἀγαθωσύνη[EN338] and ἔργον[EN339]—as though it were a vessel which had still to be filled—and therefore for the glorifying of the name of Jesus Christ in the community. According to 2 Thess. 2^{17}, the community needs to be "stablished in every good word and work." Prayer is also made that it should "be fruitful in every good work" (Col. 1^{10}) and "made perfect in every good work" (Heb. 13^{21}). For the necessary perfecting of the saints Christ has instituted apostles, prophets, evangelists, pastors and teachers (Eph. $4^{11f.}$). And according to 2 Tim. $3^{16f.}$ the saving power of the Scripture inspired by God is to be found in the fact that it sets the man of God in the right frame of mind (ἵνα ἄρτιος ᾖ[EN340]) in which to be "throughly furnished unto all good works."

If in all good works it is a matter of their participation in the good work of God, to which certain men are selected and brought by God Himself, and for which they are empowered by Him in specific actions, it necessarily follows that they are distinguished from all other human works by the fact that they are done as ordered and commanded by God, or to put it in another way, in the freedom given by God. In conjunction with the work of God, and in the service of its declaration, their works have a particular function. In the exercise of this function this particular man can and must and may and will on this [596] particular occasion say this or do that or take up this particular attitude. If he recognises and fulfils this function, his work is a good work. His speech and action and attitude are not according to his own inclination or desire or plan or caprice but according to the direction given to him and received by him. He hears this. And he obeys it, not mechanically impelled from without, but in the freedom which is given him; yet in this freedom and not another. In any other freedom he would really be a captive. He serves, not to his humiliation and shame, but to his exaltation and honour; yet only in the glory and dignity for which he is ordained as a participant in the work of God, and not therefore in any which he might fashion for himself (to his own true shame and humiliation) by serving himself or the opinion and plans of men or the dark forces of the cosmos and history. He is integrated into the communion of saints. With a particular place and commission he accompanies the people of God, the community. At his own place and time he is absolutely indispensable and responsible for the whole of its history. But he is this as a brother among brethren. And in this way he genuinely comes to himself and lives by his own faith. By this integration it may be recognised, and by integration in the doing of a particular work he himself may be assured, that all is well with his obedience and service and therefore his freedom; that the direction which he hears is not

---

[EN336] work of faith
[EN337] approval of the good
[EN338] good
[EN339] work
[EN340] so that you might be thoroughly prepared

secretly the voice of his own inclination or desire or plan or caprice. He will consider how the law and command and direction of God is received by others at other times and places. He will note the multiplicity which has characterised its declaration and reception in the history of the people of God as a whole. Thus, in order that he may hear the direction for himself here and now—the direction of God, and not that either of human tradition or his own heart or head—and to obey and serve this direction and not that of a collective or individual daemon, he will also listen to his brethren, and listen together with all or many of them, and then and on this basis exercise himself to obey. This is not because he does not trust the participation in the work of God granted to him, but because he knows that for all the particularity with which it applies to him it is granted to him only in his togetherness with them, as one of the fellowship of the saints. He will then go his own way all the more certain of his commission and all the more convinced of his freedom.

In this sense, and on all these presuppositions, we must say of man's sanctification that it already takes place here and now in works which are really good, i.e., which are praised by God and praise Him. We have had to consider rather more precisely, in the light of scriptural teaching, the way in which this happens (and does not happen). But the fact that it happens is something that we can deny only at the expense of questioning the whole divine act of atonement [597] and revelation and concealing a main aspect of the biblical witness, with serious effects upon all other aspects.

A single illustration will be enough to prove this. We surely cannot evade what is stated in the great passage Heb. 11. We need not develop this as a whole. It is sufficient to note that the chapter is dealing with faith as the confidence of things hoped for, the certainty of things not seen. But in the depiction of this faith we have to do at every point with human acts and attitudes—those of Abel and Enoch and Noah and Abraham and Isaac and Jacob and Moses and Rahab the harlot and others. Of all these it is said (v. 13) that "they died in faith, not having received the promises, but having seen them afar off, and were persuaded of them, and embraced them, and confessed that they were strangers and pilgrims on the earth." But it is also stated of them that—each in his own particular relationship to the great acts of God, and united to a great people by this common relationship—they worked actively and passively in obedience. Their acts are of great consequence in the context of that history, and they are thus depicted in rather extravagant terms. They "subdued kingdoms, wrought righteousness, obtained promises, stopped the mouths of lions, quenched the violence of fire, escaped the edge of the sword, out of weakness were made strong, turned to flight the armies of the aliens," some being praised for exploits which belong very characteristically to the Old Testament (v. 33 f.), others for their suffering and constancy in the most violent persecution (v. 35 f.). It is said of them—with reference to their faith, but to the works of their faith—that the world was not worthy of them (v. 38). The purpose behind this depiction emerges clearly in 12¹ᶠ. The New Testament community is as it were surrounded on all sides, and it is pledged and claimed—as by one mighty declaration and summons—by the existence and acts of these believers of God's former people. It cannot escape them. "Therefore, seeing we also are compassed about with so great a cloud of witnesses, let us lay aside every weight, and the sin that doth so easily beset us, and let us run with patience the race that is set before us, looking unto Jesus the author and finisher of our faith." It is Jesus who is obviously attested by this great cloud of witnesses. Being the end (τέλος) of the work of God, He is also the end of the Law of God (Rom. 10⁴). All these men with their works bore witness to Him; and it is to Him that Christians can and should and may and will bear witness with their works—their good works.

We conclude by saying that in addition to many bad there are also good thoughts and words and works. God in the doing of His work sees to it that this is the case. None of those to whom the work of God is revealed—no Christian—will doubt or contest this. He has no excuse, therefore, if his own work is not a good work. He will not try to hide the fact that he too, and he particularly, is elected and called and empowered to do good works. In accordance with his election and calling and empowering, he will do them as works of faith, conversion and love. They will certainly not praise himself or the Christian as the one who does them. But they will have the praise of God, and will praise Him. God gives it to His own that in all their sloth and corruption and disintegration they may and will do such works.

He sees to it that among His people (known only to Himself) there are genuine good works performed by its members. We may mention a few examples drawn from our own [598] observation (and well below the level of Heb. 11). There is the good assistance which one gives another. There is the good co-operation between few or many. There are good meetings and partings. There is the good attempting of big things and the good fulfilment of small. There is good conduct in difficult and testing conditions. There are good achievements in family and social life. There is the good upholding of the old and the good establishment of the new. There is good speaking and silence; good laughter and weeping; good work and repose; good seeking and finding. There are also good political resolves and decisions. There is good Christian profession. There is also good prayer, good hearing and reading and study, and sometimes good preaching—and all the other concrete things we might mention. In all these things, of course, it is not of him that willeth and runneth, but of God that sheweth mercy (Rom. 9¹⁶). But there is no point in trying to avoid the fact—we can do so only in unbelief—that these things do exist because God gives them, and in His mercy will continually give them. There is no time when the Christian should not count seriously on the fact that God gives them with the superfluity to which there are so many allusions in the Epistles. The sanctification of man decidedly consists also in the fact that God does give them, not merely in general but individually, and not magically or mechanically or when he is asleep, but for him to do. The saints of God receive and do them.

We will bring the discussion to a close by citing two questions and answers from the *Heidelberg Catechism* which are highly relevant in the present context.

Qu. 86. As we are redeemed from our plight by grace through Christ without any merits of our own, why should we do good works? *Answer*—Because Christ, having bought us by His blood, has also renewed us by His Holy Spirit, that we should show ourselves grateful to God for His benefits with our whole lives, and that He should be magnified through us. Also in order that we may have assurance of our faith from its fruits, and win our neighbours to Christ by our godly conversation.

And *Qu.* 91. But what are good works? *Answer*—Only those which of a true faith take place according to the Law of God and to His glory, and are not grounded in our own opinion or the evaluation of men.

6. THE DIGNITY OF THE CROSS

The cross—we have left to the last this indispensable element in any Christian doctrine of sanctification. It ought to be given this place (1) because it marks the limit of sanctification as the raising up of slothful man in the power of the resurrection of Jesus Christ—the point at which this event reaches out beyond itself to the second coming of Jesus Christ, the resurrection of the flesh and the Last Judgment, when the saints will be revealed as such, the contradiction will be ended between what they still are and what they are already, and they will enter into the eternal life, the light, to which as the people of God they are now moving with the whole cosmos. It ought also to be given this place (2) because under all the aspects so far considered—as *participatio Christi*[EN341], the call to discipleship, awakening to conversion and the praise of works—it is with reference to the cross that man's sanctification is seen to be his movement to that goal, and therefore set in the light of the great Christian hope.

[599]   It is at the corresponding place that the cross of the Christian is introduced in Calvin (*Instit.* III, 8) and A. de Quervain (*Die Heiligung* I, 1942, 151–221). D. Bonhoeffer has given it emphasis by speaking of it in the basic sections of *The Cost of Discipleship* already mentioned. On the other hand, it is striking that in Kohlbrügge's doctrine of sanctification (at any rate as presented by W. Kreck) the cross, while it is not ignored or uninfluential, is not given any very prominent position or role.

We refer to the cross which everyone who is sanctified in Jesus Christ, and therefore every Christian, has to bear as such, the people of God in the world being ordained to bear it. It is clear that this cross stands in the closest relationship to that of Jesus Christ Himself. The cross is the most concrete form of the fellowship between Christ and the Christian. As the bearing of the cross was and is for Jesus Christ His coronation as the one Son of Man, the royal man, so for the Christian the cross which he has to suffer is his investiture with the distinction, glory and dignity proper to him as a Christian. And this parallel has its basis in a material, historical connexion. Without the cross of Christ the Master there is no cross of the disciples, Christians. It is by the fact that He bore and suffered His cross that they are sanctified and called to discipleship and set in conversion and freed for the doing of good works. And it is by the same fact that they also come to bear and suffer their cross. It is on the basis of His exaltation in His death on the cross as the One who was rejected in our place that there takes place their elevation with its limit and goal in the fact that they too come to bear and suffer their cross.

According to all the synoptic accounts (Mk. 8[34f.] and par.) the declaration of Jesus that those who would be His disciples must deny themselves and take up the cross comes immediately after the Messianic confession of Peter and the first annunciation of the passion. Bonhoeffer is right when he lays his finger on the fact that in this annunciation as we have it in Mk. 8[31] and Lk. 9[22] express mention is made of His rejection by the elders and high-priests

---

[EN341] participation in Christ

and scribes. In the crucifixion of Jesus Christ we have to do with the particular suffering of One who is rejected and destroyed and shamed by men—and not just by any men, but by the spiritual leaders of the people of God. It is quite obvious and understandable that the disciple who had just recognised and confessed Jesus to be the Messiah should take offence at this prophecy. But his confession naturally implied his willingness to follow Jesus. And it received the answer—his protest being brushed aside by the stern saying of Jesus—that he and all those who make this profession and share this willingness, if they are to be disciples of the Rejected and Crucified, must take up their own cross and therefore in their own place enter into the passion of Jesus, the shameful passion of One who is despised and rejected.

We must be clear at the very outset that the connexion between the cross of Jesus Christ and that of the Christian, for all its direct necessity, is not a direct but only an indirect connexion. Those who have to take up their cross only follow Him in this, although finally they do follow Him in this too. In the words of 1 Pet. 2^{21}, they follow in His steps. They do not accompany Him in an equality of their cross with His. And they certainly do not precede Him in the sense   [600] that His cross acquires reality and significance only as they take up their cross. Behind this view there stands the ancient mystical notion that it is Christ's own cross that Christians have to take up and carry. This notion is quite false.

Ἀράτω τὸν σταυρὸν αὐτοῦ [EN342] is what is said in Mk. 8^{34} and par., and the continuation is that the disciple must lose τὴν ψυχὴν αὐτοῦ [EN343] (to save it). He is to do it ἕνεκεν ἐμοῦ [EN344], in the sense that he thus proves and confesses himself to be My disciple. But it is his own life, just as it is himself (ἑαυτόν) that he has to deny in the preceding verse. What Simon of Cyrene did (Mk. 15^{21} and par.), he did not do at the bidding of Jesus but under the compulsion of those who led Jesus away to be crucified. And it was Jesus Himself, not Simon, who was crucified. He gave up His own life (Mk. 10^{45}), not that of Simon.

The cross of Jesus is His own cross, carried and suffered *for* many, but *by* Him alone and not by many, let alone by all and sundry. He suffers this rejection not merely as a rejection by men but, fulfilled by men, as a rejection by God—the rejection which all others deserved and ought to have suffered, but which He bore in order that it should no more fall on them. Their cross does not mean that they have still to suffer God's rejection. This has been suffered already by Him (as their rejection). It can no longer be borne by them. Similarly the exaltation accomplished in His crucifixion and therefore in the suffering of that rejection is His and not that of His disciples or the world above which He was exalted as the Lord in His death. To His exaltation there corresponds that of His elect and called, the elevation which now comes to Christians and is promised to all men, their awakening from the mortal sleep of the slothfulness of sin. And we have seen already that this uprising of man has its basis and thrust in Him, in His exaltation to the right hand of the Father as effected in His death; that it becomes and is a fact wholly and utterly in virtue of this exaltation. Yet their elevation is not identical with His exaltation. It is only

---

[EN342] let him take up his cross
[EN343] his life
[EN344] for my sake

thanks to His exaltation, and in the strength of it, that it takes place at all. The relationship between the two is irreversible. And if their elevation consists ultimately in the fact that they have to take up and carry their cross, this is not a re-enactment of His crucifixion. It takes place in correspondence to it; with the similarity proper to a disciple following his Master; but not in any sense in likeness, let alone identity. His own crown and the dignity which comes to the disciple in discipleship are two distinct things. The crown of life, which the disciple is promised that he will receive at the hand of the King (Rev. 2¹⁰), is the goal of the way which he may go here and now as the bearer of this dignity.

[601]
When Paul says concerning himself in Gal. 2²⁰ that he no longer lives, but Christ lives in him, this does not mean that he identified himself with Christ, or gave himself out to be a second Christ. He at once interpreted the statement by that which followed: "And the life which I now live in the flesh I live by the faith of the Son of God, who loved me, and gave himself for me." Paul himself did not take part—except in so far as he received it in faith as done for him—in this self-offering of Christ, which took place for him as one who was loved by Christ. He did not mean this when he said in the preceding verse (Gal. 2¹⁹) that he was crucified with Christ ($X\rho\iota\sigma\tau\hat{\omega}$ $\sigma\upsilon\nu\epsilon\sigma\tau\alpha\upsilon\rho\acute{o}\mu\alpha\iota$ EN345), or in Gal. 6¹⁷ that he bore the marks ($\sigma\tau\acute{\iota}\gamma\mu\alpha\tau\alpha$) of the Lord Jesus, or in 2 Cor. 4¹⁰ that he bore about in the body the dying ($\nu\acute{\epsilon}\kappa\rho\omega\sigma\iota\varsigma$) of the Lord Jesus. Nor did he mean it in Gal. 6¹⁴ when he made his boast only in the cross of Christ "by whom the world is crucified unto me, and I unto the world," or in Rom. 6⁶ when he said of Christians generally that "our old man is crucified with him," or in Gal. 5²⁴ when he claimed that "they that are Christ's have crucified the flesh with the affections and lusts," or in Col. 3⁵ where Christians are summoned to mortify their members, or in other passages which refer to the dying of Christians. Both the text and the context of all these sayings completely exclude any idea of an interchangeability of Christ and the Christian, the Head and the member, the One who leads and the one who follows. They refer to a hard and painful and even mortal but redemptive attack which must and is and will be made on the Christian in fellowship with the suffering and crucified Christ, so that his whole life is determined and marked and characterised by its influence and effects. But the suffering which comes on Christians, the cross to which they are nailed, the death which they have to die, is always *their* suffering, *their* cross, *their* death, just as the salvation which accompanies it is *their* salvation, won for them and brought to them in the suffering and cross and death of Christ on their behalf ($\dot{\alpha}\nu\tau\grave{\iota}$ $\pi o\lambda\lambda\hat{\omega}\nu$ EN346). Their cross corresponds to the death of Christ. It does this with supreme realism. But it does not do more. It is not a repetition, or re-presentation, of the cross of Christ.

There is only one passage (Col. 1²⁴) which at a first glance seems rather obscure in this respect. Here Paul twice describes his suffering as an apostle as a suffering $\dot{\upsilon}\pi\acute{\epsilon}\rho$ EN347, for others—an expression which elsewhere in the New Testament is used only in relation to the suffering of Christ. He rejoices in his $\pi\alpha\theta\acute{\eta}\mu\alpha\tau\alpha$ EN348 for his readers. He fills up, or completes, or repays ($\dot{\alpha}\nu\tau\alpha\nu\alpha\pi\lambda\eta\rho\hat{\omega}$) by means of them that which is still lacking of the afflictions of Christ ($\tau\grave{\alpha}$ $\dot{\upsilon}\sigma\tau\epsilon\rho\acute{\eta}\mu\alpha\tau\alpha$ $\tau\hat{\omega}\nu$ $\theta\lambda\acute{\iota}\psi\epsilon\omega\nu$ $\tauο\hat{\upsilon}$ $X\rhoι\sigmaτο\hat{\upsilon}$). He suffers in his flesh for ($\dot{\upsilon}\pi\acute{\epsilon}\rho$) the body of Christ which is the community. The explanation is twofold. On the one

---
EN345 I have been crucified with Christ
EN346 for many
EN347 on behalf of
EN348 sufferings

hand, the community as the body of Christ, i.e., the earthly historical representation and form of the presence and action of Jesus Christ as its Head, has to exist in an earthly-historical correspondence to His afflictions, His passion (these are its ὑστερήματα[EN349]). And, on the other hand, the apostle is appointed to be the messenger to the community in Christ's stead (ὑπὲρ Χριστοῦ, 2 Cor. 5²⁰), and therefore he has to see to it in his creatureliness (ἐν τῇ σαρκί μου), not as a second head, but as a special member of the body with a distinctive responsibility, that a witness is given to what must take place as the earthly-historical correspondence of Christ's passion. What Paul is saying in this passage is that as a bearer of his own cross he may do this, and rejoices to do it, in his apostolic παθήματα[EN350]. In the verse which follows (v. 25) he tells us that he suffers as a minister to the community in accordance with the divine dispensation (οἰκονομία) which he knows that he is charged to fulfil. He rejoices in his apostolic suffering because he knows that he has this charge, and is invested with this dignity, in his suffering as a man. Even in this outstanding passage the connexion between the suffering of the Christian and that of Christ is only indirect.

We may now turn from this delimitation to the positive statement which must be made in this context. Because it takes place in Jesus Christ that man is set in this whole movement, it is integral to the event of sanctification—the *participatio Christi*[EN351], the call to discipleship, the awakening to conversion and the praise of good works—that as the life-movement of the Christian—as a human, earthly-historical life-movement—it is radically and relentlessly fixed and held and broken at a specific place. In the literal sense it is a happening which is crossed through, which is determined and characterised by a cross. The cross involves hardship, anguish, grief, pain and finally death. But those who are set in this movement willingly undertake to bear this because it is essential to this movement that it should finally, i.e., in its basis and goal, be crossed through in this way. We are necessarily outside the movement if we will not take up and bear our cross; if we try to escape the *tolerantia crucis*[EN352] (Calvin). [602]

It is not a matter merely of hardship, pain and death in themselves and in general, just as it is not merely a matter of the human life-movement in itself and as such.

It is quite in order that this man should not wish to see himself arrested and disturbed and broken; that he should try to ward off pain and death. Even the Christian does this. In themselves and as such, pain, suffering and death are a questioning, a destruction and finally a negation of human life. The Christian especially cannot try to transform and glorify them. He cannot find any pleasure in them. He cannot desire or seek them. For he sees and honours and loves in life a gift of God. And he is responsible for its preservation. He cannot be a lover of death, as the natural man may easily become in a strange reversal and unmasking of his pretended affirmation of life and avid desire for it. His Yes to life is not one which can surreptitiously change into a No. He knows

---

[EN349] lacks
[EN350] sufferings
[EN351] participation in Christ
[EN352] bearing of the cross

better than others what life is, and what he is doing when he secures himself against its negation. He affirms it just because it is for him more than a matter of life. What is at stake is that the will of God should be done, which is his sanctification (1 Thess. 4³). Because he does not love his life in itself and as such, he cannot love its negation and therefore pain, anguish and death as such. He affirms his life in this context.

But in the same context he may and can and must also affirm its negation. "For whether we live, we live unto the Lord; and whether we die, we die unto the Lord: whether we live, therefore, or die, we are the Lord's" (Rom. 14⁸). We are His possession "both in body and soul, in life and death." To be His possession, the doing of His will, sanctification, is thus that which is more than dying in the dying of the Christian. To be the Lord's includes this alternative of dying. The Christian knows better than others—than those who for different reasons have lost their zest for life and long for its end and dissolution—what he is doing when he says Yes to the negation of his life, to pain and suffering and death. He says Yes to these because his sanctification in fellowship with Jesus Christ, in His discipleship, in the conversion initiated by Him, in the doing of good works, ultimately includes the fact that he has to see and feel and experience the limit of his existence—even of his Christian existence

[603]   engaged in sanctification—as the limit of his human and creaturely life, which necessarily leads to pain and suffering and death, leading to death, and proclaiming it, and finally involving it. To save his life he must surrender and lose it. He will not seek or induce this loss. It will come to him. But as a Christian, and because it is a matter of life, he will not negate but affirm it, just as elsewhere and right up to this frontier he will not negate but affirm life. He will not affirm either for their own sake. But he will definitely affirm both, even death, ἕνεκεν ἐμοῦ EN353, for Jesus' sake. He will accept the fact that this limit or frontier is set, and that he has to note it. He will take up his cross.

"Whether we die, we die unto the Lord." It is Christ who sets this term to our life. It is not set accidentally, by fate or by an unknown God. It is not set merely with the limit of death itself, which belongs to our nature as a mark of our finitude. To be sure, natural death also belongs to the cross which the Christian has to take up. But this limit is not set according to a law of nature which the Christian has in common with all other men. It is set in his special fellowship with Jesus Christ, and therefore—because He is the King who controls this fellowship—according to the law of Him who is also Lord over nature and that which takes place according to its laws. Jesus Christ Himself has, of course, endured suffering and death as it is appointed for all men and in some form comes on all. But He endured it in obedience to His Father and the exercise of His office. He endured it in order supremely to glorify His Father and His love by taking on Himself the divine sentence of rejection on all men and thus opening the way for the actualisation of the election of all men. He endured it

---

EN353 for my sake

6. *The Dignity of the Cross*

in the act of reconciling the world with God, as the man in whom God humbled Himself in order that man should be exalted. He endured that that limit should be set for Him in the negation of His life. And in so doing He tore down the wall of partition which separated man from God. Offering and losing His life, He was the living and true and royal man, as was revealed in His resurrection. This is the law of His crucifixion. It is in accordance with this law that a term is set for Christians and they have to bear their cross. In the sphere of this lordship they are wonderfully free from any other laws, divine, human or demonic, inward or outward, spiritual or natural, Or rather, they become free from any such laws as they come under this law. They do not have to fear any overwhelming force, but only the Lord who brings them under it because He is theirs and they are His. And they cannot really fear Him—only their own disloyalty—because His law which leads them to take up their cross is the law of the grace of God directed to the world and known by them; because in the fact that He gives them to bear their cross they can see that God has given them this special light, and that they are honoured by this special fellowship with Jesus Christ.

At the end of the chapter already quoted (III, 8, 11) Calvin points out that the difference [604] between philosophical (Stoic) and Christian patience is that the latter is quite free from any suggestion of necessity. The Christian does not take up his cross, and yield to God, because it is quite futile to resist One who is so superior in strength. If we obey God only because we must, our secret thoughts are all of disobedience and evasion, and we refrain from these only because they are impossible. The Christian yields in recognition of the righteousness and wisdom of the divine providence which rules his life. He obeys a living, not a dead, command. He knows that resistance or impatience is wrong. He understands that it is for his salvation that God lays his cross on him. He thus accepts it *grata placidaque anima*[EN354], not with his natural bitterness, but in thankful and cheerful praise of God. This is a true picture, and it is extremely surprising that to underline this distinction Calvin did not make use of the insight with which the chapter as a whole begins—that the God with whom the Christian has to do, and who meets him even in suffering, is God in Jesus Christ, so that he for his part can encounter Him only with this free and willing and joyous patience, and not with the gloomy resignation of the Stoic with his *necesse est*[EN355].

The special fellowship of the Christian with Christ involves participation in the passion of His cross. As Christians take up and bear their cross, they do not suffer, of course, with the direct and original and pure obedience which for all its bitterness it was natural and self-evident for the Son of God who was also the Son of Man to render to His Father. Their obedience will never be more than the work of the freedom which they are given. It will always be subsequent. It will always be so stained by all kinds of disobedience that if in the mercy of God it were not invested with the character of obedience it would hardly deserve to be called obedience. Nor is their suffering even the tiniest of contributions to the reconciliation of the world with God. On the contrary, it rests on the fact

---

[EN354] with a grateful and peaceful soul
[EN355] 'it must be'

225

that this has been perfectly accomplished, not by them but by God Himself in Christ, so that it does not need to be augmented by their suffering or by any lesser Calvaries. Among other men, Christians are simply those to whom its truth and perfection are revealed (not hidden). They arise only as its witnesses. What they suffer is not what Jesus suffered—the judgment of God on the man of unrighteousness, the divine rejection without which the election of man cannot be accomplished. This was suffered by Jesus for the whole world and therefore for them. They exist only—and this is quite enough—in the echo of His sentence, the shadow of His judgment, the after-pains of His rejection. In their cross they have only a small subsequent taste of what the world and they themselves deserved at the hand of God, and Jesus endured in all its frightfulness as their Head and in their place. It is true—and we shall have to return to this—that they too have to suffer rejection at the hands of men. But they do not have to suffer rejection by God. On the contrary they have the sure knowledge that they are His elect. Again, they will not find, as Jesus did, that they are rejected by all men. At the very worst they will be rejected only by many, perhaps a majority. And in this as in other respects they will never be quite innocent in their suffering. They will never suffer merely through the corruption and wickedness of others, or through the undeserved decrees and buffetings of fate or the cosmic process. There is always a very definite (if sometimes disguised) connexion between the sufferings which befall them and their own participation in the transgression and guilt in which all men are continually implicated. And whereas Jesus was quite alone as the One who was rejected and suffered in their place, they can always know that even if they are rejected by ever so many they suffer as members of His community and therefore in company with at least a few others, and can count on the support and intercession, or at least the remembrance, of many more. Finally, whereas the suffering of Jesus is obviously on behalf of all other men, and for their salvation, liberation and exaltation, it is only with serious qualifications that we can say of the suffering of a Christian that it is significant and effective for others, and takes place in their favour. What it means to lay down one's life for one's friends (Jn. 15[13]) is only indicated from afar by any conceivable relationship of a human sufferer to others.

[605]

In short, the statement of the *Heidelberg Catechism* (*Qu.* 37) "that during the whole time of His life upon earth, and especially at the end, He bore both in body and soul the wrath of God against the sin of the whole human race, so that by His suffering as by a propitiatory offering He redeemed us in body and soul from eternal perdition and won for us God's grace and righteousness and eternal life," is one which cannot be referred to any Christian bearing his cross, not even to the greatest martyr. There applies to the Christian what is said in *Qu.* 44: "That in the greatest trials I have the assurance that by His unutterable anguish, pain and terror which He suffered even in soul both on and before the cross, my Lord Christ has redeemed me from the fear and pain of hell."

Between Christ and the Christian, His cross and ours, it is a matter of similarity in great dissimilarity. There is, of course, a great and strong and obvious similarity. It is because of this that we can speak of the dignity of the cross. Christians are distinguished and honoured by the fact that the fellowship with Jesus into which He Himself has received them finds final expression in the fact that their human and Christian life is marked like a tree for felling. The sign of the cross is the sign of the provisional character of their Christian existence. It is not the whole or even the heart of the matter that these men find themselves on the way with their little looking to Jesus as the author and finisher of their faith, with their little obedience in His discipleship, in their noticeable transition (which has to be renewed day by day) from the old to the new, from death to life, and with their very problematical good works; just as the life and speech and action of Jesus on His way from Jordan to Gethsemane was not the whole or the heart of the matter, the form in which He was truly Lord, apart from the fulfilment which came so terribly with the completely new development of the passion. In the life of Christians it is not just a matter   [606] of themselves and the fulfilment of their sanctification, but (since they have their activating cause in Jesus) of something far greater than themselves—of the glory and Word and work of God, compared with which they and all that they may become can never be more than dust and ashes. Or, from a different angle, it is a matter of themselves as God's witness, of their existence as individuals and as a community, but in the strict sense of the earth which is God's, of the whole world in all its blindness, need and care, which God so loved that He gave for it His only begotten Son. What are little Christians, with all the little things which may take place in the sphere of their existence in virtue of this Son of God, compared with this embracing plan and will of God? And, from another angle again, it is a matter of these little Christians, but of them only in so far as, watching and waiting with all the great world for the revelation of the glory of its Creator and Lord (2 Pet. 3^{12}), they may look and move towards it. What is all that they can see and experience and grasp and attest here and now—even on their way in fellowship with Jesus—alongside the eternal future announced from God both to themselves and to the world? What are they and have they compared with the glory of their Lord, who has risen again from death, and of whose fulness they have here and now received grace for grace, but whom they still confront as beggars, completely unworthy even in their fellowship with God by Him, sighing concerning themselves and the world which does not yet know Him, sighing for the true manifestation of that which has taken place for the world and themselves in this One? This is the limit which is set for the Christian especially, and as a sign of which he comes to bear his cross, not in identity but in similarity with the cross of Jesus. His cross points to the fulness and truth of that which he expects, and to which he hastens, as one who is sanctified in Jesus Christ. It points to God Himself, to His will for the world, to the future revelation of His majesty, to the glory in which his Lord already lives and reigns. As he comes to bear his cross, he finds himself prevented from forgetting this truth and fulness, and encouraged to take comfort in it and stretch out towards it. His cross inter-crosses his Christian life. He will not desire, or will, or try to bring it about, that this should happen. It will come unasked and unsought. As he belongs to Jesus, it is inevitable that it should come. His sanctification is fulfilled in its coming.

Calvin was at his best in this context (III, 8, 1). In what has to be thought and said concerning the Christian's cross, it is not for him a question of manufacturing a violent paradox, but of an *altius conscendere*EN356; of the recognition of the point where the sanctification of man points beyond itself from its root in the Holy One. *Quoscunque Dominus cooptavit ac suorum consortio dignatus est, ii se ad duram, laboriosam, inquietam plurimisque ac variis malorum generibus refertam vitam praeparare debent*EN357. The heavenly Father did not make things easy but hard for His only begotten Son, the One whom He loved above all and in whom He was well [607] pleased (Mt. 3¹⁷, 17⁵), so long as He was upon earth. We can say, indeed, and it is to this passage that reference is made in *Qu.* 37 of the *Heidelberg Catechism: totam eius vitam nihil aliud fuisse quam perpetuae crucis speciem*EN358. He, too, had to learn obedience by the things which He suffered (Heb. 5⁸). And beginning with Him, the Father deals with all His children according to this rule. Christ having subjected Himself to it for our sakes, we cannot be emancipated from it as those who are destined to be conformed to His likeness (Rom. 8²⁹). It works itself out in the *res durae et asperae*EN359 which we regard as hostile and evil when we experience them. (And they are this, as Calvin emphasises in opposition to the teaching of the Stoics, III, 8, 8: Poverty *is* hard, and sickness painful, and shame galling, and death terrible.) Yet in all these things it is a matter of *Christi passionibus communicare*EN360; of entering (like Him and with Him) "through much tribulation into the kingdom of God" (Ac. 14²²). The fiercer the affliction which assails us, the stronger the confirmation of our *societas cum Christo*EN361.

Of the many New Testament references we will adduce only two. The first is Phil. 3¹⁰ (which is also quoted by Calvin). What does it mean for Paul to know Christ and the power of His resurrection? The answer is that it means a knowledge of the κοινωνία τῶν παθημάτων αὐτοῦEN362 in which he finds himself placed as an apostle. What does it mean to go forward to the resurrection of the dead? The answer is that it means to be one who is made conformable to His death (συμμορφιζόμενος τῷ θανάτῳ αὐτοῦ). The second is 1 Pet. 4¹²: "Beloved, think it not strange (ξενίζεσθε) concerning the fiery trial which is to try you ... but rejoice, inasmuch as ye are partakers of Christ's sufferings; that, when his glory shall be revealed, ye may be glad also with exceeding joy."

In the light of this we can and must say a few words concerning the fact and extent that in the cross laid upon the Christian we really have to do with the fulfilment of his sanctification. The only decisive thing is, of course, the all-comprehensive fact which forms the point of departure—that as the cross of the Christian comes from Jesus it is in all its forms an awakening call and summons to look to Him, and therefore, as we have already seen, to arise. It is only

---

EN356 higher ascent
EN357 Whomsoever the Lord has chosen and deemed worthy to be in the company of his own must prepare themselves for a hard, laborious and troubled life crammed with many and various kinds of evils
EN358 his whole life has been nothing other than the appearance of a perpetual cross
EN359 hard and painful times
EN360 sharing in the sufferings of Christ
EN361 partnership with Christ
EN362 sharing in his sufferings

in this context that we can say anything more concrete if we are not to be guilty of dubious moralising.

With this backward reference and proviso we may say (1) that it is necessary and good for the Christian, and serviceable to sanctification, to be kept in the humility which is not natural to any of us, or rather to be continually recalled to it, by the cross which he has to bear. If this limit were not set for him, and palpably before him, he might easily begin to hold up his head with a proud confidence, not in God, but in his own Christianity; seeking, in the strength of the fact that he may be a Christian, to be strong in his own feelings and thought and acts, and thus jeopardising no less than everything. If he really takes up his cross, he will be prevented from doing this. Even if it consists only in an ordinary toothache, it will remind him of the limited nature of even his Christian existence, of his frailty and pettiness. It will restrain him from taking himself and his spirituality and his faith and its practical achievements with a seriousness which has no place for criticism or humour. It will summon him to seek and find his salvation and God's glory and the power of his own service only in the place *extra se*[EN363] from which they come to him and in which alone they have an unshakeable foundation. They will teach him speedily to range [608] himself again, as he ought, with other men; not merely with Christians, but with the children of men generally. The cross breaks over Christians constantly to teach even officers of the highest rank to begin again at the beginning as privates.

We may say (2) that for the Christian it is also helpful to sanctification that he should accept the punishment which in some real if hidden sense comes in and with his cross. Jesus Himself has borne the great punishment for him and for the whole world. But it is inevitable that in the following of Jesus all sorts of lesser punishments should have to be borne by the one who belongs to Him, and that he will have good reason to see and accept that these are just. It will certainly not be the sword which smites him—the sword of the wrath of God. But it will be the rod of His fatherly love. And the Christian is yet to be found who has not deserved it, who in what befalls him may rightly see only the work of an alien evil or cosmic destiny and not the answer to his own corruption. It is the latter which is directly or indirectly brought before him in the suffering which overtakes him. And it may and will remind him of the great punishment which he is spared. It may and will renew his gratitude, and give to his movement of conversion the fresh impulse and seriousness which are always so badly needed.

We may also say (3) that the cross which is really taken and carried by the Christian is a powerful force to discipline and strengthen his faith and obedience and love. In this respect it makes common cause with his impulsion by the Holy Spirit. When this is translated into the impulsion of his own spirit, even in the man seriously engaged in sanctification it may easily happen that

---

[EN363] outside of himself

he falls into what he thinks to be a spiritual roving and wandering and marauding and even plundering, or perhaps into a higher or lower form of pious idling. He is not aware of this himself. But it is noted by others, especially by the sharp eyes of worldlings. And they have then good reason to shake their heads, to laugh or to be annoyed, and in any case to dismiss Christianity as valueless. When the cross comes, he is given the opportunity, and even forced, to see it himself. As it sets for him and shows him his own limit, it causes him to be startled at himself. It forcibly teaches him to think of the one necessary thing, to focus and concentrate all his attention upon it. It presents some form of an ultimatum, for it is really the last thing which is announced in his life and thinking and conscience. When the cross comes, man's own spirit is rightly directed by the Holy Spirit as it previously refused to be—although pretending to be full of the Spirit. The Christian is taken in hand. And this is obviously to the benefit of his sanctification, his faith and obedience and love. From this crisis—which will have to come more than once and in different forms—he will obviously emerge stronger than when he was engulfed by it.

[609]   We may finally say (4)—but with particular care and restraint—that in the bearing of his cross there may be for the Christian particular verifications. That is to say, there may be particular good works of faith and love, works which are particularly well pleasing to God and which redound particularly to the praise of God. The Roman Church is quite right when in its legends and teaching concerning the saints it understands and portrays them all as great sufferers. What we are and have and think and do and attempt as Christians in good days, when the situation is calm and favourable and we are not exposed to any serious assaults from within or without, is always subject, for all its conscious zeal and sincerity, to the difficult question whether and how far it is tested, and hardened, and solid and enduring. Not every affliction or distress which comes on a man, even a Christian, has in itself and as such—however terrible it may be—the power to give this attestation, to make him the doer of an accredited work. But the fact that opportunities are often missed does not alter the fact that the cross is for the Christian the opportunity—and if he takes and bears it the power as well as the opportunity—to verify and therefore to purify and deepen his Christian existence and intensify his Christian work. When his own forces are reduced, when he is robbed of more than one of the aids which he values, when he is pushed into the corner and his back is against the wall, when he stands on unsafe and possibly crumbling ground and is thus thrown back with all the greater intensity on God and referred to the strength which comes from the covenant with Him, the Christian who takes up his cross and bears it will on this basis set his hand to the work with renewed willingness and energy, and although he may not do better or greater things, he will certainly do those which, since a limit has not yet been set, or is not yet felt or burdensome, will certainly be more tested and purified and substantial, and may indeed be better and greater, than ever before. There can be no doubt

that every genuine good work of the Christian acquires finally the fiery glow mentioned in 1 Pet. 4^{12}.

But so far we have referred only incidentally to the question what we have to understand specifically by the cross which the Christian has to carry. We must now try to take our bearings in this respect, at any rate as far as the main outlines are concerned.

In the New Testament one aspect of the cross stands with absolute dominance in the foreground—and it is a serious question for much later Christianity, including that of our own day, whether all is well if this aspect has to a large extent lost its actuality except for a few isolated instances. In the New Testament the cross means primarily persecution; the persecution of Christians by the world, by Jews and Gentiles, among whom Christians are sent "as sheep in the midst of wolves" (Mt. 10^{16}). In the New Testament, and during the centuries which followed, the Christian existence and confession and life was always latently at least (if not uninterruptedly) an enterprise which stood under the [610] threat of repression even to the point of physical violence. Later, and in our own time, the cross indicated in the New Testament has become rare, and for the most part exceptional, in this unequivocal form. At this point, therefore, we can speak only with great caution and in the light of certain analogies to persecution in the full sense. There can be no doubt that even to-day a Christian is a *rara avis*EN364, under constant threat, even in an environment which is ostensibly, and perhaps consciously and zealously, Christian. However great may be the solidarity which Christians feel and practise in relation to the world, their way can never be that of the world—and least of all that of the supposedly Christianised world. From the point which inspires them, they have to go their own way in great and little things alike, and therefore in their thought and speech and attitude they are always at bottom, although in some cases more markedly than others, aliens and strangers who will give plenty of cause for offence in different directions. To some they will appear to be far too ascetic. To others they will seem to affirm life far too unconcernedly. Sometimes they will be regarded as individualists, sometimes as collectivists. On the one hand they will be accused as authoritarians, on the other as free-thinkers; on the one hand as pessimists, on the other as optimists; on the one hand as bourgeois, on the other as anarchists. They will seldom find themselves in a majority. Certainly, they will never swim with the stream. It is only occasionally and against their true character that they can ever tolerate the official and officious. Things generally accepted as self-evident will never claim their absolute allegiance, even though they take on a Christian guise. Nor will they command their complete negation, so they can hardly count on the applause of the revolutionaries of their day. Nor will their freedom, to which we referred in our discussion of discipleship, be exercised by them in secret, but revealed openly in free acts and attitudes which will never be right to the world. And the

---

EN364 rare breed

world will not like this. They do not even need to make an explicit confession, although this will sometimes sharpen the offence that they give. To-day, however, in an age of doctrinal tolerance, this may well be allowed. But there will be all the less tolerance for the free decision and act of Christians. To this the reaction will be sour and bitter. It will be met with mistrust and repudiation, with suspicion and scorn, and even sometimes open indignation. Its disruptive tendencies will be quietly or forcefully accused and condemned. Measures will be taken to silence or destroy it, or at least to render it innocuous. Sometimes matters may be pressed even further, and counteraction undertaken which brings Christians at least in sight of the situation of Mt. 10^{16-39}, if not quite so far. They do not need to go beyond this point to be marked by the cross of rejection. Surely it is disturbing and wounding and confusing and hampering enough always to be so isolated, and subject to attack, among our fellows. How [611] much rather Christians would please than displease! How much they would prefer honour than shame for an attitude that is to them so clear and simple and necessary! But whether the shame be less or greater, they cannot cease to go the way which at the end will turn many, perhaps the majority, against them, and thus lead to their complete isolation. And even though they may not have to do with a Nero or a Diocletian, this will mean severe restriction by the limit which is so palpably and effectively set to their life-movement. Is it not surprising—when we think of the shame in which Jesus died, rejected not only by God but by men—that this particular cross seems to come upon relatively so few Christians? Or is it the case that so many succeed in evading it by refusing to go the distinctively Christian way on which they will inevitably be threatened and assailed by their limitation in this form?

Not by a long way, however, does the New Testament pretend that the sufferings of this present time are restricted to persecution. A passage like Rom. $8^{19f.}$ is shot through by the conception that the cross of Christians also consists in their particular share in the tension, transience, suffering and obscurity by which every man is in some form constricted and disturbed and finally condemned to death, and in which man also seems to find himself in a painful connexion with creation as such and as a whole. The older Evangelical hymn depicted the cross of the Christian primarily in this light. In so doing, it departed to some extent from the New Testament. But it did it very impressively. If it is in its own way right, then in relation to the cross laid on the Christian we have also to think of the afflictions of creaturely life and being which come on him either suddenly or gradually, momentarily or continually, but in the long run with overwhelming force: misfortunes, accidents, sickness and age; parting from those most dearly loved; disruption and even hostility in respect of the most important human relations and communications; anxiety concerning one's daily bread, or what is regarded as such; intentional or unintentional humiliations and slights which have to be accepted from those immediately around; the inability freely to develop one's life and talents; the sense of a lack of worthwhileness in respect of particular tasks; participation in the general adversities of the age which none can escape; and finally the dying which awaits us all at the end. If Jesus Himself was a suffering creature, and as such the Lord of all creatures, we are not only permitted but commanded to regard all the human suffering which we have only briefly sketched as a suffering with Him, in His fellowship, and therefore to understand the irruption of this suffering into the life of the Christian as the sign of this fellowship, and thus the manifestation of the supreme dignity of the Christian.

Finally, we must think of the suffering which—perhaps quite apart from persecution, or the participation in other ills of human life, but perhaps also in connexion with them—arises in all its terror from the fact that the Christian too, in spite of what he already is, still stands under the law of sin, and is still afflicted with the burden of the flesh, and is therefore subject to temptation, and is in fact tempted, always latently and sometimes acutely, notwithstanding his age or maturity or serious Christian achievements; tempted in his faith and love and hope, and therefore in the fulfilment of his relationship to God as it has been perfectly restored in the atoning death of Jesus. Temptation in the shape of intellectual or theoretical doubts is relatively the most harmless form of this cross. There too, of course, it is a question of truth. But in so far as it arises in a theoretical form it can be answered in an orderly induction by correct study and reflection. The trouble is that it then suddenly or gradually arises again in the new form whether the truth—that which is or can be known theoretically as true—is even for the Christian an authoritative and effective and illuminating truth—the truth of life. Here we have the practical doubt by which the real Christian especially is often attacked and perhaps steadily beleaguered as by an invincible enemy. He may accept and repeat the Creed. But does he really believe, at bottom, in the presence and action of the Father, Son and Holy Spirit in his own life? Has he really experienced His grace? Does he know it? Can he live in and by it? Has it really been addressed to him? Can this really be the case when in the innermost place where as a Christian he would be satisfied with even a little he is so empty and dry, so helpless in his attempt to seize and exploit the help which he knows is there, so unable to pray a prayer which is worthy of the One to whom he prays, and certain to be heard by Him? Is he not always a fool before God, an unprofitable servant? Has not God long since removed His face from him—if it ever lighted on him at all? Would he not do better to be something other than a Christian? In this form we may doubt even the truth which we know and sincerely confess. And God knows that—whether we are aware of it or not—we all stand constantly on the edge of this doubt. We must beware of transmuting and even glorifying it dialectically. Once we really know it, we will not do this. It is the sharpest form in which a limit is set to the Christian. It is the bitterest form of the cross. In this form it has been laid, with its hostile stimulation, even on what are humanly speaking the greatest of Christians. According to Mk. 15^{34} Jesus Himself experienced the cross finally and supremely in this form. He, the only begotten Son of God, had to ask: "Why hast thou forsaken me?" This is comforting.

[612]

What are our doubts and despairs, disguised or acute, compared with His dereliction, which was also and especially suffered by Him in our place? This means, however, that in fellowship with Him we have to reckon seriously with the fact that our cross will take, and may never lose, this character. In this character it cannot form part of an intellectual game. Unless we are to evade [613] our sanctification at the decisive point, we have to bear it, to see it through, in this character. The only thing is that in so doing we are not forsaken by the One who raised and answered the question whether He was not forsaken by God. At this point, then, we find ourselves in the deepest fellowship with Him.

We may conclude the discussion with two observations.

First, we must emphasise again that those who know what the cross is will not desire or seek to bear it. Self-sought suffering has nothing whatever to do with participation in the passion of Jesus Christ, and therefore with man's sanctification. The cross which we have to bear in following Jesus comes of itself, quite apart from any wish or action of our own. No one need worry that there will be no cross for him. Our only concern is not to avoid it; not defiantly or craftily to refuse to bear it; or not to cast it away again when it is only half taken up. Our only concern, since we have to suffer in any case, is not to do so like the ungodly, which means without the comfort and promise of suffering with Jesus. It must be our constant prayer, not only when adversity comes but in the good days which precede it, that this should not happen, that the Holy Ghost should make us free to accept and therefore to bear the appointed cross, i.e., to make it our own.

Second, the *tolerantia crucis*[EN365] is not an end in itself, and the direction to it, like every direction to sanctification, is not an ultimate but only a penultimate word. The dignity of the cross is provisional, indicating the provisional nature of the Christian existence and all sanctification. The crown of life is more than this. It is of the very essence of the cross carried by Christians that it has a goal, and therefore an end, and therefore its time. It signifies the setting of a term. That is why it is so bitter. But this limitation is not itself unlimited. Borne in participation in the suffering of Jesus, it will cease at the very point to which the suffering of Jesus points in the power of His resurrection, and therefore to which our suffering also points in company with His. It is not our cross which is eternal, but, when we have borne it, the future life revealed by the crucifixion of Jesus. Rev. 21⁴ will then be a present reality: "And God shall wipe away all tears from their eyes; and there shall be no more death, neither sorrow nor crying, neither shall there be any more pain: for the former things are passed away." P. Gerhardt is thus right when he says: "Our Christian cross is brief and bounded, One day 'twill have an ending. When hushed is snowy winter's voice, Beauteous summer comes again; Thus 'twill be with human

---

[EN365] bearing of the cross

pain. Let those who have this hope rejoice." There cannot lack a foretaste of joy even in the intermediate time of waiting, in the time of sanctification, and therefore in the time of the cross.

INDEX OF SCRIPTURE REFERENCES

INDEX OF SUBJECTS

INDEX OF NAMES